PEARSON SCIENCE 6

SASKATCHEWAN EDITION

Teacher's Resource

CB082298

Steve Campbell
formerly Richmond School Board,
British Columbia

Terry Johanson
Prairie Spirit School Division

Penny Mohr
Bjorkdale School
North East School Division

Christine Treptau
St. Gabriel School
Regina Roman Catholic Separate
School Division

Ted View
Miller High School
Regina Roman Catholic Separate
School Division

Nora Alexander

Steve Campbell

Douglas Hayhoe

Doug Herridge

Lionel Sandner

Jim Wiese

Beverley Williams

Ricki Wortzman

ISBN-13: 978-0-13-311152-1

EAN

9 780133 111521

PEARSON

Copyright © 2013 Pearson Canada Inc., Toronto, Ontario

Adapted from Addison Wesley Science and Technology 6 Teacher's Guide © 2000

Pearson Science 6, Saskatchewan Edition, Teacher's Resource was published previously as *Pearson Saskatchewan Science 6, Teacher's Resource*. The content of the two titles is identical.

All Rights Reserved. This publication is protected by copyright, and permission should be obtained from the publisher prior to any prohibited reproduction, storage in a retrieval system, or transmission in any form or by any means, electronic, mechanical, photocopying, recording, or likewise. For information regarding permission, write to the Permissions Department.

The information and activities presented in this book have been carefully edited and reviewed. However, the publisher shall not be liable for any damages resulting, in whole or in part, from the reader's use of this material.

ISBN-13: 978-0-13-312015-8

Printed and bound in Canada

8 18

DEVELOPMENTAL EDITOR: Lina Mockus
COORDINATING AND PRODUCTION EDITOR: Louise McCauley
COPY EDITOR: Ruth Peckover
EDITORIAL ASSISTANT: Kristiana Shin
COVER AND TEXT DESIGN: Alex Li
PRODUCTION COORDINATOR: Shonelle Ramserran
TEXT COMPOSITION: Lapiz Digital Services
ILLUSTRATIONS: Computer Composition of Canada Inc., Pronk&Associates

PUBLISHER: Reid McAlpine
MANAGING EDITOR: Lee Ensor
PROJECT MANAGER: Eileen Pyne-Rudzik, Ph.D.
RESEARCH AND COMMUNICATION MANAGER: Martin Goldberg

The authors and Pearson Education Canada would like to thank Dr. Glen S. Aikenhead, Dr. Herman Michell, and the staff of the Saskatchewan Ministry of Education for their guidance in the development of this program.

Copyright © 2013 Pearson Canada Inc., Toronto, Ontario

Adapted from Addison Wesley Science and Technology 6 Teacher's Guide © 2000

Pearson Science 6, Saskatchewan Edition, Teacher's Resource was published previously as *Pearson Saskatchewan Science 6, Teacher's Resource.* The content of the two titles is identical.

All Rights Reserved. This publication is protected by copyright, and permission should be obtained from the publisher prior to any prohibited reproduction, storage in a retrieval system, or transmission in any form or by any means, electronic, mechanical, photocopying, recording, or likewise. For information regarding permission, write to the Permissions Department.

The information and activities presented in this book have been carefully edited and reviewed. However, the publisher shall not be liable for any damages resulting, in whole or in part, from the reader's use of this material.

ISBN-13: 978-0-13-312015-8

Printed and bound in Canada

8 18

DEVELOPMENTAL EDITOR: Lina Mockus
COORDINATING AND PRODUCTION EDITOR: Louise McCauley
COPY EDITOR: Ruth Peckover
EDITORIAL ASSISTANT: Kristiana Shin
COVER AND TEXT DESIGN: Alex Li
PRODUCTION COORDINATOR: Shonelle Ramserran
TEXT COMPOSITION: Lapiz Digital Services
ILLUSTRATIONS: Computer Composition of Canada Inc., Pronk&Associates

PUBLISHER: Reid McAlpine
MANAGING EDITOR: Lee Ensor
PROJECT MANAGER: Eileen Pyne-Rudzik, Ph.D.
RESEARCH AND COMMUNICATION MANAGER: Martin Goldberg

The authors and Pearson Education Canada would like to thank Dr. Glen S. Aikenhead, Dr. Herman Michell, and the staff of the Saskatchewan Ministry of Education for their guidance in the development of this program.

6 Saskatchewan Science

Teacher's Resource Contents

UNIT 1

Diversity of Living Things

Table of Contents

Table of Contents *(continued)*

Unit Indicators Correlation Chart

Indicator	Lesson References	Assessment Opportunities
By the end of grade 6, students will be able to:		
DL6.1 Recognize, describe, and appreciate the diversity of living things in local and other ecosystems, and explore related careers.		
a. State the characteristics that define all living things (e.g., are made up of one or more cells, require energy for life processes, respond to stimuli in their environment, and have the ability to reproduce).	Lesson 1 Unit 1 Review	Work On It, p. 6 Unit 1 Review, p. 79, q. 1, 11
b. Observe and document the diversity of living things in their local habitat through journaling, a nature walk, sketching, drawing, photographing, video recording, or other means.	Lesson 4 Lesson 13 Design Project	Work On It, p. 20 Communicate, p. 62, q. 1–2 Work On It, p. 75
c. Show respect for other people, living things, and the environment when observing ecosystems.	Lesson 4 Design Project	Work On It, p. 20 Work On It, p. 75
d. Document the diversity of living things in different terrestrial and aquatic habitats (e.g., grasslands, forests, tundra, deserts, rivers, ponds, and oceans) using print, video, and/or on-line resources.	Lesson 4 Lesson 13	Work On It, p. 20 If Time Allows, p. 20 Work On It, p. 61
e. Analyze how First Nations and Métis art and storytelling highlight movement and/or behaviour of living things and reflect a worldview that values all living things.	Unit 1 Review	Unit 1 Review, pp. 79–80, q. 3, 19, 27
f. Identify examples of science and technology-related careers and workplaces which require an understanding of the diversity of living things (e.g., naturalist, zoo keeper, paleontologist, and wildlife biologist).	Lesson 6	Communicate, p. 29, q. 5
DL6.2 Examine how humans organize understanding of the diversity of living things.		
a. Construct and use a classification system to organize living things into groups and subgroups according to student-developed criteria.	Lesson 2 Lesson 3 Lesson 4 Lesson 8 Design Project Unit 1 Review	Work On It, p. 10 Get Started, p. 12 Work On It, p. 14 Work On It, p. 20 Build On What You Know, p. 20 Work On It, p. 38 Work On It, p. 75 Unit 1 Review, pp. 79–80, q. 4, 9, 22

Indicator	Lesson References	Assessment Opportunities
b. Consider personal observations and ideas as well as those of others (including differing worldviews) when constructing classification systems by asking questions, sharing stories, and responding to classmates' classification systems.	Lesson 3 Lesson 8 Lesson 14 Design Project	Get Started, p. 12 Communicate, p. 16, q. 5–6 Communicate, p. 40, q. 1, 3–4 Get Started, p. 63 Work On It, p. 64 Work On It, p. 75
c. Demonstrate how different classification systems can be used to classify the same set of objects and explain how humans develop and refine systems to meet specific needs.	Lesson 3 Unit 1 Review	Get Started, p. 12 Communicate, p. 16, q. 4 Unit 1 Review, p. 79, q. 2, 4, 10
d. Explore local First Nations and Métis methods of organizing understanding of living things (e.g., two-leggeds, four-leggeds, winged-ones, swimmers, trees, and grasses) and the criteria underlying that understanding (e.g., where animals are found, how animals move, and the uses of plants).	Lesson 13 Unit 1 Review	Think Again!, p. 62 Unit 1 Review, pp. 79–80, q. 3, 19
e. Describe how aspects of First Nations and Métis worldviews (e.g., holistic, interconnectedness, valuing of place-based knowledge) shape their systems of organizing understanding of living things.	Lesson 1 Unit 1 Review	Think Again!, p. 7 Unit 1 Review, pp. 79–80, q. 3, 19
f. Illustrate the diversity of living things on Earth by constructing a visual representation (e.g., poster, mobile, slide show, and web page) showing examples from each kingdom of the five-kingdom taxonomic model: monera, protists, fungi, plants, and animals.	Design Project	Work On It, p. 75
g. Use appropriate scientific terminology to communicate ideas about the diversity of living things (e.g., biotic, abiotic, kingdom, phylum, monera, protist, fungi, plant, animal, vertebrate, and invertebrate).	Lesson 7 Design Project Unit 1 Review	Work On It, p. 31 Communicate, p. 33, q. 1, 4 Work On It, p. 75 Unit 1 Review, p. 79, q. 4, 12
h. Critique the use of biological classification systems to aid scientific understanding of living things rather than relying on common, local, or personally chosen names.	Unit 1 Review	Unit 1 Review, p. 79, q. 1–3

Indicator	Lesson References	Assessment Opportunities
DL6.3 Analyze the characteristics and behaviours of vertebrates (i.e., mammals, birds, reptiles, amphibians, and fish) and invertebrates.		
a. Identify characteristics of vertebrates and invertebrates and classify animals as vertebrates or invertebrates from drawings, videos, pictures, lists, and/or personal observations.	Lesson 7 Lesson 8 Design Project Unit 1 Review	Work On It, p. 31 Work On It, p. 38 Work On It, p. 75 Unit 1 Review, pp. 79–80, q. 4, 13, 21
b. Compare and represent characteristics and behaviours (e.g., body shape, body description, method of respiration, method of reproduction, method of movement, and method of feeding) of student-selected examples of vertebrates.	Lesson 8 Lesson 9 Unit 1 Review	Work On It, p. 38 Work On It, p. 42 Communicate, p. 44, q. 1 Unit 1 Review, p. 79, q. 14
c. Compare and represent characteristics and behaviours (e.g., body shape, body description, method of respiration, method of reproduction, method of movement, and method of feeding) of student-selected examples of invertebrates (e.g., arthropods, annelids, cnidarids, echinoderms, molluscs, and nematodes).	Lesson 5 Lesson 6 Lesson 7 Unit 1 Review	Work On It, p. 23 Work On It, p. 28 Communicate, p. 29, q. 1–3 Work On It, p. 31 Unit 1 Review, p. 79, q. 15
d. Propose questions for inquiry that arise from personal investigations of characteristics and behaviours of animals.	Lesson 5 Lesson 7 Lesson 9 Design Project	Communicate, p. 24, q. 4–5 Work On It, p. 31 Communicate, p. 33, q. 3 Work On It, p. 42 Work On It, p. 75
e. Suggest reasons why current biological classification systems for living things are based on structural (internal) characteristics rather than solely on physical appearance or behaviour.	Lesson 14 Unit 1 Review	Work On It, p. 64 Communicate, p. 65, q. 1 Unit 1 Review, p. 79, q. 2, 6
DL6.4 Examine and describe structures and behaviours that help: • individual living organisms survive in their environments in the short term • species of living organisms adapt to their environments in the long term.		
a. Propose questions to investigate related to the structures and behaviours that help organisms survive in their environments (e.g., “What advantage are different beaks for birds?”, “Why do owls turn their heads to look sideways?”, “Why do rabbits change colour at different times of the year?”, “Why do caribou migrate?”, “Why do ground squirrels hibernate?").	Lesson 8 Lesson 11 Lesson 12 Unit 1 Review	Work On It, p. 38 Communicate, p. 40, q. 4 Work On It, p. 51 Work On It, p. 56 Unit 1 Review, p. 79, q. 5

Indicator	Lesson References	Assessment Opportunities
b. Show interest and curiosity in learning about living organisms' adaptations to different environments by journaling, participating in a nature walk, or sharing science-related information about adaptations (gathered from print or video resources or personal experience) with classmates.	Lesson 9 Design Project	Work On It, p. 42 Work On It, p. 75
c. Describe examples of structures and behaviours, including seasonal changes, which help living things survive in their environments during the lifetime of the organism.	Lesson 11 Lesson 12 Unit 1 Review	Work On It, p. 51 Work On It, p. 56 Communicate, p. 57, q. 1–5 Unit 1 Review, p. 80, q. 20, 24–25
d. Describe examples of adaptations to structures and behaviours (e.g., flippers, webbed feet, night-time vision, wide wings, camouflage colouring, migration, and hibernation) that have enabled living things to adapt to their environments in the long term.	Lesson 9 Lesson 11 Lesson 12 Unit 1 Review	Work On It, p. 42 Get Started, p. 50 Work On It, p. 51 Communicate, p. 54, q. 1, 3–4 Work On It, p. 56 Communicate, p. 57, q. 1–5 Unit 1 Review, p. 80, q. 24–25
e. Explain how scientists use fossils and the fossil record as a source of information to identify changes or diversity in species over long periods of time.	Lesson 10 Unit 1 Review	Work On It, p. 47 Unit 1 Review, p. 79, q. 7
f. Suggest reasons why specific species of organisms have or might become endangered or extinct.	Lesson 10 Unit 1 Review	Communicate, p. 48, q. 2 Unit 1 Review, p. 80, q. 20
g. Gather information from a variety of sources (e.g., Elder, traditional knowledge keeper, naturalist, textbook, non-fiction book, museum display, encyclopedia, and website) to answer student-generated questions about the structural and behavioural adaptations of living organisms.	Lesson 8 Unit 1 Review	Work On It, p. 38 Unit 1 Review, p. 80, q. 20, 24–25
h. Compare closely related animals that live in different parts of the world and propose explanations for any differences in their structures and behaviours.	Lesson 11	Communicate, p. 54, q. 2

Indicator	Lesson References	Assessment Opportunities
i. Research the advantages of particular structures or behaviours of organisms that suit different environments (e.g., how different bird beaks are best suited to obtain different types of food, how different types of foot structure are best suited for different environments).	Lesson 9 Lesson 12 Unit 1 Review	Communicate, p. 44, q. 1 Communicate, p. 57, q. 5 Unit 1 Review, p. 80, q. 20
j. Suggest reasons to explain how results of similar and repeated studies of the adaptations of organisms may vary and suggest possible explanations for variations (e.g., independent studies may reveal different responses by polar bears to temperature changes or pollution).	Design Project Unit 1 Review	Communicate, p. 77, q. 7 Unit 1 Review, p. 80, q. 25
DL6.5 Assess effects of micro-organisms on past and present society, and contributions of science and technology to human understanding of micro-organisms.		
a. Choose and correctly use appropriate tools (e.g., magnifying glasses, optical microscopes, and video microscopes) to study living organisms that cannot be seen with the naked eye.	Lesson 15	Work On It, p. 68
b. Observe and represent, using words and diagrams, characteristics of micro-organisms obtained from student- or teacher-collected water samples (e.g., bottled water, tap water, rain barrel, pond, creek, slough, and river water).	Lesson 15	Work On It, p. 68
c. Explain how micro-organisms meet their basic needs, including moving around and obtaining food, water, and oxygen.	Lesson 15	Communicate, p. 69, q. 2
d. Design and conduct an investigation of the factors that influence how quickly micro-organisms break down organic matter (e.g., build a composter in a 2 L plastic bottle and vary conditions such as the amount of water, soil, light, and combinations of waste products).	Lesson 16	LM 1-23
e. Compare cultural, historical, and scientific understandings and explanations of disease, including First Nations and Métis understandings and the contributions of scientists such as John Snow and Louis Pasteur to the germ theory.	Lesson 16 Unit 1 Review	Think Again!, p. 73 Communicate, p. 73, q. 2 Unit 1 Review, p. 80, q. 28

Unit Indicators Correlation Chart *(continued)*

Indicator	Lesson References	Assessment Opportunities
f. Critique representations or depictions of micro-organisms in a variety of texts (e.g., science-fiction, cartoons, movies, music, and poetry).	Lesson 16	Communicate, p. 73, q. 5
g. Discuss positive and negative impacts of micro-organisms for humans (e.g., food production and spoilage, fermentation, pasteurization, water and sewage treatment, human digestion, composting, disease spread and prevention, and biological warfare).	Lesson 16	Work On It, p. 72

Activity Planning Chart

Note that estimates of class times are based on 40 min per period.

Lesson	Type of Activity	Time (number of classes)	Materials Required (for each group)	Line Masters
Launch: Diversity at the Zoo	reading, guided inquiry	1 class period	notebook pen or pencil	none
1. Living Things	reading	1 class period	notebook pen or pencil	LM 1-3
2. Methods of Classifying	reading	1 class period	atlases notebook pen or pencil	LM 1-4
3. Classifying Living Things	guided inquiry	1 class period	notebook pen or pencil	LM 1-5
4. Classifying Trees	guided inquiry	1 class period	paper and pen or pencil camera (optional)	LM 1-6
5. Classifying Animals — The Invertebrates	guided inquiry, research	1 class period	research materials library and computer access notebook and pen or pencil	LM 1-7 LM 1-8
6. Classifying Arthropods	reading	1 class period	a collection of specimens or models of different arthropods (optional) videos of different insects (optional)	LM 1-9 LM 1-10
7. Investigating an Arthropod — The Mealworm	open inquiry	2–3 class periods	mealworms in a breathable container magnifying glass dry cereal blank white paper lined paper pencils Optional Materials: blunt tweezers plastic gloves	LM 1-11 LM 1-12 LM 1-13
8. Classifying Animals — The Vertebrates	guided inquiry, research	1 class period	research materials library and computer access paper and pen or pencil	LM 1-14
9. All About Fish	guided inquiry	1–2 class periods	large, clear container big enough so a fish can swim freely (small aquarium) tap water conditioner to remove chlorine thermometer water at the same temperature as the water in the aquarium or holding tank goldfish or other small fish small net pencils paper	LM 1-15 LM 1-16

Activity Planning Chart *(continued)*

Lesson	Type of Activity	Time (number of classes)	Materials Required (for each group)	Line Masters
10. A Prehistoric Vertebrate	guided inquiry	1 class period	paper and pen or pencil	LM 1-17
11. Animal Adaptations	guided inquiry	1 class period	paper and pen or pencil	LM 1-18
12. The Perfect Beak	open inquiry	1 class period	beaks: spoon, tweezers, straw food: marbles, gummi worms in dirt, navy beans, toothpicks plastic cups to hold food graph paper or computer access stopwatches or clock for timing notebook pen or pencil	LM 1-19
13. Plant Adaptations	guided inquiry	1 class period	map of Saskatchewan's ecozones ruler, pencil colour pencils notebook	LM 1-20
14. The Key to Classifying	guided inquiry	1 class period	notebook pen or pencil	none
15. The Microscopic World	open inquiry, research	2 class periods	living micro-organisms in slides or prepared slides of micro-organisms white paper pens and pencils magnifying glass microscope	LM 1-21 LM 1-22
16. The Impact of Micro-organisms	guided inquiry, research	1 class period	research materials library and computer access paper and pencil	LM 1-23
Design Project: Classifying Living Things Around Us	design	3 class periods	recording material (paper, pencil, camera, video recorder) magnifying glass Popsicle sticks guide or classification chart for local plants and animals trees classification chart from the Classifying Trees activity (optional) paper pencil	LM 1-24 LM 1-25

- The Launch activity in this unit refers to a zoo. Zoos contain a great diversity of living things. If time allows and you have the opportunity, a field trip to a local zoo may help students observe and understand first-hand some of the similarities and differences among living things.
- The project at the end of the unit involves taking students on a field trip to a field, pond, or other local habitat. You will need to make arrangements for the trip. Ensure that you obtain permission to visit the site from authorities in advance of the trip. Follow any guidelines your school board has for field trip safety and permission, as well as the safety cautions noted in this unit.
- Invite guest speakers who have an interest in, or work with, a range of plants or animals. You might invite a zoo worker, veterinarian, pet store employee, animal shelter employee, nursery worker, avid gardener, or paleontologist. Encourage students to prepare questions ahead of time.
- Students will benefit from studying as diverse a group of plants and animals as possible. Ask family, friends, other staff members, and students if they have fossils, models of animals, posters of different living things, plant or animal identification books, or simple classification keys that they are willing to have on display in your class while you are working on this unit. Contact your school board, local museum, or zoo to find out if they have any collections available for loan.
- As they progress through the unit, students will be building their understanding of the diversity of the animal kingdom. Establish a central location where they can mount and display pictures, posters, and charts of the different members of the animal kingdom. This can help to consolidate their understanding of the similarities and differences among the many members of the animal kingdom.

Materials and Equipment Needed for Unit 1

(based on 30 students)

Launch: Diversity at the Zoo	
Materials • paper • pencils • notebooks	**Equipment** • no equipment needed
1. Living Things	
Materials • poster paper • pencils • notebooks	**Equipment** • no equipment needed
2. Methods of Classifying	
Materials • chart paper • pencils • notebooks	**Equipment** • atlases
3. Classifying Living Things	
Materials • chart paper • pencils • notebooks	**Equipment** • no equipment needed
4. Classifying Trees	
Materials • paper • pencils • notebooks	**Equipment** • cameras (optional)
5. Classifying Animals — The Invertebrates	
Materials • chart paper • pencils • notebooks	**Equipment** • research materials • library and computer access

Materials and Equipment

(continued)

6. Classifying Arthropods	
Materials • poster paper • pencils • notebooks	**Equipment** • a collection of specimens or models of different arthropods (optional) • videos of different insects (optional)
7. Investigating an Arthropod — The Mealworm	
Materials • notebooks • mealworms • dry cereal • blank white paper • lined paper • pencils	**Equipment** • breathable containers • magnifying glass • blunt tweezers (optional) • plastic gloves (optional)
8. Classifying Animals — The Vertebrates	
Materials • chart paper • pencils • notebooks	**Equipment** • research materials • library and computer access
9. All About Fish	
Materials • water at the same temperature as the water in the aquarium or holding tank • tap water conditioner to remove chlorine • goldfish or other small fish • pencils • paper	**Equipment** • large, clear container big enough so a fish can swim freely (small aquarium) • thermometer • small net
10. A Prehistoric Vertebrate	
Materials • paper • pencils • notebooks	**Equipment** • no equipment needed
11. Animal Adaptations	
Materials • paper • pencils • notebooks	**Equipment** • no equipment needed

Materials and Equipment

(continued)

12. The Perfect Beak	
Materials • marbles • gummi worms in dirt • navy beans • toothpicks • graph paper • pencils • notebooks	**Equipment** • spoon, tweezers, straw • plastic cups to hold food • research materials • stopwatches or clock for timing • library and computer access
13. Plant Adaptations	
Materials • paper • pencils • notebooks • colour pencils	**Equipment** • map of Saskatchewan's ecozones • rulers
14. The Key to Classifying	
Materials • paper • pencils • notebooks	**Equipment** • no equipment needed
15. The Microscopic World	
Materials • living micro-organisms in slides or prepared slides of micro-organisms • white paper • pens and pencils	**Equipment** • magnifying glass • microscope
16. The Impact of Micro-organisms	
Materials • paper • pencils • notebooks	**Equipment** • research materials • library and computer access
Design Project: Classifying Living Things Around Us	
Materials • paper • pencils • notebooks • chart paper • Popsicle sticks	**Equipment** • research materials • library and computer access • recording material (e.g., camera, video recorder) • magnifying glass • guide or classification chart for local plants and animals • trees classification chart from Classifying Trees activity (optional)

Materials and Equipment

(continued)

Overall Unit Requirements	
Materials • 30 pencils • 30 sets of colour pencils • 30 sets of markers • 30 notebooks • 30 pens • 5 packs of loose-leaf paper • 1 pack of graph paper • 100 sheets of poster paper • 24 sheets of chart paper • 100 mealworms • 1 kg dry cereal (bran) • 30 goldfish or other small fish • 1 bottle tap water conditioner to remove chlorine • 100 marbles • 100 gummi worms in dirt • 2 bags of navy beans • 1 box of toothpicks • 6 jars of living micro-organisms or prepared slides of micro-organisms • 30 Popsicle sticks	**Equipment** • 15 atlases • 6 breathable containers • a collection of specimens or models of different arthropods (optional) • videos of different insects (optional) • 30 magnifying glasses • 6 blunt tweezers (optional) • 30 plastic gloves (optional) • 6 large, clear containers (small aquariums) • 1 large classroom aquarium • 6 small nets • 15 thermometers • 6 spoons • 6 straws • 6 plastic cups to hold food • 6 stopwatches or a clock for timing • 30 maps of Saskatchewan's ecozones • 30 rulers • 15 microscopes • camera (optional) • video recorder (optional) • 15 field guides or classification charts for local plants and animals • 15 trees classification chart from Classifying Trees activity (optional)

Addressing Student Preconceptions

Launch: Diversity at the Zoo and Lesson 1: Living Things

Students may think that items such as logs or dead leaves are non-living or abiotic. Because they were once alive, they are considered to be biotic by scientists. Anything that was once alive is biotic.

Lesson 2: Methods of Classifying

Students are likely to be familiar with at least one multi-level classification system, such as sorting addresses alphabetically. However, they may not conceptualize this as classifying.

Lesson 3: Classifying Living Things

Students divide the organisms presented in the Launch section into plants, animals, and fungi. To reveal students' preconceptions, consider asking students to subdivide each of their groups before proceeding with Lesson 3.

Lesson 4: Classifying Trees

Some students may think they are classifying plants simply by naming them. In one study, grade 6 students preferred to give specific names to plants (such as spruce, lilac, rose, or buttercup), rather than place them into more abstract categories (tree, bush, vine, or wildflower). The classification key presented is used to identify various species of trees with which students are likely to be familiar, but you may want them to organize their plants into groups before giving them specific names.

Lesson 5: Classifying Animals — The Invertebrates

In one study, only a minority of students correctly identified fish, turtles, and snakes as animals with a backbone. Before you begin this lesson, ask the class to group the following animals into those with a backbone and those without: ant, bird, cow, elephant, fish, gerbil, seal, snake, spider, and turtle. This exercise will allow you to observe any preconceptions about vertebrates and invertebrates.

Lesson 6: Classifying Arthropods

A common misconception is that spiders are a type of insect. Spiders are arthropods, and differ from insects in their number of legs and body parts. An insect collection can be helpful to emphasize this fact, and prepare students to observe a live specimen of an arthropod in the next lesson.

Lesson 7: Investigating an Arthropod — The Mealworm and Lesson 9: All About Fish

In these lessons, students observe characteristics and behaviour of live specimens. One study found that more learning occurs when live specimens are used. Students will sometimes apply human characteristics (anthropomorphize) live specimens when observing them. Encourage them to use authentic observations and avoid stems such as, "My mealworm likes ..." or "My fish wants to ..." when describing animal behaviour.

Lesson 8: Classifying Animals — The Vertebrates

Many students believe vertebrate animals have distinct limbs and heads, and may misclassify fish and snakes as invertebrates. Some students believe that a backbone makes an animal rigid and inflexible. You could lead the class through stretching, bending, and twisting exercises to enhance their awareness of their own flexibility.

Lesson 10: A Prehistoric Vertebrate

Many students are fascinated by dinosaurs, and may get an intuitive sense of structural characteristics by exploring the similarities and differences between prehistoric and modern vertebrates. They should be careful not to make assumptions about dinosaurs' appearance or behaviour based on scant evidence. Even today, scientists cannot be absolutely certain about what colour dinosaurs were. Students may also believe that dinosaurs and humans co-existed. It may be helpful to use a timeline to demonstrate when various life forms inhabited Earth.

Lesson 11: Animal Adaptations and Lesson 12: The Perfect Beak

Students may be unclear about the differentiation between structural and behavioural adaptation. They should understand that structural adaptation relates to physical features whereas behavioural adaptation relates to how the animal acts to survive. Behavioural adaptations, like structural adaptations, occur over time as animals evolve and should not be confused with changes in behaviour, which can occur instantly.

Lesson 13: Plant Adaptations

Students may believe that Saskatchewan is one ecozone. It will help them to understand that their province actually has five ecozones, ranging from the sub-Arctic (Taiga Shield Ecozone) in the north to the much more temperate Prairie Ecozone in the south.

Lesson 14: The Key to Classifying

This lesson reinforces the concept that structural characteristics are used to classify living things. To review the concept of classification, consider presenting the class with drawings of various animals (e.g., a mouse, cockroach, trout, robin, turtle, dolphin, eel, frog, penguin, worm, snail, spider, snake, and dog). Ask students to place these animals into the following categories: fish, amphibian, reptile, bird, mammal, insect, mollusc, and worm.

Lesson 15: The Microscopic World

Many people commonly use the word "bug" to refer to both insects and micro-organisms. You may like to introduce the activity with a discussion about this preconception by asking the class what "bug" means. Students may not have a clear concept of what a "flu bug" is, for example.

Lesson 16: The Impact of Micro-organisms

Students may think that all micro-organisms are harmful. It may be a surprise for them to find out that many are useful and that some are essential for life.

Design Project: Classifying Living Things Around Us

Consider focussing the project on a wetland habitat. Research reveals that as children grow up, they often develop negative attitudes toward wetlands versus woodlands and meadows. North American wetlands are an important source of biodiversity and are in great environmental danger. Attitudes toward wetlands should be positive if these areas are to survive. Before the field trip, consider asking your students if they enjoy wetlands such as ponds, rivers, bogs, and swamps. Have a follow-up discussion when you return. Alternatively, visit any ecosystem that is particularly sensitive or is being encroached on in your locale, and have a similar discussion.

Big Ideas

In this unit, students will take a close look at the special characteristics of living and non-living things. They will learn how to organize information about both living and non-living things and discuss the ways scientists use classification systems in their work. An important aspect of their study will include the ways First Nations and Métis peoples regard the environment. Students will become familiar with a value system that is founded on respect for all things on Earth. Students will use classification systems around their home, school, and community to help them study the diversity of plants and animals, with a focus on Saskatchewan ecozones.

Once you have determined students' prior knowledge, you may want to hand out LM 1-1 Unit 1 Summary and LM 1-2 Unit 1 Key Terms to help students record their understanding of the unit and key terms.

Time
1 class period
Key Terms
• diversity • biotic • abiotic • organisms
Line Masters
• none

Assessing Students' Prior Knowledge

- Invite the class to brainstorm a list of living things. Challenge them to be as specific as possible. Say something like, *Make a list of the names of as many living things as you can. If you think of a bird, for example, ask yourself, "What kind of bird am I thinking of? Is it a duck? Is it a robin?" Then write down the name of the bird you're thinking of.*
- Students could first work individually and write a list. After a few minutes, invite the class to form small groups and combine their lists. Ask each group to look for similarities and differences among the living things on the combined list.
- Walk around the room and listen to discussions to determine what characteristics students use to define similarities and differences. Encourage the groups to discuss the characteristics they find. You might wish to end the exercise by giving each group chart paper and challenging them to find a way to organize their lists.
- Once group work is finished, invite the groups to share their lists with the rest of the class. Ask students to explain how they organized their lists, and encourage discussion with the class. You could ask, *Are there other ways we can sort the living things?*
- Consider posting the lists in the class so that students can review them periodically as they work through the unit. These lists could be modified throughout the unit as the students learn more about classifying living things.

Introduce the Unit

- Explain to students that during the unit, they will explore the diversity of living things and use some characteristics to classify them. Ask, *What comes to mind when you hear the term "diversity of living things"?*
- Introduce words like "variety" and "difference" to help illustrate the meaning of diversity if students do not volunteer them. Ensure that students understand that to classify means to place items into a group, based on some common characteristic or feature.

Introduce the Design Project

- Tell students that at the end of this unit, the class will go on a field trip.
- Say something like, *By then, you will know a lot about how to identify and classify plants and animals. For your project, you will design a classification system for all the living things you see on the field trip.*
- Remind the class to record any information they find in the unit that might help them with this project.

Get Started ▶

- Read the first paragraph of Get Started to the class. Read the last sentence in the paragraph, and ask for students to suggest some things that are seen at different times of the day or year.
- Write their suggestions on the board or on chart paper.
- When no more suggestions are offered, read the second and third paragraphs. Ask students to answer the question at the end of the third paragraph.
- Write these answers down as well, then say, *These ideas are all ways in which we can classify living things. Classifying is putting things into groups.*

Time
40 min
Skills
• classifying • observing • comparing • communicating
Grouping
individuals, pairs
Materials and Equipment
(per group) • notebook • pen or pencil
Line Masters
• none

Work On It

- Ask students to work in pairs to list all the living and non-living things they can see in the illustration. Then consider the Work On It questions.
- As they work on answering these questions, challenge students to clearly indicate and label the characteristics they identify for each group of organisms they create.
- The work students do for procedure step 6 will give you a good idea of how familiar each student is with classification systems. Consider modelling a simple tree diagram on the board before the class begins this step.

Communicate

1. If you have sufficient space, ask all your students to post their charts to make it easier to compare their work with that of their classmates. Students' charts and groupings of organisms will vary. Encourage students to observe and discuss the similarities and differences of their classmates' ideas.
2. Students should be able to identify the characteristics used by their classmates to sort the organisms into groups. As students discuss which groupings they think are more helpful, ask them to clearly explain their reasons.
3. This mind map is important because students will be adding to it throughout the unit. You may wish to help them get started by reviewing the key factors of a mind map or providing them with a graphic organizer. Students' mind maps can be put in their portfolios. Remind them to use scientific words as much as possible, and to make sure they understand the meanings of the words they use.

1 Living Things

Time
1–2 class periods

Key Terms
• spirit guide • biotic • abiotic • stewardship • ecosystem

Line Masters
• LM 1-3

Indicator Assessment Chart

Indicator	Assessment Opportunities
DL6.1 a. State the characteristics that define all living things (e.g., are made up of one or more cells, require energy for life processes, respond to stimuli in their environment, and have the ability to reproduce).	• Work On It, p. 6
DL6.2 e. Describe how aspects of First Nations and Métis worldviews (e.g., holistic, interconnectedness, valuing of place-based knowledge) shape their systems of organizing understanding of living things.	• Think Again!, p. 7

Background Information

As students begin to explore the ideas of living and non-living things, they may have questions about why some things are classified as biotic or abiotic. As they go through the unit and build on their prior knowledge, their ideas will become more developed. Scientists have developed a set of characteristics that allow everything to be divided into one of the two groups. This form of identification helps scientists with consistency in their descriptions and gives them common terminology for their communications. In this lesson, the students will discuss the seven characteristics that, according to scientists, qualify something to be considered as living. They will also become familiar with the terms biotic and abiotic. They may be surprised to find that some things, such as a log or a dead leaf, are considered biotic because they were once living.

traditional ***KNOWLEDGE***

Throughout this unit, students will explore information about First Nations and Métis peoples. In this lesson, they will discuss the idea of spirit guides and learn about how they are considered to watch over a clan or family. Students will also learn that many Aboriginal people believe that humans are related to everything in Mother Earth. This belief helps them maintain an abiding respect for the sacredness of all things, living and non-living. It reinforces the idea that we all have a responsibility to ourselves and to future generations to care for Mother Earth and become stewards of the environment.

continued →

For most of Saskatchewan's First Nations and Métis people, the physical world is inseparable from the non-physical world of metaphysics, which includes spirit. This view is unlike the dualistic thinking that pervades aspects of Western thought. According to most First Nations and Métis groups, spirit is not separately defined but is a part of all created things, which includes some objects that Western science would term abiotic, such as wind, fire, and water. Thus, created things share a connectedness. Regardless of the language, be it Cree, Lakota, or Ojibwa, prayers said by many First Nations Elders often end with the phrase "All my relations." This phrase describes the connectedness that we share with all of creation.

For the Plains nations, spirit forms the fifth and perhaps the most important element. One Cree Elder, Stuart Prosper, explains that an "entity has spirit if it can take life and give life." Therefore, items that science would classify as non-living, such as rocks and fire, have the capacity to take and give life. As a result, these items are considered animate and living. Fire, for example, gives life to humans by providing us with heat and light, yet devastating fires can kill entire swaths of forested land and the organisms that live in it. For First Nations groups, a fire spirit dwells within a flame. For that reason, a flame used to light a fire for a ceremony is never blown out. To blow out a match would risk hindering the spirit in the fire. This belief about spirit forms a crucial part of First Nations and Métis ways of knowing.

Even though the concept of spirit is beyond the scope of a science program, the belief is valid and sacred in the context of First Nations and Métis ways of knowing. It is a way that people who follow their respective traditional paths understand and explain the natural world. It is important that teachers acknowledge the belief of the First Nations and Métis people without denigrating it by directly or indirectly comparing it with science in a negative light.

Any comparison drawn between the worldviews of First Nations and Métis groups and Western scientists should be made to help students understand that there are different ways of knowing the natural world. It is crucial that students learn that other established cultural ways of knowing the world have validity in their own right. To measure traditional knowledge against Western science implies that Western science is the only measurable, observable, and correct way of knowing the natural world. The traditional knowledge of First Nations and Métis people has never attempted to describe the world in a strictly empirical and measurable way, like scientific knowledge has. As a result, a direct comparison of the two systems is not a suitable measure. It would be akin to comparing stories from a faith to those of science.

The traditional knowledge of First Nations and Métis people came from their struggle to survive and was obtained through careful observation of natural phenomena over many generations. For these people, the experimental ground was life and the validity of that experiment resulted in their survival. Their traditional knowledge has great validity since that body of knowledge has helped these societies survive for countless generations in the harsh Saskatchewan climate.

Note: The concept of a spirit guide is not attributable to all First Nations, and groups to whom this idea applies may have a different term to describe a spirit guide.

Some First Nations and Métis groups believe in metaphysical entities called "protecting spirits" or "spirit guides," which they call the "grandfathers and grandmothers." These are the spirits of many powerful animals and animate entities like rocks, water, fire, and plants that protect and guide humans. Grandfathers and grandmothers are not deceased relatives or ancestors to whom these people pray. Rather some groups, like the Cree, believe that the grandfathers and grandmothers are the spirits of the animals and plants that have come to help, to teach, and to dwell with humans because they took pity on humans. In these creation stories, humans, having no remarkable adaptations like claws or fur, needed the help of spirit guides to endure harsh climes. Thus, beings like "grandfather" buffalo gave their lives so that humans might survive.

Because of these remarkable gifts, spirit is revered. Tobacco, the pipe, the stone, fire, and the buffalo are examples of the great gifts bestowed on humanity. As a result, among many First Nations and Métis groups, spirit is regarded with reverence. The physical manifestations of an animal or plant spirit are also considered sacred.

Get Started ▶

- Ask students to conduct a discussion by incorporating a Talking Circle.
- Arrange chairs in a circle. A circle has no beginning or end, which indicates that all members have equal status.
- Provide an object such as a walking stick or special stone that may be passed from student to student.
- Only the person holding the object may speak. When the object is passed, each person may speak or pass. Everyone's presence is appreciated whether they speak or not.
- Each member must respect the others in the group — no put-downs are allowed and what is said remains in the circle.
- Start the Talking Circle by asking, *Why do we need to care for Earth?*

- Ask students, *Have you ever thought about how Earth is a living, evolving thing?* Their answers will vary and will provide an opportunity to introduce the idea that First Nations and Métis people respect all living and non-living things and have a sense of responsibility to care for Earth.
- Read the first three paragraphs on page 4 of the student book and give the students a chance to discuss the idea of spirit guides. Ask them to think about how different cultures have traditions regarding the care of nature and stewardship of the environment.

Science and Living Things

- Ask students what they think are the differences between living and non-living things.
- Ask them to read pages 4 and 5 of the student book to see how closely their thinking lines up with the actual characteristics of living things.

The term "biotic" means living or once living. Things such as a log or a dead leaf are biotic because they were once living. Scientists use the terms "biotic" and "abiotic" to trace the interactions of these factors within a system. You may wish to ask your students to describe several things as biotic or abiotic and give reasons for their choices. Abiotic things include sunlight, wind, temperature, mineral soil particles, and water, sometimes in the form of precipitation. Biotic things include all living things such as plants and animals.

Time

40 min

Skills

- classifying
- communicating

Grouping

individuals, groups

Materials and Equipment

(per group)
- notebook
- pen or pencil

Line Masters

- LM 1-3

Work On It

- Ask students to copy the table from page 6 of the student book into their notebooks. You may want them to use a ruler and give them exact measurements for their rows and columns. Alternatively, hand out LM 1-3 Living Things.
- Students may need to guess their Yes or No answers and will need to discuss their answers with others. Ask them to write their answers into their notebooks.
- You may wish to provide a blank chart (LM 1-3) for this activity and have students record their answers to share with others.
- Students will need time to compare their lists with those of their classmates. You may wish to organize them so that one person from each group moves to a neighbouring group at your signal. Continue this rotation until students have had a chance to discuss their charts with several other groups.

Think Again! The Idea of Stewardship

- Ask students something like, *What responsibilities do you have? Do you help look after the environment? What kinds of things do/could you do?*
- Ask students to use the Think-Pair-Share method to process the information on student book page 7. Ask them to read the paragraphs and bullets.
- When they are finished reading, ask them to share the important points with a partner. Give them an opportunity to share their partner's thinking with the whole group.
- Expect students to be able to explain the idea of interdependence and to include some information about how Aboriginal people believe in stewardship of the land.

! The answer to the riddle is **life**. Scientists include more than just organic things in their definition of biotic items. They also include interdependence and the relationships between living things within an ecosystem as biotic factors.

Communicate

Students will have an opportunity to represent their learning by drawing and labelling an ecosystem for display in the classroom. As well as making sure every student participates, each group of four could have a reporter (to report to the whole class), a recorder (to keep track of the group's progress), a checker (to make sure the group understands the task and stays on track), and a gofer (to manage the group's materials). Students' posters should include the following criteria:

- colour representations of all parts of the ecosystem
- a clear labelling system to demonstrate biotic and abiotic elements

An ecosystem can be described as a community of living things, together with their physical environment, and viewed as a system of interdependent relationships. It includes processes such as the flow of energy and the cycling of chemical elements through components of the system.

For ESL/ELL

Some ESL/ELL students may need extra time to review the key words and phrases and the more complex ideas. It may be helpful for them to keep a notebook with specific definitions and descriptions. You may wish to provide photos of each of the objects named in the chart in the Work On It activity on student book page 6.

For Enrichment

Some students may be interested in doing more research on ecosystems and the impact that civilization has had on them. They may wish to do a Venn diagram of an ecosystem, which shows the overlap between various factors. For example, they could draw a Venn diagram of living things that move in an ecosystem. One circle would list the living things that move on the ground and one circle would list the living things that move through the air. The intersection of the two circles would include animals that do both. They could use the image on page 5 in the student book as a model for their ecosystem.

Assessment *for* Learning

What to Look For in Student Work	What to Do
Students should be able to describe the characteristics of biotic and abiotic things and list the seven characteristics of living things. Students should be able to explain why stewardship of Earth is an important concept. Students should be able to draw a large diagram with items labelled "abiotic" and "biotic."	• Review the materials on student book page 5. Reinforce the idea of stewardship and what it means (student book page 7). • Make sure students understand biotic and abiotic factors by giving plenty of examples of each and allowing the students to group them accordingly. Give students a simple diagram to get them started if they are unsure how to draw an ecosystem.
Students should also be able to describe how First Nations and Métis worldviews shape their systems of organizing and understanding living things.	• Allow students extra time to discuss differing worldviews, so that they become used to considering differing points of view.

2 Methods of Classifying

Page 8

Time

1–2 class periods

Key Terms

- taxonomy

Line Masters

- LM 1-4

Indicator Assessment Chart

Indicator	Assessment Opportunities
DL6.2 a. Construct and use a classification system to organize living things into groups and subgroups according to student-developed criteria.	• Work On It, p. 10

Background Information

In this lesson, students learn a variety of more common and familiar ways to classify objects. They explore the tree classification system, and apply this technique to the classification of transportation vehicles. There are an estimated 3 to 30 million species on Earth, and only about 1.4 million have been named and described. All things can be classified, or sorted into groups, by their shared attributes. As classification gets more detailed, the number of objects in a group will get smaller, and the objects within the groups will have more characteristics in common.

Living things are classified by structural features. This classification technique was first described by Carolus Linnaeus (1707–1778) in his volume *Systema Naturae*, published in 1735. Interestingly, he constructed his classification tree by working in reverse of standard practices, starting at the species levels and devising groups from their characteristics, rather than starting with two large groups and working down. Linnaeus also gave us the nomenclature, or naming system, for organisms.

traditional **KNOWLEDGE**

Sometimes, First Nations and Métis people use words in their language as a guide to the way items look or how they are used. This approach helps pass along knowledge about the environment over generations and aids in the transmission of important facts and characteristics of living and non-living things in the environment. All languages have examples of vocabulary that describe the purpose of an item. We use words like heart-smart or riverbend, for example.

Get Started ▶

- Invite all students in the class to sort themselves into groups based on their hair colour. Then ask, *Can you think of something else that can divide the people in your group into other groups?* Students are likely to identify attributes like gender, skin colour, or clothing type.
- Ask students to remain in their hair-colour groups and form new subgroups. Challenge them to find one more attribute that can be used to further sort all the groups.
- Ask the students, *Can you describe yourself based on the final group you're in?*
- Direct the students' attention to the photo of various groups on student book page 8 and ask, *Do you have collections or groups of things in your room? What about in your desk? How do you organize these things so you can find things when you need them?*
- After students have shared the ways in which their possessions are organized, challenge the class to think of other ways they could be organized.
- Point out the illustrations of the library shelf and the music shop on student book page 8. For each picture, ask, *What objects are classified in this picture? What characteristics are being used to classify the objects?*
- After students have discussed these examples as a class, direct them to make two lists to show the types of books and music in the illustrations. You might ask for a volunteer to describe how he or she would find a particular book or CD.
- Point out that we can "read" illustrations and diagrams just as we read text. Discuss how best to read the diagram on student book page 9. Together, look at the title and then at the various levels of information.
- Ask students why a diagram is sometimes more helpful than running text for obtaining information.

One System of Classification

- Ask the class to tell you where your school is located. Students are likely to respond with details of the school's address (street, town, province). Encourage students to add as much additional information as they can to describe where the school is: the country, continent, planet, solar system, galaxy, and universe. Record their responses on the board.
- Ask the class to look at the tree classification chart on student book page 9 and ask, *Can we put our school into any of these categories?* Students should be able to identify four categories.
- Point out that the tree classification diagram contains information similar to the school's address on the board, but that it starts with the biggest area of the address and works down.

Toolkit 5 will help students see a variety of ways they can use organizers to help them organize information as they begin to classify objects.

Time

40 min

Skills

- classifying
- making models

Grouping

individuals

Materials and Equipment

(per group)
- atlases
- notebook
- pen or pencil

Line Masters

- LM 1-4

Work On It

- Students can work individually on the activity in the student book. Direct them to copy the diagram on page 9 of the student book onto a fresh piece of paper, making sure they leave enough space to add to it. Alternatively, you may wish to use LM 1-4 Methods of Classifying.
- You may want to list the home addresses of class members on a chart at the front of the classroom so that all students have enough information to build a detailed tree classification diagram.

Think Again! What's in a Name?

Cree is a verb-based language. Names given to objects in Cree are descriptive, like in Latin. In Cree, unlike in English, a word's meaning may also describe the usage or the action associated with an object. For example, the Cree word for chokecherry is takwehiminan, which means "berry that is crushed." Even though Cree words can be long, they are very useful.

- Ask students to look at the table on student book page 10. Let them try pronouncing the Cree words to each other.
- Ask them to think about words in our language that describe an actual object (e.g., longhouse, riverbend, etc.). Ask them to make a list in their notebooks to share with the whole class.
- Make a list on chart paper to display the describing words that students suggest.

Communicate

The Communicate questions can be completed individually or in pairs. Remind students to sort the transportation vehicles into groups that make sense and to clearly label each part of their tree classification systems.

1. Answers will vary.
   a. Students' answers are likely to refer to transportation methods.
   b. Groups that students identify will likely include land vehicles, air vehicles, and water vehicles. Other possibilities are vehicles used in summer, vehicles used in winter, vehicles used year-round; vehicles for fun, vehicles for work; motorized vehicles, non-motorized vehicles.
   c. Subgroups will depend on the initial groups chosen. Some possibilities are: one-person vehicles, multi-person vehicles; vehicles with wheels, vehicles without wheels.
   d. It may be helpful to remind students that the final category should describe at least one way in which each vehicle is different from all of the other vehicles.
   e. Divide the class into pairs. Each partner should review the other's work, and then modify his or her own work if necessary.
   f. Students should be able to clearly explain the reasoning behind the categories in their classification trees.
2. Answer will vary. Students should give examples of how they might classify objects in their homes using a tree classification system.
3. Answers will vary. Students should recognize that there are some benefits to being able to classify people, but that there is a danger in stereotyping or marginalizing people by identifying them strictly by certain characteristics.

For ESL/ELL

This lesson provides a good opportunity for students to share some of the vocabulary from their first language. Ask them if they can think of words in their language that demonstrate what an object looks like or what it is used for.

For Reteaching

Provide students with a collection of 10 to 15 similar objects, such as books of different genres, pictures of different flowers, or a collection of buttons. Ask students to sort the objects into groups based on common attributes. They must continue to sort until every object is in a group on its own. Challenge students to draw the classification systems they came up with on a tree diagram.

Assessment *for* Learning

What to Look For in Student Work	What to Do
The level that students reach independently in making their classification tree is an opportunity to assess students' understanding of classification. Observe if they proceed to house numbers or stop at streets. Students should be able to organize their classification trees into groups and logical subgroups. Collect their classification charts for inclusion in their portfolios.	• If students have difficulty, try letting them do a very simple tree diagram or give them a graphic organizer to get them started. Using an Inductive Thinking activity is a good way to allow students who are visual/kinesthetic learners to experience success. Give each group of three or four students a set of objects (i.e., magazine pictures of various animals, plants, etc.) and let them group the objects in any way they choose. All group members must agree with the grouping and be able to explain why they organized the objects as they did. This activity allows students to explore the characteristics of objects, work together to decide on what is important, and experience organizing items in a hands-on way.
Answers to question 2 will demonstrate their success in identifying various kinds of classification systems used to organize information.	• Expect students to be able to make logical groupings of things around their house and then organize them into subgroups that make sense.

3 Classifying Living Things

Page 12

Time

1–2 class periods

Key Terms

- place-based knowledge
- species
- genus
- family
- order
- class
- phylum
- kingdom
- carnivorous
- structures
- multicellular
- vascular
- non-vascular
- single-celled

Line Masters

- LM 1-5

Indicator Assessment Chart

Indicator	Assessment Opportunities
DL6.2 a. Construct and use a classification system to organize living things into groups and subgroups according to student-developed criteria.	• Get Started, p. 12 • Work On It, p. 14
DL6.2 b. Consider personal observations and ideas as well as those of others (including differing worldviews) when constructing classification systems by asking questions, sharing stories, and responding to classmates' classification systems.	• Get Started, p. 12 • Communicate, p. 16, q. 5–6
DL6.2 c. Demonstrate how different classification systems can be used to classify the same set of objects and explain how humans develop and refine systems to meet specific needs.	• Get Started, p. 12 • Communicate, p. 16, q. 4

Background Information

In this lesson, students work individually to build on their understanding of the tree classification system. They consider why some characteristics are useful for classifying objects, and why other characteristics are not. The five kingdoms of living things, Monera, Protist, Plant, Animal, and Fungi, are introduced. Students are asked to sort the living things illustrated in the Launch lesson as belonging to the Plant, Animal, or Fungus kingdom.

The five major kingdoms used to classify organisms were initially proposed by R.H. Whittaker in 1969. They are:

- Monera — one-celled organisms without definite nuclei
- Protists — one-celled organisms with definite nuclei
- Fungi — multicellular non-photosynthetic organisms with nuclei that obtain nutrients from organic sources
- Plants — multicellular photosynthetic organisms with nuclei
- Animals — multicellular organisms that do not produce their own food and move by means of muscle and nerve tissues

traditional **KNOWLEDGE**

The defining characteristics of these kingdoms have changed and continue to change as new living things and new information about living things are discovered. Viruses, for example, do not fit in any of the five classic kingdoms. Some algae, such as blue-green algae, were once classified as plants, but are now more commonly included in the Protist kingdom.

In this lesson, students are introduced to the concept of place-based knowledge — a way that Aboriginal people group things according to their usefulness for particular purposes. Students should understand that various nations have different ways of describing plants and animals and that there is a wide variety of unique grouping methods.

!

Aboriginal peoples have developed ways of teaching and learning that emphasize their values and traditions. While each First Nation is unique, many use story, song, dance, and art to pass along their histories to younger generations. Many Elders are stewards of knowledge and are depended upon to keep language, tradition, and history alive.

Get Started ▶

traditional **KNOWLEDGE**

- Traditional knowledge is by nature place based. Place-based knowledge is collections of teachings passed down over time by a group of people about occurrences, organisms, weather conditions, natural phenomena, medicines, and traditional stories that are specific to a certain geographic region. Traditional knowledge is about people and their relationship to the land. Frequently, place-based knowledge is about ways that enable people to survive in a particular environment. Knowledge such as times of harvest, hunting and gathering sites, ways to tan hides, and types of medicinal plants are a few examples.
- In Saskatchewan, First Nations and Métis people have passed down insights about the land and survival from one generation to the next for many centuries. Among the FNM people, place-based knowledge has many uses. For example, teachings about the kinds of deer and when they migrate to a specific locale are forms of place-based knowledge. Groups of Dené people as well as some northern Cree have six seasons in their understanding of the yearly seasonal changes: spring, summer, fall, freeze-up, winter, and break-up. Information about types of food, medicines, climate, and plants also may be specific to the locale. First Nations and Métis use of plants, animals, and substances for healing often differed from group to group and may therefore be locally defined.

- There is a danger of attributing one local indigenous teaching to all First Nations and Métis peoples. Often, information and ways that plants and animals were used are specific to a reserve, a particular family, or an individual. When generalizations are expressed, especially when they concern specific traditional teachings that an Elder gives, another danger is misappropriation of information. Many Elders wish to be credited for their knowledge, not because it raises their profile but because they want to ensure that the information stays true to their experience and is respected. When transmitting teachings of a specific nature, it is crucial to explain from which First Nation or Métis group the information came and from whom as a sign of respect for the information and the person. Some forms of knowledge, which are given privately, remain for one's use only. For example, the Cree have teachings reserved for women since only a woman may experience that part of life's journey. Be sure to check with an Elder about what knowledge can be repeated orally, what can be repeated in writing for public reading (e.g., class notes or the Internet), and what must remain private.
- Ask your students to think of things that they could add to place-based knowledge.
- Ask the class to name as many living things as they can. List students' suggestions on the board.
- Once there is a sufficient number of examples, challenge the students to build a tree classification diagram with the items on the list.
- Start the chart by writing "Living Things" for the main heading. Remind students that for the first level of the chart, they need broad categories that will include as many organisms on the list as possible.
- Encourage students to think about the types of characteristics that they can use for categories by asking questions like, *Is that true of all the organisms in the group? Is it true for an organism's whole life? Are there any organisms not in the group that also have that characteristic?*
- Ask students to study the list of characteristics of living things on student book page 12. Ask, *Which characteristics would you choose to make a classification tree?*
- Prompt their thinking by asking further questions such as, *Can any of these characteristics separate plants from animals? Which characteristics can be found in both plants and animals?*
- Invite students to read the first two paragraphs in Get Started, and then answer the questions in the third paragraph.
- When they have finished, ask for volunteers to read their lists to the class, and then discuss their ideas as a class.
- For students who have difficulty understanding that some characteristics are more useful than others, ask, *Does a flower have to be pretty in order for it to be a flower? Do spiders eat things other than flies?*

How Scientists Classify

- Ask students to read "How Scientists Classify" on pages 12 and 13 of the student book.
- Ask them to answer the questions in the last paragraph on page 13.
- Students should understand that it is easier for scientists to classify animals by their structural characteristics and that they use this method to organize information about all living things.
- You may wish students to talk in pairs to make lists describing a variety of living things. Let them check each others' lists to look for structural characteristics.
- Ask students to examine the Tree of Life chart on student book page 13. Ask them to look at the photos and challenge them to think of more living things that could be classified under each kingdom.

There are over 1 000 000 species within the animal kingdom. Scientists believe that there are millions more still to be discovered! If your students do a search on the Internet using the phrase "five kingdoms of living things," they will come up with a range of sites suitable for their exploration.

Tree of Life #1

- Engage the class in looking at the classification chart of the five kingdoms on student book page 13. Ask, *How many of you have heard of the plant kingdom or the animal kingdom?* What do you know about these kingdoms? Encourage volunteers to share what they know.
- Many students may not be familiar with the monera and protist kingdoms. Explain that these kingdoms were created only after scientists learned more about single-celled living things. Students may be surprised to learn that mushrooms are fungi.
- Many students believe that all living things in existence have already been found and described. Emphasize that there are many unknown species. It is believed, for example, that only half of the insect species have been found. Say something like, *When new living things are discovered, they are placed into these five kingdoms. If they do not fit in a kingdom, scientists must change the way they place things into these five kingdoms, or consider making a new kingdom.*
- Ask students to work individually to classify the organisms from the illustration in the Diversity at the Zoo activity on student book pages 2–3, then share their suggestions with the class. Encourage students to support their ideas with reasons.
- Some students may be interested in collecting photographs of living things and using them to create a mobile of the five kingdoms. Encourage students to include annotated titles that will identify the main characteristics of the organisms in each kingdom.
- Invite students to add to their mobiles during the unit as they learn more about the classification of living things.

Time
40 min
Skills
• classifying • inferring
Grouping
individuals
Materials and Equipment
(per group) • notebook • pen or pencil
Line Masters
• LM 1-5

Work On It

- Ask students to read the instructions and identify some of the plants and animals in the photos on student book page 15.
- Ask students to create a table in their notebooks with four columns. Label the columns Plants, Animals, Fungi, and Not sure. Alternatively, photocopy LM 1-5 Classifying Living Things for students.
- Allow students to work in pairs or small groups to discuss in which column each of the plants, animals, and fungi should be placed.
- Students may need to use an encyclopedia or the Internet to help them identify the living things in the photos.
- Key for organisms on page 15:
  Top (from L to R): tamarack, wolverine, white spruce, brook trout, lichen
  2nd row from top (from L to R): jack-rabbit, timber wolf, house wren, spear grass
  3rd row (from L to R): caribou, fungus (*Pholiota flammans*), white-throated sparrow
  4th row (from L to R): needle-and-thread grass, lodgepole pine, beaver, badger
  5th row (from L to R): Richardson ground squirrel, pine grosbeak, white-tailed deer (fawn), coyote
  6th row (from L to R): Western kingbird, jack pine, brown trout
  7th row (from L to R): black spruce, sharp-tailed grouse, walleye, tree sparrow, lake trout, (above trout) snow goose
  Bottom row (from L to R): black bear, bison, wild wheat grass, cougar, ovenbird

Communicate

The following characteristics listed on student book page 12 are useful for classification:

- humans have lungs to breathe with
- frogs can live in water and on land
- birds have wings
- elephants give birth to live young

Bringing the class together to discuss their responses can provide an opportunity to reinforce that permanent, well-defined characteristics related to the structure of living things are useful for classification, but those that are variable or subjective (such as prettiness) are not.

1. Students may have differing opinions about which living things should be placed in which kingdoms. They may need help in identifying some of the photos.

2. The five kingdoms of living things are Monera, Protists, Plants, Animals, and Fungi.

3. Fungi are unlike plants in that they cannot make their own food and must obtain their food from other organisms. They are unlike animals because they cannot move from place to place. They are unlike both plants and animals in that they can be single celled.

4. Answers will vary. It will help students to work in groups in order to share their thinking about how they might classify animals. They may come up with ideas such as colour, size, habitat, shape, food, behaviours, etc.

5. Answers will vary. Allow students some time to share their questions with group members and with the class as a whole.

6. Answers will vary. Students may be encouraged to think about items that they think Aboriginal people may have used in daily life and how they might be grouped. After the students discuss their questions with a classmate, you may wish to record students' questions on a chart for future reference.

traditional *KNOWLEDGE*

For most First Nations and Métis groups, transmission of knowledge (teaching) involves respect for that knowledge and its keeper. Often the teaching is given to anyone who asks and respects the protocol of the person being asked, but some knowledge is restricted and conditionally given only to a chosen few. Based on these practices, students (and teachers) need to understand a few basic rules of protocol (etiquette) in asking an Elder for help. The following is protocol to observe when asking an Elder for cultural or traditional knowledge.

continued →

1) **Ask about protocol.** Often it is wise to ask Elders about the protocols they use. They know that because you are not from their communities, you may not be familiar with their customs. They would be more than happy to explain those protocols.

2) **Bring an appropriate gift or offering.** When one approaches an Elder, a Knowledge Keeper, or anyone who follows the traditional path, one needs to bring an appropriate gift or offering. For many First Nations and Métis people, Tobacco is appropriate. Tobacco has been used for many generations as a type of offering. Many, if not all, First Nations and Métis people feel that Tobacco is offered as a sign of respect. The amount of Tobacco need not be significant. It can be as little as a single cigarette. Jams and tea are offered in some communities (e.g., Air Ronge). The act of giving a gift or offering comes from the value of reciprocity — the belief in the act of giving and taking. Many First Nations and Métis groups practise this value since they believe that a teaching that is earned is valued much more than one that is gratuitously given. Often in ceremony, when an Elder or any practitioner asks the Creator for help, he or she gives Tobacco. Traditional drummers will offer Tobacco to the spirit in the animal who gave its life to make their drums.

   The Elder will often consider one's request before answering. Give the Elder time to reflect. If the Elder is able to help, he or she will keep your Tobacco. If he or she returns the Tobacco, the Elder cannot fulfil your request. Follow up the presentation of the offering with a handshake.

3) **Listen carefully.** If the request is granted, the answer one gets may teach through a story. Many Elders use the ethic of non-interference in their teaching. They do not give the teaching directly because they want learners to reflect and to discern the knowledge for themselves.

4) **Pay for their costs.** If you invite an Elder to your classroom, remember to offer gas money and an honorarium for their time, or if possible, please arrange for transportation. Many Elders are aged, and many do not drive a vehicle.

5) **Be hospitable.** Offer tea (customary for many First Nations and Métis groups) and something to eat.

Things to avoid:

- One might call to arrange a visit with an Elder, but offer the Tobacco in person and receive the teaching face to face. Never ask for the teaching directly on the phone. It is too impersonal.
- Learning from an Elder requires relationship building. Please be accepting if the Elder refuses or can't fulfil your request. Some teachings are only given if the Elder feels that you are allowed to have that knowledge. For example, men may not ask women Elders for teachings on women and reproduction.
- Listen to what Elders do not say as much as to what they do say. If they seem to avoid a specific topic, there is a reason. They will not likely tell you the reason. It is for the listener to figure out or just accept.
- Teachers may wish to contact their division offices. Some divisions have Aboriginal co-ordinators who may already have resources at their disposal and contact with Elders. The office of the Treaty Commissioner retains a list of Elders who may wish to come and present to your classroom.

BUILD ON WHAT YOU KNOW

Ask the students to read over the instructions on student book page 16 and look over the "My Tree" chart at the bottom of the page. They will be building a classification tree chart that will be referenced throughout the unit. As they learn more about classification, they will add levels to their charts. Students will need to post their charts or store them somewhere where they can be easily retrieved, so they can continue to make additions throughout the unit. It will be helpful if they start their charts fairly small so that they can add levels at a later date. You may wish them to do a rough draft of the charts that they can re-do as a final project to represent their learning at the end of the unit. Ensure the subgroups they create on their charts are distinct from each other. Encourage students to check that each thing they include in their charts can fit in only one category at each level of their charts.

You might ask your students to search for Northern Lights Food on the Internet to explore the company website. Ask students to list examples of the plant and fungi kingdoms that this First Nations company provides.

Assessment *for* Learning

What to Look For in Student Work	What to Do
Students should be able to discuss the characteristics of living things and demonstrate an understanding of criteria that are useful for classification. Expect them to be able to identify important details and sort living things into groups. As students work on their classification charts, you can observe how well they use appropriate vocabulary and terminology. At this point in the unit, they should be able to use the key terms: biotic, abiotic, stewardship, ecosystem, place-based knowledge, species, genus, family, order, class, phylum, kingdom, carnivorous, structures, multicellular, vascular, non-vascular, single-celled, and taxonomy.	• If students have difficulty sorting, review the materials on student book page 12 and provide them with further examples of characteristics to be sorted. Help students by encouraging them to use the new vocabulary in their discussions and explanations. If they are having difficulty, organize a discussion where each student must contribute a comment, using at least one of the key terms. They can prepare their comment in advance or work with a partner to decide on their term. Once they have all had a chance to contribute and listened to their classmates, they will have processed all of the terms in context.

4 Classifying Trees

Page 17

Time
1–2 class periods

Key Terms
• coniferous trees • deciduous trees

Line Masters
• LM 1-6

Indicator Assessment Chart

Indicator	Assessment Opportunities
DL6.1 b. Observe and document the diversity of living things in their local habitat through journaling, a nature walk, sketching, drawing, photographing, video recording, or other means.	• Work On It, p. 20
DL6.1 c. Show respect for other people, living things, and the environment when observing ecosystems.	• Work On It, p. 20
DL6.1 d. Document the diversity of living things in different terrestrial and aquatic habitats (e.g., grasslands, forests, tundra, deserts, rivers, ponds, and oceans) using print, video, and/or on-line resources.	• Work On It, p. 20 • If Time Allows, p. 20
DL6.2 a. Construct and use a classification system to organize living things into groups and subgroups according to student-developed criteria.	• Work On It, p. 20 • Build On What You Know, p. 20

traditional ***KNOWLEDGE***

Background Information

A classification key is a hierarchical arrangement of distinguishing features that is used to identify an organism. The simplest keys are usually based on an artificial classification system that uses only a few characteristics, chosen to make identification easy. Most field guides are artificial classification keys. They use characteristics such as habitat preference for birds, or edible and inedible for plants. These keys do not necessarily reflect evolutionary relationships, and not all members of a species will always fit the description. The arrangement of organisms into kingdoms, phyla, etc., down to species, is a natural classification system. This system reflects evolutionary relationships because their organization is based on invariant characteristics. The characteristics are usually structural features that are found in all members of the species regardless of variations in local environment or life events (barring amputations, etc.). All members of a particular species will always fit the description. The classification keys presented in the lesson are simplified natural classification keys. The smallest groups on a classification key are usually species. The smallest groups on the key in the student book are the common names of either the species or the genus (one level above species).

Students will read about specific ways that First Nations and Métis people use trees native to Saskatchewan. Students will take a closer look at birch and tamarack trees and how they are used for a variety of purposes. While the Dené First Nation is highlighted as a user of the tamarack tree in this lesson, there are over 80 First Nations bands in Saskatchewan, many of which belong to tribal councils. More information can be found on the website First Nations Bands of Saskatchewan: http://www.sicc.sk.ca/bands/.

Get Started ▶

- Bring in samples of a small leaf-bearing twig from one coniferous and one deciduous tree that grow in your area and are on the classification key. If this is not possible, find pictures of two tree species that show the leaves and branch structure. Make them available around the classroom for students to refer to.
- Ask students to find one of the tree species on the classification key. Ask them to list the characteristics for that species that are on the key in their journals. When they have finished, ask questions about the sample or pictures you provided, using the scientific terms on the key.
- If you bring in a maple twig, for example, you might ask, *Can anyone tell me why we call this leaf a simple leaf? What do we mean when we say these leaves are opposite on the twig?*
- Challenge students to explain their answers using the samples or pictures. Repeat this procedure for the other tree samples you provided.

Saskatchewan Tree Stories

traditional ***KNOWLEDGE***

- Many types of trees used traditionally by First Nations and Métis people offer medicinal and survival uses beyond the ones mentioned in the student book on page 17. Many First Nations and Métis groups have used other readily available woods, such as lodgepole pine and willow.
- The willow is a sacred plant in the practices of many Plains people. On the prairies, the Plains Cree often used the willow to fashion various structures. The sweat lodge is one such structure. Its frame was made of long young willow trees and draped with hide or canvas. The Sundance lodge employs willows bound together to fashion a dancing arena.

- Even products from the willow, such as the bark, were used for art and decorative purposes. Some groups like the Dené of northern Saskatchewan and the Northwest Territories made willow into baskets. Some of the women were so expert, they often used their teeth to cut and to make images and decorations into the skin of the willow bark. A fungus that lives on the bark of the willow, called the *willow tear*, was used in ceremony. For more information on traditional Dené art, see the website Birchbark Baskets (http://www.fortliard.com/bbb.htm).
- Lodgepole pine was used to fashion teepees. The tallest and straightest trees were chosen. The bark was stripped and tied together to form a conical structure.
- Students may wonder why it is important to identify trees. Start a discussion by asking, *Can anyone think of a job where you might need to identify trees?* Direct the discussion to include occupations such as loggers, landscapers, nut growers, and park and conservation workers.
- Other questions you might ask are, *What would happen to a bird that only lived in jack pines if you planted red pines by mistake? Would you be able to sell your lumber if you cut down ash trees when your customers wanted walnut wood? What other ways can you find that First Nations and Métis people used birch and tamarack trees?*

! Scientists have found fossil evidence of ancient forests at the South Pole. These forests were thick with 25-m-high trees that grew in numbers of over 500 per hectare. Although the climate was warmer then, these trees needed to adapt to live without sunlight for six months of the year!

Time

40 min

Skills

- observing
- classifying

Grouping

individuals
pairs
groups

Materials and Equipment

(per group)
- paper
- pen or pencil
- camera (optional)

Line Masters

- LM 1-6

Work On It

- Before going outside to identify trees, review the leaf characteristics students will be looking for. Outlining hints such as the following on the board may be helpful:
  - Make sure you look for features like the type of leaf, what shape it is, and where it is in relation to other leaves on the twig.
  - Start at the top of the classification key and work down one step at a time. For each step, decide if the leaves on the tree match the description on the key.
  - Review the decisions you make until you and your partner both feel sure you have identified the type of tree.
- You may wish to hand out LM 1-6 Classifying Trees to students so that they can sketch the leaves they find in step 4.

Communicate

Question 1 may be answered in class. The remaining questions can be assigned as individual seatwork or homework.

1. Students will suggest a variety of strategies: taking a twig to a nursery, asking a forester, or using a more detailed classification key.
2. Answers might include: the type of tree is not on the key, the tree was diseased, or the branches were damaged and the leaf position could not be seen.
3. Students should state that coniferous trees have leaves like needles or scales, and deciduous trees have wide leaves. Some students may know that deciduous trees lose all their leaves in the fall.
4. Most students will include the words "coniferous" and "deciduous." Encourage them to add the scientific terms that describe leaves: simple, compound, opposite, alternate, lobes, needles, and scales.

BUILD ON WHAT YOU KNOW

Students will add three different types of plants to their My Tree charts. Encourage them to be as accurate as they can, and to include enough detail for others to be able to understand and follow the chart.

If Time Allows

- Ask students to take photos of leaves from around their home or collect photos and use the classification key to identify the trees. As they work through the key, ask questions based on the descriptions at each level. You might ask questions such as, *Are these leaves like needles or scales, or are they wide? Are the needles arranged as single needles or are they in bunches?*

For Reteaching

To reinforce the concepts, ask students to design and put together another type of classification tree. Ask students to collect a variety of weeds, wild plants, or grasses from their yards. Caution them to get help from their parents and to take only samples of weeds and not to damage or take flowers, etc., from gardens. Ask them to try to identify their plants using the Internet. Once they have identified and grouped their plants, ask them to make a classification chart for their samples. Ask them questions like, *How did you identify your plant? What characteristics did you notice when you were grouping your samples? Why did you group them the way you did?*

For Enrichment

Challenge students to work together in small groups to design a quiz game or set of questions based on the characteristics of coniferous and deciduous trees. Invite them to pose their questions to other groups. Ask the groups to use the tree classification keys for reference when they answer the questions.

Assessment *for* Learning

What to Look For in Student Work	What to Do
Students should be able to apply and correctly use the new vocabulary and terminology learned in this lesson, specifically, "coniferous" and "deciduous."	• Keep a checklist of student responses. Include vocabulary and terminology from this and the previous lessons. Review these terms frequently for those students who need extra help.
Using key terms, students should be able to construct and use a more detailed classification system to organize living things into groups and subgroups.	• Use the students' tree classification systems to evaluate their organizational ability. If some students need help with setting up and adding to their trees, provide good models by displaying and discussing exceptional examples from their classmates.

5 Classifying Animals — The Invertebrates

Page 21

Time
1–2 class periods

Key Terms
• invertebrates • vertebrates • parasites

Line Masters
• LM 1-7 • LM 1-8

Indicator Assessment Chart

Indicator	Assessment Opportunities
DL6.3 c. Compare and represent characteristics and behaviours (e.g., body shape, body description, method of respiration, method of reproduction, method of movement, and method of feeding) of student-selected examples of invertebrates (e.g., arthropods, annelids, cnidarids, echinoderms, molluscs, and nematodes).	• Work on It, p. 23
DL6.3 d. Propose questions for inquiry that arise from personal investigations of characteristics and behaviours of animals.	• Communicate, p. 24, q. 4–5

Background Information

In this lesson, students are introduced to the main difference between vertebrate and invertebrate animals — the presence or absence of a backbone. They explore different types of invertebrate animals in a photo-essay, and then construct a classification chart using some characteristics that distinguish each animal. They read about the use of insect classification in forensics, and consider forensic entomology as a career choice.

Animals can be divided into vertebrates — those with a backbone — and invertebrates — those without a backbone. Vertebrates include groups such as reptiles, amphibians, birds, fish, and mammals. Invertebrate groups include: sponges; jellyfish and corals; flatworms; nematodes or roundworms; molluscs; arthropods; earthworms and leeches; and starfish and sea urchins. Most of the world's animals are invertebrates, and the classification of many of them is controversial. Students may be surprised to learn that invertebrates make up 98 % of all the animals in the world! The student book introduces four groups of invertebrates: sponges, worms, molluscs, and arthropods. Worms are a diverse group of organisms that are classified in different ways by different scientists. They are simply grouped together as worms here for simplicity.

Get Started ▶

- Post pictures of worms or snakes in the front of the classroom, or write "snake" and "earthworm" on the board.
- Challenge the class to come up with as many similarities and differences between these animals as they can. After students have volunteered some ideas, ask, *Does a snake have a backbone? What about an earthworm?* Students will likely know that an earthworm has no backbone, but some students may think this is also true of a snake.
- Introduce the terms "vertebrate" and "invertebrate" to the class. Invite students to feel along their lower necks for the vertebrae that make up their backbones. Explain that the presence or absence of a backbone is an important structural feature that scientists use to classify animals.
- As students begin to understand the difference between vertebrates and invertebrates, ask them to work in small groups to make a list of as many invertebrates as they can. This activity will provide an opportunity to gauge how familiar students are with this group of organisms.
- Invite the class to look at the photographs in Get Started and describe the animals. Stimulate their observations by asking questions such as: *What is similar about the animals in the photographs? What is different about the animals? What characteristics would you use to classify these animals?*

Invertebrate Phyla

- The table on student book page 22 lists the four main invertebrate phyla along with their general characteristics. It may be helpful for students to read this table and flip back to the photos on student book page 21 to note the general characteristics depicted in the photos, or to find other photos on the Internet or in reference books that represent examples of species in each phylum.

! Words that are derived from Latin often have "um" as an ending. These words are always pluralized by replacing "um" with "a." In modern English, we often still pluralize words ending in "um" with "a"; for example, curriculum — curricula; datum — data; practicum — practica.

Time

40 min

Skills

- classifying
- observing

Grouping

individuals

Materials and Equipment

- notebook
- pen or pencil

Line Masters

- LM 1-7

Work On It

- LM 1-7 Classifying Animals —The Invertebrates can be used as a worksheet for the Work On It activity.
- Do the first step of the procedure together as a class. Draw a chart on the board like the one below and ask the class to divide the animals into two groups.

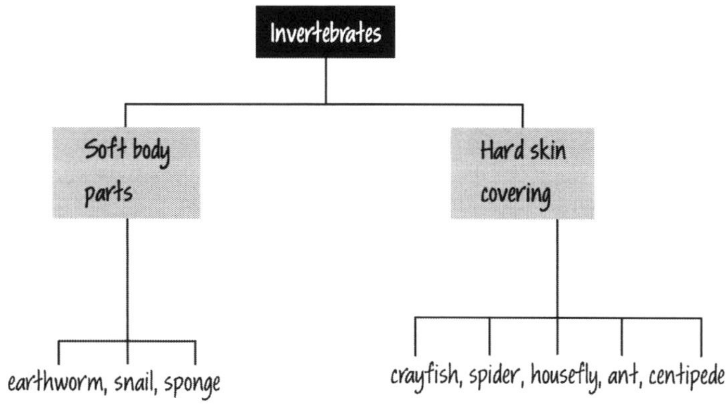

- Ask the class to look at the pictures of the animals in the first group. Ask, *What characteristic is shared by the animals in this group? Can you suggest a characteristic that will divide this group into subgroups?* Tell students to keep their ideas to themselves and to do the rest of the activity individually. Remind the class to look for characteristics that will not change in order to subdivide the groups of animals.
- Students should be able to classify the animals into the following groups:

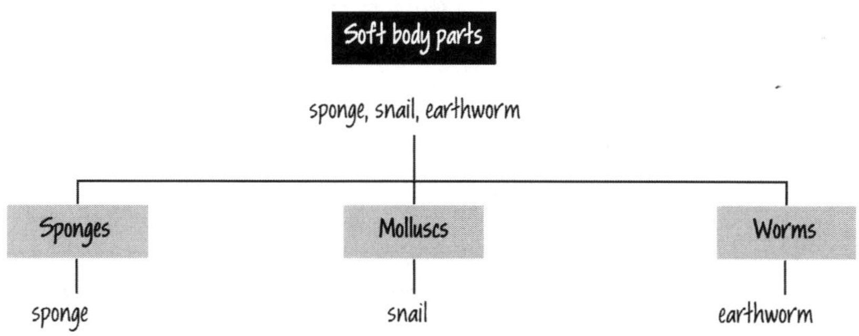

continued →

- All other animals are arthropods. This group of animals is presented in more detail in Lesson 6. For this lesson, expect students to identify the following characteristics and groups:

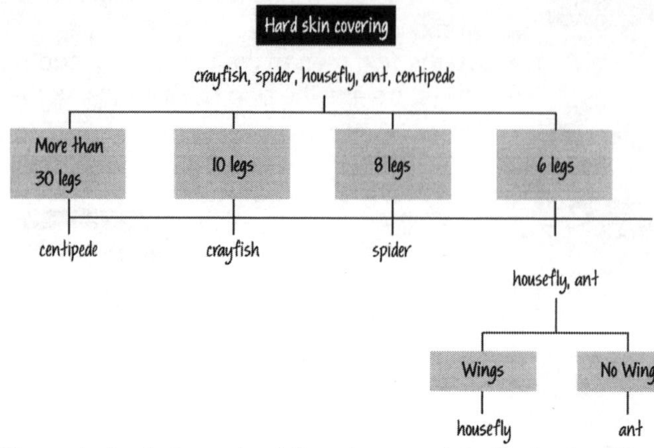

- When students have had time to complete their classification trees, gather the class together to share and discuss their groups and their characteristics. Encourage students to explain their reasons for including an animal in a group.

Octopi are very intelligent and flexible creatures. The marine biologists at the Vancouver Aquarium were dismayed to discover that someone was stealing their fish. Each night, a few very expensive fish would disappear from their tanks. The biologists set up a video camera to catch the thief in the act. Imagine their surprise when viewing the tape as they watched an octopus sneak out of a tiny hole in her tank, cross the feeding area behind the tanks, and swipe a fish or two out of one of the neighbouring tanks! She then climbed back into her own tank and settled in for the night with her sushi meal!

Communicate

1. Students should place the animals into the following groups:
   - Grasshopper: an arthropod with a hard skin covering, 6 legs, and wings
   - Moth: an arthropod with a hard skin covering, 6 legs, and wings
   - Scorpion: an arthropod with a hard skin covering, 10 legs, and no wings
   - Flatworm: a worm with soft body parts
   - Sponge: sponges
2. Students will suggest various characteristics but they should be structural, such as the presence of antennae or number of body segments.
3. Students are likely to suggest non-structural, variable characteristics such as body length, where it lives, or how long it lives.
4. Encourage students to focus their questions on invertebrates or aspects of Dr. Dennis Lehmkuhl's work. Consider asking the class to research the answers to their questions.
5. Challenge students to support their choices with sound reasoning.

BUILD ON WHAT YOU KNOW

The invertebrate animal that students add to their My Tree charts will vary.

For Reteaching

Make available a large collection of photos, illustrations, and diagrams of vertebrate and invertebrate animals. Some students may benefit from sorting the collection into the two groups: vertebrates and invertebrates. Encourage students to further classify the invertebrates, using characteristics such as body covering, body features, and number of legs. When they have finished sorting the pictures, ask them to record their work in a tree classification chart.

For Enrichment

Encourage students to find out more about invertebrates. LM 1-8 Invertebrates provides guidelines for searching references and taking notes on new information.

Assessment *for* Learning

What to Look For in Student Work	What to Do
Students should be able to identify and describe characteristics of invertebrates and classify invertebrates into phyla.	• If students are not clear about how to identify characteristics of invertebrates, you may need to reteach the section. Using the For Reteaching section above, ask them to make another classification chart.
Students should be able to clearly communicate procedures and results of the Work On It investigation.	• For those having difficulty communicating the procedures from Work On It, allow them to share their thinking with a partner. Have each partner explain their thinking to the other and then let them display and explain each other's thoughts to a larger group. If one partner gets stuck, the other partner may help by adding details.

CAREERS AND PROFILES

Dr. Dennis Lehmkuhl: Professor of Ecosystems; Biology and Taxonomy of Aquatic Insect *Page 25*

- Ask students to read the material on student book page 25 to find out how this ecologist decided to study zoology at a very early age.
- Dr. Lehmkuhl has a website that you may want students to visit. Direct students to www.dennislehmkuhl.com to have them learn more about streams, rivers, and aquatic insects in Saskatchewan.
- Ask them something like, *Have you ever thought you might be able to discover new species of animals? Would you be interested in becoming an ecologist? Why or why not?*
- Ask students, *Why does Dr. Lehmkuhl think it is important to classify things? What did he discover about dams that was important to the survival of many species?*
- Ask students to do some research to find out what other species are affected by sudden changes, such as the building of dams or flooding. Ask them to find out if there are species that have been affected this way in Saskatchewan.
- Ask them to find out what building plans have affected the environment close to their community and discuss the implications as a group. Once again, you could organize your discussion using the Talking Circle rules described in Lesson 1, Get Started in this Teacher's Resource.

6 Classifying Arthropods

Page 26

Time

1 class period

Key Terms

- adaptations
- exoskeleton
- proboscis
- jointed legs
- segmented body
- thorax
- abdomen
- specimens

Line Masters

- LM 1-9
- LM 1-10

Indicator Assessment Chart

Indicator	Assessment Opportunities
DL6.1 f. Identify examples of science and technology-related careers and workplaces which require an understanding of the diversity of living things (e.g., naturalist, zoo keeper, paleontologist, and wildlife biologist).	• Communicate, p. 29, q. 5
DL6.3 c. Compare and represent characteristics and behaviours (e.g., body shape, body description, method of respiration, method of reproduction, method of movement, and method of feeding) of student-selected examples of invertebrates (e.g., arthropods, annelids, cnidarids, echinoderms, molluscs, and nematodes).	• Work On It, p. 28 • Communicate, p. 29, q. 1–3

Background Information

In this lesson, students take a close look at an extremely diverse group of invertebrates, the arthropods. They explore the distinguishing characteristics of a number of classes of arthropods, and explore which of these characteristics apply to all arthropods and which to a particular class of arthropod. They create an information poster on one arthropod of their own choosing, which describes the animal in detail.

There are more than one million species of arthropods that have been described. Some scientists estimate that with the number of as-yet-undescribed species in the rainforests, the total number of species could be six to nine million. All arthropods have jointed appendages, which can be legs, mouths, wings, antennae, or reproductive parts. The word "arthropod" comes from the Greek "arthron" and "pous podos," and loosely means "jointed foot." Arthropods also have a hard exoskeleton, made from a material called chitin, which is attached to their bodies by muscles. Some more familiar arthropods include crustaceans (crayfish, crabs, copepods, and sow bugs), arachnids (ticks, spiders, and scorpions), chilopods (centipedes), and insects (dragonflies, grasshoppers, termites, flies, ants, bees, moths, butterflies, and beetles).

Get Started ▶

- Divide the class into seven groups and assign each group one of the following: spiders, crayfish, butterflies, bees, beetles, grasshoppers, or mosquitoes.
- If you have access to a collection of arthropod specimens, set up specimens of these animals for students to observe.
- Direct the groups to list all the information they can about their animal on chart paper.
- After a few minutes, invite each group to share its list with the class by posting it and presenting the information orally. Ask the rest of the class whether they know anything else about this species. The groups can add this information to their lists.
- After all the groups have shared their lists, challenge them to find similarities among these seven animals by saying something like, *All these different animals are in one group called arthropods. What characteristics do you think arthropods have in common?*
- Encourage students to refer to their lists while they think about the question. Students are unlikely to think of jointed appendages, so point this out to them if they do not suggest it.
- Ask the class to read the paragraph in the Get Started section, and then study the photographs of arthropods on student book pages 26 and 27. Ask, *Can anyone tell us what is similar in this group of animals? Can anyone suggest a difference that might put some of them into different subgroups?*
- Read aloud to the class the definition of adaptation in the Get Started section. Challenge students to explain how the adaptations described in the captions under each photo could help the animal to survive.
- To help students become more familiar with terminology, ask them to use LM 1-9 Classifying Arthropods to label the parts of three arthropods, using the photos on student book page 27.

All Arthropods Are Not the Same!

- Carry the discussion further by saying, *We can subdivide arthropods into smaller groups. In what ways are these animals different from one another?* Ask students to look over their lists again before they respond.
- List their responses on the board or on chart paper. Students are unlikely to suggest jointed appendages. Point this feature out to them if this is the case.
- When the list is complete, invite the students to turn to the photos in Lesson 5 on student book page 23, and ask, *Which of the invertebrate animals you classified in Lesson 5 are arthropods? How do you know?*
- Consider having students choose one animal and research how its adaptation is helpful.

Most crustaceans live in either marine or freshwater environments. A few, such as hermit crabs and wood lice (sow bugs), have adapted to life on land. Scientists believe that over half the animals in the world are crustaceans. Small crustaceans, such as krill, are eaten by many much larger animals and represent the largest biomass on the planet.

Time

40 min

Skills

- observing
- interpreting
- classifying

Grouping

individuals
pairs
groups

Materials and Equipment

(per group)

- notebook
- pen or pencil
- any other materials students may wish to use to complete procedure step 4

Optional Materials

- a collection of specimens or models of different arthropods
- videos of different insects

Line Masters

- LM 1-10

Work On It

- This activity could be approached successfully by providing the class with a video of arthropods, a specimen collection, a website, or the photographs in the student book to examine.
- Students can work individually or in small groups or pairs. Give them lots of time to observe the examples carefully, and remind them to make detailed records of their observations to refer to later.
- Encourage students to use the list of arthropod characteristics created in the Get Started section as a guide.
- In steps 3 and 4, students make a poster of similarities and differences between a pet animal of their choice and an arthropod.
- Encourage them to give precise descriptions of the characteristics of the animals, so that others will be able to see clearly the comparison between the two animals.
- Students may enjoy using the characteristics of arthropods to design and build a realistic, imaginary arthropod. LM 1-10 Design Challenge: Make an Arthropod challenges students to “adapt” an arthropod to a specific environment.

Communicate

Students can work on questions 1 to 3 in pairs or small groups. Assign questions 4, 5, and 6 as individual work, and schedule a time when students will present the posters they create in question 4 to the class.

1. Answers are likely to include any two of the following: hard outer body, segmented body, jointed legs, and specialized mouth parts.
2. The following characteristics can describe one of the animals in the photographs: has larger back legs; has a round, hard body; has very thin legs; has claw-like legs; has wide wings; has narrow wings. Answers from your students will depend on the source of the arthropod samples your class uses.
3. Jointed legs and three main body parts are the characteristics students should identify from the list as more helpful for classifying arthropods. Students should be able to explain that this is because they are structural characteristics. Students also should report that colourful wings, tiny size, and rough skin are less helpful characteristics because they are not structural characteristics of the animals, are not specific, and can be interpreted differently by different people.
4. Give students an opportunity to present their posters to the class, and to examine and discuss one another's work. Encourage them to use scientific terms and vocabulary as they describe and discuss their work.

continued →

5. This activity gives students the option of representing their learning in alternative ways. You may wish to reserve some computer time for your students to work on their presentations. Some students may work on their projects on their home computers.
6. The words students add to their mind maps will vary but should include "specimens," "abdomen," "thorax," "exoskeleton," and "proboscis."

BUILD ON WHAT YOU KNOW

As students revisit their My Tree charts, they may need some help with planning so that they can frequently add information to their charts. You may wish to model how to plan a chart by putting together a class tree chart that you can expand on as the unit progresses. The chart on student book page 27 will be helpful in demonstrating what the chart could look like.

The spruce budworm is one of the most destructive insects in Saskatchewan. There has been some controversy about the effectiveness and environmental impact of spraying. The Saskatchewan government has made the following statement: "Spraying to manage the spruce budworm is part of the provincial government's comprehensive forest insect management plan," Environment Minister Nancy Heppner said. "The program's overall approach is based on a solid foundation of effective monitoring and prompt action where unacceptable risks are identified. This approach has helped us to successfully manage budworms and will continue to serve us well as we face the emerging threat of the mountain pine beetle."
See the complete article on the Government of Saskatchewan website, Spruce Budworm Aerial Spraying Begins, at http://www.gov.sk.ca/news?newsId=f6ac6266-8142-43db-8ab6-bebb27a37664.

For ESL/ELL

Arthropods hold a fascination for most children. This lesson will provide opportunities to share common vocabulary and point out interesting facts, photos, and labels for students to share with each other.

For Reteaching

Plan a field trip to a local habitat or natural museum. Engage students in using magnifying glasses, bug boxes, and bottles outside or in making sketches at a museum. Remind students to pay attention to similarities and differences between the species they observe. If you are in a local habitat, also remind students to return all specimens unharmed.

Assessment *for* Learning

What to Look For in Student Work	What to Do
Students should be able to compare the characteristics of different kinds of arthropods by describing body shape, method of respiration, method of reproduction, method of movement, and methods of feeding. Students should be able to correctly use scientific terminology learned in this lesson.	• Use the For Reteaching suggestion above to help students become engaged in their learning. Students who have difficulty organizing their work may be motivated by observing arthropods in their natural environment. • Review terminology and ensure that students have frequent opportunities to use the vocabulary as they discuss concepts. Allow students to self-assess and explain how well they think they are able to use the terms covered in the unit to date. This exercise will help increase their engagement and encourage them to think more deeply about their own learning.

7 Investigating an Arthropod — The Mealworm

Page 30

Time

2–3 class periods

Key Terms

- larvae
- moult
- pupae
- dependent variable
- independent variable
- fair test

Line Masters

- LM 1-11
- LM 1-12
- LM 1-13

Indicator Assessment Chart

Indicator	Assessment Opportunities
DL6.2 g. Use appropriate scientific terminology to communicate ideas about the diversity of living things (e.g., biotic, abiotic, kingdom, phylum, monera, protist, fungi, plant, animal, vertebrate, and invertebrate).	• Work On It, p. 31 • Communicate, p. 33, q. 1, 4
DL6.3 a. Identify characteristics of vertebrates and invertebrates and classify animals as vertebrates or invertebrates from drawings, videos, pictures, lists, and/or personal observations.	• Work On It, p. 31
DL6.3 c. Compare and represent characteristics and behaviours (e.g., body shape, body description, method of respiration, method of reproduction, method of movement, and method of feeding) of student-selected examples of invertebrates (e.g., arthropods, annelids, cnidarids, echinoderms, molluscs, and nematodes).	• Work On It, p. 31
DL6.3 d. Propose questions for inquiry that arise from personal investigations of characteristics and behaviours of animals.	• Work On It, p. 31 • Communicate, p. 33, q. 3

Background Information

This lesson introduces the class to mealworms, the larval stage of the darkling or grain beetle. Students will observe live mealworms that are fed various kinds of cereal to find out how they eat. Students consider how the mouth parts are adapted to help mealworms survive. Students then pose their own question about mealworms, and plan and carry out an investigation to answer them. Mealworms are very simple to care for in the classroom and you may decide to keep them for the students to observe long after this particular activity.

Grain beetles are arthropods, in the subgroup insect. There are four stages in the life cycle of the grain beetle: egg, larva, pupa, and adult. Metamorphosis occurs during the pupal stage. The larval stage is four to six months long, and is the only stage where visible growth occurs. Mealworms feed on almost any dry grain (corn meal, flour, oatmeal) and can be found wherever grain is grown, stored, or processed. They can survive with little food for a long time, and their moisture requirements are so small that placing a carrot, potato, or apple slice in a colony can satisfy them. Depending on how long you keep mealworms in the class, you may find that you and your students can observe all of the stages of their life cycle, although their eggs are extremely small!

traditional **KNOWLEDGE**

Many First Nations believe that the Creator first put plants, then animals, and finally humans on Earth. They feel that humans are not as important as the plants and animals and so must be responsible to care for Mother Earth.
There is an excellent article regarding this belief at Suite101.com, Native American/First Nations History: http://nativeamericanfirstnationshistory.suite101.com. This site is a rich source of information about First Nations and Métis contemporary and traditional culture.

Get Started ▶

- Ask students to read the information on mealworms individually.
- Challenge students to note any distinct body features they see in the diagram on student book page 30, and encourage them to suggest what purposes the features serve.
- Remind students that mealworms are arthropods, and so they share the distinguishing features of all arthropods.
- Ask, *Can anyone tell us some characteristics we found in arthropods in the last lesson?* Students should suggest jointed legs and an exoskeleton.
- Some students may think mealworms should be classified as worms. Consider having the students copy the schematic of the life cycle of the darkling beetle, including the egg, larval, pupal, and adult stages from student book page 30 to help them process the whole cycle.
- Students may be interested to hear that a four-stage life cycle is called a complete life cycle.

- Ask students, *Do you know what happens when the animal goes from a pupa to an adult? What is this phase called?*
- Students may be familiar with metamorphosis in butterflies or frogs. Explain that one reason mealworms are not classified as worms is because they metamorphose into beetles.

Variables in Investigations

- Even though variables in investigations will have been covered in other units and other years, you may need to remind your students that they represent an important focus for ensuring that their results are authentic.
- Ask students, *If you were to measure the amount of sugar that can be dissolved in water, what variable would you need to control?* Their answers will give you an indication of the depth of their understanding.
- Students will often try to offer opinions or make false observations when investigating living creatures. Point out that they should avoid stems such as "My mealworm likes…" or "My mealworm wants…."
- One way to ensure authentic observations is to require students to include only facts that they can collect using their five senses.

Time

40 min

Skills

- observing
- experimenting
- interpreting

Grouping

individuals
groups

Materials and Equipment

(per group)
- mealworms in a breathable container
- magnifying glass
- dry cereal
- blank white paper
- lined paper
- pencils

Optional Materials
- blunt tweezers
- plastic gloves

Line Masters

- LM 1-11

CAUTION!

Remind students to always wash their hands after handling animals, plants, or soil. Ensure that students wash their hands once they are finished the activity.

Work On It

How Do Mealworms Eat?

- Divide the class into groups and provide them with a community of mealworms. Remind students to handle the mealworms with care so as not to harm them.
- Say something like, *Mealworms are arthropods in the subgroup of insects. What are the common characteristics of insects?*
- Suggest that students turn back to student book page 27 to review the characteristics of insects, paying attention to the three body segments.
- Students may have difficulty distinguishing the thorax and abdomen on mealworms.
- Consider posting the following hints somewhere in the classroom:
- The head includes the insect's eyes, antennae, and jaws.
- The thorax is the middle section of the insect, where the legs are attached.
- The abdomen is made up of one or more segments behind the thorax.

Finding Out More About Mealworms

- Before they begin, ask each group to fill in LM 1-11 Investigating an Arthropod — The Mealworm, then check their plan with you. Ensure they have considered all of the following before you allow them to proceed:
  - How will you know when your question is answered?
  - What variable will you change in your investigation?
  - What variables will you keep the same? How will you be sure?
  - What will you be measuring, and how will you measure it?
  - What will you do to be sure your investigation does not hurt the mealworms?

A good site for information on grain beetles and other common pantry pests is University of Nebraska-Lincoln—UNL Extension in Lancaster County—Insects, Spiders, Mice and More:
http://lancaster.unl.edu/pest/resources/pantrypests304.shtml.
This site is managed by the University of Nebraska and is an excellent source of information for students who wish to do further research on managing arthropods that have become harmful in households across North America.

Communicate

Students should present the results of their independent investigations. Remind them to make sure they discuss the following:

- what question they were investigating
- what they did
- what they observed
- what they think now

Also draw their attention to Communicate question 2. You might tell the class that you will randomly call on one person from each group to answer the question after the group's presentation.

1. Expect students to present their findings using diagrams and graphs whenever appropriate, and to use appropriate vocabulary. Focus the discussion around the questions each group investigated, the procedures they followed, and the explanations they suggested for their results.
2. Students may benefit from explaining what went well and what didn't go well to a partner before being encouraged to explain to the whole class.
3. Encourage students to look carefully and critically at their results and to suggest different ways to investigate their questions. Remind students that scientists often modify their questions or their investigations based on the results of previous experiments.
4. Encourage students to include pictures of the animal at each of its life stages. They should report that the mealworm feeds on grain only during the larval and adult stages, whereas eggs and pupae depend on their own internal reserves for food.

BUILD ON WHAT YOU KNOW

The arthropods students add to their My Tree charts will vary. Encourage students to consult reference materials and confirm that the animals they chose are arthropods. Ensure students can relate characteristics that will classify the arthropods they chose into different subgroups.

For ESL/ELL

It will be important to give ESL/ELL students extra time to explain their thinking as they design and complete investigations concerning the behaviour of mealworms. Reinforce the idea that they can use the key terms to expand their vocabulary and use authentic observations to keep their investigations simple. Giving ESL students related materials in their first language will help them become better able to read materials in English.

For Enrichment

Students have observed mealworms in some detail now and may want to observe other invertebrates. Challenge them to research nutrient and space needs of different invertebrates and then design a housing compartment for one they wish to observe. Hand out copies of LM 1-12 Design Challenge: Build an Observation Chamber. Suitable invertebrates to observe include earthworms, ants, wood lice, snails, and crayfish.

Invite interested students to consult a variety of different resource materials to research insect life cycles in depth. LM 1-13 Life Cycles can be used to guide their research. They may also wish to continue their investigation of the mealworm over time and design experiments and observations that can be completed over time. Remind them to handle all live creatures carefully and to not do anything that may harm them.

Assessment *for* Learning

What to Look For in Student Work	What to Do
Students should be able to pose and explore questions about the needs of animals and compare characteristics of invertebrates (arthropods).	• Use Teacher Modelling to give all students, and particularly struggling students, frequent good examples of the criteria needed. When posing questions, let students know why you are asking and ask them to think of questions of their own.
During their presentations, students should be able to use correct science and technology terminology, propose questions for inquiry through investigation, and communicate the procedures and results of investigations.	• Some students may need extra time and coaching when doing a presentation. Frequent opportunities to speak and discuss will help nervous students become more confident. Creating a safe learning environment, where all students take learning risks, is key to their growth. Allowing them to practice with a partner or within a smaller group may also help add to their confidence.

8 Classifying Animals — The Vertebrates

Page 34

Time
3 class periods

Key Terms
• vertebrae • cold-blooded • warm-blooded • structural characteristics

Line Masters
• LM 1-14

Indicator Assessment Chart

Indicator	Assessment Opportunities
DL6.2 a. Construct and use a classification system to organize living things into groups and subgroups according to student-developed criteria.	• Work On It, p. 38
DL6.2 b. Consider personal observations and ideas as well as those of others (including differing worldviews) when constructing classification systems by asking questions, sharing stories, and responding to classmates' classification systems.	• Communicate, p. 40, q. 1, 3–4
DL6.3 a. Identify characteristics of vertebrates and invertebrates and classify animals as vertebrates or invertebrates from drawings, videos, pictures, lists, and/or personal observations.	• Work On It, p. 38
DL6.3 b. Compare and represent characteristics and behaviours (e.g., body shape, body description, method of respiration, method of reproduction, method of movement, and method of feeding) of student-selected examples of vertebrates.	• Work On It, p. 38
DL6.4 a. Propose questions to investigate related to the structures and behaviours that help organisms survive in their environments (e.g., "What advantage are different beaks for birds?", "Why do owls turn their heads to look sideways?", "Why do rabbits change colour at different times of the year?", "Why do caribou migrate?", "Why do ground squirrels hibernate?").	• Work On It, p. 38 • Communicate, p. 40, q. 4
DL6.4 g. Gather information from a variety of sources (e.g., Elder, traditional knowledge keeper, naturalist, textbook, non-fiction book, museum display, encyclopedia, and website) to answer student-generated questions about the structural and behavioural adaptations of living organisms.	• Work On It, p. 38

Background Information

This lesson introduces students to vertebrates and their five major subgroups: fish, amphibians, reptiles, birds, and mammals. Students first explore the different ways that cold-blooded and warm-blooded animals regulate body temperature. After reading about distinguishing characteristics of the five vertebrate subgroups, students research one animal from each subgroup in more depth. Using the research of the entire class, students create a chart listing all the animals they can in the five subgroups of vertebrates.

Vertebrates can be cold-blooded, which means their body temperature is the same as their surrounding environment, or warm-blooded, which means they use energy to maintain a steady body temperature no matter where they are. Reptiles, fish, and amphibians are cold-blooded vertebrates, whereas birds and mammals are warm-blooded vertebrates.

In this lesson, consider having your class complete the chart as they read the information. When they have finished, challenge students to add two or three more examples of animals to each subgroup. When all students have finished reading and have completed the chart, ask volunteers to share their work.

Get Started ▶

- Review the word "vertebrate" with the class. Read the paragraph in Get Started aloud.
- Challenge students to come up with as many advantages to having a backbone as they can.
- Advantages include: the backbone provides protection for the spinal cord; it makes the skeleton more flexible, which allows animals a great range of movement; and it provides a place for muscles to attach, which also increases movement and strength.

Characteristics of Vertebrates

- You may wish to read this section as a class.
- When the reading is complete, ask the class to answer the questions about humans in this section, either orally or in their notebooks.
- Students should be able to relate that humans are warm-blooded mammals. They are likely to know that normal human body temperature is 37.0°C, which can be measured with a thermometer.
- Before moving on with the next sections describing the five subgroups of vertebrates, introduce students to the strategy of using a recording chart to help to organize information as they read.
- On the board, draw a table similar to LM 1-14 Classifying Animals — The Vertebrates to demonstrate how students can organize their information. Students can use this table during the Work On It activity.

Time
40 min
Skills
• observing • interpreting • classifying
Grouping
pairs groups
Materials and Equipment
(per group) • notebook • pen or pencil • research materials • library and computer access
Line Masters
• LM 1-14

Work On It

- Provide students with reference books, videos, magazines, a list of Internet sites, and any other material that describes vertebrates so they can begin their research.
- Encourage students to include diagrams, illustrations, and detailed descriptions in their work.
- Suggest that students first look at the structural characteristics that classify the animals as vertebrates, and then at the characteristics that classify the animals into subgroups.

Think Again! Structures for Life

- Ask students to read the information regarding structural characteristics on page 39 of the student book.
- Ask them to identify the ways scientists use structural characteristics when classifying plants and animals by writing these characteristics in their notebooks and sharing with a partner.
- Classification is a systematic means that scientists have employed to understand the relationship between organisms in the living world. It is based on a particular worldview of the natural world. In the First Nations and Métis worldview, a systematic classification would not necessarily be useful for survival purposes. For First Nations and Métis people, grouping is used for the practical purpose of survival, to foster a love of Earth, to promote cultural values, and to show relatedness of living things through spirit.

traditional ***KNOWLEDGE***

- The primary purpose of grouping among First Nations and Métis people is for survival. Living organisms therefore may be grouped according to uses that would enable First Nations and Métis to hunt, forage, and cure diseases. Some groups describe plants according to their uses for food and healing.
- The grouping of living things had a place in spiritual practice. For example, the Cree grouped the organisms of the natural world into winged, two-legged, four-legged, swimming things, and plants. Winged ones consisted of birds, bats, and flying invertebrates (regardless of number of legs). Four-leggeds were composed of animals such as the deer, wolves, moose, elk, badgers, and wolverines. Two-leggeds were the humans. The swimming ones consisted mainly of fish, but perhaps other animals that swim were also classed in this group. Ones that grow consisted of plants. Be aware that this type of grouping was not meant as a classification system but mainly as a way in which Elders and practitioners could refer to groups of animals in prayer.
- The Ojibwa system is very similar. According to Elder **Lillian Pitawanakwat's** teachings on her website Four Directions Learning Activities, http://www.fourdirectionsteachings.com/ojibwe_junior.pdf, organisms were grouped as follows: birds (things that fly), the crawlers, the swimmers, the trees, two-leggeds, and four-leggeds.

- The Inuit of the northern territories have a much more complex grouping method, often called a tree of life. The Inuit called things that moved the *Uumajuit*, which included many kinds of organisms such as animals, fish, mammals, and people. The *Piruqtuit* were things that were growing or *Nunarait* — things of Earth. Plants, fungi, lichens, algae, and the like were classed either as *Piruqtuit* or *Nunarait*. *Anirniliit* were the organisms that breathe and have spirit. Thus, terrestrial and flying animals, but not aquatic animals, were part of this group. Aquatic animals were classed differently because their method of breathing is different. (See Canada's Polar Life, http://www.arctic.uoguelph.ca/cpl/index.htm.)
- Teachers should be mindful that First Nations and Métis people have different motives for grouping things. It is important to not directly compare FNM ways of grouping to the Western system of classification. It is acceptable to differentiate between the two ways of knowing nature to suggest that different people have different purposes for describing nature. Traditional ways of knowing by grouping living things for survival, ceremony, or prayer have served First Nations and Métis people for millennia. Elders hope that their teachings help foster an appreciation of and love for the land.
- Ask students to make an illustration of the sacred hoop or circle of life. There are many illustrations for sacred hoops and medicine wheels on the Web.

Communicate

You may like to answer question 1 as a class to wrap up the research from the Work On It activity. Students can work in pairs for the remaining questions.

1. Humans belong in the vertebrate subgroup of mammals. Invite student pairs to present their research to the class. Remind the class to note any differences and similarities among the animals in each subgroup. Similarities may include the following points.
   - Fish: streamlined body shape for forward motion, fins, scales
   - Amphibians: bony internal skeleton, four legs, three-chambered heart, lay eggs in water or moist areas
   - Reptiles: well-developed internal skeleton, scales, breathe through lungs
   - Birds: internal skeleton made of light bones with air cavities, wings, four-chambered heart
   - Mammals: internal bone structure, young develop inside adult, most are covered with hair, breathe with lungs, four-chambered heart

   Ensure that students have presented the information clearly. Students can also add this information to the chart they made in Get Started as they were reading.

continued →

2. There are many terms in this unit that may be unfamiliar to students. Encourage students to use any words they add to their mind maps to be sure they have understood their meanings.
3. Students should explain that structural characteristics are used because they do not change throughout the life of an animal.
4. Students are likely to suggest adaptations such as thick fur and lots of body fat for an organism to live in the Arctic, and tolerance to heat and dark for animals in deep-sea hot vents. To remind students what happens to organisms when their habitats no longer exist, introduce students to the acronym MAD. Say something like, *When a habitat changes, animals go MAD.* MAD stands for Move to a new habitat that they are adapted to, Adapt to the change in their habitat, or Die out.

BUILD ON WHAT YOU KNOW

Students can choose vertebrate examples from their notes to add to their classification charts.

For ESL/ELL

You may suggest that ESL students research animals from their countries of origin.

For Enrichment

Students may be interested in finding out how warm-blooded animals such as birds and cold-blooded animals such as turtles survive over winter. Challenge them to make a poster that will explain these two different survival strategies.

Assessment *for* Learning

What to Look For in Student Work	What to Do
Students should be able to describe specific characteristics or adaptations of animals for particular habitats and to identify and describe the characteristics of vertebrates.	• This lesson is rich in content and some students may find the number of characteristics overwhelming. Break this number down into chunks and allow students time to discuss similarities and differences between the five groups of vertebrates at length in their groups.
Students should be able to explain the difference between structural and physical characteristics and give reasons why scientists use structural characteristics to classify vertebrates.	• If students are having difficulty, ask them to reflect on the details of structural characteristics, particularly bone structure, the circulatory system, and the reproductive system (student book page 39) and confer with you or a peer to review the key factors.

ASK A TRADITIONAL KNOWLEDGE KEEPER | Judy Bear: Humanity's Place

Page 41

traditional **KNOWLEDGE**

- The way that traditional knowledge enhances a student's appreciation for the land is often by the values that are imparted. Judy Bear's piece reflects many of the attitudes with which many First Nations and Métis people regard Mother Earth.
- Many of the values conveyed in Judy Bear's profile align with the fundamental concepts and connections in the provincial curriculum. The key ideas of sustainability and stewardship are two such examples. Ecologists and environmental scientists, often in co-operation with many cultural groups around the world, strive to find ways to reduce the harm that has been done to the planet. *"Of all life forms, only humans can be removed to the benefit of the planet, and only humans have the power to make changes that will reverse the damage already done to Mother Earth."* Judy's words encapsulate the fragility of Earth and the considerable harm humans have done to the planet, whether deliberately or unintentionally. This fragility hints at the lack of stewardship humans have had for Earth. On a more positive note, the Traditional Knowledge Keeper suggests that humans have the ability to reverse some of those changes.
- The concepts of constancy and change are echoed in Judy's reflection on her father, Elder Isaac Bear. She highlights that constancy and change can only be understood through observation. For example, her father's teachings are based on his observations about the land and the change in climate. At this point in the reading, teachers may help students understand that bodies of knowledge are based largely on observation.
- Observation has a place in traditional knowledge as well as Western science. Both systems emphasize different but valid ways of looking at the natural world. Scientists may look at aspects of the natural world to further our understanding of *how* things work, for example, evolution, heredity, etc. For many First Nations and Métis groups, observation of the natural world results in survival and cultural knowledge about *what* the world is. Though their motives may vary, the value of observation is fundamental to both knowledge systems.

- A last concept deeply rooted in First Nations and Métis ways of understanding is the belief in connectedness and interrelatedness of all living things. In their understanding of the world, many First Nations and Métis people believe that humans are the weakest among the living things because they rely the most on gifts that the natural world offers. Unlike the bear or the wolf, humans lack fangs and claws to rend the flesh of prey. Without the wings and talons of the eagle and the owl, people can neither catch fish nor fowl. For shelters, humans need the trees and hides of different animals. For food, plants and animals provide. In their humility, another strongly held value, First Nations and Métis people consider themselves last of all living things.
- After reading this section, ask students, *What changes over time have the Elders noticed in weather and migration patterns?*
- Ask, *How have children become disconnected from the land? What might you do to become more connected to Mother Earth?*
- Use the Talking Circle to facilitate discussion among your students. Use the rules found in Lesson 1, Get Started, for your Talking Circle.
- Following are some topics you may wish to discuss further with your class:
  - Humans depend on Mother Earth for everything for survival. Give some examples of how humans depend upon Mother Earth.
  - Of all life forms, only humans can be removed to the benefit of the planet. What do you think this idea means?
  - How can humans reverse the damage already done to Mother Earth?

9 All About Fish

Page 42

Time
1–2 class periods
Key Terms
• none
Line Masters
• LM 1-15 • LM 1-16

Indicator Assessment Chart

Indicator	Assessment Opportunities
DL6.3 b. Compare and represent characteristics and behaviours (e.g., body shape, body description, method of respiration, method of reproduction, method of movement, and method of feeding) of student-selected examples of vertebrates.	• Work On It, p. 42 • Communicate, p. 44, q. 1
DL6.3 d. Propose questions for inquiry that arise from personal investigations of characteristics and behaviours of animals.	• Work On It, p. 42
DL6.4 b. Show interest and curiosity in learning about living organisms' adaptations to different environments by journaling, participating in a nature walk, or sharing science-related information about adaptations (gathered from print or video resources or personal experience) with classmates.	• Work On It, p. 42
DL6.4 d. Describe examples of adaptations to structures and behaviours (e.g., flippers, webbed feet, nighttime vision, wide wings, camouflage colouring, migration, and hibernation) that have enabled living things to adapt to their environments in the long term.	• Work On It, p. 42
DL6.4 i. Research the advantages of particular structures or behaviours of organisms that suit different environments (e.g., how different bird beaks are best suited to obtain different types of food, how different types of foot structure are best suited for different environments).	Communicate, p. 44, q. 1

Background Information

In this lesson, students observe live fish to further understand some of the characteristics of this subgroup of vertebrates and to identify some of the adaptations that help them survive.

Fish are cold-blooded vertebrates that have gills and fins. Their shapes can vary greatly, but most are shaped somewhat like a torpedo to swim efficiently through water. Fish are found in all the waters of the world, except for the highly saline Dead Sea in the Middle East and Great Salt Lake in Utah, U.S.A. There are about 20 000 species of fish — about the same number of species as in all the other vertebrate subgroups combined. Fish are important not only as a food supply, but for controlling disease-carrying insect populations and providing a measure of environmental health. Overfishing, the increasing human population, and water pollution are threatening many fish species.

Fish are fairly easy to keep in a classroom aquarium. You may wish to start a community tank, with a variety of fish for your students to observe. Live bearers, such as guppies or platy fish, are easy to breed and your students will enjoy watching tank populations grow over time. Keeping fish in the classroom also provides an ongoing opportunity to help students understand the importance of stewardship as they experience the responsibility of caring for the community.

Get Started ▶

- Engage pairs of students in brainstorming a list of everything they know about fish.
- Challenge the students to suggest adaptations that help fish to survive.
- When they have finished, ask each member of a pair to join with a member of another pair to compare and modify their lists.
- When going on a field trip, see if you can find fish to observe in local ponds, lakes, or streams. Ask students to try to identify any fish they find by taking photographs, etc. They may also wish to find photos of local fish in the library or on the Web.

Time

40–60 min

Skills

- observing
- inferring
- interpreting

Grouping

groups of three

Materials and Equipment

(per group of three)

- large, clear container (big enough so a fish can swim freely)
- goldfish or other small fish in an aquarium
- tap water conditioner to remove chlorine
- thermometer
- small net
- water (same temperature as the water in the aquarium or holding tank)
- paper and pencils

Line Masters

- none

Work On It

- Remind students to be very careful not to harm the fish during their observations.
- Ensure they quickly transfer the fish from the holding tank to the observation chamber, so it is not out of water too long.
- Suggest to students that they read over all the questions in Work On It before they begin their observations.
- Remind them that they should record their observations with words and diagrams.
- From their work in Lesson 8 and their observations of a live specimen, expect students to answer the questions with statements similar to the following:
  - *A fish breathes through its gills. A live fish passes water through the mouth, and over its gills.* Students may observe that the fish keeps its mouth open and always keeps moving in order to do so.
  - *A fish's eyes are usually on either side of its head, so it can see in all directions around it. This arrangement allows it to see food and predators easily.*
  - *A fish's fins are positioned to help the fish move in different directions through water.* Students should be able to identify which fins are used to move forward, left, right, up, and down. They should also suggest that the shape of the fish's body helps it to move more easily through the water.
- Students are asked to come up with observations or questions about adaptations the fish have for their environment. You may wish to ensure they consider all the items in Procedure step 10 while they are observing the fish by asking, *How are the scales arranged on the fish? Why do you think they are arranged this way? (The arrangement of scales helps streamline fish so they can move easily through water.) How is the fish shaped? Why do you think it is shaped this way? (Because it has no neck, it has a streamlined body that moves well through the water.)*
- You may wish to provide stopwatches and suggest that students count the number of times the fish's gills move in a minute. They could then compare their findings with those of their classmates.

Communicate

Assign the Communicate questions for students to work on together in their small groups.

1. Diagrams should be as accurate as possible, and labelled and annotated like the following example:

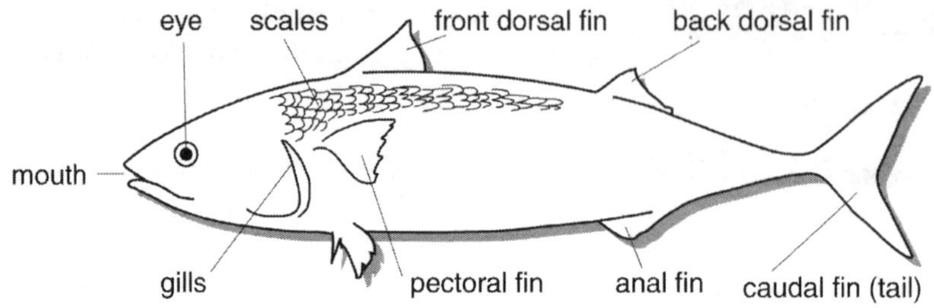

   Pectoral and Pelvic Fins
   - help the fish balance and move up and down

   Anal and Dorsal Fins
   - help stabilize fish; in some species, help the fish move forward

   Caudal Fin
   - helps the fish move forward and also acts as a rudder
2. Answers will reflect the location of the school and students' homes.
3. **a.** Students should respond that if fish habitats disappear or become polluted, fish will either move to new habitats, adapt to the new conditions of the old habitat, or die out.
   b. Invite students to share their finished posters with the class. You may like to display the posters in the school halls for other students and parents to see.
4. Encourage students to add any new scientific words they found during their research for question 1.
5. Students' charts, tables, and graphs will vary, but should clearly show the main similarities (they are all animals that need to move to get food) and differences (the presence and absence of a backbone) between vertebrates and invertebrates. Use LM 1-15 Vertebrates and Invertebrates to help students organize their work.

If Time Allows

Expect students to find that, unlike fish, whales are warm-blooded, breathe with lungs, and bear live young. Research shows that they evolved from land mammals and that their flukes (tail) were once legs and feet. This feature represents a structural adaptation over time.

For ESL/ELL

The excitement of observing live fish in the classroom will provide a rich opportunity for ESL students to practise their English. You may wish to ask them to add any new vocabulary to their notebooks.

For Reteaching

Students will enjoy making detailed observations of another vertebrate. Direct students to closely observe a pet or a zoo animal and record the adaptations that help it survive in its natural habitat.

For Enrichment

LM 1-16 A School of Fish challenges students to conduct further research on different fish species and to describe the most unique and interesting adaptations they can find in this diverse group. If students have a home aquarium, they may be interested in continuing their observations. Those who do not have a home aquarium may research on the Internet and watch live fish in public aquariums using their webcams.

Assessment *for* Learning

What to Look For in Student Work	What to Do
Students should be able to formulate questions about and identify the needs of different types of animals, describe specific characteristics or adaptations that enable vertebrates to live in a particular habitat, and compare the characteristics of vertebrates and invertebrates. Students should also be able to ask questions that specifically explore fish body shape and movement and how well fish are adapted to their environment.	• Circulate among the groups as they are observing their fish and jot anecdotal notes on their thinking. If some students are having difficulty recording their observations, you may wish to provide them with a graphic organizer to help them get started. • You may need to model good questioning for some students. You may wish to use chart paper to give some examples of questions that relate to the affective (How did it feel?), the cognitive (What are the facts?), and the metacognitive (Did your thinking change?) states.

10 A Prehistoric Vertebrate

Page 45

Time
1 class period

Key Terms
• paleontologists • fossils • fossil record

Line Masters
• LM 1-17

Indicator Assessment Chart

Indicator	Assessment Opportunities
DL6.4 e. Explain how scientists use fossils and the fossil record as a source of information to identify changes or diversity in species over long periods of time.	• Work On It, p. 47
DL6.4 f. Suggest reasons why specific species of organisms have or might become endangered or extinct.	• Communicate, p. 48, q. 2

Background Information

In this lesson, dinosaurs are presented as extinct vertebrates that we know of through their fossilized remains. By comparing an illustration of a dinosaur fossil to illustrations of skeletons of animals that are common today, students consider the changes that have occurred in animals over time.

Paleontology is the study of fossils. Paleontologists look for evidence and records of prehistoric life. Fossils are used to reconstruct the skeletons of prehistoric creatures, which are then used to support or refute hypotheses about the size, habits, and environment of these extinct creatures. Dinosaurs were abundant during the Cretaceous period in what is now Dinosaur Provincial Park, near Lethbridge, Alberta. From comparisons of dinosaur fossils to the skeletons of birds, scientists speculated that birds evolved from dinosaurs long ago. A recent find in China uncovered fossils of an unknown dinosaur with what appears to be feathers. The new dinosaur appears to be a close relative of the *Velociraptor*. Students will be interested to learn that Saskatchewan was home to many dinosaurs, including *Velociraptors*, *Triceratops*, and the king, *Tyrannosaurus rex*.

Get Started ▶

- Bring in a model of a dinosaur skeleton, or provide books or other visual material with pictures of various skeletons for the class to examine.
- Ask, *What is the main characteristic of vertebrate animals?* When students have answered, ask them to look for the backbone on a dinosaur. Then ask, *What other characteristics can you see in the dinosaur skeleton that we saw in other vertebrates?*

- Expect students to suggest things like having teeth and four legs. Students may also suggest things they have learned elsewhere about dinosaurs but cannot tell directly from their skeletons, such as laying eggs, having scales, or being cold-blooded.
- Point out that these are features that scientists have inferred from studying fossils, and they may not be correct. Explain that an inference is a guess based on previous experience and knowledge.
- Invite students to share what they know about fossils and what fossils can tell scientists. List students' key points on the board.
- Ask students, *Why is the study of fossils useful?* Record their suggestions to refer to throughout the lesson.
- Read aloud the paragraphs under Get Started while the class follows along in their textbooks. When you have finished, reread the question at the start of the second paragraph, How can paleontologists figure out what organisms were around that long ago? Invite students to share their ideas.
- Use the word "inference" to answer the question in the text by saying something like, *Paleontologists use their experience and knowledge to make inferences about what organisms were around long ago.*

Dinosaurs in Saskatchewan

- Read the three paragraphs on student book page 46 together. Ask students to look at the photographs on the page, to identify the *T. rex* fossils, and state where they were found.
- Ask students to describe what a fossil record is.
- Ask students why they think scientists need to study fossils.
- Ask students to explain to a partner what a fossil is and ask them to report back to the whole class.

Time
40 min
Skills
• observing • comparing • hypothesizing • inferring
Grouping
individuals, pairs
Materials and Equipment
(per group) • notebook • pen or pencil
Line Masters
• none

Work On It

- Before students begin to compare the different skeletons, direct their attention to the illustration of the dog's skeleton on student book page 47 and challenge them to identify the major bones. Ask, *Can you see a rib cage? a skull? leg bones?*
- You may choose to ask students to look as a class for these bones in the other skeletons. Keep prompting the class until they have identified all the bones and structures that are common to the skeletons. Then direct them to work individually to look for differences in the skeletons.
- Students could create a chart to record the similarities and differences they find.
- Set aside time for the class to share and discuss their findings. Encourage students to use appropriate vocabulary and terminology.
- Challenge students to suggest how the bone structures in each skeleton may help the animals move and eat.
- Review Venn diagrams with your students. Explain that a Venn diagram consists of two or more circles that contain characteristics of two or more different things. The circles overlap when the things have similar characteristics.

continued →

- The Venn diagram is a powerful tool for students to use because it gives a clear illustration of which characteristics are similar and which are different when comparing any two things.
- The fossil record is important for several reasons. Students can find the answers to this question by rereading the second paragraph on page 46 of the student book.

If Time Allows

Remind students that an adaptation is a special feature that helps an animal to survive. Encourage them to think about or research the habitat in which *Tyrannosaurus rex* lived, and to support their suggestions for adaptations with sound reasoning. Use LM 1-17 A Prehistoric Vertebrate to label *Tyrannosaurus rex* and help students answer the questions regarding its adaptations.

Students may be interested in finding out more about this giant crocodile and might wish to do a report on it. There is an excellent website that describes Big Bert and the search for its habitat on the Virtual Saskatchewan website:
http://www.virtualsk.com/current_issue/bert.html

Communicate

Students can work in pairs to answer the Communicate questions.

1. Most scientists believe that *Tyrannosaurus rex* was a predator, although some argue that it may have also scavenged some of its food. Its large legs and jaws with long, sharp teeth are evidence that *Tyrannosaurus rex* may have been able to run very quickly to chase down and capture its prey.
2. Students may suggest that fossils can show similarities in body structure between creatures of the past and those of today. Fossils may also help scientists prevent extinctions from happening today. Compare this answer to the suggestions students made in Get Started. Encourage the class to discuss what they learned during this lesson.
3. Students should add "paleontologist" and "fossils" to their mind maps, as well as any scientific terms they encountered to describe the skeletons.
4. Many fossils of marine animals have been found Saskatchewan and mammal bones have been found in the Cypress Hills area. Invertebrate fossils have been found in southern Saskatchewan. Some sites that students may find useful are:

   The Royal Saskatchewan Museum

   http://www.royalsaskmuseum.ca/

   The Encyclopedia of Saskatchewan

   http://www.esask.uregina.ca/

For Reteaching

Students may have difficulty recognizing the similarities in structure of the different animal skeletons shown. Visit the library and collect a variety of detailed skeleton illustrations for students to observe. Point out the obvious similarities, such as leg bones and rib cages, and ask students to find these features on skeletons in their textbooks.

For Enrichment

Many students are fascinated by dinosaurs and may wish to extend their research individually. Here is a great website for dinosaur research: Dinosaurs for Kids, http://www.kidsdinos.com/.

Assessment *for* Learning

What to Look For in Student Work	What to Do
Expect students to be able to explain their Venn diagrams, giving details about how the *Tyrannosaurus rex* skeleton was similar to and different from the human, bird, dog, and fish skeletons.	• Review the purpose of Venn diagrams for those having difficulty. Give students some simple examples so that they can see how differences and similarities between any two things are demonstrated.
Students should be able to explain how fossils provide evidence of changes in animals over geological time.	• You may wish to make anecdotal notes to use as evidence for assessing student achievement in comparing fossils with animals of the present. In this way, you will be able to assess which students need extra help.

ASK AN EXPERT — Lara Shychoski: A Saskatchewan Paleontologist

Page 49

- Ask students to read the material on student book page 49 to find out how this paleontologist first became interested in dinosaurs as a little girl.
- Ask them something like, *Have you ever thought you might become a scientist? Would you be interested in becoming a paleontologist? Why?*
- Ask students, *Why is it important to study fossils?*

Follow up:

- Ask students to do some research to find out what species are extinct or becoming extinct.
- Ask them to find out if agriculture, growing suburban areas, and/or deforestation have affected the environment close to their community. This will be an opportunity for you to facilitate a class discussion on the impact of humans on the local environment. Once again, you could organize your discussion using the Talking Circle rules described in Lesson 1, Get Started.
- You may wish to organize an outdoor education experience at the Royal Tyrrell Museum in Drumheller, Alberta. It offers excellent visitor packages that take students behind the scenes to meet the paleontologist and even allow them to sleep overnight among the dinosaurs!

11 Animal Adaptations

Page 50

Time

1 class period

Key Terms

- structural adaptations
- behavioural adaptations
- evolution
- predators
- prey

Line Masters

- LM 1-18

Indicator Assessment Chart

Indicator	Assessment Opportunities
DL6.4 a. Propose questions to investigate related to the structures and behaviours that help organisms survive in their environments (e.g., "What advantage are different beaks for birds?", "Why do owls turn their heads to look sideways?", "Why do rabbits change colour at different times of the year?", "Why do caribou migrate?", "Why do ground squirrels hibernate?").	• Work On It, p. 51
DL6.4 c. Describe examples of structures and behaviours, including seasonal changes, which help living things survive in their environments during the lifetime of the organism.	• Work On It, p. 51
DL6.4 d. Describe examples of adaptations to structures and behaviours (e.g., flippers, webbed feet, nighttime vision, wide wings, camouflage colouring, migration, and hibernation) that have enabled living things to adapt to their environments in the long term.	• Get Started, p. 50 • Work On It, p. 51 • Communicate, p. 54, q. 1, 3–4
DL6.4 h. Compare closely related animals that live in different parts of the world and propose explanations for any differences in their structures and behaviours.	• Communicate, p. 54, q. 2

Background Information

In this activity, students will learn about how animals are adapted to survive in their habitats. They will take a look at structural adaptations, which relate to animals' body parts, and behavioural adaptations, which relate to the way animals act in order to survive. They will be given examples of both structural and behavioural adaptations and will be asked to try to identify adaptations by looking at photos of various animals. Throughout the lesson, students will take a close look at the adaptations of animals native to Saskatchewan.

Many stories from First Nations and Métis people feature themes around how some animals got their unique or unusual characteristics. You may wish to read some of these stories to your students and invite them to find other stories on the Internet. Be aware that there are many contemporary First Nations and Métis authors whose works are intended for adult readers. A good link for vetting Aboriginal stories for children is BookWire: Helpful Resources: Children's Booksellers: http://bookwire.com/bookwire/Childrens-Booksellers.html. If this URL no longer functions, please try searching on the following term or phrase: BookWire Directory.

Get Started ▶

- After reading the first paragraph and looking at the photos, give students time to discuss their ideas about why some animals have special features.
- Ask something like, *What kinds of special features help animals to survive?*
- List their answers on chart paper or on the board.

Adaptation — Suiting the Environment

- Explain to the students that these special features are called adaptations. Animals may be adapted by their physical features (structural adaptation) or by the way they act (behavioural adaptation).
- After reading this section on student book pages 50 and 51, ask students to talk to a partner to see if they can think of structural and behavioural adaptations in animals.
- Ask the pairs to report their examples to the class and record them on chart paper or on the board.

Time
40 min
Skills
• observing • inferring • interpreting
Grouping
individuals, pairs
Materials and Equipment
(per group) • notebook • pen or pencil
Line Masters
• LM 1-18

Work On It

- Give the students time to examine the photos, but remind them not to read the captions just yet.
- Once they have listed their suggestions, ask them to carefully read the captions and list all of the adaptations cited. You may want them to add any new adaptations to the lists in their notebooks.
- Allow some time for students to share their lists with the class.

Think Again! Unusual Adaptations

- Ask students if they can think of any unusual structural or behavioural adaptations found in the animal kingdom.
- After having read the paragraphs on student book pages 53 and 54, ask something like, *What unusual structural characteristics can you name? What unusual behavioural characteristics can you name? How do adaptations differ between predators and prey?*
- Ask students to search the Internet to find photos or graphics of other unusual adaptations.
- Use LM 1-18 Animal Adaptations to help students do more research on unusual adaptations.

Communicate

Students will have an opportunity to revisit their *My Tree* charts, consider a variety of animals, and make up imaginary animals to explore the idea of adaptation. You may wish to have them work in groups to research the questions and present their findings.

1. Answers will vary. Researching on the Internet will help students find animals with structural and behavioural adaptations. Here's a great site to start their explorations: Arctic Wildlife: How animals are adapted to live in the Arctic:
http://www.saskschools.ca/~gregory/arctic/Awildlife.html
2. Answers will vary. Expect examples such as: animals adapted for living in hot climates may be too cold in frigid climates, predators may not be able to catch the food they need, animals adapted to living in trees may not survive in grasslands, etc.
3. Giving birth to young in a den is a behavioural adaptation. It allows the cubs to stay warm and keep out of the way of predators. Living in a hollow tree stump or log may be an effective alternative.
4. Students may need extra time to work on this activity. Although their animal is imaginary, the adaptations should be logical and help it to survive.

BUILD ON WHAT YOU KNOW

Answers will vary. Animals such as wolverines, ermine, lemmings, gophers, raccoons, Arctic terns, and pelicans might be included.

For Enrichment

Some students may be interested in creating an animal adaptation poster that illustrates both structural and behavioural adaptations of a number of unusual animals.

Assessment *for* Learning

What to Look For in Student Work	What to Do
In their answers to Work On It, students should demonstrate an understanding of animal structural adaptations by listing factors including camouflage, thickness of fur, shape of feet, shape of nose and ears, length of neck or legs, and mimicry.	• If students are having difficulty, you may wish to provide a variety of examples of animal adaptations for them to examine at length.
Students' answers to Communicate questions should also demonstrate an understanding of behavioural adaptations, including migration, hibernation, type of cry or call, hunting methods, and social interactions.	• A field trip to a local aquarium or zoo will help students see adaptations first-hand and provide opportunities for naturalist and visual/spatial learners.

ASK AN EXPERT — Ryan Fisher: On the Protection of Sprague's Pipit *Page 55*

- Ask students to read student book page 55 to find out how this Métis student is working toward his Ph.D., doing research to try to slow or even stop the extinction of Sprague's pipits.
- Ask them something like, *Have you ever thought you might be able to help a species to survive? Would you be interested in becoming a research scientist? Why?*
- Ask students, *Why is it important to study animals who are in danger of becoming extinct? How did Ryan Fisher become interested in a career as an ecologist?*
- Ryan Fisher is a Métis student, born and raised in Saskatchewan, who studies at the University of Regina. Ryan's doctoral thesis concerns the factors that influence the habitat of a small bird called Sprague's pipit. The pipit is a tiny songbird endemic to the prairies, whose numbers have been declining in some parts of Saskatchewan in recent years. Ryan's thesis work, which has been ongoing for three years, concerns the effects of human activity on the pipit population. By catching and counting the birds, he hopes that his research will lead to some understanding of the effects that humans have on the environment. Currently, his research shows that the habitat on which the bird relies — the prairie that it needs for nesting — is disappearing under pressure from some types of human development, whereas some other human activities actually benefit this bird. Working with farmers, ranchers, and landowners with the aim to preserve as much habitat as possible for these tiny animals, Ryan has made some startling findings.
- One would assume that birds would do best in untouched prairie. Ryan's study shows that these tiny birds actually thrive best in prairie ecosystems where the prairie grass is moderately grazed by cattle, but the field has never been ploughed. His research also demonstrates that pipits are able to survive and reproduce in Saskatchewan in habitats in which introduced species of plants have been grown, that is, grasses that are not endemic to Saskatchewan prairies (although not quite as well as in native prairie). Moreover, the pipits seem to fare well in fields that are used for hay production.

Follow up:

- Ask students to research other species that are extinct or becoming extinct. Ask them to find out if there are endangered species in Saskatchewan.
- Ask them to find out how conservation strategies have affected the environment close to their community. Once again, you could organize your discussion using the Talking Circle rules described in Lesson 1, Get Started.

Additional Questions

1. What does the pipit's status, classed as threatened, mean for the species in Saskatchewan?

   A threatened species is one in which the numbers of the population are dramatically declining. If preventive measures aren't taken, the population may become endangered (at risk of extirpation or extinction). If the pipit became endangered in Saskatchewan, it would mean that its population would drop below a level considered by the Committee on the Status of Endangered Wildlife in Canada (COSEWIC) to be less than acceptable. Their endangered status would mean possible and impending extirpation or extinction if their decline continued unabated.

2. Why is the decline of this songbird of concern?

   Students should state their opinions and justify their answers. Some possible answers are: loss of an organism, loss of diversity, and so on.

12 The Perfect Beak

Page 56

Time
1 class period
Key Terms
• none
Line Masters
• LM 1-19

Indicator Assessment Chart

Indicator	Assessment Opportunities
DL6.4 a. Propose questions to investigate related to the structures and behaviours that help organisms survive in their environments (e.g., "What advantage are different beaks for birds?", "Why do owls turn their heads to look sideways?", "Why do rabbits change colour at different times of the year?", "Why do caribou migrate?", "Why do ground squirrels hibernate?").	• Work On It, p. 56
DL6.4 c. Describe examples of structures and behaviours, including seasonal changes, which help living things survive in their environments during the lifetime of the organism.	• Work On It, p. 56 • Communicate, p. 57, q. 1–5
DL6.4 d. Describe examples of adaptations to structures and behaviours (e.g., flippers, webbed feet, nighttime vision, wide wings, camouflage colouring, migration, and hibernation) that have enabled living things to adapt to their environments in the long term.	• Work On It, p. 56 • Communicate, p. 57, q. 1–5
DL6.4 i. Research the advantages of particular structures or behaviours of organisms that suit different environments (e.g., how different bird beaks are best suited to obtain different types of food, how different types of foot structure are best suited for different environments).	• Communicate, p. 57, q. 5

Background Information

In this lesson, students will explore animal adaptation further by looking at a specific structural adaptation in birds — the beak. They will take a look at how various beak shapes work and try an experiment to see what shapes of beak are adapted to different foods. They will have an opportunity to identify and describe birds that are native to Saskatchewan as they research to answer questions throughout the lesson.

Beak shape is an important factor in the survival of many birds. Their beaks have adapted to the specific habitats and food sources in which the birds are found. Many bird watchers or "birders" use beak shape as a means of identifying particular species of birds. If students use field guides or Web research to identify birds, they will find that becoming familiar with beak shape is a useful way of narrowing their searches. There are literally hundreds of birds native to Saskatchewan. Students will have no problem finding many identification websites on the Internet.

Get Started ▶

- Ask students if they have ever noticed that different birds have not only different-sized, but also different-shaped beaks.
- Ask them to give you some examples of different beak shapes and list these examples on chart paper or on the board.
- Ask students to read the paragraph on student book page 56 and look at the photographs. Ask them to explain why they think each bird illustrated has a different beak shape.

Time

40 min

Skills

- measuring
- classifying
- inferring

Grouping

pairs

Materials and Equipment

(per group)

- beaks: spoon, tweezers, straw
- food: marbles, gummi worms in dirt, navy beans, toothpicks
- plastic cup to hold food
- graph paper or computer access
- stopwatch or clock for timing
- notebook
- pen or pencil

Line Masters

- LM 1-19

CAUTION!

Even though it will be tempting for students to eat some of the food items they are working with, it is important to warn them about the dangers of eating items when conducting experiments. You may wish to provide some treats specifically for eating before getting started.

Work On It

- Before you hand out the materials, ask students to copy the table under Procedure step 4 on student book page 57 into their notebooks.
- Allow the students some time to collect their materials and arrange them on their desks.
- Review how to use the stopwatches and ask the timer to try to start and then stop the stopwatch after 15 s.
- As students begin the activity, circulate among them to make sure they are on track and filling in their tables.
- Use this opportunity to review controlling variables in an experiment. Ask students to discuss why it is a good idea to change only the beak in their trials.
- Students can use LM 1-19 The Perfect Beak to complete their bar graphs.

Communicate

1. The woodpecker's beak is sturdy, long, and pointed for pecking into bark and wood to catch insects. The hummingbird's beak is long and narrow and acts like a straw to collect nectar. The duck's bill is flat and narrow and helps it strain water for food. The owl's bill is sharp, hooked, and pointed to capture and kill small animals. The kingfisher's beak is long and sturdy for snatching fish from the water.
2. Answers will vary. Expect such things as capturing fish, tearing meat, catching flying insects, breaking nuts, or collecting seeds.
3. Some examples are: The woodpecker can grasp the side of a tree with its specialized feet (structural adaptation). The hummingbird can hover in one spot to collect nectar (behavioural adaptation). The duck has a waterproof coating of feathers that hold oil and prevent it from sinking (structural adaptation). The owl has eyes that allow it to see in the dark (structural adaptation). The kingfisher is able to dive under water in order to catch its dinner (behavioural adaptation).
4. Answers will vary. Expect students to include things like: Animals that live in cold climates may have thick fur for protection, whereas those that live in warm climates may be able to get rid of heat by sweating or panting. Animals that live in jungles or grasslands may be camouflaged to help catch prey or hide from predators. Animals that live in oceans may be able to take oxygen from the water or hold their breath for a very long time.
5. Students may need help in creating data bases. You may find it most useful to help students set up a spreadsheet to record, track, and manipulate data. The Help function in spreadsheet programs will aid them as they begin to explore the use of spreadsheets.

Assessment *for* Learning

What to Look For in Student Work	What to Do
As students perform their experiments, they should be able to produce an accurate bar graph showing the best beak shape for collecting the specific foods. They should be able to explain how different beak shapes are adapted to different environments and food types.	• For those having difficulty, give them ample time to try their experiments. Review how to control variables and assist them in doing so. Encourage students to compare their results with those of other groups and discuss their findings in order to gain a deeper understanding of how adaptations help birds survive.

13 Plant Adaptations

Page 58

Time

1 class period

Key Terms

- dormant
- Taiga Shield ecozone
- boreal forest
- Boreal Shield ecozone
- parkland
- Boreal Plain ecozone
- Prairie ecozone
- taproots
- Cypress Hills Upland ecoregion
- forested plateau
- plant knowledge keepers

Line Masters

- LM 1-20

Indicator Assessment Chart

Indicator	Assessment Opportunities
DL6.1 b. Observe and document the diversity of living things in their local habitat through journaling, a nature walk, sketching, drawing, photographing, video recording, or other means.	• Communicate, p. 62, q. 1–2
DL6.1 d. Document the diversity of living things in different terrestrial and aquatic habitats (e.g., grasslands, forests, tundra, deserts, rivers, ponds, and oceans) using print, video, and/or on-line resources.	• Work On It, p. 61
DL6.2 d. Explore local First Nations and Métis methods of organizing understanding of living things (e.g., two-leggeds, four-leggeds, winged ones, swimmers, trees, and grasses) and the criteria underlying that understanding (e.g., where animals are found, how animals move, and the uses of plants).	• Think Again!, p. 62

Background Information

In this lesson, students will take a closer look at plant adaptation and, in particular, plants that are native to Saskatchewan. They will become familiar with the five ecozones of Saskatchewan and use this information to create their own tables and lists to organize these ecozones.

traditional ***KNOWLEDGE***

In examining the five ecozones of Saskatchewan, students will be afforded opportunities to learn about the First Nations and Métis peoples who live there. They will look at how local plants are used as medicine and become familiar with the ways that plant knowledge keepers pass along information orally through families. Knowledge about an ecozone's plant life was essential to the survival of tribal groups. This knowledge was acquired over time and passed along and preserved in oral structures. Stories, songs, and dances were employed to help pass along important knowledge and history in many tribes.

Get Started ▶

- Ask the students, *What adaptations do you think plants have? Can you give examples? What about plants in Saskatchewan?*
- After reading student book pages 58 and the top of page 59, ask students to discuss how plants can adapt to fire.

Ecozones of Saskatchewan

- Review the definition of an ecosystem with your students. Ask them what they think an ecozone might be. The term "ecozone" is relatively new and these particular ecozones correspond to the floristic kingdoms of botany. They help define specific areas of Saskatchewan where particular plants exist.
- Ask students to read student book pages 59, 60, and the top of page 61.
- Let them know that they will be using this information to create their own charts of Saskatchewan's ecozones.

Time

40 min

Skills

- classifying
- comparing
- communicating

Grouping

individuals, pairs

Materials and Equipment

(per group)
- map of Saskatchewan's ecozones
- ruler, pencil
- colour pencils
- notebook

Line Masters

- LM 1-20

Work On It

- Ask students to use the map on student book page 58 and the information on student book pages 59, 60, and 61 to make their charts.
- Encourage them to organize their work carefully and to add all of the factors listed in the seven steps of the procedure. You may wish to have students use LM 1-20 Plant Adaptations to take notes as they read the student book section.
- Give them time to share their charts with each other and display them in the classroom.

If Time Allows

Once students have had a chance to make a chart for Saskatchewan, they may be interested in making a similar chart for ecozones in different areas of the world.

Think Again! Prairie Plants for Food and Healing

traditional ***KNOWLEDGE***

- Many people take medications and natural products to help their health and to build their immune systems.
- Ask students something like, *Have you or anyone you know ever taken vitamins or natural foods to help improve health?*
- Let students know that many plants are held in high regard by First Nations and Métis people and some of the remedies we use today are a result of the knowledge they have passed on.
- Ask students to read the section on student book page 62 and ask them to discuss the concept of plant knowledge keepers with a partner.
- You may wish to ask students to research on the Internet to make a list of some of the plants that First Nations and Métis people use as medicine.
- For more information, teachers might wish to read *Historical Use of Native Plants As Food*, by Anna Leighton.

- For a teaching unit on this topic, consult "Nature's Hidden Gifts," by Morris Brizinski, at http://www.usask.ca/education/ccstu/units/hidden_gifts.html.

Communicate

The following questions will help students deepen their understanding of plant adaptations and personalize their knowledge of local plants. You may wish to assign the first question as homework.

1. Answers will vary. Students are likely to list types of grasses, weeds, trees, and bushes in their search. You may wish to help students differentiate between native plants found in the environment and imported plants found in gardens, etc.
2. Answers will vary. Students may start by thinking of obvious uses, such as food. Encourage them to become more creative and think about things like habitat, insulation, medicine, building material, clothing, art, dyes, etc.
3. Students will have an opportunity to personalize their learning.
   - **a.** Answers will vary. Look for suggestions such as: take only what you can carry out, leave the campsite looking like no one has been there, don't cut or chop down trees or bushes for fire or shelter, make sure you recycle all your garbage, bury any organic waste you can't carry out, and observe the environment around you rather than trying to adapt it to your needs.
   - **b.** Answers will vary. Re-use, reduce, recycle, turn out the lights, don't litter, try to eat foods that are produced locally, etc.

Assessment *for* Learning

What to Look For in Student Work	What to Do
Students should be able to describe specific plant adaptations for each of the ecozones listed in Work On It.	• For those having difficulty, help them highlight the text on student book pages 58, 59, and 60 to find adaptations of plants in various ecozones.
Students' answers to Communicate, question 3 will give you a profile of how well they understand the importance of stewardship.	• Making lists of local plants may help some students process the information and help them remember plant names and uses.

14 The Key to Classifying

Page 63

Time
1 class period

Key Terms
• physical appearance • learned behaviours

Line Masters
• none

Indicator Assessment Chart

Indicator	Assessment Opportunities
DL6.2 b. Consider personal observations and ideas as well as those of others (including differing worldviews) when constructing classification systems by asking questions, sharing stories, and responding to classmates' classification systems.	• Get Started, p. 63 • Work On It, p. 64
DL6.3 e. Suggest reasons why current biological classification systems for living things are based on structural (internal) characteristics rather than solely on physical appearance or behaviour.	• Work On It, p. 64 • Communicate, p. 65, q. 1

Background Information

This reading activity presents students with examples of characteristics that vary between groups of plants or animals. Students apply this knowledge to explain why physical appearance and learned behaviours are not used in formal classification systems.

Early observations of living things produced many errors in classification. In several species of birds, for example, the male and female birds were classified as different species. These classifications were based on the different colouration of the two sexes, for example, male and female cardinals. Although informal classification systems such as field guides often include physical appearance and learned behavioural traits, formal classification is based on structural characteristics that do not vary within a group.

Get Started ▶

- Ask the class to look back at the picture of a mealworm's life cycle on student book page 30. Ask something like, *How would you classify a mealworm if you observed it only during the larval stage?*
- Students may suggest that the larvae look like worms. Tell the class that insects are usually classified by characteristics they have in their adult stage, because characteristics that change during the life cycle of an organism are not very useful for classification.
- Extend the discussion by asking questions about other organisms. You might ask, *How do scientists classify plants? What characteristics would scientists use to classify cats and dogs into different groups?*
- Students should demonstrate an understanding that organisms are classified by characteristics that are constant, and not by features that change over time.

Physical Appearance and Learned Behaviours

- Invite students to study the photograph on student book page 63. Then ask, *What characteristics of the people in the photo are not useful for classifying humans?*
- Challenge students to explain their answers and suggest some characteristics that would be more useful.
- Ask students to look at the photos on student book page 64 and ask them, *What learned behaviours are necessary to be able to play soccer or to play a harp?*

Time

40 min

Skills

- observing
- classifying

Grouping

individuals, pairs

Materials and Equipment

(per group)
- notebook
- pen or pencil

Line Masters

- none

Work On It

- Students can read the information in this activity individually.
- Direct the class to make a chart to list examples of physical appearance and learned behaviours of people that they encounter as they read the lesson.
- When reading is complete, review as a class the characteristics students came up with. Ask, *Can anyone think of something else we could add to our list of physical appearance features? How about learned behaviours?*
- When students are listing features of physical appearance, note whether they can distinguish between inherited and behavioural characteristics.
- Ask students to add the new suggestions to their lists.
- Some students may list clothing choices as a feature of physical appearance. Challenge them by asking things like, *Are we born liking to wear red shirts, or is that something we learn?*
- Ask for volunteers to choose one example from their list and suggest how it could be useful for studying living things but not for classifying them.
- You may wish to model a response using a characteristic not included in the reading such as weight, which could be useful for studying humans and diet or humans and strength, but is not useful for classification because it changes over time.

Communicate

Assign the Communicate questions as seat work or homework.

1. Students should explain that structural characteristics refer to the inner structure of living things. Physical appearance refers to inherited characteristics that can help us to tell one individual from another. Learned behaviours are skills that living things acquire over time.
2. Answers may include: Learned — reading, language, walking, etc. Structural — jaws and teeth for biting and chewing, two arms, two legs for walking, etc.
3. Students should be comfortable with the words they add to their mind maps and understand what they mean.

For ESL/ELL

ESL students may be engaged by discussing the learned behaviours they came to class with and the new behaviours they are learning. You may wish to suggest they make a list of both types of behaviours.

For Reteaching

Some students may benefit from considering the changes that have occurred in their own bodies since they were born. Ask, *How have you grown in height and weight since you were born? What skills have you learned?* If they suggest unchanging characteristics unique to them, such as eye colour, ask questions like, *Do we all have the same eye colour as you?*

Assessment *for* Learning

What to Look For in Student Work	What to Do
Students should be able to explain the difference between inherited and learned or behavioural characteristics.	• For students who are struggling, having them discuss their personal appearance and learned behaviours to help them personalize the information.
Students should be able to demonstrate and explain how structural characteristics are used in formal classification and why physical appearance and learned behaviours are not suitable for classifying living things.	• For those having difficulty, ask them to compare their lists from Communicate question 2 with those of their classmates to help them broaden their understanding of learned and structural characteristics.

15 The Microscopic World

Page 66

Time

2–3 class periods

Key Terms

- micro-organisms
- protist kingdom
- cilia
- flagella
- pseudopods

Line Masters

- LM 1-21
- LM 1-22

Indicator Assessment Chart

Indicator	Assessment Opportunities
DL6.5 a. Choose and correctly use appropriate tools (e.g., magnifying glasses, optical microscopes, and video microscopes) to study living organisms that cannot be seen with the naked eye.	• Work On It, p. 68
DL6.5 b. Observe and represent, using words and diagrams, characteristics of micro-organisms obtained from student- or teacher-collected water samples (e.g., bottled water, tap water, rain barrel, pond, creek, slough, and river water).	• Work On It, p. 68
DL6.5 c. Explain how micro-organisms meet their basic needs, including moving around and obtaining food, water, and oxygen.	• Communicate, p. 69, q. 2

Background Information

This lesson introduces micro-organisms, and provides an opportunity for students to observe the diversity in this group of organisms. Students also explore how micro-organisms meet their basic needs.

Like all living things, the basic needs of micro-organisms include food, water, oxygen, and reproduction. This activity looks at micro-organisms of the protist kingdom. These organisms don't fit into any other kingdom. Members of this kingdom are single-celled organisms that have a nucleus, and include slime molds, euglenids, chrysophytes, dinoflagellates, and protozoans. They include animal-like, plant-like, and fungus-like organisms.

Get Started ▶

- Introduce the class to a microscope and ask students to share what they know about microscopes.
- Use LM 1-21 The Microscopic World to help students label and become familiar with the parts of the microscope.
- Tell students that the suffix "micro" means "small," then ask them to explain the meaning of the term "micro-organism."
- Explain that scientists use microscopes to see micro-organisms — organisms that are so tiny they are invisible to the naked eye.
- Challenge the class to closely describe the protists in the photographs on student book pages 67 and 68 as accurately as they can.

- Remind them that scientists use structural characteristics to classify living things. Ask, *What structural characteristics can you see? How are these organisms similar to each other? How are they different?*
- Be sure to model good handling of a microscope with students—carry the microscope with two hands, grasping the arm of the microscope in one hand and holding the base of the microscope with the other. Place the microscope on the table so that its arm is facing you.
- Demonstrate to the class how a microscope works. Model these steps:
    1. Plug in the microscope and turn on the light.
       Safety: Some microscopes use a mirror that can damage the eyes if direct sunlight is reflected from it.
    2. Rotate the nosepiece until the objective lens with the lowest power is in place. While watching from the side, use the coarse adjustment knob to move the lens to its lowest point.
    3. Place a slide on the stage and secure it with the stage clips. Centre the slide over the hole in the stage.
    4. Look through the eyepiece and turn the coarse adjustment knob to move the slide away from the lens until the object is in focus. Move the slide to see the object of interest.
    5. Turn the fine adjustment knob to improve focus.
    6. To take a closer look, switch to the medium power lens. Students should avoid using the highest power lens so as not to damage it. Use only the fine adjustment knob to focus the image at higher powers.

Time

40 min during 2 class periods

Skills

- observing
- classifying

Grouping

pairs, groups

Materials and Equipment

(per group)
- living micro-organisms in slides or prepared slides of micro-organisms
- white paper
- pens and pencils
- magnifying glass
- microscope

Line Masters

- none

CAUTION!

Some microscopes use a mirror. Remind students to take care not to reflect sunlight directly into their eyes.

Work On It

- Ask students to look at the labelled photo of a microscope on student book page 67, and then identify these parts on a microscope in the classroom.
- Ensure that students know how to hold the microscope, illuminate a slide, and focus the microscope before they begin work.
- Encourage students to study the photographs on student book pages 67 and 68 to identify some of the characteristics of protists while they wait to look through the microscope.
- Students are likely to be very excited to see live micro-organisms moving around on their slides. They may need a full period just to find a variety of protists and observe their actions.
- It may be difficult to find protists in pond water. A few that may be visible are filamentous algae; small quick ciliates, such as *Opalina*, *Vorticella*, *Daphnia;* and a few diatoms. If you are concerned that you may not see any protists in pond water, order prepared samples from a science supply company.
- Remind students to record their observations by drawing diagrams in pencil and including point-form descriptions.
- Some students may benefit from guidance in the accuracy of their diagrams. As they draw, ask questions such as, *What is the overall shape of the organism? Does your drawing show the relative proportions of the different features of the living thing?*
- Remind students to use the microscopes carefully, clean them, and put them away when finished.

! What is a basic need? You may wish to engage the students in a debate regarding their basic needs. Some things are simple, such as food, air, and habitat. Other things may encourage discussion: cellphones, computers, friends, learning, homework, etc.

Communicate

Bring the class together to discuss their observations and answer question 1. Assign question 2 to small groups, and reserve class time for the presentations.

1. Expect students to suggest similarities such as: all specimens are composed of only one cell, all have a nucleus, and all are invisible to the naked eye.
2. Although their presentations will focus on different species, students should include information similar to the examples below.

Amoeba

Feeds: Eats algae and other organic matter by surrounding and engulfing them. Food particles are then enclosed in vacuoles, into which enzymes are released to digest the food.

Moves: Extends pseudopods, which can form anywhere on its surface.

Breathes: Oxygen and carbon dioxide diffuse through the cell membrane.

Gets rid of waste: Passes wastes out through its cell membrane.

Reproduces: Forms a sphere, slowly constricts through its middle, and then splits into two identical cells.

Paramecium

Feeds: Eats bacteria, algae, and yeast by beating its cilia to move them into a small groove that leads to its mouth. Food then passes through the gullet where a food vacuole is formed. Enzymes enter the food vacuole and digest the food.

Moves: Cilia on the outer body beat at an angle, propelling the organism forward and rotating it as it moves.

Breathes: Oxygen and carbon dioxide diffuse through the cell membrane.

Gets rid of waste: Expels undigested food through its anal pore.

Reproduces: Uses both asexual and sexual reproduction. In asexual reproduction, it spreads itself equally to either end and splits. In sexual reproduction, it exchanges genetic material with another paramecium.

Dinoflagellate

Feeds: Some can produce their own food through photosynthesis and store it as starch. Others absorb nutrients from the surrounding water.

Moves: Makes a swimming motion, propelled by its two flagella.

Breathes: Absorbs carbon dioxide from and eliminates oxygen into the surrounding water.

Gets rid of waste: Passes wastes out via vacuoles.

Reproduces: Divides into two new organisms, each with one flagellum. Each new organism eventually grows a second flagellum.

BUILD ON WHAT YOU KNOW

Answers will vary. Ask students to explain their choices for the two additions to their chart.

For Reteaching

Students may benefit from observing photographs, diagrams, and illustrations of protists on CD-ROMs, websites, and other reference materials. Encourage students to look for similarities to and differences from the organisms that they observed under the microscope.

For Enrichment

Ask students to bring in a sample of pond water, and examine a drop under the microscope to look for different micro-organisms. Challenge them to identify the organisms they find. Provide students with copies of LM 1-22 Observing Micro-organisms.

Assessment *for* Learning

What to Look For in Student Work	What to Do
Students should be able to describe and explain the various parts of a microscope.	• For struggling students, play the microscope game: List all of the parts of the microscope and their descriptions. Cut them up and ask students to pair up to match the labels to their descriptions and glue them onto a diagram of a microscope.
Students should be able to observe and describe microscopic living things using correct terminology.	• For students who are encountering difficulties using the scientific terminology for micro-organisms, ask them to practise with a partner by using a tape recorder to record the more difficult terms.
Students should be able to describe how micro-organisms meet their basic needs.	• If students have difficulty describing how micro-organisms meet their basic needs, help them take an alternative point of view by comparing the way humans meet their needs to the way an animal living in a drop of water would meet its needs.

16 The Impact of Micro-organisms

Page 70

Time
1–2 class periods

Key Terms
• microbiology • pasteurization

Line Masters
• LM 1-23

Indicator Assessment Chart

Indicator	Assessment Opportunities
DL6.5 d. Design and conduct an investigation of the factors that influence how quickly micro-organisms break down organic matter (e.g., build a composter in a 2 L plastic bottle and vary conditions such as the amount of water, soil, light, and combinations of waste products).	• LM 1-23
DL6.5 e. Compare cultural, historical, and scientific understandings and explanations of disease, including First Nations and Métis understandings and the contributions of scientists such as John Snow and Louis Pasteur to the germ theory.	• Think Again!, p. 73 • Communicate, p. 73, q. 2
DL6.5 f. Critique representations or depictions of micro-organisms in a variety of texts (e.g., science-fiction, cartoons, movies, music, and poetry).	• Communicate, p. 73, q. 5
DL6.5 g. Discuss positive and negative impacts of micro-organisms for humans (e.g., food production and spoilage, fermentation, pasteurization, water and sewage treatment, human digestion, composting, disease spread and prevention, and biological warfare).	• Work On It, p. 72

Background Information

This lesson takes a deeper look at micro-organisms and how they affect us. Students will read about characteristics of micro-organisms and understand that, while they can be harmful, they are also essential for life.

Learning about micro-organisms will help students understand more about good hygiene and why we have processes in place to make sure our food is safe. Micro-organisms such as bacteria, fungi, protozoa, algae, and viruses can be both helpful and harmful. Some of them can cause illness or disease, but most of them are helpful to us. Millions of micro-organisms live on and in our bodies and most are either neutral or actually help us in a variety of ways, such as aiding in digestion.

Get Started ▶

- Ask students if they think micro-organisms are harmful or useful. You could have them vote by a show of hands. Let them know that both views are correct.
- Ask students, *How do you think diseases such as flu or colds spread?* Harmful micro-organisms are spread from one person to another by touch.
- Ask also, *How do our bodies fight against disease?* There are helpful micro-organisms in our bodies that help with digestion and others that help build our immune systems.
- Ask students to read the paragraph on student book page 70 and then do a Think-Pair-Share with the chart on the bottom half of the page. Ask them to read the bullets to each other and see how many they can report back to the class without looking.

Good or Bad?

- Ask students to read the section under this subheading to see if they can find examples of useful or harmful micro-organisms.
- You may want to search the Internet for background information on the germ theory.
- Ask students if they have seen any movies or read any books in which micro-organisms were the "stars." Have a class discussion about whether the portrayal of the micro-organism was realistic and whether the micro-organism was helpful or harmful.

Micro-organisms and the Spread of Disease

- Students may read the four bullets and give examples that go with each one.
- In 2009, there was an outbreak of the H1N1 virus, also called the swine flu. You may wish to discuss this or other recent outbreaks, such as SARS, with the class. There is a lot of information on the Internet about such outbreaks. MedLINE and the CDC are good sources of information.
- You may wish to cover methods of preventing the spread of disease—thorough and often hand washing, sneezing into an arm or tissue instead of the hand or air, cooking food thoroughly, storing food safely, drinking water from reputable sources (if unsure of the water, treating it with a filter), using insect repellents, getting rid of standing water on properties (to avoid West Nile Virus), and so on.
- Malaria is a classic example of a disease spread by insects. You can ask interested students to research malaria and write a short report.

Time
40 min
Skills
• classifying • inferring
Grouping
pairs
Materials and Equipment
(per group) • research materials • library and computer access • paper and pencil
Line Masters
• none

Work On It

- Ask students to create a table similar to the one on student book page 72. They may do a rough draft in their notebooks and then make a final copy on poster or chart paper to present to the class.
- Students can make their travel brochures and print them for use by friends or relatives who are planning to travel, so that they will have an authentic audience for their work. You may suggest that they include a caveat such as: *This list is not exhaustive. Please consult your doctor or medical professional for advice on practising hygiene in foreign countries.*

Think Again!

- Review the concept of timelines for the students and give them some examples of a variety of timelines to examine. A great website for examples of timelines is the Timeline Index: http://www.timelineindex.com/content/home.php
- The suggestions for timeline inclusions are not exhaustive and students should be able to fill in several more dates after researching on the Internet. Some other important contributions are:
  1595 — Sacharias Jansen — Invented the microscope.
  1890 — Emil von Behring and Kitasato Shibasaburo — Developed an effective diphtheria antitoxin.
  1897 — George Nuttall — Demonstrated that flies can spread plague bacilli.
  1928 — Sir Alexander Fleming — Discovered penicillin.
- Ask students to share their timelines by displaying them in the classroom or hallways.

Communicate

Questions 2–6 give students a variety of ways to represent their learning about micro-organisms. You may want them to choose one or two of the activities suggested and to complete them at home.

1. Answers will vary. Expect students to be able to explain that coughing and sneezing in class can cause the spread of harmful micro-organisms. Remind them that the best way to prevent the spread of germs is to stay home if they are sick and to wash hands thoroughly and frequently using soap and hot water.
2. You may wish to create a bulletin board in the classroom or hallway to display student posters.
3. One way to preserve puppet shows is to record them. The show can then be run for the students who presented it and they can look for ways to self-assess.
4. Students may start their rap by writing rhyming lines and then put the lines to a beat. A program like Garage Band is very useful for creating back beats over which students can write their raps.
5. Students may need some help organizing their computer slide presentations. If you have iMacs, they can use an application called Keynote.
6. Cartoon strips are an excellent way for students to organize the big ideas in their learning. Students can also use cartoon storyboards as a way of organizing text and illustrations about what they have learned.

For Enrichment

Students can use LM 1-23 The Impact of Micro-organisms to create an in-class pop bottle composter. Ask them to follow the directions to set up their composters and observe them over time. Remind them to control variables in their investigations to ensure a fair test.

Assessment *for* Learning

What to Look For in Student Work	What to Do
Students should understand the impact of micro-organisms and be able to describe both positive and negative impacts in detail using proper terminology in their explanations.	• For students having difficulty with their presentations, allowing them to demonstrate their learning in a variety of ways — puppet shows, dance, story, etc. — may help them to be more successful.

DESIGN PROJECT

Classifying Living Things Around Us

Page 74

Time

3 class periods

Skills

- observing
- classifying

Grouping

pairs

Materials and Equipment

(per pair)

- recording material (paper, pencils, camera, video recorder, markers, chart paper)
- magnifying glass
- Popsicle sticks
- guide or classification chart for local plants and animals
- trees classification chart from the Classifying Trees activity (optional)

Line Masters

- LM 1-24
- LM 1-25

Indicator Assessment Chart

Indicators Met in Design Project
DL6.1 b. Observe and document the diversity of living things in their local habitat through journaling, a nature walk, sketching, drawing, photographing, video recording, or other means.
DL6.1 c. Show respect for other people, living things, and the environment when observing ecosystems.
DL6.2 a. Construct and use a classification system to organize living things into groups and subgroups according to student-developed criteria.
DL6.2 b. Consider personal observations and ideas as well as those of others (including differing worldviews) when constructing classification systems by asking questions, sharing stories, and responding to classmates' classification systems.
DL6.2 f. Illustrate the diversity of living things on Earth by constructing a visual representation (e.g., poster, mobile, slide show, and web page) showing examples from each kingdom of the five kingdom taxonomic model: monera, protists, fungi, plants, and animals.
DL6.2 g. Use appropriate scientific terminology to communicate ideas about the diversity of living things (e.g., biotic, abiotic, kingdom, phylum, monera, protists, fungi, plant, animal, vertebrate, and invertebrate).
DL6.3 a. Identify characteristics of vertebrates and invertebrates and classify animals as vertebrates or invertebrates from drawings, videos, pictures, lists, and/or personal observations.
DL6.3 d. Propose questions for inquiry that arise from personal investigations of structural characteristics and behaviours of animals.
DL6.4 b. Show interest and curiosity in learning about organisms' adaptations to different environments by journaling, participating in a nature walk, or sharing science-related information about adaptations (gathered from print or video resources or personal experience) with classmates.
DL6.4 j. Suggest reasons to explain how results of similar and repeated studies of the adaptations of organisms may vary and suggest possible explanations for variations (e.g., independent studies may reveal different responses by polar bears to temperature changes or pollution).

Background Information

In the Design Project, students go on a field trip and observe the diversity of living things in a habitat such as a pond, field, or wetland near the school. They record the characteristics of all the living things they observe. When they return to class, they design a classification tree for the living things they observed.

traditional ***KNOWLEDGE***

Many Aboriginal people have a particular way of being in nature. Because of their deep respect for all things, living and non-living, they are careful not to disturb the environment as they move through it. This respect may allow them to become effective observers of the goings-on in natural surroundings. If students keep this in mind, they are much more likely to see living things on their field trip. The **Things To Remember** list on student book page 75 will help them to be respectful as they move through the environment and collect data.

Get Started ▶

- Review with students some of the features of the habitat they are about to visit.
- Challenge students to begin a classification tree of the living things they expect to see, and to describe what kinds of features they would use to place organisms into groups.
- Read the paragraph in Get Started as a class. Invite volunteers to choose an organism in one of the pictures, and describe it using characteristics that would be useful for classification.

CAUTION!
Students should be reminded to use the buddy system while on the field trip and stay with a partner, so that they are never alone. They should also be careful to wash their hands thoroughly with soap and warm water after handling animals, plants, or soils.

Work On It

On a Field Trip

- When you arrive at the area where students will conduct their study, review the guidelines for the field trip on student book page 75 and outline the boundaries of the area where they will work.
- Ensure students understand the type of observing and recording they are expected to do.
- Students should have either a guidebook to local plants and animals or their student book with them to use the Tree Classification Chart as they work.
- Assign a time limit, and then send students to begin their observations.

Back in Class

- When students are back in class, consider starting their classification systems, described in step 1 of the Procedure, as a class.
- Circulate around the room to make sure all the pairs have successfully organized their lists into plants, animals, and fungi before they continue independently.
- Remind students to look back over the unit as they work for the characteristics that were used to divide living things into groups.
- You may need to remind students to use the scientific terms for living things that they learned in this unit. Make sure that their classification tree is clear and easy to follow.

Communicate

Set aside time for students to present and explain their classification trees for question 1. When the presentations are complete, assign the rest of the questions for individual homework.

1. Students can be expected to explain their groupings and the reasoning they used to organize their classification systems in their presentations.
2. Students should state in their answers that structural features were used to group the living things. A complete answer should give examples and explain how these features were helpful.
3. Answers will vary, but students' subgroups should be similar because they all visited the same habitat.
4. Answers will vary. Students may report that they resolved their differences in their combined lists by asking for clarification of their group members' observations, and making sure they used structural features only.
5. Expect students to describe structural features of their five suggestions that are similar to the groups on their classification systems.
6. Students should be able to describe how living and non-living things in the ecosystem they visited are interdependent.

7. Answers will vary. Students should be able to describe how a major change, such as a fire or flood, might affect the living things in the environment. They should be able to describe how some things may adapt whereas others may not survive.

For ESL/ELL

For safety's sake, you may wish to pair ESL students with others who are more proficient in English. You might organize students into trios for this activity so that all students get a chance to discuss their findings within their groups.

For Reteaching

Some students may benefit from working directly from the classification trees in the student book. Direct students to turn to the classification chart on student book page 13 and ask them to divide the organisms on their lists into different kingdoms. Then ask them to turn to student book pages 18 and 19, and use the classification charts there to identify the trees on their lists. The charts on student book pages 13 and 21 can be used to classify any invertebrate and vertebrate animals they observed.

Unit 1 Summary

Page 78

Students may wish to use this unit summary as a study guide. The Unit Summary is available on LM 1-1.

Unit 1 Review

Page 79

Explain Your Stuff

The short-answer questions provided on this page could be used as an end-of-unit test or an in-class review of the unit, among other possibilities. Examples of the types of answers you may expect are presented below.

1. Scientists use structural characteristics to classify living things because these characteristics remain consistent throughout the lives of organisms.
2. Scientific classification systems help organize the vast diversity of living things so that people can make sense of them. They are also helpful for seeing similarities and differences among living things.
3. Everything on Earth has a spirit flowing through it. Aboriginal people use place-based knowledge to group the things in their environment which have a practical purpose to aid in survival.
4. A snake and an earthworm are similar in that they are both members of the animal kingdom, which means they move and must consume food to survive, and they are both cold-blooded. They are different because a snake is a vertebrate and an earthworm is an invertebrate.
5. The main difference between warm-blooded and cold-blooded animals is how they regulate their body temperature. Warm-blooded animals use energy to maintain their body temperature at a specific level. Cold-blooded animals do not maintain their body temperature at any specific level — their bodies are the same temperature as their surrounding environment. A warm-blooded animal has a wider area where it can live than a cold-blooded animal because it does not rely on the environment to maintain its body temperature. However, a warm-blooded animal must consume food regularly so that its body has sufficient energy to maintain its warm temperature.
6. A person's ability to play basketball is not a useful characteristic for classifying that person scientifically because it is a learned behaviour that can be affected by environment as well as instruction and practice. Not all humans have the same opportunity to learn this behaviour. A useful characteristic for classifying humans is bone structure.

7. This fossil helps us understand the ways in which animals change over time when we compare it to structures of animals living today. Studying the similarities and differences between it and animals of today helps scientists to infer how similar animals may have lived in the past.
8. Students' description of the micro-organism should include the following points: long, rectangular-shaped cell with a number of small bodies inside, and one long flagellum.
9. Students will need to organize their Tree of Life carefully to ensure that all the different groupings are located in logical places and flow from one to another in an easy-to-understand manner.
10. Answers will vary. Expect students to be able to explain that classification helps us organize information and objects so that we can find them when we need them. It helps us identify and learn about living and non-living things around us and organize this information so that it is easier to use.
11. Living things are made up of one or more cells, respire, require energy, respond to stimuli, grow and develop, reproduce, and excrete.
12. Five groups of living things are monera (bacteria), protists (algae, amoebas), plants (trees, grasses, weeds, flowers), animals (horses, dogs, humans), and fungi (mushrooms).
13. Two types of animals are vertebrates, such as fish, amphibians, reptiles, and birds, and invertebrates, such as sponges, molluscs, worms, and arthropods.
14. Five types of vertebrates are fish, amphibians, reptiles, birds, and mammals.
15. Four types of invertebrates are sponges, molluscs, worms, and arthropods.
16. Micro-organisms are difficult to see with the unaided eye.
17. Single-celled organisms are composed of one cell, whereas multicellular organisms are made up of more than one cell.
18. Biotic things are those that are living or were once living. Abiotic things are not living and never were living.
19. For Aboriginal peoples, everything on Earth has spirit flowing through it. Everything is living or alive with spirit.
20. Answers will vary. Expect students to give examples of how some organisms will adapt and survive whereas others will not.
21. The vertebrate (dog) has an interior skeleton, is warm-blooded, lives on land, has hair, breathes through lungs, eats a variety of food, gives birth to live young, and the female nurses its young. The invertebrate (ant) lives on land or water, has a segmented body, has an exoskeleton, breathes through special organs, and reproduces by laying eggs.
22. Coniferous trees have leaves that are like needles or scales. Deciduous trees have wide leaves.

23. Answers will vary. Expect answers such as: Structural characteristics of a dog include canine teeth and fur. Behavioural characteristics of a dog include that it hunts in packs (wild) and barks.
24. Answers will vary. Expect answers such as: Rabbits remain still to avoid predators, some change colour to match their surroundings, they have large ears to detect predators, and large rear legs for quick escapes.
25. Answers will vary. Expect answers such as: To survive in a cold environment, some animals have adapted by developing blubber, thick fur, and hibernating. To survive in a hot environment, animals have adapted by developing a low need for water and methods of heat dispersion, such as panting and sweating.
26. Answers will vary. Expect answers to include ideas such as: Diversity helps living things to adapt and survive changes in the environment.
27. Answers will vary. Expect answers to include ideas such as: Stewardship and relations with Mother Earth can include many of the same things. Both ideas relate to the responsibility that all people have to care for Earth and to ensure its healthy survival for future generations.
28. Answers will vary. Expect answers to include ideas such as: Microscopes have helped science, medicine, and society by allowing scientists to study and understand both harmful and useful micro-organisms. They have helped us study diseases, learn about how they spread, and helped us create vaccinations to fight sickness and death. They have also helped us learn about how micro-organisms such as yeast help us process food.

How Did You Do?

Self-evaluation allows students to communicate their learning and their feelings about it. Seeing how students view their learning can give you insight and information on which to base your programming decisions.

Ask students to answer these questions individually, then to share their answers with the class. Some students will likely find some areas of this unit easier than other areas. This exercise may help students identify who can give them assistance to understand difficult concepts.

Unit 1 Line Masters

Table of Contents

Table of Contents *(continued)*

Name: ________________________________

Unit 1 Summary

Something I know and understand before starting the Diversity of Living Things Unit.	Lesson(s) where I learned about this idea or learned more about this idea.	Important points about the Diversity of Living Things
		Living (biotic) things depend on non-living (abiotic) things for survival. The groups are interconnected.
		Classification systems help organize our understanding of the world. The tree classification system can be used for both biotic (living) and abiotic (non-living) things.
		From observations in their local environment, Aboriginal peoples may describe plants or animals according to their uses in daily living or for survival.
		Scientific classification systems are based on structural characteristics.
		Trees can be classified as deciduous or coniferous.
		Invertebrates are a group of organisms without backbones, such as sponges, worms, arthropods, and molluscs.

Copyright © 2013 Pearson Canada Inc.
The right to reproduce this page is restricted to the purchasing school.

Something I know and understand before starting the Diversity of Living Things Unit.	Lesson(s) where I learned about this idea or learned more about this idea.	Important points about the Diversity of Living Things
		Arthropods have a hard outer body covering, jointed legs, specialized mouth parts, and a segmented body.
		Vertebrates are a group of organisms with a backbone. Some are warm-blooded (birds, mammals) and others are cold-blooded (fish, reptiles, and amphibians).
		Fossils reveal similarities and differences among animals that lived long ago and animals that are alive today. They can tell us a lot about the changes in animals over time.
		Adaptation is changes that occur in a species over many, many years and ensure the survival of the species.
		Structural adaptations involve an animal's body parts. Behavioural adaptations include migration, hibernation, hunting style, and whether an animal lives alone or not.
		First Nations and Métis people on the prairies have used plants for medicine and daily living. Certain people are plant knowledge keepers who have place-based knowledge of plants.

Copyright © 2013 Pearson Canada Inc.
The right to reproduce this page is restricted to the purchasing school.

Something I know and understand before starting the Diversity of Living Things Unit.	Lesson(s) where I learned about this idea or learned more about this idea.	Important points about the Diversity of Living Things
		Some species of plants have interesting adaptations, such as root systems that can survive fires, drought, and harsh weather.
		Saskatchewan has ecozones with unique characteristics.
		Micro-organisms are so small that you need a microscope to see them. Protists are complex microscopic organisms.
		Micro-organisms can cause disease but are also useful to humans in many ways.

Copyright © 2013 Pearson Canada Inc.
The right to reproduce this page is restricted to the purchasing school.

Name: ______________________________

Unit 1 Key Terms

Word	I know nothing about this word.	I can spell this word correctly.	I have seen/heard it before.	I can define it as it relates to science.
abdomen				
abiotic				
adaptations				
behavioural adaptations				
biotic				
boreal forest				
Boreal Plain ecozone				
Boreal Shield ecozone				
carnivorous				
cilia				
cold-blooded				
coniferous trees				
Cypress Hills Upland ecoregion				
deciduous trees				
dependent variable				
diversity				
dormant				
ecosystem				
evolution				
exoskeleton				
fair test				
family				
flagella				
forested plateau				
fossils				
fossil record				
independent variable				
invertebrates				
jointed legs				
kingdom				

Copyright © 2013 Pearson Canada Inc.
The right to reproduce this page is restricted to the purchasing school.

Word	I know nothing about this word.	I can spell this word correctly.	I have seen/heard it before.	I can define it as it relates to science.
larvae				
learned behaviours				
microbiology				
micro-organisms				
molluscs				
moult				
multicellular				
non-vascular				
organisms				
paleontologists				
parasite				
parkland				
pasteurization				
physical appearance				
place-based knowledge				
plant knowledge keepers				
Prairie ecozone				
predators				
prey				
proboscis				
protist kingdom				
pseudopods				
pupae				
segmented body				
single-celled				
species				
species, genus, family, order, class, phylum, and kingdom				
specimens				
spirit guide				
sponges				
stewardship				
structural adaptations				
structural characteristics				
structures				

Copyright © 2013 Pearson Canada Inc.
The right to reproduce this page is restricted to the purchasing school.

Word	I know nothing about this word.	I can spell this word correctly.	I have seen/heard it before.	I can define it as it relates to science.
Taiga Shield ecozone				
taproot				
taxonomy				
thorax				
vascular				
vertebrae				
vertebrates				
warm-blooded				

Copyright © 2013 Pearson Canada Inc.
The right to reproduce this page is restricted to the purchasing school.

Name: ________________________________

Living Things

Fill in the table with Yes or No to indicate whether the objects are biotic or abiotic.

Object	Breathes	Requires energy	Responds to stimuli	Grows and develops	Can reproduce	Excretes waste	Biotic/ abiotic
Rock							
Tree							
Dog							
Computer							
Desk							
Water							
Gold							
Sunlight							
Clouds							
Wooden ruler							
Hamburger							
Cotton fabric							
Glass							
Paper							
Grass							
Ant							

Look around your classroom and list all the biotic and abiotic objects that you see.

Biotic	Abiotic

Copyright © 2013 Pearson Canada Inc.
The right to reproduce this page is restricted to the purchasing school.

Name: ___________________________

Methods of Classifying

Add more levels to the tree chart to show the locations and addresses where you and some of your classmates live.

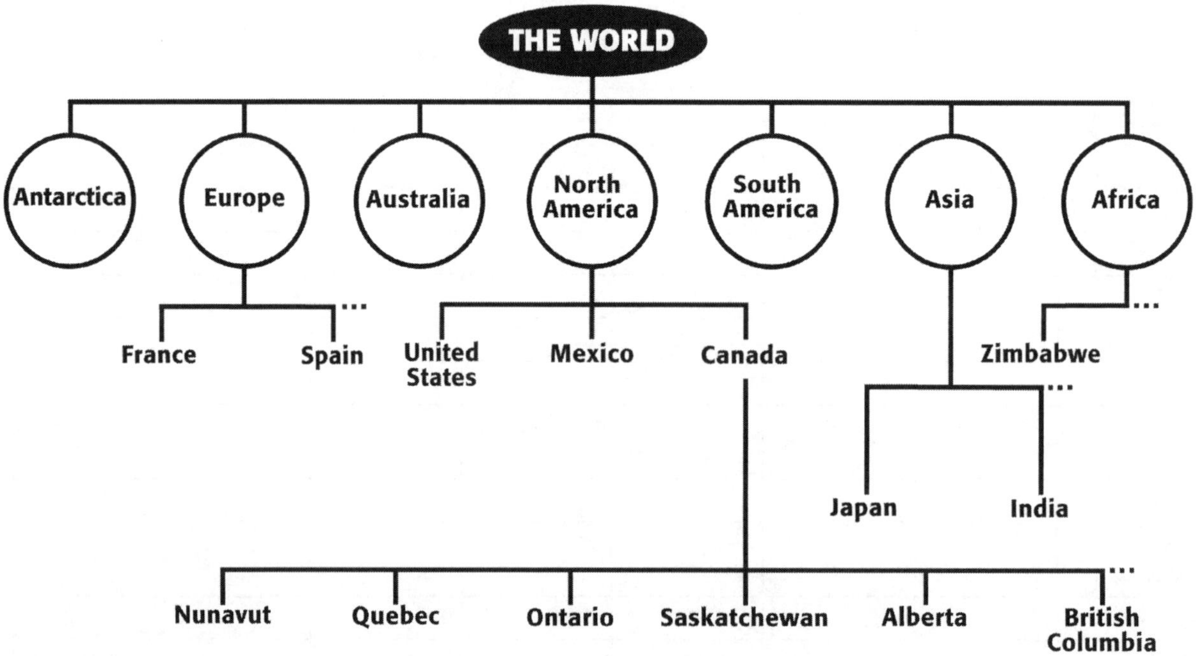

Copyright © 2013 Pearson Canada Inc.
The right to reproduce this page is restricted to the purchasing school.

Name: ______________________________

Classifying Living Things

Use the illustration on page 15 of the student book to classify Saskatchewan's organisms into one of the following categories.

Plant	Animal	Fungi	Not sure

Copyright © 2013 Pearson Canada Inc.
The right to reproduce this page is restricted to the purchasing school.

Name: ______________________________

Classifying Trees

With a partner, choose at least four different types of trees in your schoolyard or local park. Sketch one type of leaf in each section below and its placement on the branch. Try to identify your sample sketches back in the classroom.

1	2
3	4

Copyright © 2013 Pearson Canada Inc.
The right to reproduce this page is restricted to the purchasing school.

Name: ______________________________

Classifying Animals — The Invertebrates

Separate these illustrations by cutting them out. Follow the procedure on page 23 of your student book to place them on a classification tree. Use the tree at the bottom of this page to get started.

Sponge

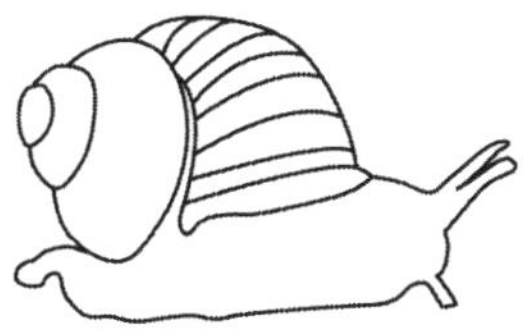
Snail

Earthworm

Crayfish

Ant

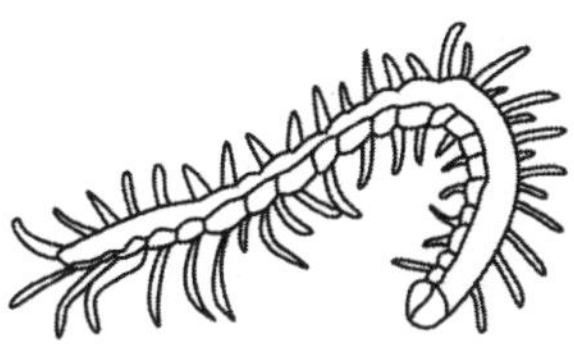
Centipede

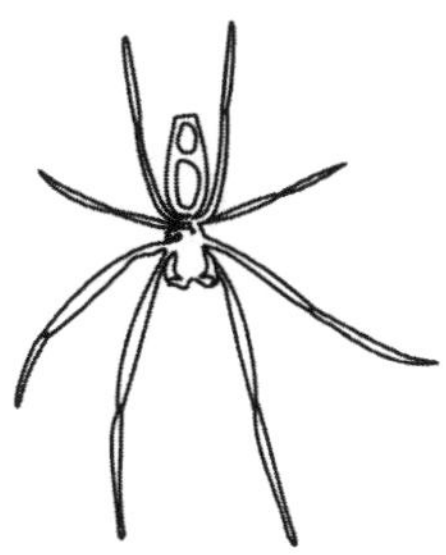
Spider

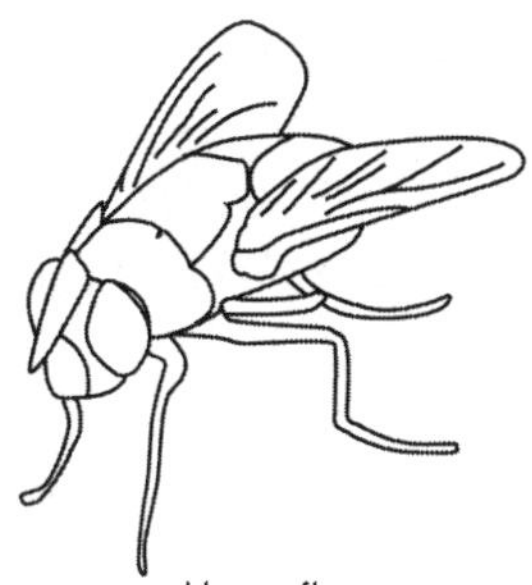
Housefly

Copyright © 2013 Pearson Canada Inc.
The right to reproduce this page is restricted to the purchasing school.

Name: ___________________________________

Invertebrates

You have learned that there are four classes of invertebrates: sponges, worms, molluscs, and arthropods. What are the features of each class?

Materials

- several reference sources, including the "Diversity of Living Things" unit
- a collection of photos, illustrations, or diagrams of invertebrates
- chart paper

Procedure

1. Using your reference sources, make a list of the characteristics or features that are used to place animals into each class of invertebrates.

2. Choose one class you would like to learn more about. Find photographs or diagrams of as many animals in this class as you can.

3. Make drawings of the animals you have found. Clearly show and label the characteristics that each shares with all other members of its class.

4. When you have finished, look over the drawings you have made. How similar are the animals? How different are they?

What Did You Find Out?

What did you learn about the diversity of invertebrates? Think about the characteristics that the animals in the class you chose have in common. Do you think these features help the animals to survive? Why or why not? Write down your thoughts.

Copyright © 2013 Pearson Canada Inc.
The right to reproduce this page is restricted to the purchasing school.

Name: ____________________________

Classifying Arthropods

Use page 27 of your student book to label the illustrations on this page.

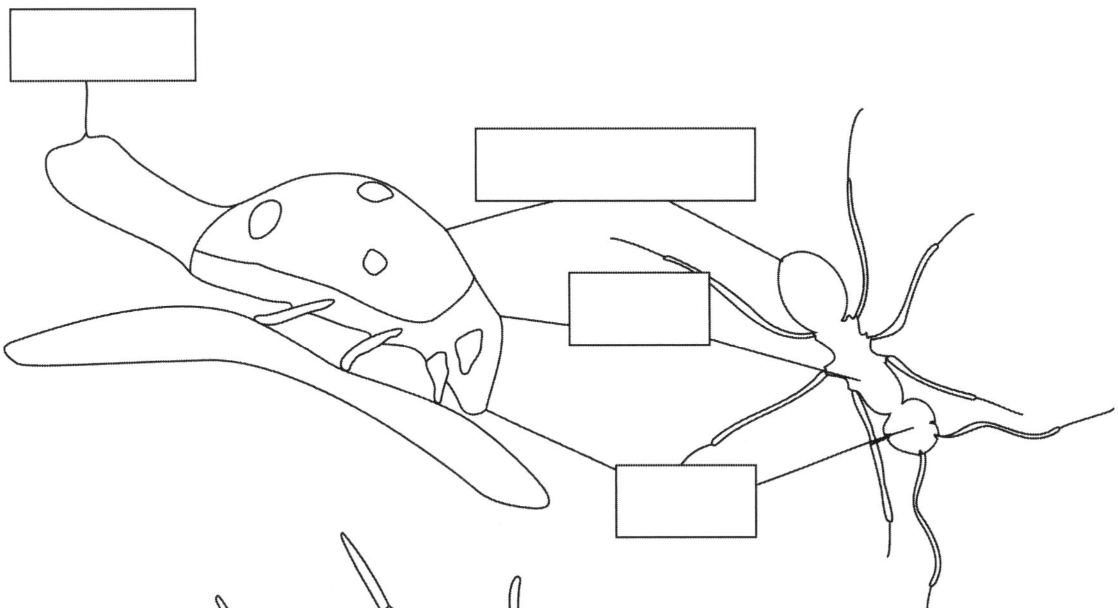

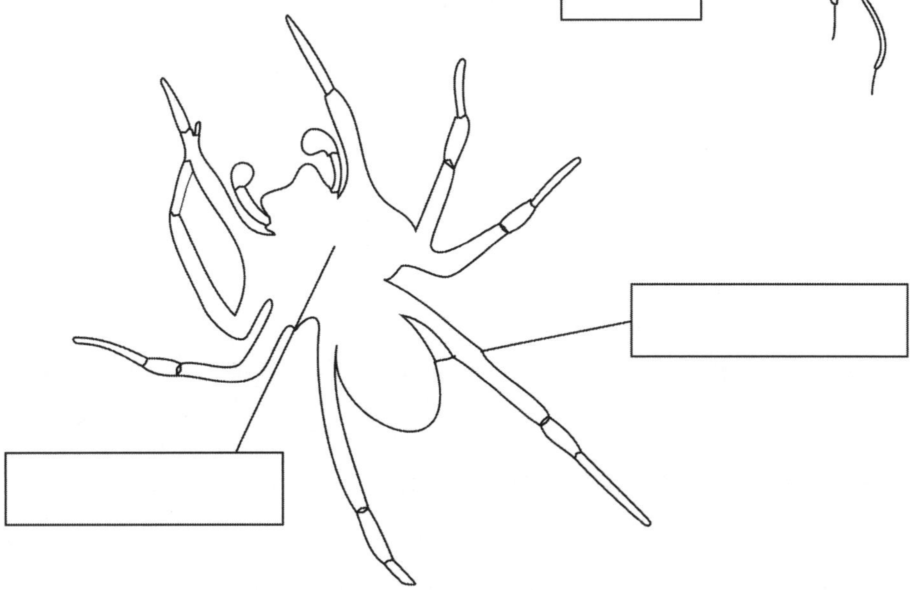

Use your labelled diagrams to help identify the similarities and differences among the animals in the photos on page 28 of your student book. Make a list of these similarities and differences.

Copyright © 2013 Pearson Canada Inc.
The right to reproduce this page is restricted to the purchasing school.

Name: ___________________________________

Design Challenge: Make an Arthropod

The Task
Moviemakers, cartoonists, and other creative people often invent realistic creatures that don't really exist. Can you invent a realistic arthropod?

Plan Your Design
1. Work with a group. Choose a specific environment where your arthropod will live. Write a clear description of the environment. Include things like plants, water, temperature, and other living things in the environment.

2. Design an arthropod that could live in this environment. What features does it need to have to be an arthropod? What adaptations does it need to survive in its environment?

3. Make a list of these features and adaptations. Ask your teacher to check your work.

Build Your Design
4. Draw a diagram of your arthropod. Remember to label all its features and adaptations.

Test Your Design
As a group, go through this list to see if your arthropod can survive.

A. It's getting late and your arthropod is hungry! What does it eat?

B. Your arthropod spots some dinner, but it is on a big rock high above. How does your arthropod get to it?

C. Almost there, but now someone thinks your arthropod is dinner! How does your arthropod protect itself?

D. Phew! Got away safe and got some food too! Now how about something to drink? How does your arthropod find water?

If you now want to make a change in your design, note the change on your plan.

Communicate
After you've designed your arthropod, draw a picture showing your arthropod in its habitat. Write a short description of it. Include a name for it, and explain the adaptations that help it survive.

Copyright © 2013 Pearson Canada Inc.
The right to reproduce this page is restricted to the purchasing school.

Name: ________________________________

Investigating an Arthropod — The Mealworm

1. This is what I would like to find out about mealworms:

2. Here are the steps in my procedure:

3. Here is how I controlled the variables to make sure my investigation is a fair test:

4. Here is how I measured what happened:

5. Here is what happened:

Copyright © 2013 Pearson Canada Inc.
The right to reproduce this page is restricted to the purchasing school.

Name: ___________________________________

Design Challenge: Build an Observation Chamber

The Task

Earthworms and ants live most of their lives underground. How can you observe how these invertebrates live? How about designing a device to help you?

Plan Your Design

1. With a partner, brainstorm everything you know about ants or earthworms. You and your partner will design and build an observation chamber that will let you observe earthworms or ants in their own environments. Remember that the animals need to be able to survive in whatever set-up you design. If you aren't sure how they meet their basic needs, do some research first.

2. Draw a diagram of your observation chamber. Clearly label it to show how it will work, and how it will meet the animals' basic needs. Now make a list of the materials you will need to build your observation chamber. What materials do you need to gather to build your observation model?

3. Ask your teacher to check your work.

Build Your Design

4. Build your observation chamber.

Test Your Design

A. First, set up your chamber with everything your animals need. Remember that no harm should come to your animals.

B. When your chamber is ready, carefully add your animals, and test how well you can observe them in the environment.

C. Do you need to make any changes in your design? If you do, take the animals out carefully and make all the changes before putting them back in.

Communicate

Observe your animals for several days. Keep records of your observations. You may think of other things you could change to make your observation chamber more suitable for your animals. Be sure to return your animals to their natural habitats when you are finished. Share your findings with the class.

Copyright © 2013 Pearson Canada Inc.
The right to reproduce this page is restricted to the purchasing school.

Name: ___________________________________

Life Cycles

Insects have a life cycle of several different stages. Insects such as butterflies have a four-stage life cycle. Insects such as grasshoppers have only a three-stage life cycle. In this activity, you will compare these two types of life cycles.

Materials

- reference materials
- pens and pencils
- paper

Procedure

1. Find the life cycle of a butterfly in your reference material. Look up and record the following things:
   - the four stages of the butterfly's life cycle
   - what each stage looks like
   - what happens in each stage
   - how long each stage lasts
   - a picture of an adult butterfly

2. Find the life cycle of a grasshopper in your reference material. Look up and record the following things:
   - the three stages of the grasshopper's life cycle
   - what each stage looks like
   - what happens in each stage
   - how long each stage lasts
   - a picture of an adult grasshopper

What Did You Find Out?

Present the results of your research to the class. Be prepared to answer questions on the differences and similarities between the two kinds of life cycles.

Copyright © 2013 Pearson Canada Inc.
The right to reproduce this page is restricted to the purchasing school.

Name: ________________________________

Classifying Animals — The Vertebrates

Research one animal from each group and fill in the table with the following information:

	Fish	Amphibian	Reptile	Bird	Mammal
Body shape and description					
Warm- or cold-blooded					
How it breathes					
Adaptations for survival					
How it feeds					

Compare your table with those of your classmates to find similarities and differences within the same subgroups of vertebrates. Record your findings below.

Copyright © 2013 Pearson Canada Inc.
The right to reproduce this page is restricted to the purchasing school.

Name: ____________________________________

Vertebrates and Invertebrates

Compare the characteristics of vertebrates and invertebrates. How are they the same? How are they different? Record your findings below:

Characteristics of invertebrates	Shared characteristics	Characteristics of vertebrates

Copyright © 2013 Pearson Canada Inc.
The right to reproduce this page is restricted to the purchasing school.

Name: ______________________________

A School of Fish

All fish have fins and breathe through gills. These adaptations help fish in their aquatic habitats. But not all fish are exactly the same. In this activity, you will compare and contrast the characteristics of fish.

Materials
- reference materials
- pens or pencils
- paper

Procedure
1. Make a list of different aquatic habitats in which fish survive. How are these habitats different from each other? What challenges do fish face in each of these habitats?

2. Choose a fish species that lives in each of the different habitats on your list.

3. For each fish species, look through your reference material and answer the following questions:
   - How does it move?
   - How big is it?
   - What does it eat? How does it eat?
   - What special adaptations does it have to survive in its habitat?

4. Draw a diagram of each fish species. Make sure you label the features that are used to classify it as a fish, and any special adaptations it has for its habitat.

What Did You Find Out?
Share your findings in a poster. Be sure your information is clear enough for everyone to understand.

Copyright © 2013 Pearson Canada Inc.
The right to reproduce this page is restricted to the purchasing school.

Name: ____________________________________

A Prehistoric Vertebrate

Look carefully at the picture of the ***Tyrannosaurus rex*** skeleton here and on page 46 of your student book. Make a list of any special adaptations it has.

Adaptations:

How did these adaptations help ***Tyrannosaurus rex*** to survive?

Copyright © 2013 Pearson Canada Inc.
The right to reproduce this page is restricted to the purchasing school.

Name: ______________________________

Animal Adaptations

Unusual Adaptations

Research to find out three interesting and unusual adaptations that animals around the world have made to survive in their habitats. Compare your findings with those of your classmates.

Animal:

Habitat:

Food sources:

Structural adaptation:

Behavioural adaptation:

Animal:

Habitat:

Food sources:

Structural adaptation:

Behavioural adaptation:

Animal:

Habitat:

Food sources:

Structural adaptation:

Behavioural adaptation:

Copyright © 2013 Pearson Canada Inc.
The right to reproduce this page is restricted to the purchasing school.

Name: ____________________________________

The Perfect Beak

Once you and your partner have completed the food collection table, fill in the bar graph below.

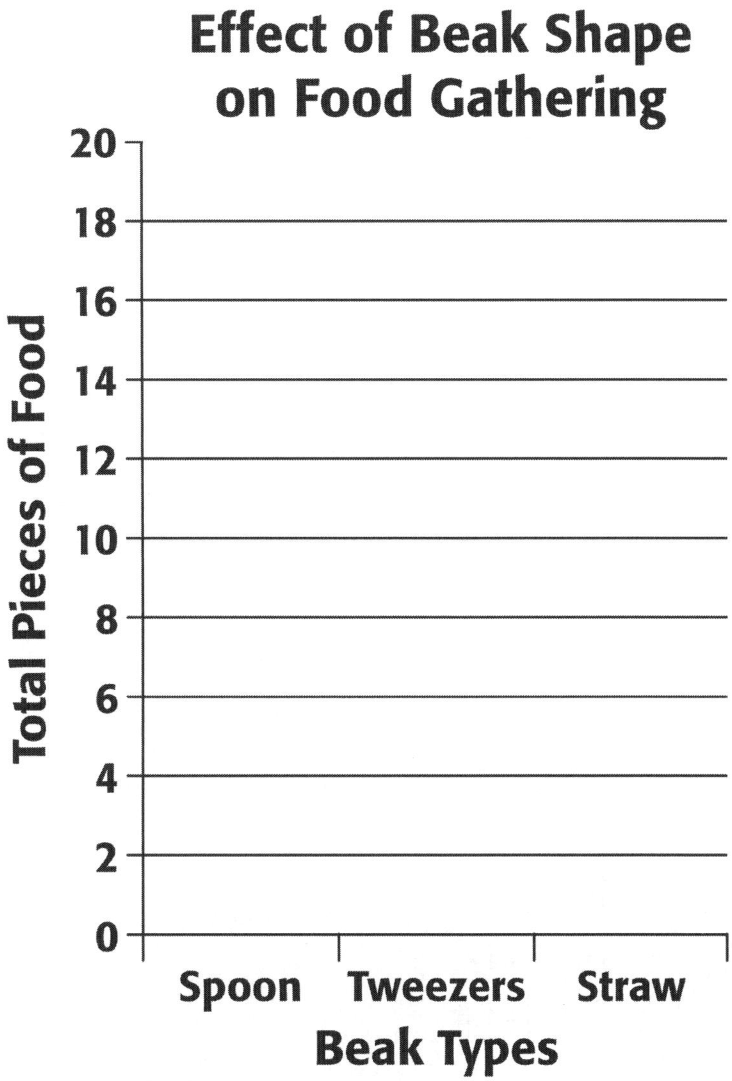

Compare your findings with those of your classmates to create a master bar graph of all of your findings.

Copyright © 2013 Pearson Canada Inc.
The right to reproduce this page is restricted to the purchasing school.

Name: ______________________________

Plant Adaptations

Use this map to label the ecozones of Saskatchewan. Label your map with important characteristics of each ecozone.

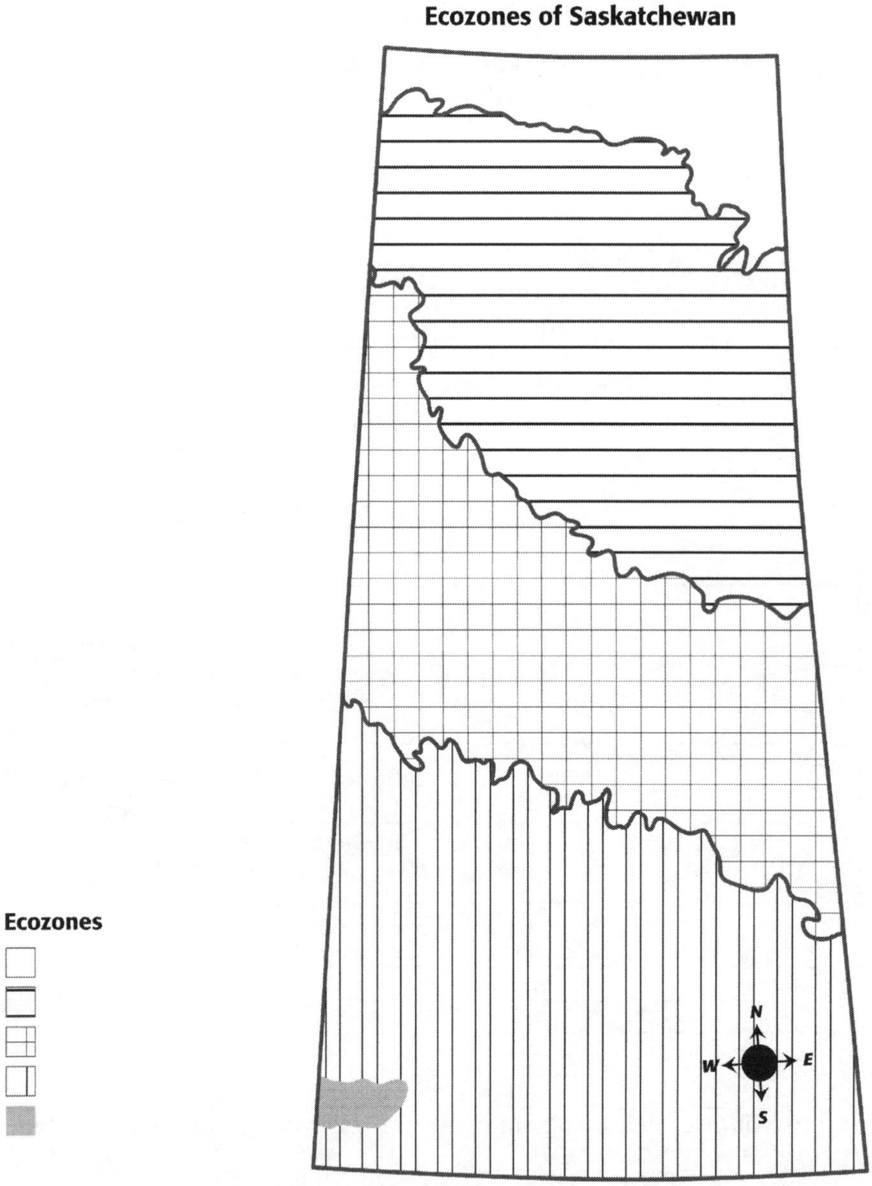

Copyright © 2013 Pearson Canada Inc.
The right to reproduce this page is restricted to the purchasing school.

Name: ______________________________

The Microscopic World

Label the microscope and describe what each part does.

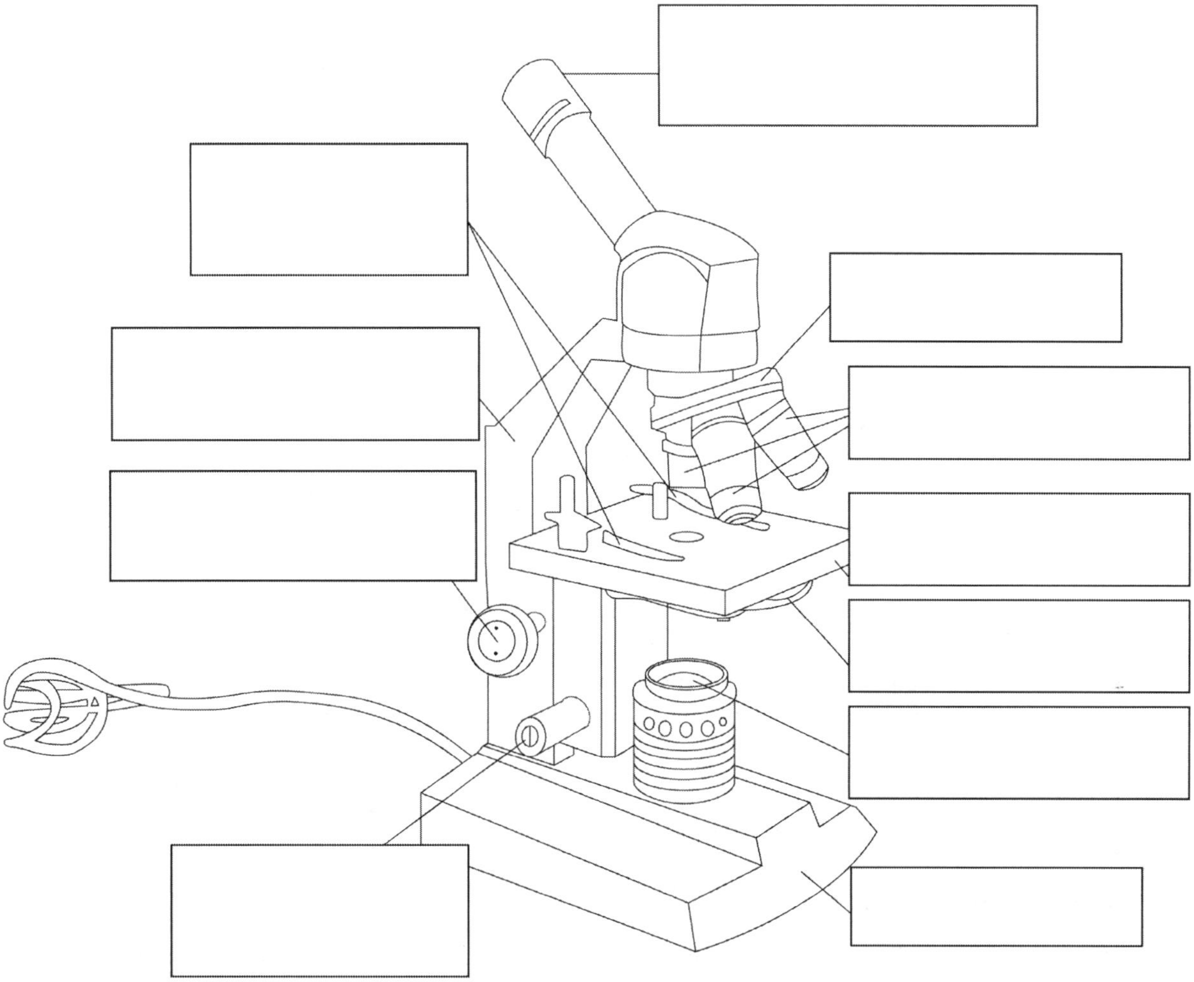

Copyright © 2013 Pearson Canada Inc.
The right to reproduce this page is restricted to the purchasing school.

Name: ___________________________

Observing Micro-organisms

You can observe micro-organisms by looking at them under a microscope. Follow the steps below to make your own microscope slide to observe the micro-organisms in pond water.

Materials

- microscope
- cover slips
- distilled or tap water
- medicine dropper
- microscope slides
- paper towel
- pond water
- sharp pencil

Procedure

1. Hold a microscope slide by its edges between your thumb and index finger, and check if it is clean. If you need to, clean it by putting a drop of distilled or tap water on it, then gently dry it with paper towel. Clean a cover slip in the same way.

2. Place a small drop of pond water in the middle of the slide with the medicine dropper.

3. Carefully place one edge of the cover slip on the microscope slide at a 45° angle.

4. Use the tip of the pencil to slowly lower the other edge of the cover slip onto the drop of pond water. This procedure will prevent air bubbles from getting under the cover slip.

5. Your slide is now ready to observe under the microscope. Follow the directions your teacher gives you to use the microscope properly.

What Did You Find Out?

Consult a classification key for pond micro-organisms to see if you can identify the micro-organisms you observed. Share your findings with your classmates.

Copyright © 2013 Pearson Canada Inc.
The right to reproduce this page is restricted to the purchasing school.

Name: ___________________________________

The Impact of Micro-organisms

Classroom Composting

Conduct an investigation of the factors that influence how quickly micro-organisms break down organic matter.

Materials per group
- four 2-L pop bottles with lids on
- garden soil — Do not use potting soil because you need the micro-organisms found in garden soil to break down the organic waste.
- finely chopped organic waste material: vegetable greens, fruit peels, etc.
- scissors
- tape

Procedure
1. Carefully cut the top one-third of each pop bottle most of the way around. Leave a piece to act as a hinge.
2. Place one cup of garden soil into each bottle.
3. Place one cup of organic waste into each bottle.
4. Place one more cup of garden soil on top of the organic waste so you have three distinct layers.
5. A fair test: Decide on one variable to test for each bottle. You could place one bottle in the window, one bottle in partial shade, one bottle in complete shade, and one bottle in darkness. Alternatively, you could put varying amounts of liquid in each bottle and put them all in the same place. Make sure you control the variables.
6. Seal the bottles with tape.
7. Place one strip of masking tape down the side of each bottle.

Copyright © 2013 Pearson Canada Inc.
The right to reproduce this page is restricted to the purchasing school.

8. Carefully measure the height of the waste in each bottle and mark it on the masking tape. As the micro-organisms in the soil break down the waste, the level of waste in each bottle should drop over time.

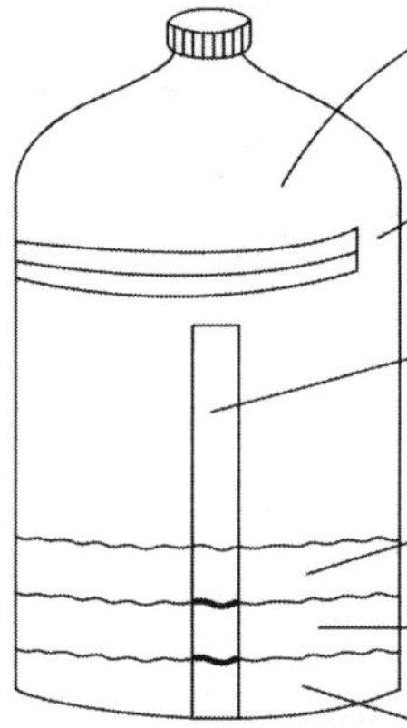

Observations

A. What happened to the levels of soil and waste in the bottles over time?

B. Were there any differences between the four bottles? Describe any differences.

Analysis

C. Give an explanation for any differences you noticed in the bottles.

Conclusion

D. What do micro-organisms need to thrive?

Copyright © 2013 Pearson Canada Inc.
The right to reproduce this page is restricted to the purchasing school.

Group Members: ____________________

Design Project Planner: Classifying Living Things Around Us

Your Plan to Classify the Living Things Around Us

If you need more space, use the back of this sheet.

A. The task that needs to be solved is:

B. This task can be solved by:

The materials needed are:

C. Design your classification system. Use a sheet of chart paper to do this. Include on your chart how you separated your groups.

D. Test your classification system. Combine your list of living things with lists from other class members, and organize them into groups using your classification system. Do you need to make any changes in your system? Draw your revised system on a fresh sheet of chart paper.

E. Explain how your classification system works.

F. Present your classification system to the class.

Copyright © 2013 Pearson Canada Inc.
The right to reproduce this page is restricted to the purchasing school.

Student name(s): ____________________________

Design Project Rubric: Classifying Living Things Around Us

Areas of Assessment	1	2	3	4
Basic Concepts The classification system uses structural characteristics.	The classification system does not use structural characteristics.	The classification system uses structural characteristics but is somewhat unclear.	The classification system uses structural characteristics and is clear.	The classification system uses structural characteristics, is clear, and accurately identifies and uses formal phyla and classes.
Skills The student collects and records data through investigation to present a classification system.	Data records and the classification system are incomplete and difficult to follow.	Data records and the classification system are complete but do not clearly identify characteristics used for classification.	Data records and the classification system are complete and accurate, and identify characteristics used for classification.	Data records and the classification system are complete and accurate, and use and identify characteristics of formal phyla and classes.
Communication In the presentation to the class, the student incorporates accurate records of the living things observed and gives reasons for the classifications used using appropriate vocabulary.	During the presentation, the explanation of the classification system is not very clear or precise.	During the presentation, the explanation of the classification system is somewhat clear and precise.	During the presentation, the explanation of the classification system is mostly clear and precise.	During the presentation, the explanation of the classification system is very clear and precise.
Relating of Science and Technology to Each Other and to the World Outside the School The student is able to identify the plants and animals in a given plot using a classification key.	Plants and animals are identified only by imprecise names or descriptors, e.g., bugs, grasses.	Plants and animals are identified by some accurate names and some common names, e.g., cedar trees, insects.	Plants and animals are identified by accurate names, e.g., red maple, monarch butterfly.	Plants and animals are identified by accurate names and the student differentiates between similar living things, e.g., white pine, red pine, Scotch pine.

Copyright © 2013 Pearson Canada Inc.
The right to reproduce this page is restricted to the purchasing school.

Name: ________________________________

Unit 1 Test

True/False

1. For each of the following, indicate whether the statement is true (T) or false (F).

a) T F All living things are biotic.
b) T F All micro-organisms are harmful to humans.
c) T F Scientists believe that there are millions of plants and animals that have not been identified yet.
d) T F Plants can adapt to their environment in order to survive.
e) T F Invertebrates have no backbone or spine.
f) T F First Nations and Métis people do not classify living and non-living things.
g) T F A tree classification system is used only for classifying trees.
h) T F Using behavioural adaptations is the best way to classify animals.
i) T F All arthropods have three body parts: a head, a thorax, and an abdomen.
j) T F Ninety-eight percent of all animal species have no backbone.

Multiple Choice

Circle the letter that best answers the question.

2. The difference between cold-blooded and warm-blooded animals is:
a) Cold-blooded animals are cold and warm-blooded animals are warm.
b) Cold-blooded animals live in cold places and warm-blooded animals live in warm places.
c) Warm-blooded animals use energy to maintain their body temperature and cold-blooded animals do not.
d) Cold-blooded animals could survive in very cold climates whereas warm-blooded animals could not.

3. Fossils help us learn about
a) what dinosaurs were around long ago
b) how animals have changed over time
c) how ancient peoples lived
d) what ancient animals ate

Matching

4. Draw an arrow to match the arthropod on the left with the correct characteristics on the right.

centipede	jointed body parts, 8 legs
spider	jointed body parts, 6 legs
ant	many similar body parts, 30 legs

Copyright © 2013 Pearson Canada Inc.
The right to reproduce this page is restricted to the purchasing school.

Fill in the Blanks

Complete the following sentences.

5. Some First Nations and Métis people believe they have a ____________ _____________ to watch over their clan or family.

6. ______________ is just another word for organizing or grouping things together.

7. Most classification systems organize plants, animals, and other living things into five large groups called ______________.

8. First Nations people across Canada have been using the ____________ tree to make canoes for thousands of years.

9. ____________ are mostly found in the oceans, have no nervous system or organs to breathe with, filter food from the water, and are found in many different colours.

10. _______________ are special features that help living things survive in different habitats.

11. The baby stage of the mealworm is called the _____________.

12. Fish, amphibians, and reptiles are _______ -blooded animals.

13. Lara Shychoski is someone who studies fossils. A person who does research on fossils is called a(n) ___________________.

14. The ______________ kingdom includes organisms that don't fit in any other kingdom.

Short Answer

15. What types of features are used to classify living things?

____

____

16. Why are some characteristics better than others for classifying living things?

____

____

____

17. Why do scientists need to classify living and non-living things?

____

____

Copyright © 2013 Pearson Canada Inc.
The right to reproduce this page is restricted to the purchasing school.

18. How do First Nations and Métis peoples view our responsibility to Mother Earth?

____

____

____

19. Describe an investigation you conducted to learn about mealworms.

____

____

____

____

20. Give three examples of how classification is used in everyday life.

____

____

____

____

21. Describe a micro-organism and explain how it meets its basic needs.

____

____

____

____

____

Copyright © 2013 Pearson Canada Inc.
The right to reproduce this page is restricted to the purchasing school.

22. Draw a classification tree that shows the five main classes of vertebrates. Note a characteristic of each class on your tree.

23. How are vertebrates and invertebrates similar? How are they different?

____

____

____

24. Give three examples of how First Nations and Métis peoples have used place-based knowledge to help them survive.

____

____

____

Copyright © 2013 Pearson Canada Inc.
The right to reproduce this page is restricted to the purchasing school.

Answers to Unit 1 Line Masters

LM 1-3 Living Things

Object	Breathes	Requires energy	Responds to stimuli	Grows and develops	Can reproduce	Excretes waste	Biotic/ abiotic
Rock							abiotic
Tree	X	X	X	X	X	X	biotic
Dog	X	X	X	X	X	X	biotic
Computer							abiotic
Desk (plastic)							abiotic
Water							abiotic
Gold							abiotic
Sunlight							abiotic
Clouds							abiotic
Wooden ruler (was a tree)	X	X	X	X	X	X	biotic
Hamburger (was a cow)	X	X	X	X	X	X	biotic
Cotton fabric (was a plant)		X	X	X	X	X	biotic
Glass							abiotic
Paper (was a tree)	X	X	X	X	X	X	biotic
Grass		X	X	X	X	X	biotic
Ant	X	X	X	X	X	X	biotic

Copyright © 2013 Pearson Canada Inc.
The right to reproduce this page is restricted to the purchasing school.

LM 1-5 Classifying Living Things

Plant	Animal	Fungi	Not sure
tamarack	wolverine	lichen	
white spruce	brook trout	fungus *Pholiota flammans*	
spear grass	house wren		
wild wheat grass	white-throated sparrow		
black spruce	beaver		
jack pine	badger		
needle-and-thread grass	white-tailed deer (fawn)		
lodgepole pine	coyote		
	brown trout		
	snow goose		
	lake trout		
	ovenbird		
	tree sparrow		
	cougar		
	walleye		
	bison		
	black bear		
	sharp-tailed grouse		
	Western kingbird		
	Richardson ground squirrel		
	pine grosbeak		
	caribou		
	jack rabbit		
	timber wolf		

Copyright © 2013 Pearson Canada Inc.
The right to reproduce this page is restricted to the purchasing school.

LM 1-7 Classifying Animals — The Invertebrates

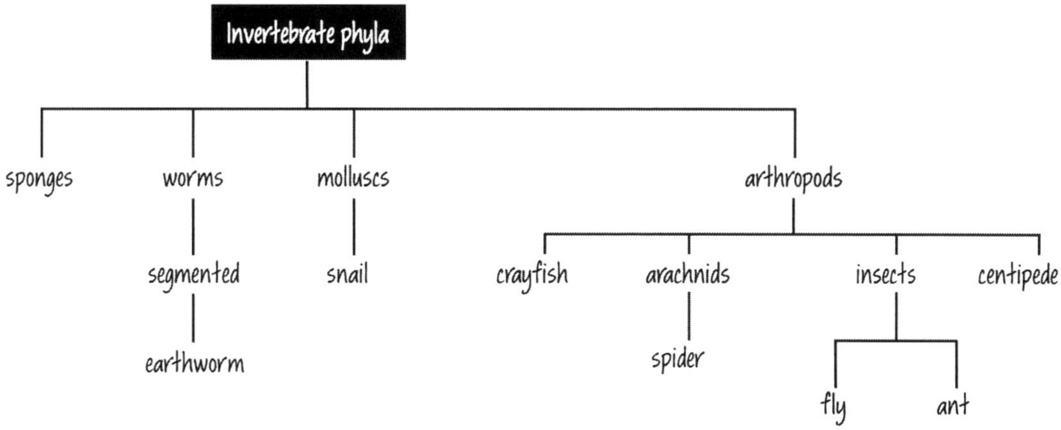

LM 1-9 Classifying Arthropods

Answers are found on page 27 of the student book.

LM 1-15 Vertebrates and Invertebrates

Characteristics of Invertebrates	Shared Characteristics	Characteristics of Vertebrates
have no backbone	can be found on land or in water	have a backbone
some have no nervous system	breathe/respire	all have a nervous system
some are single-celled	reproduce (create offspring)	all are multicellular
none are warm-blooded	expel waste	some are warm-blooded
	respond to stimuli in their environment	
	don't have cell walls	
	require energy to live	

LM 1-17 A Prehistoric Vertebrate

Answers will vary. Expect students to be able to describe adaptations such as:

- large hind legs for running fast to catch prey
- long teeth for catching, killing, and cutting prey
- long tail for balance while running
- long neck to help lunge at and catch prey
- large, powerful jaws to bite and kill prey
- small front legs and claws for feeding and holding prey once it is caught and killed
- large nasal cavity for enhanced sense of smell
- well-protected eyes, so that they are not harmed when biting at prey

LM 1-20 Plant Adaptations

Answers are found on page 58 of the student book.

Copyright © 2013 Pearson Canada Inc.
The right to reproduce this page is restricted to the purchasing school.

LM 1-21 The Microscopic World

Answers are found on page 67 of the student book.

- The ocular lens is used to look through in order to view the object being magnified.
- The stage holds the slide, or any object being viewed, and moves up and down to adjust focus.
- Stage clips are used to hold a slide in place on the stage.
- The base provides a stable support on which the microscope sits.
- The arm connects the ocular lens to the base of the microscope.
- The nosepiece holds the three objective lenses and allows the user to rotate the lenses to obtain varying degrees of magnification.
- The three objective lenses allow varying degrees of magnification. The user should always start with the lowest magnification and work toward the highest magnification.
- When using the highest magnification, the user should be careful not to allow the lens to press directly on the slide because it may break the slide or damage the lens.
- Usually used first, the coarse adjustment knob allows the user to primarily focus the object being viewed.
- The fine adjustment knob allows the user to fine-tune the focus and adjust the depth of field of the object being viewed.
- The light source (sometimes a mirror) allows light to be reflected up through the stage, slide, specimen, objective lens, and ocular lens to the eye. It illuminates the object being viewed for better visibility. When using a mirror for this purpose, care should be taken not to reflect direct sunlight into the microscope because doing so could cause damage to the user's eye.
- The diaphragm has different-sized apertures, or holes, that can be rotated to let varying amounts of light through the stage.

LM 1-26 Unit 1 Test

1. a) T
b) F
c) T
d) T
e) T
f) F
g) F
h) F
i) F
j) T

2. c)

3. All statements are correct.

4. centipede many similar body parts; 30 legs
spider jointed body parts; 8 legs
ant jointed body parts; 6 legs

5. spirit guide

6. classifying

7. kingdoms

8. birch

9. sponges

10. adaptations

Copyright © 2013 Pearson Canada Inc.
The right to reproduce this page is restricted to the purchasing school.

11. larva
12. cold
13. paleontologist
14. protist
15. Scientists most often use structural characteristics to classify living things.
16. Structural characteristics are better than other characteristics, such as behavioural, for classifying living things because they stay the same throughout the life of the living thing, are shared by all members of the species, and are easily recognized so they can be used by scientists all over the world.
17. Scientists classify living things to help them identify plants and animals.
18. Many First Nations and Métis peoples believe that all things are sacred and alive with spirit. Since humans are related to everything on Mother Earth, we have a responsibility to respect and care for her.
19. Recommended activities were to:
    - observe the mealworm with a magnifying glass
    - draw a diagram of its structure, including the head, thorax, and abdomen
    - observe and record how the mouth parts work for eating dry cereal
    - describe how the mouth parts are adapted to eating

    Students were also asked to plan and conduct their own investigations, so answers will vary.
20. Answers will vary, but may fall into categories such as:
    - identify items (e.g., objects, plants, animals, etc.)
    - organize and/or find items
    - study relationships between items
21. A micro-organism is a living thing that is so small that you need a microscope to see it. It meets its basic needs by feeding, breathing, moving, getting rid of waste, and reproducing.

22. Characteristics may include the following:

Vertebrates

	Fish	Amphibians	Reptiles	Birds	Mammals
outer covering	covered with scales	soft, moist skin	dry skin	feathers	hair
cold-/warm-blooded	cold-blooded	cold-blooded	cold-blooded	warm-blooded	warm-blooded
breathe	gills	lungs	lungs	lungs	lungs
move	fins, tail	four legs	four legs	wings, legs	legs
reproduce	lay eggs	lay eggs	lay eggs	lay eggs	give birth, nurse live young
eat	no teeth	most have teeth	most have teeth	beak or bill	teeth

23. Vertebrates and invertebrates are similar in that they are living organisms (feed, breathe, move, get rid of waste, reproduce). Many other answers are possible based on individual characteristics (e.g., many but not all have legs, eyes, a mouth, etc.). They are different mainly in that invertebrates do not have backbones whereas vertebrates do.

Copyright © 2013 Pearson Canada Inc.
The right to reproduce this page is restricted to the purchasing school.

24. Three examples of how First Nations and Métis peoples have used place-based knowledge to help them survive should include:

- using the birch tree for canoes, fire lighting, moose calls, mats, baby carriers, baskets, spears, bows, arrows, snowshoes, and sleds
- the prairie turnip is a starchy plant used for stews
- plants for healing and pain relief including sweetgrass, willow, sage, and coneflower

Copyright © 2013 Pearson Canada Inc.
The right to reproduce this page is restricted to the purchasing school.

UNIT 2

Understanding Electricity

Table of Contents

Table of Contents *(continued)*

Unit Indicators Correlation Chart

Indicator	Lesson References	Assessment Opportunities
By the end of grade 6, students will be able to:		
EL6.1 Assess personal, societal, economic, and environmental impacts of electricity use in Saskatchewan and propose actions to reduce those impacts.		
a. Provide examples of the types of energy sources used to provide heat and light to homes in the past and describe ways in which electricity-based technologies have changed the way people work, live, and interact with the environment in Saskatchewan.	Lesson 1 Unit 2 Review	Communicate, p. 88, q. 1–4 Unit 2 Review, pp. 155–156, q. 2, 7, 10, 29, 30, 33
b. Describe how electrical energy is generated from hydroelectric, coal, natural gas, nuclear, geothermal, biomass, solar, and wind sources and categorize these sources as renewable or non-renewable.	Lesson 4 Lesson 5 Unit 2 Review	Work On It, p. 103 Work On It, p. 106 Unit 2 Review, p. 155, q. 8
c. Locate and categorize by type the large-scale electrical energy generation facilities in Saskatchewan and explain how electrical energy is transmitted from those facilities to locations throughout the province.	Lesson 5 Unit 2 Review	Communicate, p. 107, q. 2, 3 Unit 2 Review, p. 155, q. 9, 11
d. Identify factors that affect electrical energy consumption at home, school, and in the workplace and propose methods of decreasing electrical energy consumption that can help to conserve natural resources and protect the environment.	Lesson 16 Unit 2 Review	Work On It, p. 149 Communicate, p. 151, q. 1, 2 Unit 2 Review, p. 156, q. 31, 32
e. Explain potential dangers of electricity at home, school, and in the workplace and suggest ways in which individuals can minimize those dangers.	Lesson 14 Unit 2 Review	Work On It, p. 140 Communicate, p. 142, q. 1, 2 Unit 2 Review, p. 156, q. 27, 28
f. Research employers and careers related to electrical energy generation, distribution, and conservation in Saskatchewan.	Lesson 11 Unit 2 Review	Work On It, p. 128 Unit 2 Review, p. 156, q. 23
EL6.2 Investigate the characteristics and applications of static electric charges, conductors, insulators, switches, and electromagnetism.		
a. Conduct investigations to determine the attraction and repulsion of electrostatically charged materials and represent the results of those investigations using drawings, sketches, tables, charts, and/or other representations.	Lesson 2 Lesson 3 Unit 2 Review	Work On It, p. 89 Communicate, p. 94, q. 1 Work On It, p. 96 Unit 2 Review, p. 155, q. 3
b. Describe how results of similar and repeated investigations into the characteristics of static electric charges (e.g., the rubbing together of different substances) may vary and suggest possible explanations for identified variations.	Lesson 2	Work On It, p. 89 Communicate, p. 94, q. 1

Indicator	Lesson References	Assessment Opportunities
c. Identify natural and man-made applications of static electric charge and discharge (e.g., lightning, photocopiers, laser printers, air filters, and electrostatic paint sprayers).	Lesson 2 Lesson 3 Unit 2 Review	Communicate, p. 94, q. 2 Work On It, p. 96 Unit 2 Review, p. 155, q. 5, 6
d. Pose questions related to the physical properties of conductors, insulators, simple circuits, and electromagnets (e.g., "How can we determine if an unknown material is a conductor or an insulator?", "How does a switch work in a simple electric circuit?", "What materials work best to create an electromagnet?").	Lesson 6 Lesson 13 Unit 2 Review	Work On It, p. 110 Work On It, p. 137 Unit 2 Review, p. 156, q. 15–17
e. Make predictions, based on observed patterns of events, related to the physical properties of conductors, insulators, simple circuits, and electromagnets and conduct investigations to test those predictions.	Lesson 7 Lesson 10 Lesson 12	Work On It, p. 112 Communicate, p. 114, q. 1, 2 Work On It, p. 124 Communicate, p. 126 Work On It, p. 131
f. Identify appropriate tools, instruments, and materials (e.g., bulbs, batteries, and wires) to use when investigating the properties of conductors, insulators, simple circuits, and electromagnets and use those tools and apparatus in a manner that ensures personal safety and the safety of others.	Lesson 6 Lesson 7 Lesson 8 Lesson 12 Design Project	Work On It, p. 110 Communicate, p. 114, q. 1, 2 Work On It, p. 118 Communicate, p. 119, q. 2 Communicate, p. 133, q. 4, 5 Work On It, p. 153
g. Test the conductivity of a variety of solids and liquids, following a given set of procedures, to identify which materials are conductors and which are insulators, and draw conclusions about the types of materials that work best as conductors and which work best as insulators.	Lesson 7	Work On It, p. 112 Communicate, p. 114, q. 1, 2
h. Explain the role of switches in electrical circuits.	Lesson 8	Communicate, p. 119, q. 3
i. Describe the operation of an electromagnet and contrast magnets and electromagnets.	Lesson 12 Unit 2 Review	Electricity and Magnetism Are Related. Check It Out!, pp. 130, 131 Unit 2 Review, p. 156, q. 24
j. Plan a set of steps to carry out a fair test of a science-related idea related to electromagnets, such as how to increase the strength of an electromagnet.	Lesson 12 Unit 2 Review	Work On It, p. 131 Unit 2 Review, p. 156, q. 25
k. Use evidence gathered through research and observation to answer questions related to the physical properties of conductors, insulators, simple circuits, and electromagnets.	Lesson 6 Lesson 12	Work On It, p. 110 Communicate, p. 111, q. 3, 4 Communicate, p. 133, q. 2–4

Indicator	Lesson References	Assessment Opportunities
l. Describe the operation of common technologies based on properties of static electricity, current electricity, or electromagnetism.	Lesson 3 Lesson 10 Lesson 13 Lesson 15 Unit 2 Review	Work On It, p. 96 Communicate, p. 98, q. 1 Work On It, p. 124 Communicate, p. 126 Communicate, p. 139, q. 1, 2 Communicate, p. 146, q. 1–4 Unit 2 Review, pp. 155–156, q. 6, 26
EL6.3 Explain and model the properties of simple series and parallel circuits.		
a. State the required characteristics of a simple electric circuit (e.g., a source of electrical energy, a closed path to conduct electrical energy, and a load to convert the electrical energy into another form of energy).	Lesson 6 Unit 2 Review	Communicate, p. 111, q. 1 Unit 2 Review, p. 155, q. 13
b. Compare a variety of electrical pathways by constructing simple circuits.	Lesson 6	Work On It, p. 110
c. Contrast a closed circuit, open circuit, and short circuit.	Lesson 8	Work On It, p. 118
d. Propose questions to investigate, and practical problems to solve, related to simple series and parallel circuits (e.g., "What happens when a light bulb is removed from a series or parallel circuit?", "How can I create a simple circuit using only a battery, light bulb, and one wire?", "How are light circuits in a house wired?").	Lesson 10 Unit 2 Review	Work On It, p. 124 Communicate, p. 126 Unit 2 Review, p. 156, q. 21
e. Construct and test various combinations of simple electric circuits to determine similarities and differences between series and parallel circuits.	Lesson 9	Work On It, p. 120
f. Draw electrical circuit diagrams to represent simple series and parallel circuits using appropriate symbols (e.g., battery, conductor, light bulb, motor, switch).	Lesson 8 Lesson 9 Unit 2 Review	Work On It, p. 118 Communicate, p. 119, q. 2 Work On It, p. 120 Unit 2 Review, p. 156, q. 19, 20
g. Construct simple circuits to demonstrate how electrical energy can be controlled to produce light, heat, sound, motion, and magnetic effects.	Lesson 6 Lesson 9 Design Project Unit 2 Review	Work On It, p. 110 Work On It, p. 120 Work On It, p. 153 Unit 2 Review, pp. 155–156, q. 12, 18
h. Design, construct, and troubleshoot an electrical circuit that meets one or more student-specified criteria.	Lesson 6 Design Project Unit 2 Review	Work On It, p. 110 Work On It, p. 153 Unit 2 Review, pp. 155–156, q. 14, 22

Activity Planning Chart

Note that estimates of class times are based on 40 min per period.

Lesson	Type of Activity	Time (number of classes)	Materials Required (for each group)	Line Masters
Launch: Electricity is Everywhere	discussion	1 class period	chart paper 5 sticky-note pads notebook pencil or pen	none
1. The Shocking History of Electricity	reading	1 class period	chart paper or cardboard scissors colour pencils highlighters	LM 2-3
2. Static Electricity	guided inquiry	1–2 class periods	3 balloons 1 m of string 1 sheet of paper towel water aluminum pie plate Styrofoam™ plate thumbtack 3 different kinds of dry cereal ruler tape pencil with an eraser on its end timeline (from Lesson 1)	LM 2-4
3. Making Static Electricity Useful	guided inquiry	1 class period	1 wool cloth 1 piece of paper 1 mL pepper 1 sheet of damp paper towel 1 plastic Petri dish with lid scissors tape	LM 2-5
4. Where Does Electricity Come From? Renewable Resources	reading	1 class period	chart paper notebook ruler pencil or pen	LM 2-6 LM 2-7
5. Where Does Electricity Come From? Non-renewable Resources	reading	1–2 class periods	chart paper notebook + and – charts from Lesson 4 ruler pencil or pen computer	LM 2-8
6. Light Up the Class	design	1 class period	2 light bulbs 2 light bulb holders 6 wires with alligator clips 1 6-V battery 1 switch	LM 2-9

(continued)

Lesson	Type of Activity	Time (number of classes)	Materials Required (for each group)	Line Masters
7. Go with the Flow	guided inquiry	1 class period	1 piece of wood 1 glass of water 1 glass of salt water 1 metal spoon 1 quarter 1 pen 6-V battery or D-cells LED (light-emitting diode) 3 wires with alligator clips (each wire about 30 cm long)	LM 2-10
8. Key Features of Electrical Circuits	reading	1 class period	2 light bulbs 2 light bulb holders 6 wires with alligator clips (each wire about 30 cm long) 6-V battery 1 switch paper and pencil	LM 2-11 LM 2-12
9. Different Needs, Different Circuits	guided inquiry	1 class period	2 light bulbs 2 light bulb holders 6 wires with alligator clips (each wire about 30 cm long) 6-V battery	LM 2-13
10. Fixing Electrical Problems	guided inquiry	1 class period	notebook pencil or pen	LM 2-14
11. Careers in Electricity	open inquiry	1–2 class periods	notebook pencil or pen computer reference materials	LM 2-15
12. Electricity and Magnets	guided inquiry	1 class period	40 staples Styrofoam™ plate compass bar magnet 6-V battery 2 insulated copper wires with bare ends (1 m each) 1 iron nail 1 pencil 1 plastic marker	LM 2-16
13. Electromagnets at Work	reading	1 class period	notebook pencil or pen	LM 2-17

Activity Planning Chart

(continued)

Lesson	Type of Activity	Time (number of classes)	Materials Required (for each group)	Line Masters
14. Electricity — Use It Safely	design	2–3 class periods	poster paper notebook pencil or pen markers or colour pencils computer reference materials	LM 2-18
15. Talking Around the World — Thanks to Canadians	open inquiry	2 class periods	notebook pencil or pen computer reference materials	LM 2-19
16. Conserving Electricity	reading	1 class period	notebook pencil or pen	LM 2-20
Design Project: A New Electrical Device	design	2–3 class periods	any materials used throughout Unit 2	LM 2-21 LM 2-22

- Depending on your location, there are a number of people and places that you can contact to visit on a field trip, or have a presenter come to your classroom. You can locate your closest power generation plant for a field trip, or arrange for a tour of SaskPower's head office or branch in your area. Also, the Saskatchewan Science Centre and SaskPower may have travelling kits and presentations available for school use.
- If you have the space available in your school, set up a centre with old appliances that apply different energy transformations, and that can be taken apart and studied using the appropriate safety guidelines.
- Some of the materials in this unit can be substituted for materials that are easy to make or find. The following list of substitutions will work for most of the lessons in this unit:
  - It is recommended that students use "mini-lamp" light bulbs because they are durable and their filaments will not become detached. Other light bulbs will also work, such as 60-W or 40-W bulbs, small lamp bulbs, and Christmas lights.
  - Bulb holders are not necessary but they make light bulbs easier for students to handle and use in circuits.
  - Alligator clip wires are recommended for safety and easier handling, but you can use regular wires with exposed ends.
  - If switches are not available, a homemade switch can be created using two thumbtacks pressed into cardboard. Attach a paper clip to one thumbtack so that it can touch the other thumbtack.

- A 6-V battery has easily accessible electrodes to which students can attach wires, but other types of batteries, such as D-cells, can also be used.

- Note: Compact fluorescent light bulbs (CFLs) are not used in this unit because they are more expensive than conventional light bulbs and because they contain mercury. Disposal of these light bulbs in the garbage is not recommended. However, comparing CFLs and conventional filament light bulbs could be an interesting and valuable extension to the ideas presented about energy transformation and conservation in this unit.
- It is important to know that LEDs will only light up if they are connected properly. The shorter wire (cathode) is the "–" connector and the longer wire (anode) is the "+" connector to the battery.

Materials and Equipment Needed for Unit 2

(based on 30 students)

Launch: Electricity is Everywhere	
Materials • chart paper • 5 sticky-note pads • notebook • pencil or pen	**Equipment** • none
1. The Shocking History of Electricity	
Materials • chart paper • colour pencils • highlighters	**Equipment** • 15 pairs of scissors
2. Static Electricity	
Materials **Station 1:** • 20 balloons • 10 m of string • 10 sheets of paper towel • tape **Station 2:** • 30 aluminum pie plates • 30 Styrofoam™ plates **Station 3:** • 30 balloons • 3 kinds of dry cereal	**Equipment** **Station 1:** • 10 rulers **Station 2:** • 30 pencils with erasers on the end • 30 thumbtacks
3. Making Static Electricity Useful	
Materials • 30 wool cloth pieces • 30 pieces of paper • 30 mL pepper • 30 sheets of damp paper towel • tape	**Equipment** • 30 plastic Petri dishes with lids • 30 pairs of scissors
4. Where Does Electricity Come From? Renewable Resources	
Materials • chart paper • notebook • pencil or pen	**Equipment** • 30 rulers

Materials and Equipment

(continued)

5. Where Does Electricity Come From? Non-renewable Resources	
Materials • chart paper • notebook • pencil or pen	**Equipment** • + and – charts from Lesson 4 • computers • 30 rulers
6. Light Up the Class	
Materials • none	**Equipment** • 30 light bulbs • 30 light bulb holders • 90 wires with alligator clips (each wire about 30 cm long) • 15 6-V batteries • 15 switches
7. Go with the Flow	
Materials • 10 pieces of wood • 10 glasses of water • 10 glasses of salt water	**Equipment** • 10 metal spoons • 10 quarters • 10 pens • 10 6-V batteries or D-cells • 10 LEDs (light-emitting diodes) • 30 wires with alligator clips (each wire about 30 cm long)
8. Key Features of Electrical Circuits	
Materials • paper and pencils	**Equipment** • 30 light bulbs • 30 light bulb holders • 90 wires with alligator clips (each wire about 30 cm long) • 15 6-V batteries • 15 switches
9. Different Needs, Different Circuits	
Materials • none	**Equipment** • 30 light bulbs • 30 light bulb holders • 90 wires with alligator clips (each wire about 30 cm long) • 15 6-V batteries

Materials and Equipment

(continued)

10. Fixing Electrical Problems	
Materials • notebook • pencil or pen	**Equipment** • none
11. Careers in Electricity	
Materials • notebook • pencil or pen	**Equipment** • computers • reference materials
12. Electricity and Magnets	
Materials • 600 single staples • 15 Styrofoam™ plates • 15 pencils	**Equipment** • 1 compass • 1 bar magnet • 15 6-V batteries • 30 insulated copper wires with bare ends (1 m each) • 15 iron nails • 15 plastic markers
13. Electromagnets at Work	
Materials • notebook • pencil or pen	**Equipment** • none
14. Electricity — Use It Safely	
Materials • poster paper • notebook • pencil or pen • markers or colour pencils	**Equipment** • computers • reference materials
15. Talking Around the World — Thanks to Canadians	
Materials • notebook • pencil or pen	**Equipment** • computers • reference materials
16. Conserving Electricity	
Materials • notebook • pencil or pen	**Equipment** • none
Design Project: A New Electrical Device	
Materials • any materials used throughout Unit 2	**Equipment** • any equipment used throughout Unit 2

Materials and Equipment

(continued)

Overall Unit Requirements	
Materials • chart paper • 5 sticky-note pads • 50 balloons • 10 m of string • 40 sheets of paper towel • 30 aluminum pie plates • 30 Styrofoam™ plates • 3 kinds of dry cereal • 30 wool cloth pieces • 30 pieces of paper • 30 mL pepper • 10 pieces of wood • 10 glasses of water • 10 glasses of salt water • 600 single staples • poster paper • notebooks • pencils or pens • markers or colour pencils • highlighters • tape	**Equipment** • 30 pairs of scissors • 10 rulers • 30 pencils with erasers on the end • 30 thumbtacks • 30 plastic Petri dishes with lids • 30 light bulbs • 30 light bulb holders • 90 wires with alligator clips (each about 30 cm long) • 15 6-V batteries • 15 switches • 10 metal spoons • 10 quarters • 10 LEDs (light-emitting diodes) • 1 compass • 1 bar magnet • 30 insulated copper wires with bare ends (1 m each) • 15 iron nails • 15 plastic markers • computers • reference materials

Addressing Student Preconceptions

Launch: Electricity is Everywhere

Students consistently confuse electrical current with electrical energy. Students might do a mind map of electricity to show how it is related to other forms of energy they see in the launch illustration. (In grade 3, they should have studied Invisible Forces.)

Lesson 1: The Shocking History of Electricity

It is important that students understand the history of electricity in relation to Saskatchewan and their current lifestyles. Most students will not connect their daily routines with using electrical energy. Also, many students at this age are just starting to understand the concepts of history and time, so they may still have difficulties connecting historical events with a certain time frame. The timeline project gives students a tool for visualizing the order of inventions and discoveries to help them understand the history of these inventions and discoveries.

The definition of electricity as the flow of charges is not formally part of the curriculum. However, it might come up naturally in this lesson. If it does, it might help students to understand the subtle, but important, difference between electrical current—the flow of charges—and electrical energy—the energy that those moving charges have.

Lesson 2: Static Electricity

Most students should have experience with static electricity but may not know how it is connected to lightning or current electricity. Students may confuse static electrical attraction with magnetic attraction, especially when they think of a balloon sticking to the wall or a charged comb sticking to their hair.

This lesson initiates a discussion about opposite charges and how they behave toward each other. Students may have questions about what makes one charge opposite to another, which could lead to a lesson about positive and negative charges at an atomic level. However, the concepts of atoms and electrons are not curriculum topics until grade 9, so they do not need to be discussed in detail at this time.

Lesson 3: Making Static Electricity Useful

After completing the centres in the Work On It activity in Lesson 2, students should have a good understanding that in static electricity, opposite charges attract and like charges repel. Many people do not think of static electricity as a useful form of electricity, so they do not know that static electricity is used in various machines and tools, such as photocopy machines, laser printers, and paint sprayers.

Lesson 4: Where Does Electricity Come From? Renewable Resources and Lesson 5: Where Does Electricity Come From? Non-renewable Resources

Many students think of electrical energy as synonymous with electrical current. In fact, we use the term "electricity" to refer to both concepts. The question to ask is, Where does the energy come from to produce electrical current? Students may have various preconceptions about the positive and negative effects of the various sources of energy.

Students may be aware of the terms "renewable resources" and "non-renewable resources" from previous units of study, but they likely did not learn how these resources were used to generate power. By the end of these two lessons, students should have a better understanding of the uses of these resources and form personal opinions about them.

Lesson 6: Light Up the Class

It is important that students predict the outcome of each Electro Problem before trying it. This way, they are more open to changing their preconceptions. It is important to allow them plenty of time to try the different configurations. Many grade 6 students believe that the current comes out of both ends of the battery and meets (clashes) at the bulb, where it is consumed. Many students also believe that current comes out of one end of the battery, goes through the bulb, and then dies before going in the other end of the battery. If you have access to an ammeter, which measures current, you can demonstrate, after students make their predictions, that the amount of current on both sides of the bulb is the same. It is the energy that is used up, not the current, but few students understand this concept. The Communicate questions allow you to sample typical student understanding of electrical current.

Lesson 7: Go with the Flow

The concept of conductors and insulators has been introduced in previous grades when studying forces, light, or sound. This lesson relates the characteristics of conductors and insulators to electrical energy. Some students may not realize that electrical devices and even wires use conductors and insulators to direct electrical current to the right places.

Lesson 8: Key Features of Electrical Circuits

Students easily learn to draw circuit diagrams, but typically have a difficult time relating them to real circuits they build. One study showed that students did not recognize circuit diagrams if they were turned upside down. You might like to try this test with your students. Another challenge is for students to see inside a light bulb. If they notice that the filament is a wire, like the other wires in a circuit, they can understand more easily how the current moves through a complete loop, including the filament in the bulb.

Lesson 9: Different Needs, Different Circuits

One study suggests that students need thorough experience with series circuits before encountering parallel circuits. So, you might like to stop the class in the middle of this lesson and evaluate students' understanding of the series circuit. When doing the Work On It activity on page 121 of the student book, you could ask students to predict which light bulb will shine the brightest when two light bulbs are connected in a simple circuit. When students see during the activity that both light bulbs shine equally brightly, you can point out that current is not consumed or used up as it travels around the circuit. However, the energy is shared between the two bulbs, making them dimmer than in the one-bulb circuit.

Lesson 10: Fixing Electrical Problems

This lesson provides students with the opportunity to apply and review new concepts of electrical circuits as they troubleshoot the problems.

Lesson 11: Careers in Electricity

Students usually think of an electrician when they are asked to give an example of a job that involves electricity. In this lesson, students will learn that there are many other occupations in the field of electricity.

Lesson 12: Electricity and Magnets

Before students read this lesson in the student book, you may wish to test their preconceptions of magnets. Although most students may have played with magnets, research indicates that few students had any idea about magnetic poles, and that many students lack experience with magnetic repulsion. Students only think of magnets as attracting each other. In the pre-lesson review, let students work in groups with two magnets per group. The activity in this lesson allows students to study the magnetic effect of an electrical current. Few students will anticipate this effect and may not recognize it, even after seeing it. This shows the need for continual reinforcement and questioning if permanent conceptual change is to take place.

Students may confuse static electrical attraction with magnetic attraction, especially when they think of a balloon sticking to a wall or a charged comb sticking to their hair.

Many students have preconceptions about electricity and magnetism even after seeing demonstrations. In one study, a majority of grade 6 students thought that the wire had to be un-insulated before it would produce a magnetic field. You may wish to test this idea and compare it to the demonstration of the insulated wire affecting a compass.

Lesson 13: Electromagnets at Work

After the investigation in Lesson 12, students may still not understand how people can use electromagnets in technology. Grade 6 students generally understand that most machines contain motors, but they do not understand the inner workings of a motor. The objective of this lesson is to inform the students that motors use electromagnets to function, but students do not need to know the specific process of how motors work.

Lesson 14: Electricity — Use It Safely

Students should have a basic knowledge of many of the safety tips in this lesson from experience and classroom instruction. It is expected that, using the new information acquired in this unit, students will have a better appreciation for these safety tips and a fuller understanding of the causes and effects of the examples brought up during the lesson.

Lesson 15: Talking Around the World — Thanks to Canadians

Students should be able to interpret the information in this lesson and on their timelines to develop a clearer understanding of the role of new technologies in the world and how these electrical devices impact their lives.

Lesson 16: Conserving Electricity

From the information in this unit, students should have a solid understanding of the impact of electricity on their lives, but they may not realize that their electrical consumption is different than that of people in other parts of the world. This lesson gives them an opportunity to look critically at their electrical usage.

Design Project: A New Electrical Device

By using the information they learned in this unit, students should be able to creatively design an electrical device and identify the electrical components in their design. Students may be very ambitious with their design, but will need to be reminded that their idea should be created within the parameters of their knowledge and materials (i.e., they should not be constructing a circuit board for an alarm clock). As a result, some of their designs may need to be altered so they use materials available to them.

Big Ideas

Page 81

This unit will present many of the characteristics and features of electrical energy. Students will manipulate series and parallel circuits and develop models of electromagnets as they learn how these devices are used in technology. Students will also take a detailed look at the properties of electrostatic charge, conducting and insulating materials, and circuit diagrams, including switches.

Through discussions of historical discoveries, generation methods, career choices, and conservation ideas, students will not only gain understanding of how electricity impacts their daily lives, but also gather evidence of how electricity has impacted the lives of all people living in Saskatchewan, including First Nations and Métis communities. By the end of this unit, students should be able to critically discuss and form opinions about many aspects of electricity, including resource gathering and development practices, the impacts of technological advances, and safety and conservation methods.

Once you have determined students' prior knowledge, you may want to hand out LM 2-1 Unit 2 Summary and LM 2-2 Unit 2 Key Terms.

Electricity is Everywhere

Page 82

Time
1 class period
Key Terms
• none
Line Masters
• none

Assessing Students' Prior Knowledge

- Divide the class into groups of four to six students.
- On the board, write, *What do you know about electricity?* Ask students to talk about this question in their groups, and to write down their ideas.
- Start a mind map on a piece of chart paper by writing the word "electricity" in the centre.
- After students have finished their discussions, choose a student from each group to contribute one idea to the mind map. If a student suggests something someone else disagrees with, enter that idea in a different colour. Continue asking for and recording ideas until students have nothing else to add.
- Keep the mind map posted in the classroom. Come back to any misconceptions that students may have as they arise in the unit.

Introduce the Unit

- Students may be so familiar with using electricity that they may not think about it. Explain that they are going to find out:
  - how light, sound, and motion can be produced from electricity
  - what static electricity and lightning are
  - how energy is produced in Saskatchewan and how it impacts the environment
  - how to build and test electrical circuits
- Start a discussion about electricity by asking, *Has anyone experienced a power failure? What happened?* Allow students to describe their experiences. If no one volunteers, direct the class to imagine a power failure. Ask students what they would miss the most without electricity.
- Continue the discussion by asking, *How did you receive news during the blackout? Did your TV or computer still work? Were you able to make food on the stove or in the microwave? Could you use a hair dryer or fan? Did your doorbell work?*
- Ask students to bring different electrical items from their homes, with parental permission, that they can study, manipulate, and take apart. When taking apart electrical devices, be sure to use proper tools and make sure that the devices do not have a power source. Create an Electrical Device Station in your classroom with these items. Be sure to include items that have different functions of light, sound, and movement.

Introduce the Design Project

- Inform the class that at the end of this unit, they will be designing and building an electrical device of their own that will perform an everyday task.
- Encourage students to set aside a part of their notebooks to jot down ideas for their electrical devices as they progress through this unit.
- During the Design Project, students should have access to all the materials presented during the unit. Make the materials used in investigations available for students for this project.

Get Started ▶

- Use a Think-Pair-Share format to prepare an initial list of examples of electricity use found in the illustrations on pages 82–83 of the student book. Ask students to work independently to come up with their own ideas, then pair up with one partner to compare lists before they share their lists with the class.
- While the students are sharing their lists with the class, either write a list on the board or ask students to write the suggestions they did not have into their notebooks as the class shares ideas.

Time
30 min
Skills
• classifying • observing • comparing • communicating • predicting
Grouping
groups
Materials and Equipment
• chart paper • sticky-note pads • notebook • pencil or pen
Line Masters
• none

Work On It

- Divide the class into groups of three or four students. Give each group one piece of chart paper and half of a pad of sticky-notes. If the groups need more sticky-notes, tell them to cut the ones they have in half.
- The groups should record all the electrical examples they have onto the sticky-notes (one per note), then work together to separate their examples into categories. If your class has already completed Unit 1: Diversity of Living Things suggest that students consider a tree classification system to categorize the uses of electricity in the illustration.

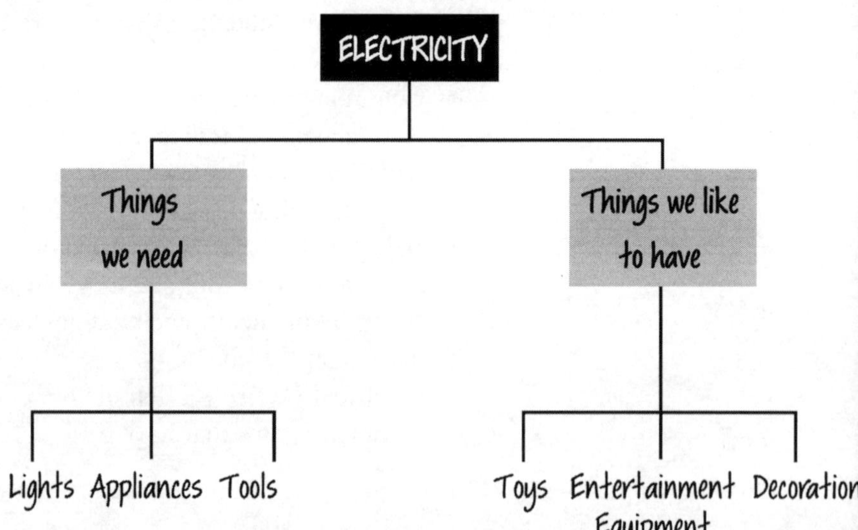

Communicate

After the groups have finished, each group will share their classification system with the class by presenting their chart. When all the presentations are complete, ask questions like, *Is there a category you would now add or change for your list? How are your categories the same as or different from those of other groups?* If time permits, allow the students to take their charts back and reclassify their electrical examples in a new way by moving around the sticky-notes.

1. Students should copy their categorized lists into their notebooks. They can use the categories that their group came up with or adjust their categories according to new information they learned when the class shared.
2. Student pictures should fit the context of one of the illustrated situations and display an understanding of what components are needed for an electrical device. The illustration should show the function of the device and a power source.
3. Students should give you their predictions about power sources, which will be discussed in Lessons 4 and 5. You may get answers such as the Sun, hydroelectricity, nuclear power, or coal power.

1 The Shocking History Of Electricity

Page 84

Time

1 class period

Key Terms

- static electricity
- prosthesis
- batteries

Line Masters

- LM 2-3

Indicator Assessment Chart

Indicator	Assessment Opportunities
EL6.1 a. Provide examples of the types of energy sources used to provide heat and light to homes in the past and describe ways in which electricity-based technologies have changed the way people work, live, and interact with the environment in Saskatchewan.	• Communicate, p. 88, q. 1–4

Background Information

Before electricity, people relied more on human power to survive, work, and entertain themselves. When it came to food storage, pioneers used root cellars and preservation methods such as meat smoking and pickling. These methods are still in use today. Ice boxes were also used: people would store large chunks of ice from a frozen lake underground and then transfer it to an insulated box for use.

Traditional Aboriginal food storage methods included drying and smoking meats to preserve them over the winter.

Luigi Galvani, an Italian physiologist, was interested in natural phenomena, including muscle tissue contraction and electricity. When he was experimenting with a dissected frog, he found he could make its leg twitch by touching the leg with two different metals. Galvani thought the electricity came from the animal itself. Even though Galvani may have been incorrect about the origins of the electrical charge, his experiments led to the understanding that the nervous system carries electrical charges generated by organic tissue.

Alessandro Volta proposed that Galvani was in fact observing the effects of an electrical current generated between the two different metals. Volta demonstrated this to be true using the "crown of cups" device. In this device, electricity is produced in saltwater reservoirs connected with two different metals. Volta subsequently developed the "voltaic pile," considered to be the first chemical battery, which eventually led to the development of modern batteries. Michael Faraday used the voltaic pile to derive his quantitative laws of electricity.

Get Started ▶

- Ask the class to brainstorm devices that did not exist 200 years ago. Create a table with the headings "Past" and "Present." List students' suggestions in the "Present" column. For each device they identify, ask, *Can you think of a device that would have done the same job 200 years ago?* Record their answers in the "Past" column. Ask students to compare the two columns. Ask, *Why couldn't we have used today's devices 200 years ago?* Direct their discussion to the discovery that many of today's devices require electricity to operate.
- Ask students to read the first paragraph of Get Started, and then to draw what they think a device to keep food cold might have looked like 200 years ago. In their drawings, look for some kind of container to hold food and a means of keeping it cool. Most students will suggest a device that uses ice.
- Encourage students to discuss the advantages and disadvantages of their appliance. During the discussion, ensure that students recognize that electricity is necessary for modern refrigerators to operate.

An Electrical Discovery

- Read the section and ask students to predict what they think the connection is between the frog's leg and electricity. Ask, *What possible experiment could be done with a frog and electricity?* Students may give a number of creative answers, including ideas of dissection or regeneration. Try to guide your students to think about useful forms of electricity that are present today.
- Some students may question the inhumane treatment of animals in experiments, which leads them to Communicate question 4. In this case, take time to talk about how experimenting practices have changed to become more aware of animal rights.

Electrical Muscles

- This section of reading explores the work of Luigi Galvani. Galvani was one of the first scientists to experiment with current electricity. Encourage students to describe Galvani's work in their own words, either orally or in writing.
- Ask the students if they know any famous or local people who have artificial limbs. Make the connection between the frog's leg and a prosthetic limb by asking, *How are the movements of the frog's leg like the movements of a prosthesis?* Students should be able to make the connection that the frog's leg moved because the lightning created a muscle impulse in the leg. This effect is similar to one type of prosthesis known as a myoelectric prosthesis. A myoelectric prosthesis works by using the electrical impulses generated from the muscles in the residual limb. The impulses are read by electrodes that move the artificial limb.

Building Batteries

- This section explores the work of Alessandro Volta. Volta is credited with constructing the first electrochemical cells, a precursor to batteries. The electrical unit known as the volt was named in his honour.
- Read the section and talk to the students about batteries. Ask, *What types of devices have batteries? How would these devices be different if they needed to be plugged in?* Students may mention items such as a TV remote control, a hand-held game, or a flashlight. Students should be able to conclude that if these items needed to be plugged in, they would be less convenient to use.

Time

30 min. The timeline will be added to throughout the unit.

Skills

- classifying
- making models
- interpreting
- comparing
- measuring

Grouping

pairs

Materials and Equipment

- chart paper
- scissors
- colour pencils
- highlighters

Line Masters

- LM 2-3

Work On It

- In this activity, the students will be creating a timeline that will be used throughout this unit in the Build On What You Know sections.
- This activity is meant to get the students thinking about the inventions that have advanced our knowledge about electricity. In the Design Project, the students will add their own inventions to their timelines.
- Students should first jot down the following notes: about 600 BCE—ancient Greeks; 1752—Benjamin Franklin; 1786—Luigi Galvani; 1796—Alessandro Volta; 1967—Richard Keefer. These notes should include a brief outline of what each person invented or discovered. Use Line Master 2-3 Timeline Template to create or guide the creation of the timeline. Be sure that the students leave enough space on their timelines to add more inventions.

Think Again! Electricity in Saskatchewan

- Students should begin to understand how important electricity is in daily life. This reading should be used to connect the previous reading on historical North American and European inventors to the development of electricity in Saskatchewan.
- After reading this section, ask students to think about a way to do a common task without the use of electricity. Refer to the three pictures on page 88 of the student book. Ask students to think of examples that are powered by animals, humans, or the environment. These examples can be imagined or realistic, such as using a kerosene lamp or candle for light, or using a fire to heat a house.

Communicate

Through discussion, students have explored how appliances have changed due to electricity. They have also read about early experiments concerning electricity. They now have the opportunity to demonstrate their understanding.

1. Encourage students to use examples from their daily lives, which might include televisions, radios, computers, batteries, hair dryers, and lights.
2. Suggest that students imagine that although there is no electricity, they still must do everything they normally would do. Look for students to demonstrate their understanding of their dependence on electricity by both identifying problems they might encounter without electricity and suggesting solutions to these problems.
3. Students in a group should be able to use their answers to the previous questions to support their presentations. If students have difficulty developing their presentations, suggest that they focus on one particular part of the day. Ask them questions like, *What was school like in the past? How would dinnertime be different? What would your weekend look like? What would be different in your house?*
4. Students can talk about this question in a group to gain a better understanding of how experimenting can have positive and negative impacts. The experiments in this lesson brought up ideas about the humane treatment of animals. In Lessons 4 and 5, the discussion will be about how electricity generation impacts the environment. For this question, students' answers may vary but should indicate that the student understands that experimentation has both positive and negative aspects.

BUILD ON WHAT YOU KNOW

Even though there are no specific inventors listed about electricity in Saskatchewan, students can still record the following dates: 1890—electricity in Regina, Moose Jaw, and Prince Albert; 1940—electricity to rural areas.

You may want to inform the class that the first electrical refrigerator for home use, called the Domelre (a contraction of DOMestic ELectric REfrigerator), went on sale in Chicago in 1913, and Clarence Birdseye introduced the first electrical freezer in 1929.

For ESL/ELL

To better support learning, encourage students to use text and pictures of the appropriate electrical inventions on their timelines. You may wish to consider constructing a timeline on a large banner in the classroom. Students can add their entries and share them with the rest of the class after you have checked their work.

Ask students to create an electricity dictionary. They may use drawings or pictures, as well as words. Students may wish to add to their dictionaries as they progress through the unit.

For Enrichment

Students could research ancient farming techniques to discuss in class. Students could also design a farm tool that uses no electricity but performs an electrical task.

Assessment *for* Learning

What to Look For in Student Work	What to Do
Students should have an understanding that the discovery of electricity and the invention of electrical devices improved our lives. Through the lesson questions, you should be able to see indicators that students are comparing historical and modern lifestyles.	• Students who are having difficulty with this concept can create a visual Venn diagram that directly compares a historical lifestyle to a modern lifestyle in terms of electricity use.

2 Static Electricity

Page 89

Time
1–2 class periods
Key Terms
• none
Line Masters
• LM 2-4

Indicator Assessment Chart

Indicator	Assessment Opportunities
EL6.2 a. Conduct investigations to determine the attraction and repulsion of electrostatically charged materials and represent the results of those investigations using drawings, sketches, tables, charts, and/or other representations.	• Work On It, p. 89 • Communicate, p. 94, q. 1
EL6.2 b. Describe how results of similar and repeated investigations into the characteristics of static electric charges (e.g., the rubbing together of different substances) may vary and suggest possible explanations for identified variations.	• Work On It, p. 89 • Communicate, p. 94, q. 1
EL6.2 c. Identify natural and man-made applications of static electric charge and discharge (e.g., lightning, photocopiers, laser printers, air filters, and electrostatic paint sprayers).	• Communicate, p. 94, q. 2

Background Information

In the Saskatchewan grade 9 Curriculum, students will be introduced to the structure of an atom and learn that positive and negative charges are caused by the loss and gain of electrons. The grade 6 unit presents static charge in terms of its behaviours and characteristics. To meet curriculum indicators, positive and negative charges are referred to as opposite charges in these lessons.

Static electricity is electricity that "stays." This means that it collects on a person or material and builds up. We study electricity by looking at the behaviours created by these charge build-ups. Students should be exposed to a variety of situations that show examples of static charge. Rubbing feet on the carpet, touching metal and getting a shock, or dust bunnies collecting under the bed are all examples of static electricity. Through the Work On It stations, students should be able to conclude that opposite charges attract each other and similar charges repel each other.

Lightning is the formation of static electricity on a large scale. During a storm, clouds move rapidly and frozen raindrops continually bump into each other. As this continues, static charges in the cloud build up until the negative charges are so excessive that they are attracted to the positively charged ground. These negative charges are then released to the ground in the form of lightning.

continued →

traditional KNOWLEDGE

Natural phenomena such as lightning storms have always been held in great respect by First Nations and Métis peoples. The Thunderbird is a central component to many Aboriginal oral traditions. The Thunderbird is a powerful spirit that waters Earth and helps the growth of plants. Lightning is believed to flash from its eyes or beak, and the beating of its wings causes thunder.

Time

90 min

Skills

- making models, observing, interpreting, experimenting, comparing, controlling variables, predicting

Grouping

individuals and groups

Materials and Equipment

Charging Balloons (for a group of 3)
- 2 balloons
- 1 ruler
- 1 m of string
- 1 sheet of damp paper towel
- tape

A Little Bit of Lightning (for a group of 3 or for one person)
- 1 aluminum pie plate
- 1 Styrofoam™ plate
- 1 thumbtack
- 1 pencil with an eraser on its end

Dancing Cereal (for one person)
- 1 balloon
- 3 different kinds of dry cereal

Line Masters

- none

Get Started ▶

- Read the section as an introduction to the Work On It stations.
- Ask students to create a T-chart like the one below in their notebooks, or create a large one on the board.
- Ask students to think of examples of static electricity and then write their ideas in either column depending on whether they are sure the cause is static electricity or if they only think the cause might be static electricity.

I know this is static electricity.	I think this is static electricity.
-shock from walking on a carpet -hearing a crackling sound when you pull your sheet off your bed	-paper sticking together -balloon sticking on a wall

- After they have shared their lists with the class, ask students to keep their lists for later use.

Work On It

- This lesson is broken up into three static electricity stations. These investigations can be completed as three stations that are rotated or done as three separate investigations.
- These stations are sensitive to the conditions in the classroom. If the classroom is humid, the static charges will not build up as well. Consider the time of year for this investigation. It is best done during the winter. You may need to bring in a dehumidifier to create a dry environment.

Students should be reminded to clean up their stations when they are finished with the material so the next group can start the experiment immediately from the beginning, without seeing completed models or experiments before they start. Remind students to also check their equipment before they get started so no material is broken or missing when they need to use it.

Charging Balloons

In this centre, students will create a model of two balloons that will be attracted to one another when one balloon is charged and the other is not. When both balloons are charged, they will repel each other. The purpose of this centre is for students to formulate the rule that opposite charges attract and similar charges repel.

- Students should follow the procedure as outlined in the student book to create the model. In step 3, they will draw a diagram of the model and predict what will happen when one or both balloons are charged.
- Students should continue to follow the procedure. In step 6, their model should show balloons that are attracted to each other. In step 7, students should find that their balloons follow each other and have an invisible connection. If students do not obtain these results, ask them to wipe both balloons with a damp towel and try again, but this time to increase the length of time they charge their balloon by 30 s.

Using the damp cloth decreases the build-up of static charge on the balloons so students can start the investigation under the same conditions every time. Be sure that their towel is only lightly dampened and that the balloon is dry before they continue with the investigation.

- Students should continue to follow the procedure. In steps 10 and 11, students should find that their model and observations are the opposite of earlier observations. The balloons are similarly charged. Therefore, they repel each other.
- The question posed in step 12 is directed to lead students to the idea that when one balloon is charged by rubbing it in hair, it will have a different charge than the balloon that is not rubbed in hair. In step 13, the rule that the students should derive is that opposite charges attract and similar charges repel. Students may not arrive at these answers right away. The Think Again! section reviews this idea, and students have an opportunity in the Communicate section to answer these questions again.

A Little Bit of Lightning

In this centre, students will build a model that creates a small electrostatic charge. This charge looks and behaves like lightning on a smaller scale. The purpose of this centre is to identify that lightning has similar characteristics to other electrostatic charges.

Variables are mentioned in this investigation. Variables are the conditions in which the investigation is performed. The variables in this centre include the height from which the plate is dropped, where the plate lands, and how much students charge the plate, which will depend on the material from which their clothes are made. An explanation about independent variables is found in the ! feature on page 132 of the student book.

- After students reflect on how lightning is made, they should follow the procedure to create the model shown on student book page 91.

continued →

- It is important for students to follow directions carefully. In steps 3 and 4, they first transfer static electricity to the Styrofoam™ plate to charge it, then they transfer the charge to the aluminum plate when they drop it. If the aluminum plate touches something else, the charge will transfer from the model into whatever it touched.
- When the model is properly created, students should receive a small static spark from the aluminum plate. If they touch the Styrofoam™ plate, they will not receive a spark because the Styrofoam™ plate is not an electrical conductor. In step 7, students should receive a second spark when they lift up the aluminum plate because the aluminum plate draws static charge from the finger that touches it.
- For steps 8, 9, and 10, students should find that there are not many changes in the results unless they touch the plate to an insulator.

Dancing Cereal

In this centre, students will investigate the characteristics of static electricity by comparing how different materials react to a charge. The purpose of this experiment is for students to learn that materials that are lighter and have a drier texture accumulate more static charge than heavier materials do. When collecting the material for this centre, choose cereals that have different sizes, densities, and weights.

- Students should charge their balloons by rubbing them in their hair. If they find that they have minimal or no results in this investigation, they should charge their balloons for a longer period of time.
- Before continuing, students should create a table similar to the one below and make their predictions. Remind students that their predictions and observations should reflect the five senses—what will they see, hear, feel, smell, and taste. (Not all sensations will be present in each experiment.)

Cereal/Material	**Predict what will happen…**	**Observations**
puffed wheat	-pieces will float up and stick to the balloon	-pieces stuck to the balloon but fell off after 5 s
Cheerios™	-pieces will stick to the balloon for 3 s	-pieces moved a bit but did not lift up
cereal 3		
hole-punch paper	-pieces will stick to the balloon	-pieces stuck to the balloon even when it was carried away
choice 2		
choice 3		

- Students should follow steps 4, 5, and 6 of the procedure to fill out their table. In step 6, students should note that the cereals reacted differently according to their size, density, and weight. Their choices in step 7 and their answers in step 8 should also reflect their understanding of differences in size, density, and weight.
- The additional activity on the next page could be used as a demonstration to introduce the lesson or as a fourth centre, if needed. In this experiment, you will show that a static charge can be used to make a light bulb light up.

CAUTION!
Do not use electricity from a wall outlet for this experiment.
Handle the glass light bulb with care to avoid breaking it. The bulb can be wrapped in sticky, transparent tape to reduce the chance of injury if it breaks.

Electricity with a Balloon

Materials

- fluorescent light bulb
- balloon

Procedure

1. Turn off the lights in the classroom.
2. Blow up the balloon and charge it using your hair.
3. Hold the balloon near the end of the light bulb. Observe what happens to the light bulb. The light bulb should light up.

- Try to keep as much material as possible from the investigations so that the items can be used for the Design Project. Many students will focus on using only the tools from the lessons dealing with circuits. Remind students that they can also use the characteristics of static electricity to create their inventions.

Think Again! Attracting and Repelling

- Students should be making connections between their centre investigations, attraction and repulsion of static charge, and lightning. Ask students to recall all three centres. After reading the section, ask them to state in their own words what they observed in each centre.

Communicate

Take a second look at the T-chart developed at the beginning of this lesson. Students should be able to reclassify some of the examples of static electricity according to the characteristics and behaviours of the objects they studied in this lesson. While students are completing the Communicate questions, ask them to revisit the three centres to gather their information.

1. This question is an opportunity for students to improve their answers in the Work On It activity according to the new information presented in the Think Again! section. For Centre 1, students' answers should include the rule that opposite charges attract and similar charges repel. For Centre 2, their answers should express the idea that lightning is a form of static electricity. Centre 3 answers should mention how size, density, and weight may affect static charge.
2. The following are forms of static electricity that the students should be able to identify:
   - You rub your feet on the carpet, then touch something made of metal and get a shock.
   - You don't use fabric softener when you wash your clothes, and they stick together when you take them out of the dryer.
   - On a cold evening, your jacket crackles when you take it off.
   - Dust gathers under your bed.

   Other suggestions may be acceptable as long as students can explain their responses, for example, When you turn on your TV and run your hand over the screen, the screen crackles.

BUILD ON WHAT YOU KNOW

Students should add Nikola Tesla, who invented the Tesla coil in 1891, to their timelines.

For Reteaching

Ask students to create a log or journal in which they record all the examples of static electricity they observe in a week.

For Enrichment

Use LM 2-4 The Great Pop Can Race to create a racecourse based on the principle of static attraction or repulsion.

Assessment *for* Learning

What to Look For in Student Work	What to Do
The student should understand the characteristics of attraction and repulsion of static charges.	• Ask the student to independently demonstrate the first centre for you and orally relate his or her observations to you during the experiment.
The student should understand that lightning has the same properties as other examples of static electricity and therefore is a form of static electricity.	• If the student is having difficulty, draw a diagram or ask the student to draw a diagram that outlines the attraction of static electricity in the clouds to the opposite charge on the ground.
The student should understand that static electricity builds up more easily in a dry atmosphere and on materials that are lighter and less dense.	• If the student does not understand this concept, ask the student to review Communicate question 2 and answer the question "why" for all the static electricity examples (i.e., dust gathers under your bed because the dust particles are attracted to one another and are light enough to be drawn together).

ASK AN ELDER | Danny Musqua: The Thunderbird and Waskwanehpigan

Page 95

- In the cultures of many First Nations and Métis peoples, lightning is often portrayed as a giant luminous bird whose eyes issue lightning. This celestial being, called the Thunderbird, is the herald of spring. Though the snow may have melted, and the migratory flocks have returned, for many of the Plains peoples, spring hasn't truly arrived until there is lightning followed by a storm. When lightning is spotted, then the Plains peoples agree that the season of life has come.
- For these peoples, the entity embodied in the Thunderbird is sacred and revered. Thus, any references to this teaching, discussed in the course of the *Saskatchewan Science* program, mustn't be taken lightly. Teachers must convey respect for the traditional explanation of the natural phenomenon of lightning and should not dismiss it out of hand, though it might contrast with the Western science explanation. However, in Elder Danny Musqua's profile, it is made clear that even though the belief in the Thunderbird was common, many Elders had different explanations or thoughts regarding lightning and thunder. Emphasis on this point helps students understand that many thinkers among the Ojibwa (and other First Nations and Métis groups) had divergent views on natural phenomena. This point also helps students understand how two differing views might co-exist.

3 Making Static Electricity Useful

Page 96

Time
1 class period

Key Terms
• none

Line Masters
• LM 2-5

Indicator Assessment Chart

Indicator	Assessment Opportunities
EL6.2 a. Conduct investigations to determine the attraction and repulsion of electrostatically charged materials and represent the results of those investigations using drawings, sketches, tables, charts, and/or other representations.	• Work On It, p. 96
EL6.2 c. Identify natural and man-made applications of static electric charge and discharge (e.g., lightning, photocopiers, laser printers, air filters, and electrostatic paint sprayers).	• Work On It, p. 96
EL6.2 l. Describe the operation of common technologies based on properties of static electricity, current electricity, or electromagnetism.	• Work On It, p. 96 • Communicate, p. 98, q. 1

Background Information

The Saskatchewan curriculum does not require students to know the inner workings of a photocopier or any other machine that uses static electricity. However, it is important for students to know that these devices are applications of static electricity.

A photocopier works on the basic static electricity principle that opposite charges attract. A bright light reflected from mirrors shines the image of the original paper onto a light-sensitive drum. The light is transmitted through the white areas of the sheet being copied and neutralizes the charges on these parts of the drum. Light is absorbed by the dark areas, so they remain charged. Then the drum rolls into the toner, which has an opposite static charge to the charge on the drum. The toner sticks to the dark areas on the drum. Then the drum rolls onto a blank piece of paper, and the toner is fused to the paper by heat to create the duplicate image.

In this lesson, there are opportunities to discuss other machines that use static electricity. Here are some examples that may be talked about:

- A laser printer works on the same principle of static charge as a photocopier. Instead of a large light, there is a small laser that receives the page data, which consists of tiny dots and spaces.

Data is received one horizontal line at a time. The laser emits a beam that is reflected from a movable mirror. The mirror moves across a positively charged drum and reflects a pulse of light from the laser for every dot and no pulse for every empty space. It thereby discharges the points on the drum that correspond to dots from the laser beam, creating a negative electrostatic image. In some laser printers, the drum has a negative charge and the laser beam creates a positive electrostatic image. Then, like the photocopier, the image is transferred from the drum and pressed onto paper with ink.

- An ionizing air purifier cleans the air by shooting out electrons that contact particles of dust and debris in the air. These electrons create a charge on the particles. The particles are collected by a plate in the purifier that has an opposite charge.
- Electrostatic paint sprayers use static electricity by charging all the paint particles with the same charge. When they leave the container, the particles repel each other and spread apart. The surface being painted is oppositely charged to the paint, so the particles are attracted to the area being painted.

Get Started ▶

- Before reading this section, ask students, *How do you think we can use static electricity to do an everyday task?* If the students conclude from the photo on page 96 of the student book that static electricity is used in photocopiers, challenge them by asking how.
- Review the characteristics of static electricity that they learned about in the previous lesson:
  - Opposite charges attract, like charges repel.
  - Lighter objects are attracted to heavier ones.
- Read the section. Ask students to look at the materials list and predict what they might be doing in the investigation before reading the procedure.

Time

60 min

Skills

- making models
- observing
- interpreting
- experimenting
- comparing
- controlling variables

Grouping

individuals

Materials and Equipment

- 1 plastic Petri dish and lid
- 1 wool cloth
- 1 piece of paper (works best with heavy, stiff paper)
- scissors
- 1 mL (1/4 teaspoonful) pepper
- tape
- 1 sheet of damp paper towel

Line Masters

- none

Work On It

- Like the activity in Lesson 2, this investigation is sensitive to the conditions of the classroom. If the classroom is humid, static charge will not build up as well. Consider the time of year for this investigation. You may need to bring in a dehumidifier to create a dry environment.

(!) The quality of the results in this investigation depends on how closely students follow the procedure. If students are having difficulty getting their model to work, encourage them to talk to the students who are successful to find out what they are doing differently. The results can be affected by having a complicated cut-out shape, not rubbing the lid long enough, rubbing too aggressively and not paying attention to the paper cut-out, starting with a charged lid, or leaving the pepper flipped for too long.

- The final outcome of this investigation is to have a picture that transferred from the cut-out to the lid. Even if their product is not exact, students should see indicators from their original cut-out in the pepper that is sticking to the lid.
- Students' answers to the question in step 9 should be similar to the following explanation: When the lid is rubbed with wool, a charge is created on the lid. The paper acts as an insulator that does not allow the charge to expand beyond the exposed parts of the lid. The pepper sticks to the lid because it has an opposite static charge, and is not attracted to the parts of the lid that have no charge.
- In step 10, the purpose of the question is for students to see the similarity between their pepper picture model and the way photocopiers make copies. Students should realize that any light material that has a static charge can be used instead of pepper. Students' answers may vary but can include a photocopier, tools such as an electrostatic dust mop, or any of the machines mentioned in the Background Information section.

Think Again! Using Static

- After reading this section, take the students on a tour to see the photocopier in your school. Ask students to try to identify the parts of the machine that were mentioned in the reading.

Communicate

Discuss the investigation results with the class and encourage students to correct and expand on their answers to the questions asked during the experiment.

1. Now that the students have read the Think Again! section, they should be able to make the connections between the investigation and how a photocopier works. Tell them to refer to the questions they answered in steps 9 and 10. Students' answers should conclude that photocopier toner is like the pepper in the experiment, and the bright light on the copier helps create an image that has charged and uncharged parts. The toner sticks to the charged parts of the image just like the pepper sticks to the charged parts of the lid, thereby copying the image.
2. Discuss this question in groups or as a class. Some possible ideas that students may suggest to reduce static build-up are to put more moisture in the air with a humidifier or vaporizer, to use fabric softeners or antistatic dryer sheets to control static cling, or to use static discharge straps at the backs of their cars or trucks that stay connected with the ground so that the vehicle does not build up a charge. Controlling static charges is usually more for convenience than a necessity, but some static charges can build up to dangerous levels that can cause gas explosions. For example, an explosion can occur at a gas station, if a spark from a static charge comes into contact with a flammable liquid, or your computer can be damaged if a static spark gets too close to the circuit boards.
3. For the mind map, you may want to share the map below as a starting point for students, or complete the entire map together as a class.

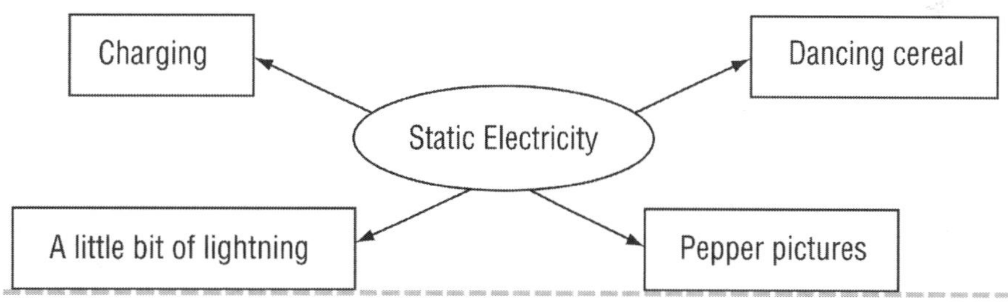

BUILD ON WHAT YOU KNOW

An optional entry to the timeline is Chester Carlson, an American inventor who patented a process called electrophotography in 1937. His device was an early model of the photocopier. It was renamed Xerography in 1938.

For Reteaching

Read the descriptions of how other machines use static electricity in the Background Information section. Ask students to research, draw a diagram, or make a model of one of the machines mentioned.

For Enrichment

Use Line Master 2-5 Making Static Electricity Useful — Getting Rid of Static to research the methods used to reduce static electricity.

Assessment *for* Learning

What to Look For in Student Work	What to Do
Students should be able to understand that static electricity can be harnessed to perform useful tasks. They should also be able to identify some machines that use static electricity.	• Go over the mind map created in Communicate question 3 and ask the student to identify the characteristics of static electricity.

4 Where Does Electricity Come From? Renewable Resources

Page 99

Time

1 class period

Key Terms

- renewable energy resource
- hydroelectricity
- generator
- reservoir
- solar energy
- passive solar heating
- active solar heating
- geothermal energy
- water pollution
- heat exchange
- noise pollution
- biomass
- biomass energy generation

Line Masters

- LM 2-6
- LM 2-7

Indicator Assessment Chart

Indicator	Assessment Opportunities
EL6.1 b. Describe how electrical energy is generated from hydroelectric, coal, natural gas, nuclear, geothermal, biomass, solar, and wind sources and categorize these sources as renewable or non-renewable.	• Work On It, p. 103

Background Information

Electricity is generated by transforming some other form of energy into electrical energy. The resources used for generating electricity can be either renewable or non-renewable. Renewable energy resources are never used up. These resources include energy from natural sources such as water, the Sun, and wind. Five forms of renewable energy discussed in this lesson are hydroelectricity and solar, geothermal, wind, and biomass energy.

In 1994, electricity in Canada was produced mainly using hydroelectric energy from flowing water (56 %) and thermal energy—steam produced from burning coal (18 %), petroleum products (7 %), and nuclear fuel (uranium, 14 %). The remainder was generated using natural gas (4 %) and other sources (1 %). A generator is a machine with a wheel that is made to rotate by a source of energy. The rotating wheel transforms the energy from the source into mechanical energy, which is converted into electrical energy by an electromagnetic motor (see Lesson 13). The source of energy used depends on which resources are most readily available in the area.

Get Started ▶

- In this lesson, students will create a chart that identifies the positive and negative aspects of each energy source. The Work On It section provides a description and an example of a + and – chart.
- Read about each form of energy as a class. When they have read about their activity in the Work On It section, students should reread the Renewable Energy Resources section with the purpose of gathering information to create their + and – charts.

! An electrical generating facility can be referred to as a power station, power plant, or powerhouse. The term "energy centre" is also a good synonym because generation plants convert different forms of energy, such as thermal energy, mechanical energy, and gravitational potential energy into electrical energy.

Renewable Energy Resources

Hydroelectricity

- Hydroelectric power is the most widely used method of electrical generation in Canada. Hydroelectric power uses the gravitational potential energy of falling water to create motion in the generator.
- The amount of power generated is controlled by the volume of water that falls through the dam and the height from which it falls. A dam maintains a constant electrical output by controlling the amount of water that falls and therefore, the amount of electricity generated.
- There are many government plans and incentives to help reduce the environmental impact of dams and reservoirs, as well as new initiatives to create dam-less hydro that runs with the river's current, without the need to create a reservoir.
- Some examples of positives are: the reservoirs are used for recreational activities and farm irrigation, there is always water available to turn the generator, running water does not create pollution, the power plants are inexpensive to run, and they can be started and stopped quickly and easily.
- Some examples of negatives are: dams are expensive to build, they require long transmission lines that are expensive, they cannot be built everywhere, and building dams has a high impact on the surrounding environment and local communities due to flooding.

traditional ***KNOWLEDGE***

- Use LM 2-6 Case Study — The Loss of Mistaseni Rock to learn about a Saskatchewan community that was affected by the development of a hydroelectric dam.

Solar Energy

- Solar energy is converted to electricity by photovoltaic cells, which are made of material like silicon, a semiconductor. When sunlight strikes the panel, the material emits electrons. When enough electrons build up, electric current is generated.
- Some examples of positives are: solar energy is available everywhere, solar panels are simple to use, they can be added to homes, there is no visible pollution, and they are becoming less expensive to manufacture and install.
- Some examples of negatives are: the Sun doesn't always shine, solar cells are expensive, and they take up a lot of space, so they are only used on a small scale.
- Use LM 2-7 Design Challenge: Build a Solar Oven for the students to generate their own solar energy.

Geothermal Energy

- Geothermal energy can be obtained from shallow pools (hot springs) at the surface of Earth's crust, hot-water deposits below Earth's surface, or from tapping right into molten rock known as magma. Many such places are located in regions of the world that have the greatest seismic activity, which limits the choice of locations.

- The world's largest source of geothermal power is in The Geysers in northern California.
- Some examples of positives are: geothermal energy is reliable, has few environmental impacts, and produces little to no air pollution.
- Some examples of negatives are: geothermal energy can only be used in areas close to the power plant, locations are difficult to access, and there is a risk of water pollution — the temperature of the ground water can increase the temperature of the water in neighbouring lakes and streams and water may be contaminated by chemicals used in the power generating plant.
- **A Saskatchewan Story**—The Craik Sustainable Living Project was founded in 2001 with the goal of reducing the ecological footprint of the town by using more environmentally friendly technologies and ways of living. By developing an eco-centre, outreach programs, an eco-village, and community action, the citizens of Craik are using alternative methods for energy generation and conservation, along with many other initiatives. For more information, visit the website Craik Sustainable Living Project, http://www.craikecovillage.ca/index.html.

Wind Energy

- Electricity is created when wind rotates a turbine that generates mechanical power that is converted into electricity.
- Since wind is an unreliable source of energy, it is usually used with another form of electrical generation, such as solar energy, to maintain a constant flow of electricity.
- Some examples of positives are: wind is a free resource, it produces no emissions, and it can be set up faster than dams or power plants.
- Some examples of negatives are: wind speed is unreliable, turbines can break down, birds flying by are at risk, it is expensive to make electricity, it requires a lot of land, and produces noise pollution.

Biomass

- Biomass energy is similar to fossil fuel energy in the sense that it is a stored and contained form of energy. Unlike fossil fuels, biomass is considered renewable because you can obtain it from trees and plants, and society is continually producing organic waste.
- Biomass is either converted into electricity by burning and the steam produced turns a generator, or the methane gas it produces by rotting is used to fuel the generators.
- Some examples of positives are: biomass energy reuses organic waste material, there is a large supply of this resource, it helps reduce waste in landfills, and it is cheap.
- Some examples of negatives are: developing a new biomass power plant is expensive, we need to be cautious of what is burned, and it is a new process so there are few regulations.

Time

60 min

Skills

- classifying
- inferring
- interpreting
- comparing

Grouping

pairs

Materials and Equipment

(per pair or group)
- notebook
- chart paper
- ruler
- pencil or pen

Line Masters

- none

Work On It

- Before reading the Work On It section, describe the following situation to students. *You are in a store and you have $20 to buy a gift for your best friend. How will you decide which gift is the best to buy?* With the class, brainstorm different ways to make this decision. Make a list of students' suggestions, then use it to identify any ideas that involve making the decision based on the pros and cons of each choice. Convert their suggestions into a + and – chart to illustrate how this method can be used in a variety of situations to make a decision.
- Use the example of buying a bicycle on page 103 of the student book to model the + and – chart with the class. Copy the chart onto the board and ask students to suggest additional pros and cons for buying a bicycle. Extend the example of deciding whether to buy a bike by asking the class, *Is there anything else you need to think about? Would this consideration go in the plus or the minus column?*
- Students will now create their own + and – chart to sort the information they read about renewable energy sources. They will be considering five different methods of generating electricity and the effects of these methods on the community and the environment. Explain to students that they should create a separate chart for each type of energy source they read about. You may want to draw their attention to the subheadings by writing them on the board: Hydroelectricity, Solar Energy, Geothermal Energy, Wind Energy, and Biomass Energy.
- Students can do this activity in pairs or larger groups. If you decide that the class will be working in pairs, ask each pair to fill in a + and – chart for all five of the energy resources presented in the student book.
- You might ask each group to identify the similarities and differences among the five energy resources in the student book, then have a volunteer from each group report to the class.
- See the activity below for another option for completing this lesson.

For Lessons 4 and 5, create a jigsaw activity. Assign one of the eight resources outlined in the two lessons to a "home group" of students. The home group learns about one resource using the information in the student book and from any additional research, and completes the + and – chart for that resource. This group of students is now the expert for this resource. Then create new expert groups with one student from each home group. Ask the experts to report to their new groups or to the entire class about their resource.

Communicate

These questions can be completed individually or in groups. You may also consider deferring these questions until after Lesson 5 is completed.

1. A renewable resource is an energy resource used for generating electricity that can be used over and over again or be replaced easily. For a non-renewable resource, answers may vary but should identify that a non-renewable resource is something that cannot be replaced.
2. Answers will vary but should show that students understand that electricity is produced from other sources. Students should also demonstrate an understanding that each energy resource is used to turn a turbine or generator in order to produce electricity. Also, students should be able to determine whether their resource is renewable and identify a variety of positive and negative impacts their power generation plant may have on the environment, the resource itself, and the people using it.

For Enrichment

Interested students could research some more dates to add to their timeline. The following could be added to the timeline.

- Hydro-Quebec's James Bay LG 1 Dam was completed in 1995.
- Charles Fritts built the first solar cell in 1883.
- The Centennial Wind Power Facility in Swift Current, SK opened in 2006.
- The Craik Sustainable Living Project was founded in 2001.

For ESL/ELL

Develop large + and – charts on the board as you read each section.

Assessment for *Learning*

What to Look For in Student Work	What to Do
Students should be able to identify and form personal opinions about renewable energy resources (hydroelectric, geothermal, biomass, solar, and wind).	• Ask students to write a persuasive opinion paragraph that outlines why one of the five resources may be used over another or to create a poster about that resource.

5 Where Does Electricity Come From? Non-renewable Resources

Page 104

Time

1–2 class periods

Key Terms

- non-renewable energy resource
- fossil fuels
- nuclear energy
- coal

Line Masters

- LM 2-8

Indicator Assessment Chart

Indicator	Assessment Opportunities
EL6.1 b. Describe how electrical energy is generated from hydroelectric, coal, natural gas, nuclear, geothermal, biomass, solar, and wind sources and categorize these sources as renewable or non-renewable.	• Work On It, p. 106
EL6.1 c. Locate and categorize by type the large-scale electrical energy generation facilities in Saskatchewan and explain how electrical energy is transmitted from those facilities to locations throughout the province.	• Communicate, p. 107, q. 2, 3

Background Information

Electricity can be generated by producing steam. Steam is typically produced using nuclear fuels such as uranium, or by burning coal or natural gas. Uranium, coal, and natural gas are examples of non-renewable energy resources because they cannot regenerate or be remade. The electricity supply in Canada is produced mainly from water-powered (hydroelectric) and steam-powered generators. In 1996, 10 % of the electricity in Canada was produced from nuclear energy sources.

Get Started ▶

- Read about each form of energy as a class to gain a primary knowledge base, just as in Lesson 4.

Non-renewable Energy Resources

Nuclear Energy

- A nuclear power plant works on basically the same principle as a coal-burning or a geothermal power generation plant. A fuel is used to heat water to steam. The steam is then used to rotate a turbine to create mechanical energy that is converted to electrical energy. The main difference is in the fuel used for this process. In nuclear power plants, steam is produced by nuclear fission—the splitting of an atom.

- The fuel in nuclear power plants is usually the element uranium. Uranium is used because it is radioactive, that is, it naturally breaks down at an atomic level and releases energy. However, uranium emits dangerous levels of radiation that can affect humans and the materials holding the uranium fuel rods.
- Nuclear power plants and uranium mines undergo heavy licensing procedures and regulations in order to maintain operations. Many nuclear power plants can only be used for a certain number of years before they need to be decommissioned due to increased radiation levels in surrounding areas. In 2009, all of the uranium mines in operation in Canada were located in northern Saskatchewan. However, most of the operating nuclear power plants were located in Ontario.
- Nuclear energy sources are used because they are readily available and have low development and production costs compared with other resources. However, as environmental costs begin to be considered more seriously, renewable energy resources such as solar energy and wind energy may begin to play a more important role.
- Some examples of positives are: uranium can be found in many places, it is inexpensive compared to other resources, and burning it as a fuel produces no air pollution.
- Some examples of negatives are: nuclear power plants are expensive to build and maintain, they need to be decommissioned after 40–60 years, nuclear waste is dangerous and needs to be stored for thousands of years, and the resource (uranium) will eventually be used up.

Coal

- Coal is the solid remains of ancient organic material.
- Coal is the fuel burned in some steam-producing power plants to turn the turbine in the generator to make electricity.
- Coal is used because it can be easily ground into a fine powder that is combustible. Coal powder is injected into a flame and creates a continuous fire that heats water to steam. The result of burning coal is smoke, which pollutes the air with increased levels of nitrogen, carbon dioxide, sulphur dioxide, and nitrogen oxides.
- Some examples of positives are: coal is cheap to use, a large amount of it is available for use, and it can be use to make other materials such as fertilizers and paints.
- Some examples of negatives are: coal mining can be dangerous, mining is disruptive to the environment, coal creates air and water pollution, and it will eventually be used up.

Natural Gas

- Natural gas is the vapour emitted during the decomposition of ancient organic material. Natural gas is usually found in underground reservoirs or pockets and is primarily made up of methane.

- Natural gas can be used to heat water to steam that rotates turbines or it can be used directly to rotate the turbines. This is done by superheating the gas in pressurized pipes and then using it as a form of wind energy to turn the turbines.
- Some examples of positives are: natural gas produces less air pollution than coal and is also used as a resource for home heating.
- Some examples of negatives are: mining natural gas can be dangerous, mining is disruptive to the environment, the resource is flammable and can explode or cause a fire.

Time

60 min

Skills

- classifying
- inferring
- interpreting
- comparing

Grouping

pairs

Materials and Equipment

(per group)
- notebook
- + and – charts from Lesson 4
- chart paper
- 1 ruler, pencil or pen

Line Masters

- none

Work On It

- Review the + and – charts created during the previous lesson.
- In this lesson, students will continue to learn about the different kinds of electricity generating plants that operate in Canada. The students will create + and – charts for the three non-renewable resources. In Communicate question 1, they will compare the different ways of generating electricity using renewable and non-renewable resources.
- Remind students that they should create a separate chart for each type of energy resource they read about. You may want to draw their attention to the subheadings by writing them on the board: Nuclear Energy, Coal, and Natural Gas.

Think Again! SaskPower and You

- You may want to use the information in this section for a separate lesson specific to the power plants in Saskatchewan. The Ask an Expert profile fits in well with the discussion of locations and creates a connection between the power plant and receiving electricity in the home.
- Go to the SaskPower website. Go to "Power & our environment" to find the Transmission and Distribution electrical system map or refer to this link:
  http://www.saskpower.com/poweringyourfuture/today/transmission.shtml
  Photocopy the map for students and ask them questions that they will need the map to answer. For example, *Where are most of the wind turbine sites located in Saskatchewan? Which power plant is located the farthest north in Saskatchewan? How many transmission lines run in and out of Meadow Lake? What kind of power plant is at Shand?*
- In addition to the facilities listed in the table, SaskPower also has cogeneration plants and other expansion projects the students can add to their table.

Communicate

You may want the students to complete these questions in pairs.

1. Students should compare their + and – charts to form their own opinions about power generation. At this point, students should be able to identify some of the common impacts (positive and negative) of power generation and give personal reasons for their answers. To further expand on the discussion brought up in this question, refer to the Extension Activity below.
2. To complete this table, students can go to the SaskPower website and click on Power & our environment to find the Power Generation Facilities link or go to: http://www.saskpower.com/poweringyourfuture/today/generation.shtml

   See the completed table below.

Generation method	Facility	Location	Generating capacity
Coal burning	Shand	Estevan	279 MW
	Boundary Dam	Estevan	813 MW
	Poplar River	Coronach	572 MW
Natural gas (peak season only)	Queen Elizabeth	Saskatoon	218 MW
Hydroelectric	Saskatchewan River Systems: Coteau Creek Nipawin System E.B. Campbell	 Elbow Nipawin Nipawin	 186 MW 255 MW 288 MW
	Island Falls	On Manitoba/ Saskatchewan border	101 MW
	Athabasca Water Systems: Waterloo Wellington Charlot	 Uranium City (all)	 8 MW 4.8 MW 10 MW
Wind power	Centennial Wind Power	Swift Current	150 MW
	Cypress	Cypress	11 MW
	SunBridge	Gull Lake	11.2 MW

3. You may want to give students some topics to research, such as years of operation, how many turbines the plant has, whether the plant has any environmental programs or initiatives, whether it has ever been upgraded, or other interesting facts. Students can choose to present their reports using a variety of methods, such as a computer slide presentation, a poster, a model, or an oral report. Student information should expand on what is found in the table.

BUILD ON WHAT YOU KNOW

The first CANDU reactor was built in Douglas Point, Ontario in 1965.

For ESL/ELL

Develop large + and – charts on the board as you read through each section.

For Enrichment

If you live near one of the power generation plants listed above, plan a field trip to the location. Use LM 2-8 Town Meeting Simulation to create a simulated town meeting about energy generation.

Assessment *for* Learning

What to Look For in Student Work	What to Do
Students should be able to identify and form personal opinions about non-renewable energy resources (nuclear, coal, and natural gas).	• Ask students to write a persuasive opinion paragraph that outlines why one of the three non-renewable resources may be used over a renewable resource, or create a poster for a resource.
Students should be able to give examples of power generation facilities in Saskatchewan.	• Orally review the power generation facilities in Saskatchewan using the SaskPower website.

ASK AN EXPERT | Jaclyn Mann: Distribution Engineer at SaskPower

Page 108

- When reading this profile, ask students to draw and label the bottom picture that depicts the path electricity follows to get to a house. You may also want to ask students to draw a map of the area of Saskatchewan for which Jaclyn plans electricity distribution.
- Some questions to ask the students are:

  From reading Jaclyn's profile, can you think of some choices she needed to make in the past in order to be successful in her career? Student answers may vary but may include that she had to move away from home, and that she might not be able to do all the activities outside of work that she wants to.

  Look at the list of the duties that Jaclyn is responsible for. What do you think would happen if Jaclyn did not perform her tasks to the best of her ability? Student answers should be specific to the duties mentioned. For example, if Jaclyn did not properly forecast the electrical load, there may be a power shortage, or if Jaclyn did not read the power quality properly, there might be a power failure or low current levels.

  From the diagram at the bottom of the page, what other jobs do you think may be needed to get electricity to your house? Students could identify jobs repairing, wiring, and monitoring power lines and transformers.
- To see a more detailed transmission diagram, go to the Transmission and Distribution link on the SaskPower website or go to the following link:

  http://www.saskpower.com/poweringyourfuture/today/transmission/generationplant.shtml

6 Light Up the Class

Page 109

Time
1 class period

Key Terms
• current electricity • circuit • electrical energy • source • path • load • transformations • light bulb

Line Masters
• LM 2-9

Indicator Assessment Chart

Indicator	Assessment Opportunities
EL6.2 d. Pose questions related to the physical properties of conductors, insulators, simple circuits, and electromagnets (e.g., "How can we determine if an unknown material is a conductor or an insulator?", "How does a switch work in a simple electric circuit?", "What materials work best to create an electromagnet?").	• Work On It, p. 110
EL6.2 f. Identify appropriate tools, instruments, and materials (e.g., bulbs, batteries, and wires) to use when investigating the properties of conductors, insulators, simple circuits, and electromagnets and use those tools and apparatus in a manner that ensures personal safety and the safety of others.	• Work On It, p. 110
EL6.2 k. Use evidence gathered through research and observation to answer questions related to the physical properties of conductors, insulators, simple circuits, and electromagnets.	• Work On It, p. 110 • Communicate p. 111, q. 3, 4
EL6.3 a. State the required characteristics of a simple electric circuit (e.g., a source of electrical energy, a closed path to conduct electrical energy, and a load to convert the electrical energy into another form of energy).	• Communicate, p. 111, q. 1
EL6.3 b. Compare a variety of electrical pathways by constructing simple circuits.	• Work On It, p. 110
EL6.3 g. Construct simple circuits to demonstrate how electrical energy can be controlled to produce light, heat, sound, motion, and magnetic effects.	• Work On It, p. 110
EL6.3 h. Design, construct, and troubleshoot an electrical circuit that meets one or more student-specific criteria.	• Work On It, p. 110

Background Information

A simple or series circuit contains an energy source, such as a battery, a path, such as wires, and a load that uses electrical energy, such as a light bulb. Electric current flows from the battery through the wire to the light bulb, then back to the battery. In a general sense, this path is what we refer to as electricity. Much of the electrical energy (voltage) is given off by the light bulb as light and heat. Even though students are not expected to understand the details of current and voltage in these circuits, they should be able to design, construct, and describe the components of these circuits. They should also understand that electricity moves through the entire circuit.

It is important to note that the solutions in this book are drawn using standard symbols. In this lesson, students will not know how to draw these symbols because they are addressed in Lesson 8. Please refer to Lesson 8 if you have difficulty reading the diagrams in this lesson.

Get Started ▶

- Ask students to read the Get Started section. Bring out the materials seen on page 109 of the student book to show students.
- Present each item to the class and demonstrate correct handling techniques. Care should be taken not to drop the light bulbs. Batteries should only be connected for a minimal amount of time to conserve their energy. Alligator clips on the ends of wires should only be used to connect electrical devices.
- Explain to the class that they will be using this equipment to solve five electricity problems.

Electricity on the Move

- Review with the class the main concept of static electricity: Static electricity stays in one place and builds up.
- Students should refer to the T-chart about static electricity that they created in Lesson 2. Ask students if there are any items on their T-charts that they are still unsure are examples of static electricity. Some of the responses will likely include turning on a flashlight, turning on the TV, and using batteries.
- Tell students that these examples are forms of current electricity. Compare static electricity and current electricity for the class. Both types of electricity are similar because they both describe energy in the form of electric charge. However, the main difference between them is that static electricity moves when it has built up whereas current electricity always moves unless it is stopped.

- The Work On It activity is the introduction to the concepts needed to complete the design project. When students are creating their device, remind them to refer to this lesson to review the components of a circuit: source, path, and load.

Time

60 min

Skills

- making models
- experimenting
- hypothesizing
- controlling variables
- predicting

Grouping

pairs

Materials and Equipment

(per group)
- 2 light bulbs and light bulb holders
- 6 wires with alligator clips (each wire about 30 cm long)
- 6-V battery
- 1 switch

Line Masters

- none

CAUTION!

Make sure your hands are dry when touching electrical appliances and switches.

Work On It

- Encourage students to explore and design their own solutions rather than look for the "right" answers throughout this activity. It is helpful if students check their results with you after each problem.
- Here is a possible solution to Electro Problem 1:

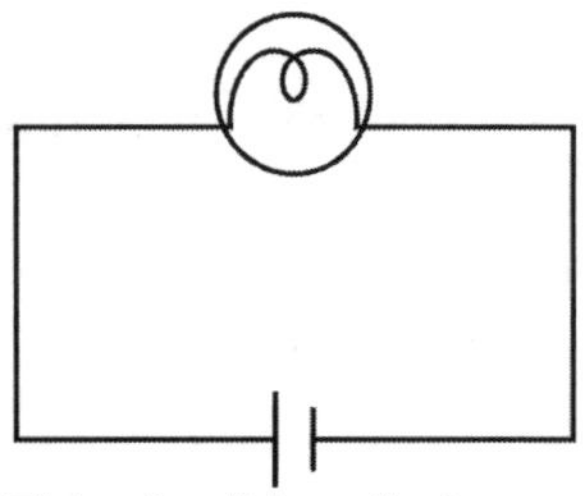

This circuit is called a series circuit. Whatever solution students create, you should be able to trace at least one complete path from one battery terminal to the other.
- You may wish to stop the class at this point and ask, *What is needed to make the light bulb go on?* The responses you receive should include an energy source, wires to allow the electricity to move between the energy source and the light bulb, and a complete circuit or path for the electricity to move in.
- The solution to Electro Problem 2 may look like this:

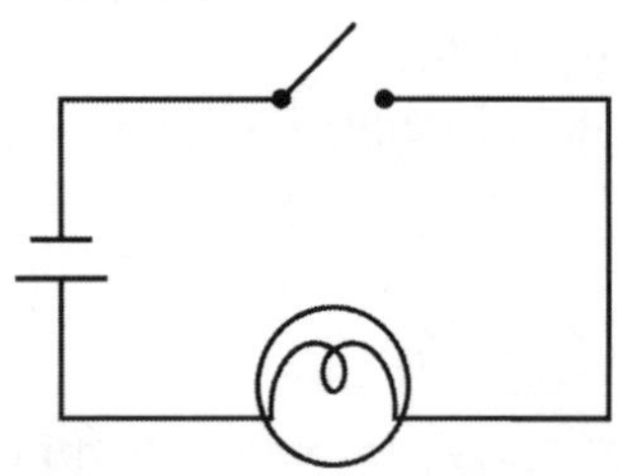

Students' solutions will be similar to Electro Problem 1 except that a switch has been inserted. Students should recognize that a complete path is created when the switch is closed, causing the light bulb to go on.
- A solution to Electro Problem 3 could look like this:

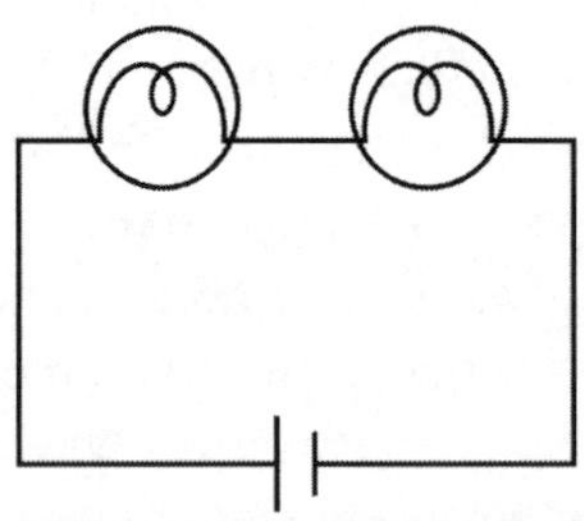

Although there are two light bulbs, this circuit is also a series circuit. Ask students, *What will happen if you unscrew one of the bulbs?* Ask them to test their predictions. Students should observe that a complete path is needed for either light bulb to go on.

- A solution for Electro Problem 4 could look like this:

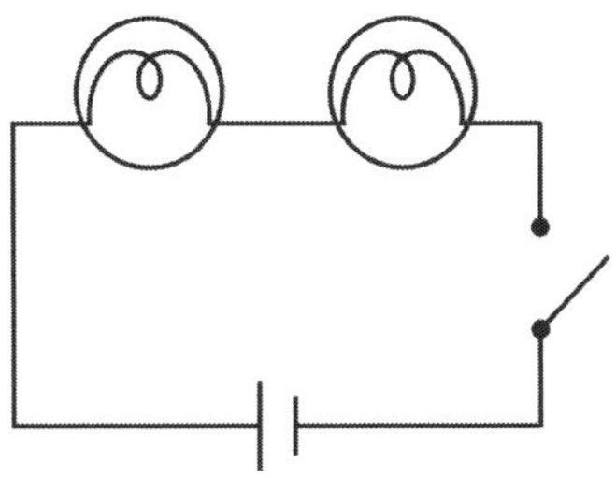

Students should observe that this circuit looks similar to Electro Problem 3 and acts in similar ways when a light bulb is unscrewed. Students should also recognize that a complete path is created only when the switch is closed.

- One possible solution to Electro Problem 5 is:

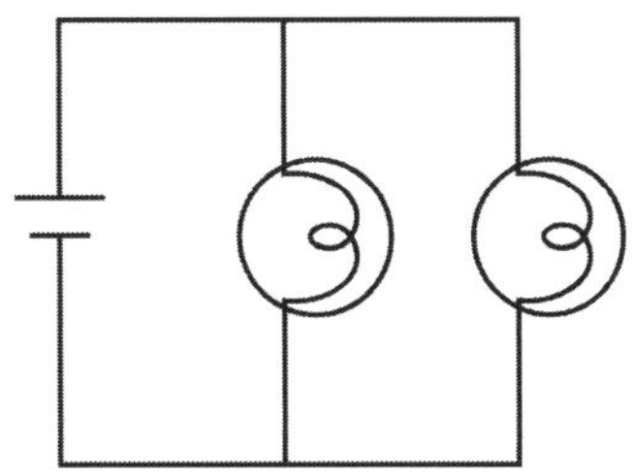

A parallel circuit has two paths in which electricity can flow. Ask students, *What do you predict will happen when one of the light bulbs is unscrewed?* Ask them to test their predictions. Students should observe that whenever either light bulb in a parallel circuit is connected in a complete electrical path, it stays on.

This diagram of a light bulb shows that the light we see is closely linked to the transformation of electricity to heat. Ask the students if they know any other transformations that use electricity.

- To better understand the idea of transformations, students can complete the activity on LM 2-9 Exploring Energy Transformations.

Think Again! Needs and Uses of Electricity

- Have an oral discussion about the first two questions presented in this section (page 110 of the student book). Students should come to the conclusion that a circuit runs in a circle, so electricity follows the path of that circle to make the lights go on.
- Ask students to look back at the illustrations on pages 82 and 83 of the student book. Ask them to talk in pairs or groups about some of the uses of electricity. For example, in the house picture, the electricity is used to turn on the lights, make the hair dryer blow, heat up the food, and play music. These devices all transform electrical energy into another form of energy that is useful. Once students have finished their discussions, finish the reading on page 111 of the student book to identify the five transformations of electrical energy.

Communicate

Students have had an opportunity to investigate the nature of electrical circuits through experimentation. These questions consolidate what they have discovered.

1. The minimum material required is one wire, one light bulb, and a battery. Many students will believe they need two wires and maybe a switch.
2. Students should be able to reclassify the images on student book pages 82 and 83 either independently or as a class according to the transformations mentioned in the Think Again! section (student book page 111). Students may find that many devices have more than one transformation and can have more than one classification.
3. Student answers may vary but should include the notion of electricity flowing from one battery terminal through the circuit and back to the other battery terminal.
4. Left to right, top row:
   (i) The light bulb will not light up because the path is incomplete.
   (ii) The light bulb will not light up because the path is incomplete.
   (iii) The light bulb will light up if the wire on the left is touching the metal part of the light bulb. Otherwise, the bulb will not light.
   (iv) The light bulb will not light up because the wire on the left is not connected to the battery terminal.

Bottom row:
(i) The light bulb will light up because the circuit is complete.
(ii) The light bulb will not light up because the circuit is incomplete.
(iii) The light bulb will not light up because the wire on the right is touching the light bulb holder, which is not a conductor.
(iv) The light bulb will not light up because of incorrect connections between the battery and the light bulb.

After completing this activity, ask students to reflect on the problems they worked on and answer the following questions:

- Which Electro Problem did you find the easiest? Describe how you solved it.
- Which Electro Problem did you find the most difficult? Describe how you solved it.
- What is one thing you have learned about electrical circuits that you didn't know before?

BUILD ON WHAT YOU KNOW

Thomas Edison invented the light bulb in 1879.

For ESL/ELL

ESL students may benefit from having items such as wires, batteries, and switches labelled. Also, students may need to create and use labelled diagrams to demonstrate what they observed and discovered.

For Enrichment

Students can research how a CFL light bulb illuminates and compare it to the light bulb model shown on page 111 of the student book.

Assessment *for* Learning

What to Look For in Student Work	What to Do
At the end of the activity, students will be able to construct a simple circuit, identify a working simple circuit, and describe what is needed for a light bulb to go on. Students should be able to identify the five energy transformations and give examples of each.	• Ask students to draw diagrams of the circuits they created so they are able to trace the connections with their fingers. • Choose another picture in which the students can identify an energy transformation or assign LM 2-9 Exploring Energy Transformations.

7 Go with the Flow

Page 112

Time
1 class period

Key Terms
• light-emitting diode (LED) • conductors • electricity • insulators

Line Masters
• LM 2-10

Indicator Assessment Chart

Indicator	Assessment Opportunities
EL6.2 e. Make predictions, based on observed patterns of events, related to the physical properties of conductors, insulators, simple circuits, and electromagnets and conduct investigations to test those predictions.	• Work On It, p. 112 • Communicate, p. 114, q. 1, 2
EL6.2 f. Identify appropriate tools, instruments, and materials (e.g., bulbs, batteries, and wires) to use when investigating the properties of conductors, insulators, simple circuits, and electromagnets and use those tools and apparatus in a manner that ensures personal safety and the safety of others.	• Communicate, p. 114, q. 1, 2
EL6.2 g. Test the conductivity of a variety of solids and liquids, following a given set of procedures, to identify which materials are conductors and which are insulators, and draw conclusions about the types of materials that work best as conductors and those that work best as insulators.	• Work On It, p. 112 • Communicate, p. 114, q. 1, 2

Background Information

The terms "conductor" and "insulator" are used to describe materials through which energy moves easily (conductors), or less easily or not at all (insulators). Students will know from experience that certain materials support the movement of sound and heat energy, and other materials prevent this movement. For example, a metal pot handle heats up along with the pot but a plastic handle will not. Similarly, there are materials that do the same for electrical energy. These materials can be in any state of matter (solid, liquid, or gas), but solids are commonly used because they are easiest to manipulate.

Get Started ▶

- Read the section and time the students for one minute as they write down as many electrical devices as they can think of.
- Ask students to form groups to compare their lists and find out what common materials are used to make these devices.

- Without discussion, ask students to write a prediction in their notebooks as to why they think certain materials are used in electrical devices. This prediction will be discussed after the investigation in the Work On It section.

A light-emitting diode (LED) is an alternative light source used when there is a lower amount of electric current available. LEDs can be found in many electrical devices, such as alarm clocks, hand-held games, display signs, and interior car lights. LEDs have advantages over regular light bulbs because they do not have a filament so they do not get hot, they have durable outer shells, and they can fit into small spaces.

When working with the LEDs in this lesson, be aware that LEDs will only light up if they are connected properly. The shorter wire (cathode) is the "–" connector and the longer wire (anode) is the "+" connector to the battery.

Time

60 min

Skills

- classifying
- making models
- inferring
- observing
- experimenting
- hypothesizing
- comparing
- controlling variables
- predicting

Grouping

groups

Materials and Equipment

(per group)
- 1 metal spoon
- 1 piece of wood
- 1 quarter
- 1 pen
- 6-V battery or D-cells
- 1 glass of water (distilled if possible)
- 1 glass of salt water
- 1 LED
- 3 wires with alligator clips (each wire about 30 cm long)

Line Masters

- LM 2-10

CAUTION!
Make sure your hands are dry when touching electrical appliances and switches.

Work On It

- Students can use LM 2-10 Go with the Flow to write up their experiment using the scientific method.
- When students have constructed their electrical tester (step 2), make sure that they test it by touching the two free ends of the alligator clips together before moving on to step 3. The LED should light up.
- In step 3, students are expected to prepare a table and make predictions. You may wish to prompt responses by asking questions like, *What materials have you seen used in electrical devices?* (Answer: Wires or metals.) *Do you know any materials that can protect you from electricity?* (Answer: Rubber and plastic.) Encourage students to write down their predictions after they have thought about these questions.
- Allow students to continue the experiment by testing the materials listed. Their tests will show that the spoon, the quarter, and the glass of salt water will cause the LED to light up, whereas the wood and the pen will not cause the LED to light up. The glass of water may or may not cause the LED to light up, depending on how many impurities are in it. A glass of distilled water will not cause the LED to light up, but if the water has enough minerals or other impurities in it, the LED will light up.
- When the students are choosing their own materials to test, they should look for materials that have similar characteristics as the materials already tested, which cause the LED to light up or not light up.

If Time Allows

Ensure that students choose an object that they have already tested that caused the LED to light up. Students should find that increasing the distance between the two wires in the material should decrease the brightness of the LED depending on how conductive the material is.

Like the electric eel, there are other animals that take advantage of living in an environment that is a conductor. Fish such as the electric ray and the electric catfish use electricity like the electric eel to hunt prey, repel enemies, and navigate. Some species of sharks, like the hammerhead, cannot emit electricity, but can feel the weak electrical impulses of other fishes' muscular movements. This sense is called electroreception. Other species that have this sense are the platypus, the echidna, and some species of salamanders.

Think Again! Conductors and Insulators

- At the atomic level, a material that is used for conducting electricity will have loosely bound electrons in the outermost orbits of its atoms. These electrons can move freely and are repelled by other free-moving electrons. When a like electric charge is introduced, it creates a domino effect by repelling the electrons closest to it, thereby generating a current. An insulator works in the opposite way. Electrons in an insulator are bound tightly in the atom, so they will not allow an electrical charge to flow.
- Most common conductors are made out of metallic materials. Elements such as copper, gold, silver, and aluminum are commonly used as electrical conductors. Some non-metallic conductors are salt water, plasma, and graphite. Common materials such as glass, rubber, plastic, ceramics, and pure water are insulators.

Communicate

1. A conductor is any material that allows electrons to flow through it. Examples of conductors are salt water and most metals, such as copper and aluminum. An insulator is anything that prevents or reduces the flow of electricity. Good insulators are rubber, plastic, wood, glass, and ceramics.
2. The Venn diagram should resemble the following but may vary according to student experience.

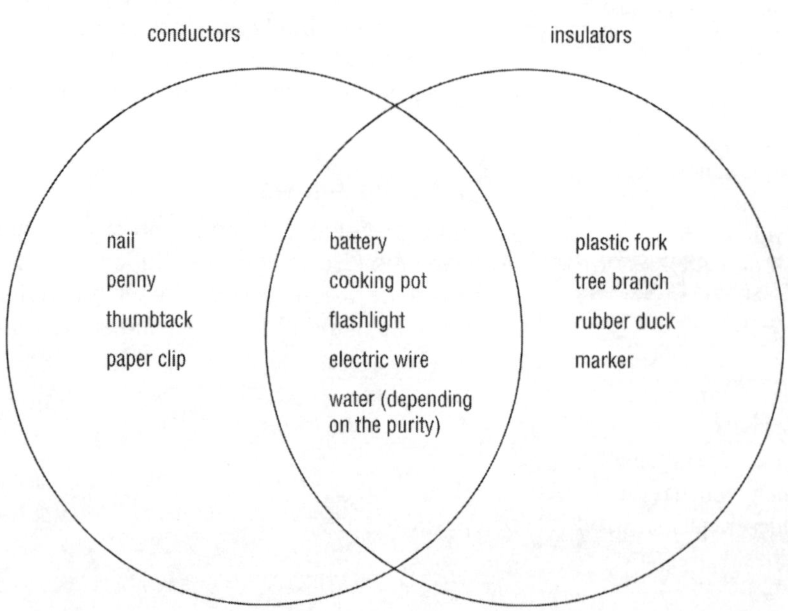

3. Since impure water is a conductor, it can transfer electricity from the lightning to the person in the water. Therefore, it is not safe to be in a lake when there is a thunderstorm.
4. Answers may vary, but students should show use of the vocabulary introduced in this lesson. One possible answer could be, *Humans are conductors of electricity, so we are at risk of electric shock. Insulators help people stay safe because they minimize or block electricity from entering a human so we can use electricity safely.*

For ESL/ELL

Have cards or sticky-notes that are labelled "conductor" and "insulator." When the students have completed their tables in the Work On It activity, ask them go back and place labels on the proper items to support vocabulary development.

For Reteaching

Set up a station with a pre-made electrical tester. Choose any number of objects that are both conductors and insulators for testing. Ask students who need additional support to go to the station independently and attempt to classify the objects according to their observations using the tester.

Assessment *for* Learning

What to Look For in Student Work	What to Do
Students should be able to predict and identify the physical properties of conductors and insulators and identify common materials used for both.	• Remove the batteries from a flashlight and ask the student to dismantle the flashlight as much as possible without breaking it. Ask the student to identify the conductors and insulators in the flashlight and explain how each part helps make the flashlight work.

8 Key Features of Electrical Circuits

Page 115

Time

1 class period

Key Terms

- wire
- primary cell
- secondary cell
- switch
- fuse

Line Masters

- LM 2-11
- LM 2-12

Indicator Assessment Chart

Indicator	Assessment Opportunities
EL6.2 f. Identify appropriate tools, instruments, and materials (e.g., bulbs, batteries, and wires) to use when investigating the properties of conductors, insulators, simple circuits, and electromagnets and use those tools and apparatus in a manner that ensures personal safety and the safety of others.	• Work On It, p. 118 • Communicate, p. 119, q. 2
EL6.2 h. Explain the role of switches in electrical circuits.	• Communicate, p. 119, q. 3
EL6.3 c. Contrast a closed circuit, open circuit, and short circuit.	• Work On It, p. 118
EL6.3 f. Draw electrical circuit diagrams to represent simple series and parallel circuits using appropriate symbols (e.g., battery, conductor, light bulb, motor, switch).	• Work On It, p. 118 • Communicate, p. 119, q. 2

Background Information

Electric circuits are usually presented in technical diagrams using standard symbols. Students are not expected to draw perfect diagrams, but they should be able to use the correct symbols when drawing a circuit. One area of confusion for students may be the use of wires. The correct way to draw wires in electric circuits is to use straight lines with right angles.

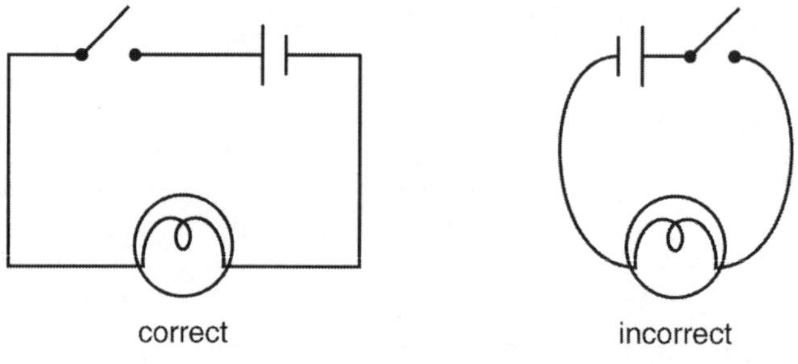

Get Started ▶

- The students should look back at their Electro Problem drawings in Lesson 6. Ask the class to look at each others' Electro Problem drawings. Ask the students, Do you notice any differences in each other's drawings? If you were given only the drawing of your neighbour's circuit, could you recreate it? As students are looking at other drawings, they should notice that there are differences in the symbols used and some drawings may be easier to read than others.
- Ask the class to read Get Started, or read it aloud to the class. Ask students, *Can you think of anything you have learned about electrical circuits that could be confusing?* Students may answer that they are uncertain whether "light" means a light bulb or an LED. Another example you might suggest is whether a switch is in the on or off position.
- Divide the class into pairs or groups. Give each pair a large piece of chart paper to use as their "electrical placemat." This mat will provide a place for students to record what they learn about electrical symbols. Encourage students to include additional information not in the lesson, to use colour, and to make connections between the symbols as they gain a better understanding of them.

What's in a Circuit?

- The students should read the section and record any new terms or symbols onto their placemats.
- Remind students that when they finish their mats, they will be completing the questions in the Work On It section with another pair of students. They should then be prepared to discuss their work with the other pair joining them and as a class.
- *After the students are finished the reading, you may want to provide them with some of the extra information given below.*

Conducting Material: The Path

- Any conductor can provide a path for electricity. This is why there are safety regulations on many electrical devices because the electricity will flow in any path found to complete the circuit. Humans have harnessed this idea by creating wires that are usually highly conductive metals insulated by plastic.

(!) The phrase "short circuit" is commonly used to describe any electrical malfunction. However, the term actually means that there is a shorter path for the electricity to follow. This can happen if the wire insulation is frayed or removed and the wires touch, or if a tree branch falls on a power line. Both of these examples give the electric current another path to follow that is shorter than the path that the current should be on.

Electrical Device: The Load

- The load is the converter device that changes electricity into a form of energy that we can use. Many electrical devices make more than one energy transformation of electrical energy to heat, light, sound, motion, or magnetism to perform their tasks. For example, an alarm clock has loads for both light and sound, whereas a remote control toy such as a car would probably have a load device for motion and for light.
- For most of the activities in the student book, students will be using the symbol for light. However, it is important for students to know that electricity can power more than just lights. Encourage students to use all the loads presented in the student book in their circuit diagrams.
- The motor and electromagnet devices will be better explained in Lessons 12 and 13.

Energy Source

- The symbol used for the energy source will be the same even if the circuit is using a wall outlet and not a battery, but it is important that students realize that there are two different types of energy sources.
- You may want to refer to Lessons 3 and 4 on electrical generation facilities to remind students that these facilities are their power source whenever they plug something into a wall outlet.
- To learn more about batteries, consider completing LM 2-11 Lemon Battery.

Switch or Control

- The symbol used for a switch is the same even if the switch being described is a specific type of switch. For most activities in this unit, the switch is a toggle switch, but it will depend on the materials you have available. Switches are described as either being closed, meaning that the circuit is complete and electricity is flowing, or open, meaning that the circuit is incomplete and there is no current.
- Toggle, rocker, slide, and popper switches all work by connecting two metal pieces. When the switch is off, the two metal pieces are disconnected.
- A reed switch works with magnetic fields to open and close the circuit. When a magnet comes close to a metal switch, it closes the circuit and electricity can flow. When the magnet is removed, the circuit opens and the flow of electricity stops. This type of switch is found in burglar alarms, flip phones, and toy sound effects.
- A tilt switch can be found in a thermostat. As the temperature drops, the bimetallic strip bends and moves the switch in one direction. Then the mercury rolls toward the switch and connects the two wires. The thermostat turns on the furnace. As the room heats up, the bimetallic strip moves the other way. The mercury rolls back and disconnects the wires. The furnace turns off.

- A photoelectric cell switch has a conducting material that can sense a change in light and radiation. This type of switch can be seen in automatic doors that open when people block the light source or in alarms that work when lights are turned on or off.
- To further learn about switches, consider completing the For Enrichment activities below.

Putting It All Together

- Circuit diagrams are professionally used for engineering and electrical work. Therefore, it is important to have diagrams that are clear, neat, and easy to understand and read. Stress to your students that their diagrams should always be drawn like the diagram on student book page 118, with straight lines and right angles.

(!) A fuse is a safety mechanism used in most electrical devices, specifically in those that have high voltage levels. Fuses are designed to allow a specific amount of electricity to pass through them. If the electric current is in excess of this amount, then the fuse will break the circuit and stop the flow of electricity. Most electrical devices have regulations about what type of fuse is needed to prevent the device from overheating. Common locations of fuses are cars, home fuse boxes (there fuses work on a switch so they don't need replacing), and electricity poles to stop a power surge from entering your house.

Time

30 min

Skills

- inferring
- interpreting
- comparing

Grouping

groups

Materials and Equipment

(per group)
- 2 light bulbs
- 2 light bulb holders
- 6 wires with alligator clips (each wire about 30 cm long)
- 6-V battery
- 1 switch
- paper and pencil

Line Masters

- none

CAUTION!

Make sure your hands are dry when touching electrical appliances and switches.

Work On It

- Place your original pairs into groups of four and let them work together to complete the Work On It questions.
- During the group discussion for step 1, ask students to come up to the board and write the confusing terms down. This will prepare you for question 1 in the Communicate section, and give you a good method to survey the class for overall understanding.
- Ask students to continue with steps 2 and 3 by looking at their solutions for the Electro Problems from Lesson 6 and referring to student book pages 109–111. Encourage students to try to draw their circuits individually, then come together as a group to compare their answers. The actual circuit diagrams for these are back in Lesson 6 of this teacher's resource, pages 206 and 207.
- Before the students complete Communicate question 2, correct their circuit diagrams for the Electro Problems.
- Students can explore the idea of batteries through LM 2-11 Lemon Battery. Follow the tips below to help make the experiment successful.

Electrical Lemon Battery

- This experiment is very sensitive to the particular materials used, and should be tested ahead of time.
- Use pre-1981 nickels and pre-1996 pennies. Nickels made after 1981 contain 75 % copper. Pennies made after 1996 are made of zinc and copper. Alternatively, substitute copper wire and steel wire, or zinc and copper metal strips.

continued →

- The amount of membrane and the thickness of the lemon skin can also affect results. Rolling the lemon on a table beforehand will break membranes and make the juice more accessible. Cut through the skin with a knife before inserting the two metals, and ensure they are both in contact with the lemon juice.
- Lemon batteries will produce a current of 50–1500 mA. Use only a low-current, low-voltage LED. The glow of the bulb is unlikely to be visible in room light, so turn off the overhead lights. Alternatively, the LED may be replaced with a voltmeter in order to demonstrate the current in room light.
- You may choose to increase the current generated by connecting two or three lemons in a series circuit. The current from two lemons in which zinc and copper strips are inserted will reliably light a low-current LED. This form of lemon battery is best set up as a demonstration, and is most convincing in a darkened room.

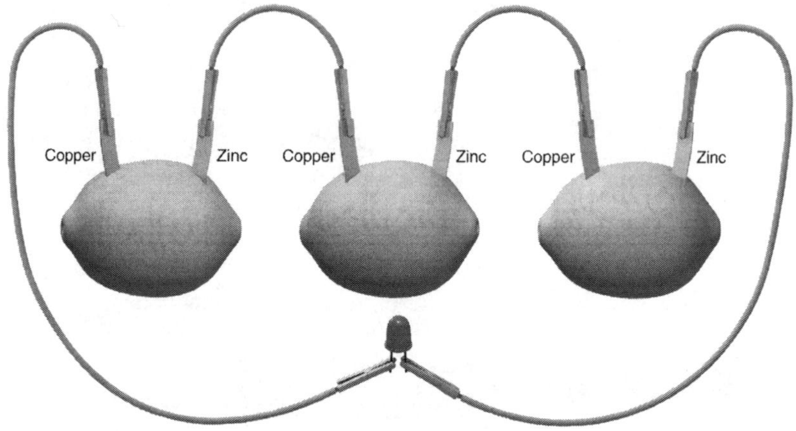

- The energy transformation in this activity is from chemical energy (from the food) into light energy (in the LED bulb).

Communicate

Students should be developing an understanding of the various symbols and types of electrical devices they may encounter in their investigations. Any problems should be listed on the board and a discussion of question 1 should assist in clarifying any misconceptions.

1. Answers may vary, but students should demonstrate their understanding of at least the bolded words and electrical symbols used in this lesson.
2. a.

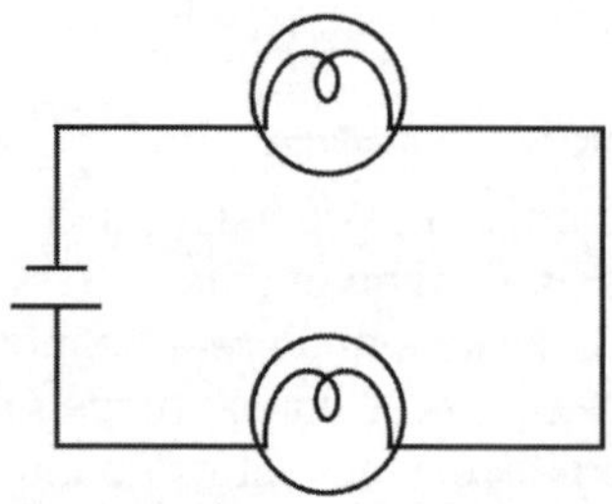

b.

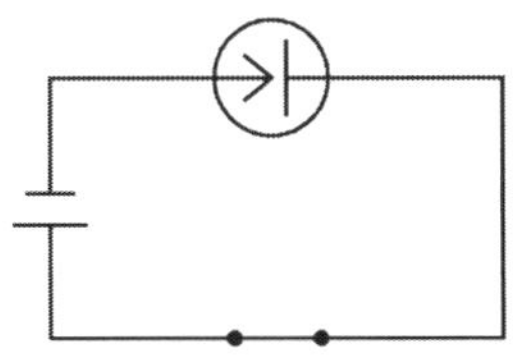

c.

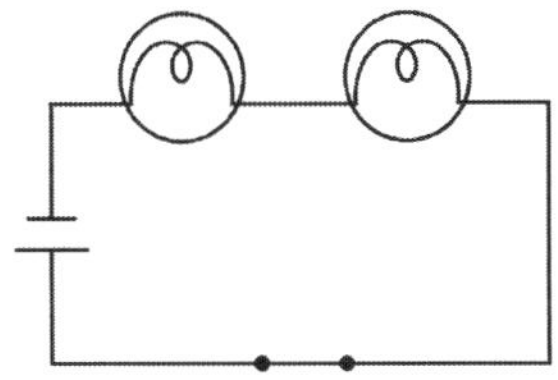

d.

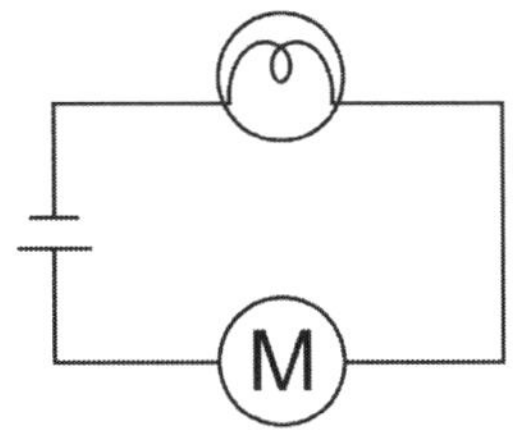

e.

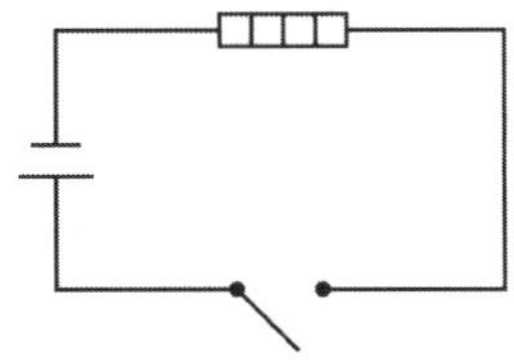

f.

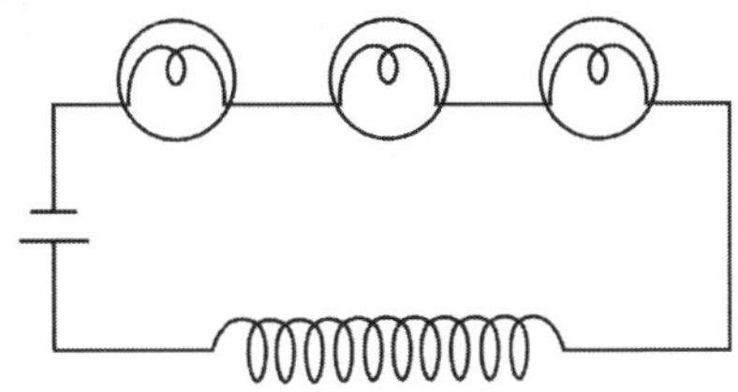

g.

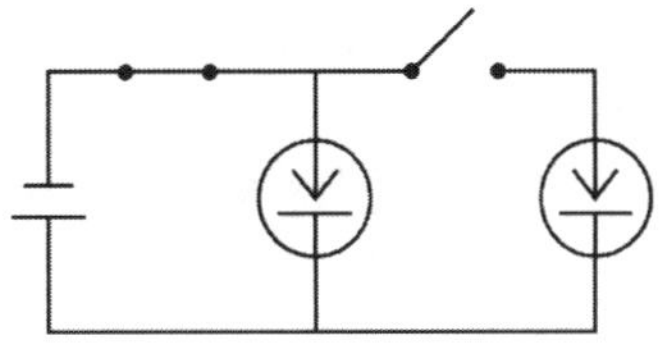

3. The design for the device should use a reed-type switch to turn on the security light. The device should act like a security device and not require someone to turn it off and on. After students complete question 3, ask them to describe different types of switches they could use in the security light and how each switch would change the function of the device.

Design Challenge

When students are creating their design projects, they will need to refer to the symbols in this lesson in order to draw their designs. Encourage the students to keep their placemats for future reference.

For ESL/ELL

Some ESL students may benefit from labelling the terms or symbols that are new to them, in their first language as well as in English, on their placemats. The concepts may come more easily when there are fewer new terms to learn.

For Communicate question 2, some ESL students may be given a reduced number of circuits to draw because it may take them longer to link terminology with the symbols.

For Reteaching

Students having trouble with the symbols of electrical circuits can complete LM 2-12 Picture That Circuit.

For Enrichment

Students can explore different switches by going on a switch scavenger hunt where they need to find an example of each switch mentioned on student book page 117. Alternatively, give them a piece of cardboard, two thumbtacks, and a paper clip and tell them to use the materials to make their own working switch.

Assessment *for* Learning

What to Look For in Student Work	What to Do
Students should be able to draw a diagram of a simple circuit using correct symbols. They should also be able to identify specific electrical instruments and use the appropriate vocabulary (i.e., a circuit uses wires, a battery is an energy source, and a light is a load). Students should also be able to identify a switch in a circuit and understand that a switch stops or starts current in a circuit.	• If a student is having difficulty, take one or more of the circuits described in Communicate question 2 and ask the student to first build the circuit using equipment, then review the symbols for drawing the circuit. • Consider assigning one of the For Enrichment activities described above.

9 Different Needs, Different Circuits

Page 120

Time

1 class period

Key Terms

- series circuit
- parallel circuit

Line Masters

- LM 2-13

Indicator Assessment Chart

Indicator	Assessment Opportunities
EL6.3 e. Construct and test various combinations of simple electric circuits to determine similarities and differences between series and parallel circuits.	• Work On It, p. 120
EL6.3 f. Draw electrical circuit diagrams to represent simple series and parallel circuits using appropriate symbols (e.g., battery, conductor, light bulb, motor, switch).	• Work On It, p. 120
EL6.3 g. Construct simple circuits to demonstrate how electrical energy can be controlled to produce light, heat, sound, motion, and magnetic effects.	• Work On It, p. 120

Background Information

All circuits studied will be series or parallel circuits or a combination of the two. A series circuit has one loop that can be traced from one battery terminal through the wires and light(s) to the other battery terminal. A parallel circuit has a branch somewhere in the circuit. If you were to trace the circuit, you would find you have a choice between two different paths. These paths would eventually re-connect after you passed the light bulb. The advantage of the parallel circuit is one light bulb will stay on if the other is removed or burns out.

Get Started ▶

- Divide the class into small groups and ask them to read Get Started.
- On the board, write, *What things are required to make an electrical circuit?* Direct the class to discuss this question in their groups, and come up with a list of answers.
- When they have finished, ask one member from each group to present the group's ideas. Students should come up with the answers "an energy source (battery), a path (wires), a load (light bulb), and a circuit or complete path."

Time
60 min

Skills
• making models • observing • interpreting • experimenting • hypothesizing • comparing

Grouping
pairs

Materials and Equipment
(per pair) • 2 light bulbs in light bulb holders • 6 wires with alligator clips (each wire about 30 cm long) • 6-V battery

Line Masters
• none

CAUTION!

Although the electricity from a battery should not be dangerous, remind students to handle all equipment carefully and to work in a dry area.

When students are working to create a parallel circuit, ensure that the battery is not connected until you have checked their work, to avoid electrical shock.

Work On It

Series Circuit

- Students should be able to easily set up this type of circuit at this stage in the unit. However, this may be the first time they will use the proper vocabulary: series circuit.
- At step 4, their model should look similar to the image on student book page 120. The circuit diagram should look like the following.

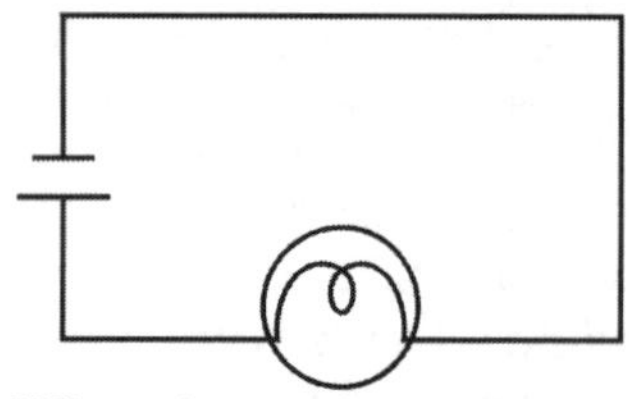

- When the students disconnect the wires, they should notice that the light turns off.
- To add a second bulb to the circuit, students must use an additional wire. Ask them, *Can you still trace a path back to the start with this circuit?* Once students have successfully completed their circuits, ask if they notice any difference in the brightness of the bulbs in this circuit compared to the circuit with only one bulb.
- At step 7, their model should look similar to the top image on student book page 121. Students should notice that both light bulbs turn on. The circuit diagram should look like the following.

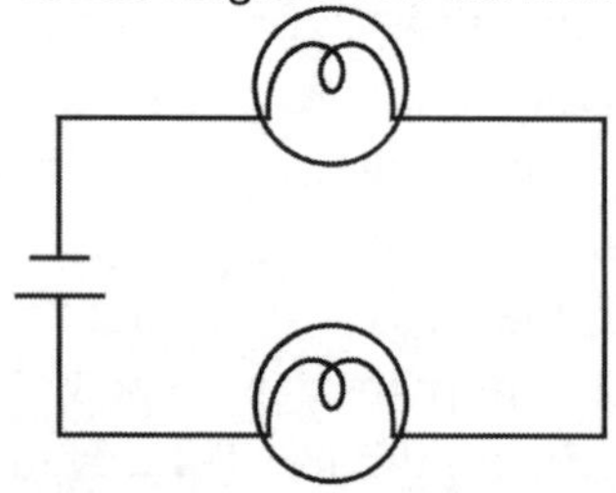

- When the students unscrew one light bulb, they should notice that the other one turns off as well. Some students may conclude that the light bulb was part of the circuit and when it was unscrewed, the circuit was broken and the electricity stopped flowing. For students who did not grasp this concept right away, it is readdressed in the Think Again! and Communicate sections.

Parallel Circuit

- Students who found a solution to Electro Problem 5 on student book page 110 may recognize a parallel circuit.
- Step 2 is very important. If they do not make a good connection, students will have difficulty getting the circuit to work. Remind students to check their connections carefully by comparing them to the image of the three-way connection on student book page 121 before proceeding.
- By the end of step 4, the circuit should look like the illustration at the top of the next page.

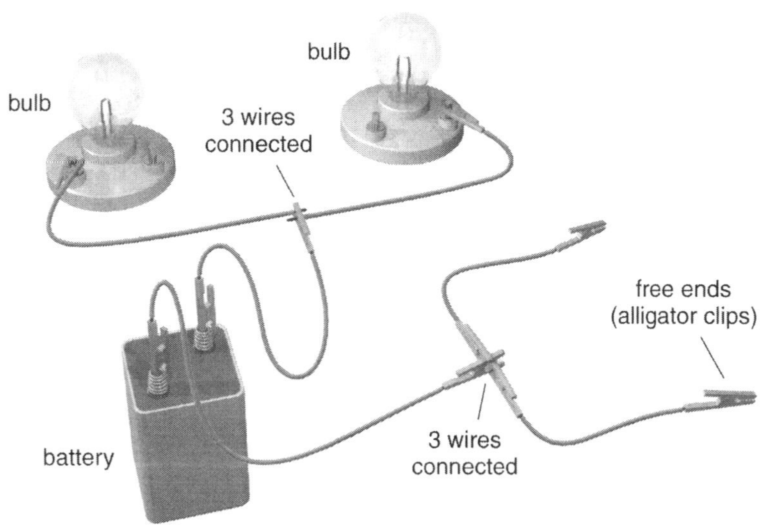

- At step 5, their model should look similar to the bottom image on student book page 121. Students should be able to trace two complete loops. If both lights do not turn on, the circuit may have a loose connection or it has not been set up properly, so students may need to start this procedure over again. The circuit diagram should look like the following.

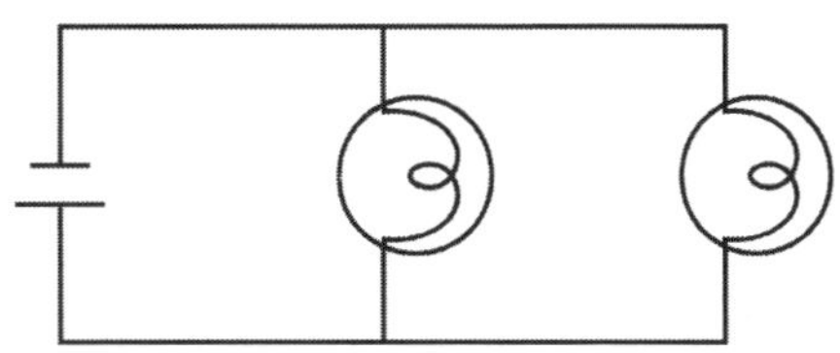

- Students will find that the second bulb stays on when one bulb is unhooked. This is because the electricity still has one complete path to flow on. Some students may also notice that the brightness of the remaining bulb stays the same.
- Review work done on circuits to date by having a Jeopardy-style review. The table below suggests some answers to give students and potential questions they might ask.

Answer	**Question**
rubber	What is an insulator?
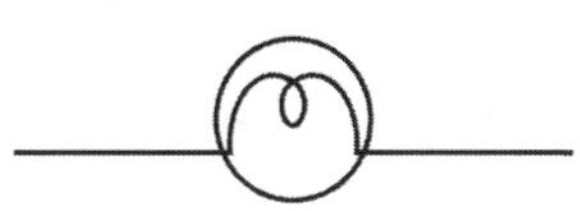	What is the symbol for a light bulb?
wind energy	What is an example of renewable energy?
circle	What type of path must a circuit follow?
toggle	What is one kind of switch?
invented the light bulb	Who is Thomas Edison?

Think Again! Making Connections

- As you read this section, bring up visual examples in class. Ask students to identify the circuits in the school. Examples of parallel circuits include lights in the classroom, computers, and electric carts. The stereo, the fan, and any hand-held battery-operated equipment are all examples of series circuits.

If Time Allows

This section is useful for those students who noticed that there was a difference in the brightness of the bulbs when the number of bulbs in the circuit was altered. When more loads are added to a series circuit, the resistance increases because the same amount of current is shared by more that one load. Since parallel circuits have more than one path, there is less resistance so the lights burn equally brightly even when there are more loads. Houses run on parallel circuits for this reason—so that all the different electrical devices can function at the same time and receive the same amount of electricity.

Communicate

These questions can be discussed as a class or in small groups. Encourage students to use the appropriate vocabulary in their answers. In Communicate question 3, students will be making a list of other loads that can use these circuits. Encourage students to refer to this list when they are brainstorming ideas for their Design Projects.

1. When one bulb was unhooked in the series circuit, there was no longer a complete path for the electricity. When one bulb was unhooked in the parallel circuit, there was still a complete path between the battery and the second light bulb.
2. The two types of circuits require the same equipment (battery, wires, bulbs), involve the same energy transformations, and require a complete path for the bulb to light. In a series circuit, removing one bulb causes the other bulb to go out. In contrast, you can remove one light bulb in a parallel circuit and the other bulb stays on. Two bulbs connected in a series circuit shine less brightly than two bulbs connected in a parallel circuit.
3. Answers may vary but can include a fan, a motor, a heater, a TV, a doorbell, or any other device that makes one of the five energy transformations.
4. Encourage students to think about devices in which it is useful to have all the electrical parts on at once. Suggestions may include electric motors, appliances, electric toys, or heating units.
5. Parallel circuits are useful in devices that have more than one load and in which it is useful to know when one particular load is not working. Students might suggest outdoor lights, lights in a marquee sign, or the fluorescent light fixtures in buildings such as schools.

For Enrichment

Have materials available to students for constructing a simple alarm system. You may wish to put together small kits containing wires, batteries, and switches. Then assign LM 2-13 Design Challenge: Design an Alarm System. Encourage students to think about the differences between parallel and series circuits. You may wish to supply bulbs or buzzers to substitute for the radio.

Assessment *for* Learning

What to Look For in Student Work	What to Do
Students should be able to identify, construct, and compare series and parallel circuits. Students should be able to draw circuit diagrams from a model using the appropriate symbols and terminology. Students should be able to identify common uses of circuits and expand beyond devices that produce light to devices that produce heat, sound, and motion.	• Ask students to work backwards by drawing a circuit diagram using correct symbols and then choosing the correct materials to create the circuits they drew. Students could also use this approach as a mini-test with each other if several students are having difficulty with this lesson.

10 Fixing Electrical Problems

Page 123

Time
1 class period
Key Terms
• troubleshooting
Line Masters
• LM 2-14

Indicator Assessment Chart

Indicator	Assessment Opportunities
EL6.2 e. Make predictions, based on observed patterns of events, related to the physical properties of conductors, insulators, simple circuits, and electromagnets and conduct investigations to test those predictions.	• Work On It, p. 124 • Communicate, p. 126
EL6.2 l. Describe the operation of common technologies based on properties of static electricity, current electricity, or electromagnetism.	• Work On It, p. 124 • Communicate, p. 126
EL6.3 d. Propose questions to investigate, and practical problems to solve, related to simple series and parallel circuits (e.g., "What happens when a light bulb is removed from a series or parallel circuit?", "How can I create a simple circuit using only a battery, light bulb, and one wire?", "How are light circuits in a house wired?").	• Work On It, p. 124 • Communicate, p. 126

Background Information

One of the processes required for any activity related to designing electrical circuits is troubleshooting. This process is used to solve problems that occur when something is not designed correctly or breaks down, and when someone is not exactly sure what is wrong. A car mechanic troubleshoots when he or she listens to the description of your car's problem and the sounds the car makes before attempting to work on it. Troubleshooting usually involves following a systematic procedure that eliminates a variety of possible problems. Usually, but not always, the most obvious problems are eliminated first. For example, if you phone a computer help line, the help desk person usually makes sure your computer is plugged in and the screen is turned on. Even though these steps may seem simple, many problems can be attributed to missing the obvious.

Get Started ▶

- Ask students to think of a time when they or a family member had a problem that the student solved. Encourage students to use examples in which something that was not working had to be fixed. You may wish to ask students to work in pairs, and ask each student to describe a situation to a partner.
- Ask two or three students to describe their own or their classmate's experience to the class. Potential scenarios: being locked out of the house and climbing through a window, or the chain coming off a bicycle.
- Focus the discussion on examples where troubleshooting was used to solve the problem. Introduce the word "troubleshooting," then direct students to read Get Started.

Problem Solver

- Read the Problem Solver section, then bring out a pre-made electrical device that is not working. Some suggestions are to bring a series circuit with one light bulb slightly unscrewed or a parallel circuit with wires not connected properly, or use the first sample problem on student book page 124.
- Use your electrical device to demonstrate the method of going through each question in order on the troubleshooting guide on page 123 of the student book. After each question, ask, *How can I check if that is the problem?* For example, the first question asks if the wires are connected to the battery. When you ask how to check that, your students should respond by telling you to check the wire connection to the battery and possibly reconnect the wires.
- Go through each question in the guide until the students have found the correct answer. If students begin to guess other solutions out of order, emphasize that it is important to follow all the steps in sequence when troubleshooting a problem.

Time

60 min

Skills

- classifying
- inferring
- interpreting
- comparing
- communicating
- predicting

Grouping

individuals and groups

Materials and Equipment

(per individual)
- notebook
- pen or pencil

Line Masters

- none

Work On It

- If the answer to the question in the Question column in the troubleshooting guide is Yes, the Response column should explain what to do to check and fix the problem. Answers for the troubleshooting guide should look similar to the ones in the table on the next page.
- Remind students that their troubleshooting guide will help them prevent any electrical problems when creating their Design Projects. They should be reminded to refer to the table they created in this section.

Question	Response
1. Are the wires to the battery connected?	Check connections to the battery. Reconnect if necessary.
2. If there is a switch, is it on?	Check if the switch is on or stuck. Turn the switch on, off, and on.
3. Are all the connections in the circuit attached properly?	Check all connections in the circuit. Reconnect if necessary. Check to see if anything is blocking part of the circuit.
4. If the circuit is a series circuit, is there only one complete loop?	Trace a path from one battery terminal, through the circuit, and back to the other battery terminal. If one full loop is not possible, rebuild the circuit.
5. If the series is a parallel circuit, do any of the wires start and end at the same place?	Ensure none of the wires start and end at the same place. Rebuild the circuit if some wires are not properly attached.
6. Does the electrical device (like a light bulb) work?	Remove the electrical device and replace it with another electrical device that you know works. If the second device doesn't work, the problem is not the device. Recheck your answers for questions 1 to 5.

- Students can work either in groups or individually to solve the problems. The answers are not as important as the process of looking for a solution. Remind the class to follow each step in the troubleshooting guide in order. Students should be able to identify the step in the troubleshooting process that solves each problem. The answers to the problems are on the next page.

Problem	Solution	Troubleshooting Step
1	Battery poles are reversed.	1
2	The switch is open.	2
3	The switch is not connected properly.	3
4	The wire is not connected to the battery.	1
5	The speaker is wired incorrectly. The circuit is incomplete.	5
6	The wires are connected incorrectly on the third bulb.	5
7	The switch is in the off position.	2

- You may choose to bring in troubleshooting guides for various appliances in your house. Students can use these samples to complete their troubleshooting guides.

Communicate

Students have an opportunity to use their troubleshooting skills in this contextualized problem. You may wish to divide the class into small groups. Ensure that any students with language challenges work with students with stronger writing skills. To answer the question, students are given a diagram of the lamp that has no problems in it. Students should work backwards to assess a possible problem using their troubleshooting guide and relay three of these possibilities to the customer in letter format. Some possible solutions may be: the wires are not properly connected to the battery, the switch is blocked or off, there is a break in the circuit, or the light bulb has burned out. Students should be able to identify a problem and provide a solution on how to fix it.

BUILD ON WHAT YOU KNOW

The first illuminated glass sign was invented by John B. Studley of Nova Scotia in 1858. Gas burners were placed behind the glass sign rather than electric light bulbs. Add Studley to the Electric Timeline.

For ESL/ELL

This lesson may be a good time to review interrogative sentences because questions can be a challenge for ESL students. ESL students may benefit from a review of interrogative sentences without using Who, What, Where, When, Why, and How? Show students how questions can be formed by reversing the order of the verb and noun in a statement.

For example: The wires to the battery **are** connected. **Are** the wires to the battery connected?

For Enrichment

Troubleshooting skills are also a part of the design process. Ask the class to work on LM 2-14 Design Challenge: Build a Flashlight. Remind them to use their troubleshooting skills when they test their designs.

Assessment *for* Learning

What to Look For in Student Work	What to Do
Students should be able to predict possible solutions using their prior knowledge about simple circuits and understand the electrical work that each of the devices depicted is supposed to do.	• Ask students to create their own diagrams of circuits that have problems that can be solved using the troubleshooting guide. Then ask them to present their problems to the class or work in groups and solve each other's problems.

CAREERS AND PROFILES

Leonard Roberts: Journeyman Electrician

Page 127

Leonard Roberts is a member of the Lac La Ronge Indian Band (LLRIB) and his profile may be used by teachers to demonstrate several key points:

- Leonard exemplifies many traits that have allowed him to be successful despite the terrible tragedy of his accident. He serves as a role model for young First Nations and Métis youth. He displays courage, determination, and perseverance which are the cornerstones of his success. Leonard had to earn his General Educational Diploma (GED) before he could attend college. He finished his grade 12 equivalency before beginning the academic path to success.
- The aim of education isn't solely to enable students to be successful in university, and university training is not always the foundation for a career. As well as providing a well-rounded background, it is important that schools allow students to learn many different skills. Colleges like the Saskatchewan Institute of Applied Science and Technology (SIAST) promote learning a trade, which in our province is in high demand. Co-op programs, like the one Leonard took, also allow students to work while studying. Thus, teachers could encourage students, both male and female, to extend their vision of possible future studies to trades as well as university.
- The science of electricity and the application of technology is another theme that runs throughout this profile. Teachers may use this profile to discuss the difference between science and technology. Science is a body of knowledge garnered through considered observation, a collective system of thought which has great predictive value, whereas technology is the means, knowledge, tools, or resources that help humans meet a need. The body of knowledge that we have about electricity, its nature and its characteristics, laws of electrical charges, etc., has been gleaned through observation and experiment. The technological aspect of electricity is different. Electricians do not need to know about the make-up of atoms in order to do their job, but they definitely need an understanding of series and parallel circuits, resistance, current electricity, direct current, etc., to do their job well. Science and its application are related, but one can exist independently of the other.

Additional questions for Leonard Roberts' profile:

1. *How is science different from technology?*

   Science is a body of knowledge garnered through considered observation, a collective system of thought which has great predictive value, whereas technology is the means, knowledge, tools, or resources that help humans meet a need.

2. *In what way(s) is science and technology related?*

   Science is the knowledge about natural phenomena that we gain through observation and experiment. Technology can make use of that knowledge. Sometimes the reverse occurs, when application of a technology adds more insights to the body of science. For example, the bow and arrow is a technology that has existed for millennia. Early FNM and other cultural groups did not use scientific principles, as we know them, to make these devices. Rather, the devices were created through necessity, careful observation, and trial and error. However, today we might use scientific principles such as thrust, lift, and drag to explain how an arrow's shape helps it fly.

11 Careers in Electricity

Page 128

Time

1–2 class periods

Key Terms

- none

Line Masters

- LM 2-15

Indicator Assessment Chart

Indicator	Assessment Opportunities
EL6.1 f. Research employers and careers related to electrical energy generation, distribution, and conservation in Saskatchewan.	• Work On It, p. 128

Background Information

In Saskatchewan, the majority of power consumption is handled by the crown corporation SaskPower, which regulates the generation, distribution, and conservation of electricity. There are also privately owned corporations located in Swift Current and Saskatoon that handle the power needs for their communities. There are many occupations in the field of electrical energy, with a wide variety of specific skills and educational requirements. People in these careers can work in the private sector or for the government. There is also an abundance of careers that are not specific to electrical power but that rely heavily on knowledge of electricity and electrical circuits. Any computer technology career relies on electricity to power computer systems. A teacher needs electricity to communicate lessons properly. Any office assistant needs electricity to organize files on a computer, use the phone or fax machine, and communicate with other people in the office.

Get Started ▶

- Ask students to list some jobs that their parents have. Write their lists on the board and choose one to discuss with the class.
- Ask your students questions about some of the careers listed, such as, *What do you think are some of the responsibilities this person has? What kinds of skills does this person need to be good at this job? What type of education do you think this person needs?*
- Tell the students that they are going to be looking at careers specific to electricity in this lesson. Read the Get Started section.

Using and Providing Electricity

- Most electrical careers can be classified as part of generation, distribution, or conservation of electricity.
- Jobs related to electricity generation are usually at power generation plants. Employees are responsible for acquiring the fuels and materials needed for electricity production, running the power plants that generate electricity, and regulating the safe production of electricity.
- A job in the distribution field involves installing and monitoring electrical power lines and transmission stations, providing direct customer service, and troubleshooting any electrical problems at a city or house level.
- A career in electricity conservation would involve monitoring safe practices, educating people on conservation methods, regulating electricity use based on environmental impact, and providing programming to help inform customers.

Time

90–120 min

Skills

- classifying
- comparing
- communicating

Grouping

individuals

Materials and Equipment

(per person)
- notebook
- pencil or pen
- computer and resource books

Line Masters

- LM 2-15

Work On It

- Students can use LM 2-15 Careers in Electricity — Occupation Profile to organize and help guide their research.
- Before students start their research, it is important that they have an understanding of the differences between the three career fields. You may want to brainstorm examples before students start researching, or assign specific jobs for their research.
- Examples of electricity generation jobs are plant operators, power dispatchers, labourers, engineers and scientists, computer systems analysts, and fabricators.
- Examples of distribution jobs include line installers, line repairers, meter readers, labourers, technicians, engineers and scientists, operators, fabricators, customer service representatives, mechanics, and contractors.
- Examples of conservation jobs include electrical inspectors, engineers and scientists, analysts, and trainers.
- The following is a sample profile for a job in the distribution field.

<u>Title:</u> Electrical Fitter
<u>Description:</u> An electrical fitter installs and assembles electrical control systems. The fitter needs to know what parts are required and how to make, alter, and connect electrical parts.
<u>Useful Skills:</u> An electrical fitter should be good at math and mechanics, have good hand-eye coordination, and be able to do precise and detailed work.
<u>Education:</u> Secondary education is needed, with a Level 3 certification and apprenticeship experience.

- It is important for students to know that there are many more jobs that have electrical aspects to their occupations. You may want to ask students to research a fourth career in electricity that requires electrical knowledge.
- Invite a local electrician or a SaskPower employee to your classroom to talk about his or her job and how it contributes to the generation, distribution, or conservation of electricity.

Communicate

1. Students should be forming personal opinions about careers in the field of electrical energy. Students should notice that most jobs they have looked at require a similar set of skills, especially when they compare their research with that of other students. A career in energy conservation may have more requirements for knowledge about the environment, whereas jobs in electricity generation and distribution require a background in mathematics, physics, and technical skills.

2 and 3. These questions give students an opportunity to compare the jobs they researched. Each group can present three job profiles to the class. You may also choose to have this class communication before the students answer question 1.

4. This question can be completed as a personal journal or a classroom discussion. Students should be able to understand that the opening and closing of power generation facilities affect the demand for skilled electrical workers in all three fields.

For Enrichment

Ask students to conduct a simulated job fair. They could create posters that reflect their research of occupations. Then give each student a personal profile with a limited amount of education, skills, and interests, and ask students to find jobs at the job fair for which they would be qualified. You could even conduct mock interviews and hire students to the posted positions.

Assessment *for* Learning

What to Look For in Student Work	What to Do
Students should be able to demonstrate through discussion and research that they have an understanding of some jobs in the electrical field.	• Consider expanding student learning through the For Enrichment options.

12 Electricity and Magnets

Page 130

Time

1 class period

Key Terms

- magnetism
- magnetic poles
- magnetic force
- permanent magnets
- temporary magnets
- electromagnets
- fair test
- independent variable

Line Masters

- LM 2-16

Indicator Assessment Chart

Indicator	Assessment Opportunities
EL6.2 e. Make predictions, based on observed patterns of events, related to the physical properties of conductors, insulators, simple circuits, and electromagnets and conduct investigations to test those predictions.	• Work On It, p. 131
EL6.2 f. Identify appropriate tools, instruments, and materials (e.g., bulbs, batteries, and wires) to use when investigating the properties of conductors, insulators, simple circuits, and electromagnets and use those tools and apparatus in a manner that ensures personal safety and the safety of others.	• Communicate, p.133, q. 4, 5
EL6.2 i. Describe the operation of an electromagnet and contrast magnets and electromagnets.	• Electricity and Magnetism Are Related. Check It Out!, pp. 130, 131
EL6.2 j. Plan a set of steps to carry out a fair test of a science-related idea related to electromagnets, such as how to increase the strength of an electromagnet.	• Work On It, p. 131
EL6.2 k. Use evidence gathered through research and observation to answer questions related to the physical properties of conductors, insulators, simple circuits, and electromagnets.	• Communicate, p. 133, q. 2–4

Background Information

The relationship between magnetism and electricity is an important phenomenon in our world. Devices such as televisions and computers rely on this relationship. This relationship was discovered by Danish teacher Hans Christian Oersted. By placing a wire over a compass and running an electrical current through the wire, he noticed that the compass needle deflected. He correctly reasoned that the deflection was the result of a magnetic field created around the current-carrying wire. This magnetic field interacted with the compass needle in the same way as a magnet did.

Get Started ▶

- Draw different arrangements of pairs of bar magnets on the board: a north pole near a south pole, two north poles near each other, and two south poles near each other. Ask the class to write a prediction of what will happen in each situation into their notebooks.
- Read the Get Started section and pause after each question to demonstrate the arrangement it asks about by putting two bar magnets on an overhead projector. Ask students to check their original predictions and correct them according to the demonstration results.

Electricity and Magnetism Are Related. Check It Out!

- Before doing the Steps in Oersted's Experiment demonstration in the next section, ask students to copy the questions at the top of page 131 of the student book into their notebooks. Ask students to independently answer each question as you are conducting the demonstration. You may want to repeat the demonstration a number of times so students have plenty of opportunity to write their answers to these questions.
- Consider reviewing the principles of how a compass works before students answer the questions from the student book. You could ask, *What is a compass? How does a compass work?* Ensure that students understand that a compass contains a magnetic needle.
- Student answers to the questions at the top of student book page 131 (Steps in Oersted's Experiment) should be as follows:

  How does a compass work? It shows direction by using a magnetic needle that points north.

  How did the magnet affect the compass? It moves the needle.

  How does current electricity work? It moves in a circuit to create a flow of electricity.

  What happens when the unhooked wire is passed over the compass? Nothing happens.

  What happens when the wire carrying the electric current is passed over the compass? The compass needle moves.

  What rule could you write to explain what happened in this experiment? An electric current has the same behaviours as a magnet.
- Before continuing, ensure that students realize that the movement of electricity through the wire generates a magnetic field.

Temporary Magnets

- You may want to write the words "permanent" and "temporary" on the board. Ask students to give you synonyms of each term to demonstrate their understanding of these two terms.
- By breaking down the word "electromagnet" into its root words "electro" and "magnet," ask students to define the term. Their definition should include the word "temporary" or a synonym.
- Students' definitions may vary but should include the same concepts as the following definition: "An electromagnet is a temporary device because it can be switched on and off. It uses an electric current to create a magnetic field with a north pole and a south pole."

! In Lesson 2, students learned the rule that opposites attract. This rule also applies to magnetism — opposite poles attract each other and similar poles repel each other. This simple rule is the basis for some of the most complicated devices that use electromagnetism.

Work On It

! Before students start the activity, remind them that they must conduct a fair test. Tell them, *A fair test means you change only one factor or variable at a time. Then, if you see anything different, you know it was caused by the one variable that you changed.* You may wish to go over the variables students should keep constant and list them on the board. A good test would always use the same nail, wires, and battery; the electromagnet would be placed in the staples for the same amount of time and on the same part of the nail; the number of staples in the pile would be kept the same, as would the shape and size of the pile. Direct students to decide how they will communicate their findings so their classmates will understand them.

Time

60 min

Skills

- making models
- observing
- experimenting
- hypothesizing
- comparing
- measuring
- controlling variables
- predicting

Grouping

pairs

Materials and Equipment

(per pair)

- 6-V battery
- 2 insulated copper wires with bare ends (1 m each)
- 1 iron nail
- 1 pencil
- 1 plastic marker
- 40 staples
- Styrofoam™ plate

Line Masters

- LM 2-16

- Students can use LM 2-16 Electricity and Magnets to write up their experiment using the scientific method.
- Ask the students, working in pairs, to complete step 1 of the procedure and record their findings in the table before they complete their predictions for the rest of the table. You may want to complete step 1 as a class in order to make sure the students have all created the model properly.
- At the end of step 1, students should have observed that when the nail touches the staples, a certain number of staples will stick to the nail as long as there is an electric current running through the wire. They may have also noticed that they pick up more staples by using the wire as the contact point instead of the tip of the nail. This is a good time to remind the students about how to conduct a fair test. Tell the students to choose the contact point that they will use for the rest of the experiment.
- In step 2, students will predict why the staples attached to the nail. Most students should recognize that they have created a temporary magnet, and the electric current has created a magnetic field in the nail that attracts the staples.
- Students should copy the table for their data, shown in step 3, and record their findings for the ten-coil row. Students should complete the table with their predictions.

CAUTION!

The nail used in the electromagnet will get hot very quickly. Ensure that students connect the battery only when they are testing their electromagnet. Do not leave the wire connected to the battery for a long time.

- For the remainder of the experiment, students will be testing the characteristics that create a stronger electromagnet by changing one variable in the experiment at a time. First, they will change the number of coils, then they will change the core material around which the coils are wrapped.
- In steps 5 and 6, students will predict which material will pick up more staples and they will create a new table to display their findings. They will only be wrapping the new materials with 40 coils, so their new table should look similar to the following:

Material	Predicted number of staples picked up	Actual number of staples picked up
Marker		
Pencil		

- If you have enough materials, ask students to conduct Oersted's experiment independently.

Communicate

1. The graph should show that the number of staples that were picked up increased as the number of coils increased.
2. As stated in the answer to question 1, students should conclude that the number of staples increased as the number of coils increased because more coils increased the magnetic field of the electromagnet, so it was able to attract more staples.
3. The nail picked up the most staples, the pencil likely picked up some staples, and the marker picked up the fewest or none. Materials that are magnetic and conductors of electricity, such as iron, nickel, and cobalt, make better cores to wrap the wire around than non-magnetic insulating materials such as plastic.
4. An electromagnet will be stronger if it has a larger number of coils that are carrying an electric current and if the coils are wrapped around a magnetic core. Students' answers may vary but should identify the same features.
5.

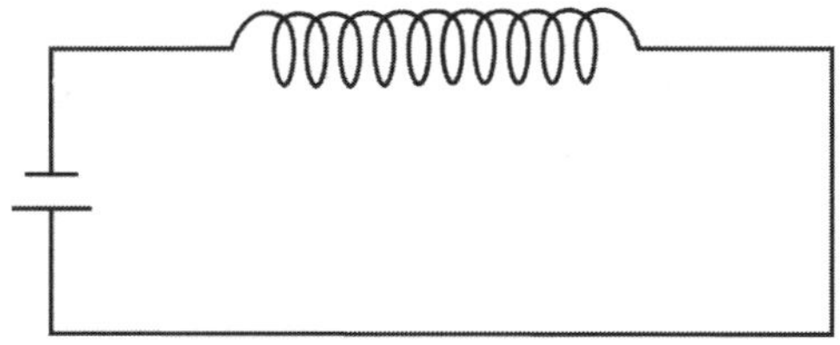

6. Students should be able to suggest a variety of devices. One example is lifting and moving large metal objects such as cars.

BUILD ON WHAT YOU KNOW

Add Hans Christian Oersted to the timeline for his discovery in 1820 of electric currents making a compass needle move. Oersted is an example of a non-scientist, in this case a teacher, making an important scientific discovery.

For Reteaching

Venn diagrams can be useful to explore the relationship between magnetism and electricity. Draw two overlapping circles on chart paper. Label one circle Electricity and the other circle Magnetism. Read the following statements aloud, and ask the class to place each one on the Venn diagram, in the correct circle:

- moves a compass needle
- causes a light bulb to go on
- has a north pole
- travels through a metal wire
- is part of a circuit
- can be used to move objects
- has internal parts that repel and attract

Assessment *for* Learning

What to Look For in Student Work	What to Do
Students should be able to make correct predictions about physical properties and identify appropriate materials used in electromagnets. Students should also be able to state how to make an electromagnet stronger. Students should be able to compare magnets and electromagnets.	• Go over the experiment questions and results as a class. Also consider completing the For Reteaching assignment.

13 Electromagnets at Work

Page 134

Time

1 class period

Key Terms

- commutator

Line Masters

- LM 2-17

Indicator Assessment Chart

Indicator	Assessment Opportunities
EL6.2 d. Pose questions related to the physical properties of conductors, insulators, simple circuits, and electromagnets (e.g., "How can we determine if an unknown material is a conductor or an insulator?", "How does a switch work in a simple electric circuit?", "What materials work best to create an electromagnet?").	• Work On It, p. 137
EL6.2 l. Describe the operation of common technologies based on properties of static electricity, current electricity, or electromagnetism.	• Communicate, p. 139, q. 1, 2

Background Information

An electromagnet consists of wire coiled around a solid core material, usually iron. The wire coil, or solenoid, generates a magnetic field when electricity is passed though it. This magnetic field acts on the core material, producing microscopic changes that greatly increase the magnetism of the wire coil. Changing the core material or the number of coils can modify the magnetic field that is induced. The best core material is magnetic material such as iron. A magnetic field generated by an electromagnet disappears when the electricity is turned off, making electromagnets extremely useful devices. Electromagnets are used in relays and circuit breakers, in certain brakes and clutches, and to lift and move metal parts and scrap metal.

Get Started ▶

- Read the Get Started section and ask students to identify the items in the photos.
- Lead a discussion on the function of each device and ask students to predict how a temporary magnet may be used in each one.
- Continue reading the next section, or go to the Work On It section to begin creating your KWL chart.
- If electromagnets are a part of students' design plans, students will have to consider that electromagnets can only be on for a limited time due to safety concerns about heated wires.

The purpose of a synchrotron is to accelerate the speed of a particle beam by using magnetic and electric fields. With this technology, scientists are able to study specific details about materials at an atomic level. The first Canadian synchrotron was built in 2004 in Saskatoon. It has a circumference of 171 m and can generate 2.9 GeV (gigaelectronvolts) of energy. The world's largest synchrotron, located in Switzerland, has a circumference of 26 659 m and an energy output of 7000 GeV.

Lifting and Driving

- Read the section and ask students to journal or discuss how their experiment from last class was like a crane.
- Ask students to independently predict how motors create motion. Use the format of a Think-Pair-Share to talk about their answers. First the students think alone, then pair with one person to talk about their ideas before they share their thoughts with the class. Students on the right track will predict that motors make some use of an electromagnet.

Motion in Motors

- In this section, it is not important that students be able to outline the steps of how a motor creates motion. The key ideas that the students should learn in this section are that an electromagnet and a permanent magnet work together to create a rotational movement. The "opposites attract" rule is the force that drives this motion, and electricity is used to create the electromagnetic effect.
- While reading this section, you may wish to have a horseshoe magnet and a model of an electromagnet available to demonstrate the five stages of how motors create motion. These stages are illustrated and described on student book pages 135–136.
- Read the section as a class, then ask students to read the section a second time to fill out their KWL charts.

Time

60 min

Skills

- classifying
- communicating

Grouping

individuals

Materials and Equipment

(per person)
- notebook
- pen or pencil

Line Masters

- none

Work On It

- The KWL chart gives students an opportunity to organize the new information they are learning in this lesson and make connections between this information and previous lessons. This activity can be done independently, in groups, or as a class depending on whether students have previously used a KWL chart and how comfortable they are with the new information.
- Ask students to create the KWL chart in their notebooks (or on large chart paper) and fill in the columns as described in the procedure.
- You may choose to ask students to create the first two columns of the KWL chart before they read Get Started. Then you can use the sections on Lifting and Driving and Motion in Motors as a model for completing the last column of the chart before they continue with the Think Again! reading section.
- Students' answers in the first column, Know, should reflect the major points in Lesson 12 and can be used as a review of those points. Students may answer that electromagnets are temporary magnets, they have wires coiled around a magnetic material, the wires have electricity running through them, the rule for magnetic poles is that opposites attract, etc.

- To complete the second column, Want, you may choose to have a class discussion in which students join all their questions together or look at the photos in this lesson to identify some questions. Some common questions may be, *How is an electromagnet used in a motor? Who invented electromagnets? Who invented motors? How are electromagnets used in speakers? How do scientists make sure the electromagnets in motors don't get too hot?*
- It is likely that not all the questions in the second column will be answered. This gives you a good opportunity to ask students to do some independent research to find answers to any remaining questions.
- Answers in the last column, Learned, should demonstrate an understanding of the electromagnets used in motors and sound devices. Students' answers may differ but should contain the bolded key ideas from both the Motion in Motors and the Think Again! sections.

While watching a thunderstorm, William Sturgeon began to question the cause of lightning. This led him to begin to study science and mathematics. In 1825, he demonstrated the use of the first electromagnet by lifting nine pounds (4 kg) using a seven-ounce (200-g) piece of iron wrapped with wire. Then, after making improvements to Volta's cell in 1828, Sturgeon introduced the first commutator for the electric motor in 1836.

Think Again! Electromagnets and Sound

- You may want to remind students that energy has different forms. Whereas electrical energy travels in a circuit, other forms of energy, such as sound, light, and heat, travel in waves.
- After students have completed their KWL charts, read this section as a class. In Communicate question 1, students will be returning to this section to read independently and to add to their KWL charts.
- You may want to share this information with your students:

  In sound amplification, the permanent magnet surrounds the electromagnet instead of being just at two contact points, like in the motor. Just like in the motor, a commutator is used to change the charges in the electromagnet. When the electromagnet has an opposite charge to the magnet, it will stay in the same spot. When the charge on the electromagnet is reversed, the electromagnet is forced to move up because there is nowhere else to go. When the charge on the electromagnet is changed again, the electromagnet returns to its original spot. This creates the up-and-down motion needed to create a sound wave.

- In this section, it is not important that students describe how electromagnets create and amplify sound. The key ideas that the students should know from this section are that the same movement of an electromagnet in a motor can be manipulated to serve other functions. The use of electromagnets benefits a variety of people and is being used to develop new technologies. Some examples of devices that use electromagnets are speakers, hearing aids, power generating plants, and MRI machines.

try this at **HOME**

- Use this activity to reinforce how important motors are in our daily lives. Student lists may vary but can include a fan, fridge, car, lawn mower, vacuum cleaner, sewing machine, washer, dryer, water pumps, etc.
- The answers to the questions may vary but should demonstrate students' understanding that motors play a large role in their daily lives. Motors reduce manual labour and simplify many tasks, without the user even being aware of their presence.
- Be sure the students understand that a motor is not an electromagnet. It is just one of many devices that use electromagnets.

Communicate

Students may answer these questions orally as a class or in groups.

1. Students have a chance now to continue to add to the third column of their KWL charts with the information presented in the Think Again! section. You may want to assign this question with the Work On It section.
2. Students can critically think to create their own inventions that contain electromagnets. Student answers will vary but should outline a device that has been altered to use an electromagnet to lift heavy loads, have motion and movement because of a motor, or amplify sound.

BUILD ON WHAT YOU KNOW

Samuel Morse was a portrait painter until a chance conversation on a cross-Atlantic voyage in 1832 sparked his interest in electromagnetism. In 1837 he invented the telegraph. Students should also add Michael Faraday to their timelines. Faraday developed the first generator in 1831, which led to the development of the first electric motor. Reese Hutchinson manufactured the first electric hearing aid in 1898. The first electromagnet was created in 1825 by William Sturgeon.

For ESL/ELL

The KWL chart can be completed as a class and displayed. You may want to create a word wall using the new vocabulary introduced in this lesson and the previous lessons.

For Enrichment

Use the LM 2-17 Design Challenge: Build a Motor to help students understand how an electromagnet can create motion.

Assessment *for* Learning

What to Look For in Student Work	What to Do
Students should be able to think of questions about using magnets and electricity and answer those questions.	• Ask students to create questions or a quiz using the information from the lesson that they can give to each other.
Students should be able to identify technologies that use electricity and electromagnets, and have a simple understanding of how these devices are used in technology.	• Go on a scavenger hunt at school, on the Internet, or in the community to identify devices that use electromagnets.

14 Electricity — Use It Safely

Page 140

Time
2–3 class periods
Key Terms
• none
Line Masters
• LM 2-18

Indicator Assessment Chart

Indicator	Assessment Opportunities
EL6.1 e. Explain potential dangers of electricity at home, school, and in the workplace and suggest ways in which individuals can minimize those dangers.	• Work On It, p. 140 • Communicate, p. 142, q. 1, 2

Background Information

Electrical energy can be dangerous if used improperly. Every year, there are over 1000 reports of electricity-related injuries. It is important that the public be educated in order to reduce the risks of injury from using electricity.

Get Started ▶

- As you are reading the section, ask students to brainstorm ways in which information can be relayed to other people. Some suggestions are: commercials, billboards, Internet sites, magazine articles, books, live performances, etc.
- Choose a number of examples from this list and ask the students, *What kind of information is being delivered by this method? Who is the audience? What is the purpose of giving this information?* For example, if the method of receiving information is listening to a radio announcer, the kind of information may be news, music, pop culture, or advertisements. The audience may be the general public, and the purpose of the information is to inform and entertain.
- As they continue reading the section, students will learn that they will be making a safety poster. Use the model above to define the purpose of their assignment. The information being delivered is electrical safety, the audience is the students at the school, and the purpose is to inform.

Time

120–180 min

Skills

- interpreting
- communicating

Grouping

individuals

Materials and Equipment

(per person)
- poster paper
- notebook
- pencil or pen
- markers or colour pencils
- computer
- resource books

Line Masters

- LM 2-18

Work On It

- The procedure steps and questions may be completed as a class discussion as you are setting up the assignment.
- For this project, you may choose to assign one particular safety tip to each student or adapt their poster's purpose by assigning them a specific audience. Posters for older students may need more data and information, posters for younger students would need a lot of pictures, and a parent audience may benefit from a brochure instead of a poster. You may wish to use LM 2-18 Electricity — Use It Safely: Poster Rubric to help you assess the posters. You may wish to distribute this LM to students so they know how they will be assessed.
- Other suggestions on how to adapt this assignment are:
  - Let the students choose their method of communication, such as a computer slide presentation, a commercial, a board game, or a rap song.
  - Ask a group to focus on a specific location such as a home, school, farm, or office.
  - Ask each student to focus on only one bullet in a tip.

There are a number of websites available with electrical safety tips, quizzes, and games.
Some suggested sites are:
SaskPower: Penny's Safety Tour
http://www.saskpower.com/safety/club/tutorial/pennytour.shtml
Queensland Government: Living Safely with Electricity
http://www.deir.qld.gov.au/electricalsafety/livingaroundelectricity/living-safely/activities/index.htm
SaskPower: Farm Safety
http://www.saskpower.com/yourfarm/safety/safetyquiz.shtml

Communicate

1. The groups should be able to identify potential electrical problems in the school, such as having too many cords in one plug, having electrical items close to water supplies, or using cords that are frayed. Metal playground equipment can be a conductor of lightning. For each problem, students' solutions should reflect an understanding of not just safety but also properties of conductors and insulators; for example, metals and humans are conductors.
2. Answers will vary but should show a connection between the person, or audience, and his or her surroundings. Students should be able to give reasons for their decisions. For example, a parent should remember that an electrical outlet has a current running through it. Young children are at the same height and level as the outlets. If they stick their fingers in an outlet, they could be electrocuted.

For ESL/ELL

Students may need additional support identifying some of the machinery in the tips. Bring in some pictures or find a website that better explains the terminology.

For Enrichment

Hold a safety fair in the school and ask students to prepare a display to explain electrical safety tips.

Assessment *for* Learning

What to Look For in Student Work	What to Do
Students should be able to identify potential electrical dangers in a variety of environments and suggest ways to minimize those dangers.	• Have a local representative from a power company present to the class about electrical safety.

15 Talking Around the World — Thanks to Canadians

Page 143

Time

2 class periods

Key Terms

- walkie-talkie
- fibre optic communications

Line Masters

- LM 2-19

Indicator Assessment Chart

Indicator	Assessment Opportunities
EL6.2 I. Describe the operation of common technologies based on properties of static electricity, current electricity, or electromagnetism.	• Communicate, p. 146, q. 1–4

Background Information

Canadians have played a significant role in the development of global communications. From telephones to faxes to satellite communication, Canadians are world leaders in using electrical devices to send signals. This lesson outlines some of these successes. Students should be encouraged to find other examples of Canadian inventions.

Get Started ▶

- Read Get Started aloud, then divide the class into groups of three or four students. Give each group a piece of chart paper. Pose the following question: *What communication devices require electricity?* Give the groups two minutes to list as many devices as they can.
- When time is up, ask students to circle any device that they know was invented by a Canadian. Some students may not be able to circle anything at this point. You could suggest that students use a different colour to circle those devices they think might have been invented by a Canadian.
- Share all suggestions as a class.
- You may want to remind students to refer to this lesson when they are brainstorming ideas for their Design Projects.

From Bell to Cellphones

- Ask students to read the next sections in groups or pairs. Ask the groups to create point-form notes as they read to identify the important discoveries outlined in the reading.
- You may need to review the expectations of point-form note taking in your class before you get started. Suggested expectations may be that the notes are in order of the reading, they are not complete sentences, usually one or two notes are used to summarize a paragraph, and correct spelling and dates are important.
- When the students have completed the reading, ask them to pair up with another group to ensure they all have similar and correct notes.

- Ask the class to review the list of Canadian inventors on page 145 of the student book and add to the list in their notebooks using the information they gathered.

Time

120 min

Skills

- communicating

Grouping

pairs

Materials and Equipment

(per pair)
- computer access
- reference materials
- pencil or pen
- notebook

Line Masters

- LM 2-19

Work On It

- Either assign or allow the students to choose an inventor in this lesson. Use the timeline as a reference for inventors.
- Use LM 2-19 Interview the Inventor to help guide student research and scripts. Encourage students to extend beyond the questions on the line master to make their interview unique.
- Ask students to present their interviews to the class or to groups.
- Instead of an interview, each student could research and write a biography about their inventor.

Communicate

1, 2, and 3. Answers will vary but should indicate that the student is critically thinking about the development and use of new technologies and how they positively and negatively impact the community and the environment.

4. Ask students to think about different methods of making signals—light, sound, motion, etc. Then, when they are doing their research, they can focus on inventions that have a certain signalling method.

BUILD ON WHAT YOU KNOW

Alexander Graham Bell, from Ontario, invented the telephone in 1876.
Cyril Duquet of Quebec designed a phone receiver in 1878.
Reginald A. Fessenden sent the first wireless voice message in 1900.
Italian inventor Guglielmo Marconi sent the first radio transmission across the Atlantic Ocean in 1901.
The following inventions are listed in the table on student book page 145:
In 1924, Sir William Stephenson of Manitoba found a method to send pictures over a phone line.
In 1927, Edward Samuel Rogers, Sr., of Ontario invented the first plug-in radio.
In British Columbia, Donald L. Hings created the first walkie-talkie in 1942.
In 1972, Canada launched the world's first geostationary satellite.
In Saskatchewan, SaskTel completed the installation of a fibre optic network in 1984. At the time, this network was the longest in the world.
In 1987, Anita Luszszak, a 15-year-old Alberta student, developed a pulsating generator.
Pierre Couture of Quebec developed a version of the electric car in 1998, and British Columbia inventors were creating a fuel cell for electric cars.
Since 2008, electric vehicles are travelling the roads of British Columbia.

For ESL/ELL

For Communicate question 1, ESL students may want to consider the advantages and disadvantages of an invention that would automatically translate and/or interpret English for them.

Assessment *for* Learning

What to Look For in Student Work	What to Do
Students should be able to identify and describe examples of electrical technology that were developed by Canadians.	• Choose one of the inventions listed on page 145 of the student book and ask students to search on-line for any information they can find about that invention.

CAREERS AND PROFILES — Donna Cavers: SaskPower Eneraction *Page 147*

- This profile can be used as a lead-in to Lesson 16 about conserving electricity.
- After you read this profile, ask students to think of ways in which they already conserve electricity. If they cannot think of any, refer to the three ways mentioned in the profile.
- Ask the students questions like, *How can electricity conservation benefit people? How can it benefit the environment? How can it benefit the electricity supplier?*
- After a class discussion, ask students to think of another program that Donna could use to promote and educate about electricity conservation. What are some incentives that Donna could offer?
- For more information, go to the Eneraction link on the SaskPower website or follow the link below:
  SaskPower eneraction

http://www.saskpower.com/eneraction/?linkid=saskpower_eneraction

16 Conserving Electricity

Page 148

Time
1 class period

Key Terms

- watts
- kilowatts
- kilowatt hours

Line Masters

- LM 2-20

Indicator Assessment Chart

Indicator	Assessment Opportunities
EL6.1 d. Identify factors that affect electrical energy consumption at home, school, and in the workplace and propose methods of decreasing electrical energy consumption that can help to conserve natural resources and protect the environment.	• Work On It, p. 149 • Communicate, p. 151, q. 1, 2

Background Information

Different countries consume different amounts of electrical energy per capita. These differences are due to various social and economic factors, including the overall level of development, the availability of energy sources, and the cost of living. Students are not expected to understand these issues, but rather to become aware of the differences in energy consumption around the world. The kilowatt hour (kWh) is a useful unit for making this comparison. An electrical energy bill usually provides the total number of kilowatt hours used each month. Some students may have seen an electrical energy meter connected to their family dwelling, which measures the amount of electrical energy used.

Energy conservation is becoming a bigger priority for electricity companies across Canada. The main reason is because it is cheaper to conserve energy than to develop new energy sources. As a result, energy conservation programs, such as SaskPower Eneraction in Saskatchewan, have a high profile in many provinces. Students can play an active role in conserving energy by making small changes in their own energy use. Using ideas discussed in this lesson, students develop a personal plan to help conserve energy.

Get Started ▶

- Before reading the section, ask students to think of all the devices they have used from the time they woke up in the morning that require electricity. After you have drawn up a list, read the first section.

! In 2009, one kilowatt hour of electricity cost $0.09 in Saskatchewan.

Using Kilowatt Hours

- Read this section to introduce the concept of a kilowatt hour.
- Use the list you drew up of all the electric devices students have used since they woke up today. Identify as many of the items you can on the table on page 148 of the student book and record the kilowatt hours. You may need to alter the list to correspond with examples in the table.
- Use the class list to model how to determine energy cost. For example, if the students listed five light bulbs, a computer, and a radio, your calculation would look like this:

  light bulbs: 5 × 0.5 kWh = 2.5 kWh

  computer: 1 kWh

  radio: 0.2 kWh

  Total: 3.7 kWh × $0.09/kWh = $0.33

  So, using these items costs $0.33 per hour.
- To check for understanding, students can independently calculate the caption question on page 149 of the student book. Tell students to assume that all appliances are in use for 1 h.

  fridge: 1.5 kWh

  light bulb: 0.5 kWh

  computer: 1 kWh

  dishwasher: 1.4 kWh

  Total: 4.4 kWh × $0.09/kWh = $0.396 or $0.40
- Remind students that this amount of money might not seem like a lot, but when some devices run every hour of every day for a month, the cost adds up.

Time

60 min

Skills

- classifying
- interpreting
- comparing
- measuring

Grouping

individuals

Materials and Equipment

(per person)
- notebook
- pen or pencil

Line Masters

- none

Work On It

- The information used in this lesson is taken from the book *Material World: A Global Family Portrait*. This book examines the characteristics of different cultures and identifies key features of what would be considered an "average family" for the culture. You are encouraged to review this book and modify the stories as appropriate to your teaching environment.
- Before reading Work On It, students should construct a table to record the information about electrical consumption by the two families. A table similar to the one below will be useful:

Electrical appliance	Energy usage

- Students should then read the stories and use the tables to record the energy consumption of the two girls. After each student has filled in her or his table, ask students to compare their work with a partner.

continued →

- The table should look similar to the following:

Electrical appliance	Energy usage
Batsuury's family uses:	
1 light bulb	0.5 kWh
black-and-white television	1 kWh
electric kettle	0.1 kWh
Total energy consumed	1.6 kWh
Jennifer's family uses:	
stove	1 kWh
plasma television	1.5 kWh
shower	1 kWh
hair dryer	0.2 kWh
radio	0.2 kWh
refrigerator	1.5 kWh
dishwasher	1.4 kWh
Total energy consumed	6.8 kWh

- After completing this activity, students should have a greater appreciation for the amount of energy the average Canadian uses in relation to average families in other parts of the world. For Procedure step 3, students should be encouraged to discuss these differences and why they occur. Students may identify access to more appliances or lifestyle as factors contributing to the difference in electrical consumption.
- For Procedure step 4, answers may vary, but students should support their answers. For example, if a student states that we use too much energy and should reduce our consumption, ask, *Are you willing to give up video games?*
- To improve students' understanding of differences in electricity usage around the world, discuss why some countries have access to more electricity than others. Factors may include access to natural generators (such as waterfalls, coal), wealth of the country (to create nuclear power stations), and physical terrain impediments (such as deserts).

try this at **HOME**

- For this activity, you can challenge students to record their electricity usage for an entire day.
- Students can refer to the energy cost calculator on the SaskPower website or follow the link below:
  SaskPower Cost Calculator
  http://www.saskpower.com/calculator/residential/

Communicate

You may choose to split this lesson into two work periods and focus on the Communicate questions next class.

1. Suggest that students use LM 2-20 Conserving Electricity — Action Plan to help guide this project. The students can brainstorm their lists in groups or with partners. You may want the groups to share their lists before they choose the idea that they will use for their action plan. It may be helpful first to develop an example of an action plan with the class. Suggest that students make goals that can be easily achieved. Encourage them to suggest specific actions rather than vague goals such as reducing the electricity bill by 10 %. Then ask students to develop independent action plans.

   After students have finished Communicate question 1, ask them to complete the following statements:

   I think my action plan will work because ______________________.

   One thing that might cause my action plan not to work is __________.

   My action plan is important to me because ____________________.

   Note: The calculated energy savings for Saskatchewan are based on the following information: Electricity from SaskPower costs $0.09/kWh. According to the 2006 census, there were about 390 000 households in Saskatchewan.

2. Individual student answers will vary. However, student answers should reflect an understanding that their action plans may have a positive or negative impact on the community or on natural resources. For example, if students reduced the amount of time they watch TV, their actions would positively affect the environment because their households would require less electricity to be generated. This plan may not directly affect a person's job, but some students may realize that by watching less TV, the ratings of a show might go down and the show may get cancelled, causing certain people to lose jobs.

For ESL/ELL

Ask students what they think *conserving* means. Write "conserving" on the board and ask students for its root word. Ask students to add the following suffixes to make new words from "conserve": -es, -ed, -ing, -tion. In pairs, students can write the rule for adding a suffix to words ending in "e".

For Reteaching

Ask students to make up their own energy story using the energy usage table provided on page 148 of the student book.

Assessment *for* Learning

What to Look For in Student Work	What to Do
Students should be able to identify factors that affect energy consumption in different locations. They should also be able to propose various methods of conserving electricity.	• Choose another story or picture book to identify energy usage and outline ways in which the characters can conserve energy.

DESIGN PROJECT

A New Electrical Device

Page 152

Time

3–4 class periods

Skills

- making models
- communicating
- controlling variables

Grouping

groups

Materials and Equipment

(per group)

- Materials may vary depending on the designs, but you should provide students with materials that they have used throughout the unit.

Line Masters

- LM 2-21
- LM 2-22

CAUTION!
You may want to remind the students about some of the safety tips learned in this unit, such as not leaving electromagnetic wires hooked to a battery source and not handling electrical devices with wet hands.

Learning Expectations

Indicators Met in Unit Project

EL6.2 f. Identify appropriate tools, instruments, and materials (e.g., bulbs, batteries, and wires) to use when investigating the properties of conductors, insulators, simple circuits, and electromagnets and use those tools and apparatus in a manner that ensures personal safety and the safety of others.
EL6.3 g. Construct simple circuits to demonstrate how electrical energy can be controlled to produce light, heat, sound, motion, and magnetic effects.
EL6.3 h. Design, construct, and troubleshoot an electrical circuit that meets one or more student-specific criteria.

Background Information

The devices that students design will need to have an energy source, wires, a switch, and a signal mechanism. While the students are thinking about ideas of tasks, remind them that they are limited in time and the materials that they have to use. Designing anything very complex is not necessarily a good idea for this project.

The types of switches that can be used may vary, but a reed or pressure switch may be the most useful. These switches can be operated by pressure from either the hand or foot. A simple reed switch can be constructed by placing two metal conductors on a spring or clothespin. The circuit is closed by pressing the two pieces together.

Get Started ▶

- Read the introduction about Elijah McCoy aloud to the class. Engage students' interest in the Design Project by saying, *You are about to become an inventor too, by designing a device that will perform or simplify an everyday task.*
- Ask the students to brainstorm possible tasks for which an electrical device could be used. Students should be thinking about a simple repetitive task that they do every day. Some suggestions include:
  - a new way of turning on the lights or shutting the door
  - a communication device to signal a code
  - a device that will signal that the school bell will ring
  - a magnetic pencil getter
  - a motion that will pass a note
- You may want to suggest that students focus only on the part of their device that involves the transformation of energy or completes the function. For example, if students design an alarm that signals when their favourite TV show starts, part of their design will include a TV or timer. Tell the students to assume they have this part and to focus on creating the electrical circuit that will work as the alarm.

Work On It

- As a class, read the introductory paragraph of Work On It and discuss the criteria for the device. Clarify anything students are unsure of before they begin to design their devices.
- Give students a copy of LM 2-21 Design Project Planner: A New Electrical Device to work with.
- Use LM 2-22 Design Project Rubric: A New Electrical Device to assess the Design Project. You may also wish to distribute this LM to students.
- Students should work through the procedure to develop their devices. Encourage students to be as specific as possible. When students have completed their designs on paper, check that each device will work and the required materials are available. Each device should have a battery, properly connected wires, and some type of switch. It should be able to perform a task that involves energy transformation.
- During the building and testing phases, students may need assistance with troubleshooting. Encourage them to refer to the troubleshooting guide on student book page 123 to help solve any problems.
- When they have completed their devices, students should answer the questions in procedure step 4, either orally or in writing. Students should be able to explain how their devices function and describe the task the device performs. Students should also be able to identify which of the five energy transformations (light, sound, heat, motion, magnetic) occur(s) in their devices. If they have used a light bulb as a signal, the energy transformations that students will mention are chemical to electrical (in the battery), and electrical to light and heat (light bulb). They should also suggest a purpose for their devices in the future that might include a new and improved model for a more complicated task. They may also discuss whether they could have used more recycled materials in their devices to make them more environmentally friendly.

Communicate

1. Student demonstrations may vary, but should have the following features: the device should serve a purpose, contain at least one energy transformation, and other students should be able to re-create it.
2. Answers may vary but should include ideas that were brought up when seeing their classmates' devices, or ideas that would be possible with unlimited materials and resources.
3. When adding their names to the Electric Timeline, students should also include the type of invention they built and the date on which they completed it.

For Reteaching

Ask students to re-create another group's device by using the other group's design plans.

For Enrichment

You may choose to have all the devices focus on tasks in the classroom, then ask the students to use their devices for a selected amount of time in the class. Also, students can create commercials for selling their devices to others.

Assessment *for* Learning

What to Look For in Student Work	What to Do
Students should be able to identify and use the appropriate tools to create their devices. Students should be able to identify the energy transformations that electricity can control, and to design their devices based on these parameters. They should also be able to properly construct the devices and troubleshoot any problems.	• Draw labelled or unlabelled circuit diagrams for devices that apply energy transformations, and ask students to construct these devices.

Unit 2 Summary

Page 154

Students may wish to use this unit summary as a study guide. The Unit Summary is available as a line master (LM 2-1).

Unit 2 Review

Page 155

Explain Your Stuff

The short-answer questions provided on this page could be used as an end-of-unit test or an in-class review of the unit, among other possibilities. Examples of the types of answers you may expect are presented below.

1. Students could use any examples from their timelines, such as Alessandro Volta's Voltaic pile in 1796, the invention of the Tesla coil by Nikola Tesla in 1891, or the first telephone, invented in 1876 by Alexander Graham Bell. Students should also be able to tell you why these inventions are important.
2. Fire and natural light were the primary sources of heat and light in homes in the past.
3. Students could describe any of the static electricity experiments they completed that demonstrate attraction and repulsion. For example, the dancing cereal was attracted to the charged balloon and jumped off the table to connect with the balloon. Another option is for students to invent their own experiments that identify the same characteristic of attraction as the experiments in Lessons 2 or 3 — a charged material that attracts an oppositely charged material.
4. The rule is that opposite charges attract and like charges repel.
5. Lightning is produced when charges in the clouds are attracted to opposite charges in the ground or in neighbouring clouds. Static electricity is used in photocopiers and laser printers, but also in items such as dust mops and air filters.
6. Students' answers will vary but should indicate an understanding that static and current electricity are different methods of receiving the same type of energy; for example, as I walked into my house, I turned on the lights while pulling off my toque and saw that my hair was standing up.
7. Students' answers should reflect the positive changes that electricity has brought. The following is a sample answer: Electricity has connected Canadians' lives by introducing and improving communication technology like telephones, satellites, and computers. It has also made various tasks in our lives easier with devices such as microwaves and flashlights.

8. Renewable energy resources:

   Hydroelectricity comes from water flowing over a dam to generate electricity. Solar energy comes from radiation from the Sun to create electrical current. Geothermal energy comes from heated water and air that rotate a generator. Wind energy comes from using wind to turn a generator. Biomass energy comes from organic waste as a fuel to make steam to turn a generator.

   Non-renewable energy resources are nuclear power, coal, and natural gas. All three resources are used as a direct heat source or an indirect source (by heating water to create steam) to rotate the generator.

   We use most of these resources as energy sources to rotate generators that make electricity. Students' descriptions may also include the advantages and disadvantages of using each resource.

9. Refer to the table on student book page 107. Some examples are Shand, located in Estevan, which uses coal as a power source. Athabasca Water Systems, located near Uranium City, generates hydroelectricity.

10. Student answers will differ but should reflect an independent opinion regarding power generation. A sample answer could be: Generating plants are beneficial to Saskatchewan because they are the primary source of power for our province. Some power plants also offer public benefits, such as lakes and reservoirs for recreational use, or greenhouses and environmental education programs. Unfortunately, these benefits also have consequences, such as harming habitats and historical heritage sites, and as a result, altering the environment for animals, plants, and people.

11. Most of Saskatchewan receives its energy from hydroelectric and coal-burning power plants.

12. Electricity is transformed into light, heat, sound, motion, and magnetic energy sources.

13. A circuit is a circular path in which an electric current flows.

14. a. will not work because the batteries are connected incorrectly. The first battery needs to be reversed.

    b. will work.
    c. will not work because the switch is open.
    d. will work.

15. A conductor is a material that will allow electricity to flow through it. Examples of good conductors are metals such as copper and aluminum, and also other substances such as salt water.

16. An insulator is a material that will stop the flow of electricity through it. Examples of good insulators are rubber, plastic, wood, and glass.

17. A switch is connected to a complete circuit and can be manipulated to open and close the circuit in order to control the flow of electricity. A closed switch completes the circuit and allows the current to flow.

18. Answers may vary, but students should give a rational explanation for their choice. One possible answer is that the best switch to use in a solar light is a photoelectric cell because it detects changes in the intensity of sunlight and switches on when it gets dark. It stores its own energy to turn on the light.

19.

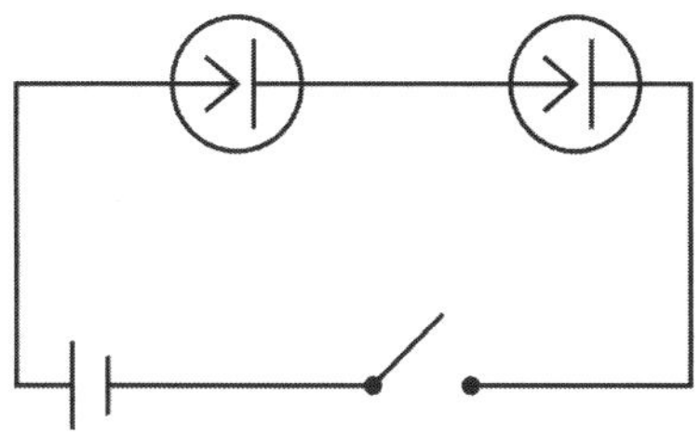

20.

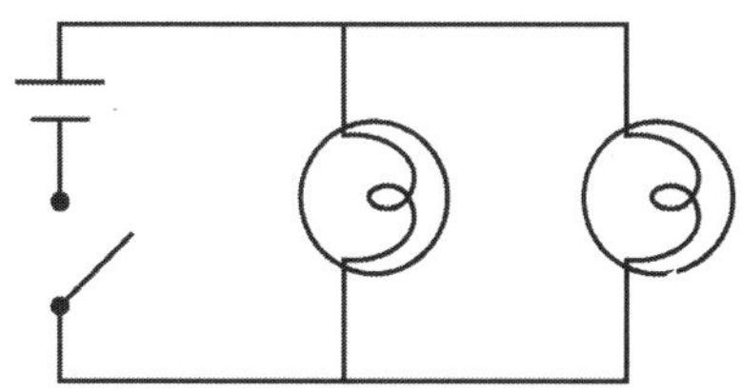

21. Series circuits are used when a number of different units need to go on or off simultaneously. These circuits are often included in machinery in which all parts must operate, and the machine does not work if one part has failed. Parallel circuits are used when devices need to operate independently. These circuits are used to light buildings, where it is advantageous not to lose the entire circuit if one bulb fails.

22. The circuit can be fixed by adding a second wire to connect the light bulbs and by closing the switch.

23. Student answers may vary but students should be able to correctly identify the area of the electrical industry. If students are having difficulty, suggest that they look back at the profiles in this unit. From the profile examples, students' answers should be: distribution engineer—distribution, journeyman electrician—distribution, performance evaluation leader—conservation.

24. Electricity and magnetism are different forces. When a metallic material is wrapped with a wire carrying electric current, the combination creates a magnetic field and forms a temporary magnet.

25. The electromagnet would pick up more staples if the core material were changed to a metallic material and/or the number of coils around the core were increased.

26. Electromagnets are used in cranes, motors, speakers, and hearing aids.

27. Student answers will vary but should show an understanding of electrical dangers. For example, water is a conductor of electricity, lightning strikes higher places, and improper wiring can lead to wires overheating or electric currents being exposed.

28. Student answers will vary but should show an understanding of electrical safety. For example, do not place electrical items near water sources, stay indoors during lightning storms, do not plug too many items into your outlets, and make sure your plugs are not broken and your cords are not frayed.

29. Student answers may vary but may include: Fessenden's invention of wireless voice messages contributed to the development of radios, televisions, and cellphones.

30. In this question, students should be able to use their knowledge of + and – charts from Lessons 4 and 5. Some possible benefits may be that inhabitants will be able to keep up with current events in the world, they will have a new means of entertainment, and they might learn about other cultures. Some possible consequences may be that they will see examples of things they cannot have, they may become frustrated about being exposed to an unfamiliar technology, and they may become disinterested in local customs and entertainments.

31. Students' answers will vary but may include ideas like availability and accessibility, how much electricity the device uses, time spent using technology that requires electricity, responsibilities that require using the technology, and interest in using the technology.

32. Expect students to relate to practical suggestions for home or school that they included in their answers and brainstorming in Lesson 16.

33. When the students look back at their timelines, they should be able to easily identify five items that they use regularly. If they have difficulty, suggest that they think of the current version of an invention (e.g., a Voltaic pile is now a battery) or something in which the original invention is now used (e.g., a Tesla coil is used in televisions). Students should be able to critically form personal opinions and imagine their lives without these inventions.

How Did You Do?

Self-evaluation allows students to communicate their learning and their feelings about it. Seeing how students view their learning can give you insight and information on which to base your programming decisions.

Ask students to answer these questions individually, then to share their answers with the class. Some students will likely find some areas of this unit easier than other areas. This exercise may help students identify who can give them assistance to understand difficult concepts.

Unit 2 Line Masters

Table of Contents

Table of Contents *(continued)*

Name: ______________________________

Unit 2 Summary

Something I know and understand before starting the Understanding Electricity unit.	Lesson(s) where I learned about this idea or learned more about this idea.	Important Points about Understanding Electricity
		Luigi Galvani discovered electricity when he saw a spark jump from metal to a frog's muscle and the frog's leg moved.
		Static electricity is electricity that does not move, but can be observed to have an effect on other objects.
		Electricity can come from a variety of renewable and non-renewable energy resources.
		The progress of electricity and energy generation has significantly affected many First Nations and Métis peoples who depend on the land where the generation and transmission facilities are constructed.
		The decision to use one energy resource over another is complex.
		Electrical circuits require a battery, wires, and an electrical device to operate. Ideally, they also have a switch to control how they operate.

Copyright © 2013 Pearson Canada Inc.
The right to reproduce this page is restricted to the purchasing school.

Something I know and understand before starting the Understanding Electricity unit.	Lesson(s) where I learned about this idea or learned more about this idea.	Important Points about Understanding Electricity
		Electricity can be changed into other forms of energy like heat, light, sound, motion, and magnetic energy.
		Conductors allow electricity to flow and insulators to stop electricity from flowing.
		Electrical symbols are used to describe the set-up of electrical circuits.
		Two types of circuits are series and parallel circuits. Which type of circuit is used depends on the situation.
		If an electrical circuit is not working, you have to fix it using a process called troubleshooting.
		Electricity is an important part of everyday life. People need to learn how to use it safely.
		Current electricity flowing through a wire creates a magnetic force. This force can be used in electromagnets and motors.

Copyright © 2013 Pearson Canada Inc.
The right to reproduce this page is restricted to the purchasing school.

Something I know and understand before starting the Understanding Electricity unit.	Lesson(s) where I learned about this idea or learned more about this idea.	Important Points about Understanding Electricity
		Canadian inventors had an important role in the development of electronic communications.
		Electricity usage varies throughout the world. We must all do our part to conserve electricity.

Copyright © 2013 Pearson Canada Inc.
The right to reproduce this page is restricted to the purchasing school.

Name: ______________________________

Unit 2 Key Terms

Word	I know nothing about this word.	I can spell this word correctly.	I have seen/heard it before.	I can define it as it relates to science.
active solar heating				
batteries				
biomass				
biomass energy generation				
circuit				
coal				
commutator				
conductors				
current electricity				
electrical energy				
electricity				
electromagnets				
fair test				
fibre optic communications				
fossil fuels				
fuse				
generator				
geothermal energy				
heat exchange				
hydroelectricity				
independent variable				
insulators				
kilowatt hours				
kilowatts				
LED				
light bulb				
light-emitting diode				
load				
magnetic force				
magnetic poles				
magnetism				
noise pollution				

Copyright © 2013 Pearson Canada Inc.
The right to reproduce this page is restricted to the purchasing school.

Word	I know nothing about this word.	I can spell this word correctly.	I have seen/heard it before.	I can define it as it relates to science.
non-renewable energy resource				
nuclear energy				
parallel circuit				
passive solar heating				
path				
permanent magnets				
primary cell				
prosthesis				
renewable energy resource				
reservoir				
secondary cell				
series circuit				
solar energy				
source				
static electricity				
switch				
temporary magnets				
transformations				
troubleshooting				
walkie-talkie				
water pollution				
watts				
wire				

Copyright © 2013 Pearson Canada Inc.
The right to reproduce this page is restricted to the purchasing school.

Name: ______________________________

Timeline Template

Copyright © 2013 Pearson Canada Inc.
The right to reproduce this page is restricted to the purchasing school.

Name: ___________________________________

The Great Pop Can Race

Let's see who can make the best race model!

Materials

1 empty pop can
1 balloon

Procedure

1. Blow up your balloon and tie the end.
2. Charge the balloon with your hair or shirt.
3. Put the empty can on its side and hold the balloon close to the can.
4. Describe what happens. Draw a diagram to better explain your description.

5. Join together in a group of five or six and construct an obstacle course on the floor, then race your pop cans.

What Did You Find Out?

Can you give an explanation about what is happening to the can and balloon?

Copyright © 2013 Pearson Canada Inc.
The right to reproduce this page is restricted to the purchasing school.

Name: ____________________________________

Making Static Electricity Useful — Getting Rid of Static

Using resource material or the Internet, research to find methods to reduce static electricity build-up. Help guide your research by filling in the blanks of the following statements.

Example: Increasing humidity will take away static charges by adding water to the air. This will help reduce static shock when you walk into a room.

1. ____________________ will take away static charges by ____________________ ____.
This will help ____.

2. ____________________ will take away static charges by ____________________ ____.
This will help ____.

3. ____________________ will take away static charges by ____________________ ____.
This will help ____.

4. ____________________ will take away static charges by ____________________ ____.
This will help ____.

Choose one of the following projects to complete in order to educate others about how to get rid of static build-up.

- create a poem or rap
- design a bookmark
- make a poster
- develop your own experiment
- create a computer slide presentation
- make a brochure

Copyright © 2013 Pearson Canada Inc.
The right to reproduce this page is restricted to the purchasing school.

Name: ____________________________________

Case Study — The Loss of Mistaseni Rock

The creation of dams and reservoirs has had huge impacts on ecosystems and agricultural land. Many archaeological and heritage sites of First Nation origin have also been affected. One example is the Mistaseni (Cree for "Big Rock"). This rock was considered to be of great cultural significance to the Plains Cree. The Mistaseni rock measured 10 m × 6 m × 2.5 m above ground. Its mass was approximately 400 t. The Plains Cree grew to worship Mistaseni. The valley surrounding the rock became the setting for sacred ceremonies, such as the Sun Dance. Many Plains Cree made long pilgrimages to the valley. In the 1850s, geologists visited the area and found the rock decorated with offerings such as beads, Tobacco, and fragments of cloth.

The Mistaseni was located near the Resort Village of Mistusinne, south of Elbow, Saskatchewan. The rock was destroyed during the construction of the Gardiner and the Qu'Appelle River dams across the South Saskatchewan and Qu'Appelle rivers, respectively. Construction of the dams began in 1958. The new reservoir, Lake Diefenbaker, was filled in 1967. For six years, a team of archaeologists and a group of entertainers conducted a campaign to save the Mistaseni. This team was led by the late Zenon S. Pohorecky, professor of anthropology and archaeology at the University of Saskatchewan. They hoped the rock could be removed from the valley intact before flooding. However, in December 1966, the Prairie Farm Rehabilitation Act (PFRA) engineers destroyed the Mistaseni using 60 sticks of dynamite.

In 1968, a cairn was built in Elbow, Saskatchewan as a tribute to Mistaseni. The cairn contains small pieces of the original rock. Other pieces were included in the memorial to Chief Poundmaker, on the Poundmaker First Nation Reserve, near North Battleford. Some pieces are also stored at the Canadian Museum of Civilization in Ottawa.

Questions

1. What was the importance of the Mistaseni to the Plains Cree people?

Copyright © 2013 Pearson Canada Inc.
The right to reproduce this page is restricted to the purchasing school.

2. Why was the rock destroyed?

3. Before the rock was destroyed, what was the hope of many concerned protesters?

4. What are the negative results from this action?

5. What are the positive results from this action?

6. Do you think the loss of this heritage site was worth the development of the dams and the hydroelectric power plants located at this site? Explain your answer.

Copyright © 2013 Pearson Canada Inc.
The right to reproduce this page is restricted to the purchasing school.

Name: ____________________________________

Design Challenge: Build a Solar Oven

The Task

Wouldn't it be fun to roast marshmallows using the Sun's heat? How about designing a solar oven to do the job?

Plan Your Design

Work with a group. You will design and build a solar oven that can roast a marshmallow. First, you will design your oven on paper. Don't forget to label your design. Then, make a list of materials you will need to build it.

Ask your teacher to check your work.

Build Your Design

Build your solar oven.

Test Your Design

If the weather isn't very sunny outside, you can test your solar oven with a heat lamp. Do you need to make any changes to your design? Make them now.

Communicate

When your design is complete, demonstrate how it works to your classmates. Be prepared to answer any questions about your solar oven.

Copyright © 2013 Pearson Canada Inc.
The right to reproduce this page is restricted to the purchasing school.

Name: ______________________________

Town Meeting Simulation

The Problem ...

Your community has called a meeting to discuss the possibility of building a new power generation plant to help with the growing demand for electricity. You will be attending the community meeting as a specific person who is directly affected either positively or negatively by this new power plant. Your assigned character will be arguing either for or against the power plant according to the role card that you are given. You will need to research your role to find out as much as you can about the opinions your character might have about a new power generation plant. In order for this simulation to work, you will have to set aside your own personal opinions and take on the opinions of your character, even if you might not agree with them.

Your Role ...

As a springboard for your research into your role, start by answering the questions below. Be sure to expand on your answers to the best of your ability so that you will have a lot to contribute to the meeting.

* Who is your character and how would he or she feel about a new power plant?
* What kinds of power generation plants might your character be more interested in building? Why? What kind of power generation might your character not be interested in? Does the kind of power generation make a difference to your character?
* How would a new power plant benefit your character? How might it have a negative impact on your character?
* What are the benefits of the new power generation plant to your community? What are the negative impacts to the community?
* What kinds of questions would your character want to ask during the meeting?

After the Meeting ...

1. What was the final decision?
2. Did the decision reflect the viewpoint of your character?
3. How did you feel about the decision that was made? Did it reflect the viewpoint of your character? Why or why not?

Copyright © 2013 Pearson Canada Inc.
The right to reproduce this page is restricted to the purchasing school.

Role Cards

You work for a nuclear power company and your job is to distribute electricity to a community. * Why should the community use your energy source over another kind? * What are the benefits to the community of using your energy source? * What other information can you present that will help the community decide to use your energy source?	You work for a hydroelectric company and your job is to distribute electricity to a community. * Why should the community use your energy source over another kind? * What are the benefits to the community of using your energy source? * What other information can you gather that will help the community decide to use your energy source?	You work for ______________ company and your job is to distribute electricity to a community. * Why should the community use your energy source over another kind? * What are the benefits to the community of using your energy source? * What other information can you gather that will help the community decide to use your energy source?
You work for SaskPower. You are a distributor of electricity. A new generation plant would mean more power for distribution in Saskatchewan. * Which energy source is the most reasonable for SaskPower? * What kinds of jobs might this new plant create? * What kinds of environmental issues should be considered?	Your job is to help with energy conservation. You want to make sure the new energy source will be environmentally friendly. * Which energy source do you think would be the best? * What do the people of the community need to know about the environmental impacts of the energy sources that are being offered?	You are an environmentalist, so you are concerned with how people treat Earth and its resources. * What is your opinion about the new power generation facility? * What would you suggest to make sure that the community is acting in the best interests of the environment?
You are a self-employed electrician. You work with electricity every day and see the need for an electricity source closer to the town. * How could you benefit from the building of a new power plant? * How might a new power plant affect your current job? * What other information can you present that will help the community decide that a new power plant closer to home is a good idea?	You are an unemployed job seeker. You have little experience with electricity but are good at working with your hands. A new power plant would give you a good chance to find a job. * What kind of power plant would you want to work in and therefore want to promote to the town? Why? * What kinds of concerns might you have about starting to work for a company like this? * What other information can you present that will help the community decide that a new power plant closer to home is a good idea?	You are a ______________ ______________ ______________ ______________ ______________ * What is your opinion about a new power generation facility? * How could it benefit you? * What are your concerns? * What information do you want to bring to the meeting? * ______________ ______________ ______________

Other options for roles: a First Nations community member concerned about construction close to the reserve, a farmer who generates his own power and sometimes sells it to the local power company, a student concerned about the future of the community, a community member hoping to help advance the progress of the town

Copyright © 2013 Pearson Canada Inc.
The right to reproduce this page is restricted to the purchasing school.

Name: ______________________________

Exploring Energy Transformations

Go on a scavenger hunt of your school or home to discover transformations of electrical energy into different forms of energy. Use the table to find items that produce different energy transformations.

Can you find something that...	Identify the correct transformation.	Draw or describe the device.
… turns on and off?		
… you can control the volume of?		
… turns on automatically?		
… moves in two directions?		
… gets hot?		
… has a remote switch?		
… uses a battery?		
… produces two different energy transformations?		
… produces three different energy transformations?		

Copyright © 2013 Pearson Canada Inc.
The right to reproduce this page is restricted to the purchasing school.

Bonus

Can you find an electrical device that uses magnetic energy?

What Did You Find Out?

Are you able to identify the five different energy transformations? Write a definition of the term "transformation."

Copyright © 2013 Pearson Canada Inc.
The right to reproduce this page is restricted to the purchasing school.

Name: ______________________________

Go with the Flow

Question (What are you trying to find out?)

Hypothesis (What do you think the answer is?)

Materials (List the materials you will use.)

Procedure

Follow the procedure outlined on pages 112–113 of your student book.

Observations (Fill in the table with your data.)

Material	Prediction	Observation
Metal spoon		
Piece of wood		
Quarter		
Pen		
Glass of water		
Glass of salt water		

Copyright © 2013 Pearson Canada Inc.
The right to reproduce this page is restricted to the purchasing school.

Analysis (What did you learn?)

A. What are the characteristics of the materials that turn the LED on?

B. What are the characteristics of the materials that do not turn the LED on?

C. Compare the data you collected to your hypothesis. What improvements can you now make to your original hypothesis?

Copyright © 2013 Pearson Canada Inc.
The right to reproduce this page is restricted to the purchasing school.

Name: ____________________________________

Lemon Battery

Can foods act like a battery?

Materials

1 lemon
1 D-cell battery
1 pre-1996 penny
1 pre-1981 nickel
2 wires with alligator clips
1 LED

Procedure

1. Connect the two wires to the metal ends of the LED.
2. Before you connect the lemon, test your model by completing the circuit by connecting the ends of the wires to the battery. If the LED does not light up, it may be connected to the battery incorrectly. Switch the wires to touch the opposite ends of the battery.
3. Take the lemon prepared by your teacher and locate the two pre-cut slits. Insert the penny into one slit and the nickel into the other slit.
4. Connect the wires to the two metals. If your LED does not light up, switch one end of each wire to connect to the other metal.
5. In the space provided, draw a diagram of your model and give a description of what you saw.

Copyright © 2013 Pearson Canada Inc.
The right to reproduce this page is restricted to the purchasing school.

Analysis (What did you learn?)

A. What in the lemon allows it to light up the LED?

B. Identify and describe any energy transformation you think is occurring.

C. Can you think of any other foods that you could use instead of the lemon?

What Did You Find Out?

From this model, can you describe how a battery works?

Copyright © 2013 Pearson Canada Inc.
The right to reproduce this page is restricted to the purchasing school.

Name: ______________________________

Picture That Circuit

You have learned the symbols for electrical circuits. Here are some exercises for you to practise these symbols. Before you know it, you'll be an expert!

1. Draw the symbol for each electrical device:

Open switch	LED	Wire

2. What electrical devices do these symbols represent?

3. Draw a circuit that has one battery, three light bulbs, and one switch that will turn all the lights on or off at the same time.

Copyright © 2013 Pearson Canada Inc.
The right to reproduce this page is restricted to the purchasing school.

4. Explain in words how this circuit works.

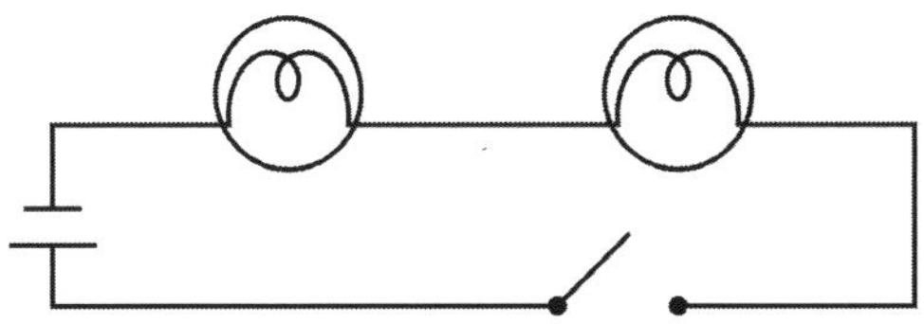

What Did You Find Out?

Are you now able to recognize the symbols for electrical circuits? Create two questions, like the ones here, to give to a classmate to solve.

Copyright © 2013 Pearson Canada Inc.
The right to reproduce this page is restricted to the purchasing school.

Name: ________________________________

Design Challenge: Design an Alarm System

The Problem

Your brother keeps going into your room and taking your stuff. He always gets in and out without getting caught! You need an alarm system. What if you designed something that would make your battery-operated radio go on whenever he came into the room? Then, when you heard the music, you'd be able to catch him!

Plan Your Design

Work with a partner. Plan a design you think will work. These questions might help you start.

- What kind of electrical circuit would work best?
- What kind of switch will turn on your circuit only when someone enters the room?
- What materials will you need to make your alarm?

Draw your design and label all parts. Make a list of the materials you will need.
Ask your teacher to check your work.

Build Your Design

Build your alarm system.

Test Your Design

Test your alarm system. Remember: You want your battery-operated radio to come on when your brother enters your room. How will you test this? Make any changes to your design, if necessary.

Communicate

Demonstrate your alarm system to the class. Explain how your alarm system works.

Copyright © 2013 Pearson Canada Inc.
The right to reproduce this page is restricted to the purchasing school.

Name: ______________________________

Design Challenge: Build a Flashlight

The Problem

It's a blackout and you don't have a flashlight. What are you going to do? Why, build one of course, using materials from around the house!

Materials

white glue
paper clips
bulbs
cardboard
heavy-duty aluminum foil
masking tape
D-cell batteries
wire
paper towel tube

Plan Your Design

Work with a group. Design your flashlight. Include a diagram that explains how your flashlight works. Make sure to label all parts.
Ask your teacher to check your work.

Build Your Design

Build your flashlight. Don't forget to add a switch.

Test Your Design

Test your flashlight. Does it work? If not, make any necessary changes.

Communicate

Demonstrate and explain to another group how your flashlight works.

Copyright © 2013 Pearson Canada Inc.
The right to reproduce this page is restricted to the purchasing school.

Name: ______________________________

Careers in Electricity — Occupation Profile

Generation

Title: ______________________________

Description: ______________________________

____

Useful skills: ______________________________

____

Education: ______________________________

____

Distribution

Title: ______________________________

Description: ______________________________

____

Useful skills: ______________________________

____

Education: ______________________________

____

Conservation

Title: ______________________________

Description: ______________________________

____

Useful skills: ______________________________

____

Education: ______________________________

____

Copyright © 2013 Pearson Canada Inc.
The right to reproduce this page is restricted to the purchasing school.

Name: ____________________________________

Electricity and Magnets

Question (What are you trying to find out?)

Hypothesis (What do you think the answer is?)

Materials (List the materials you will use.)

Procedure

Follow the procedure outlined on pages 131–133 of your student book.

Observations (Fill in the table with your data.)

Number of coils around the nail	Predicted number of staples picked up	Actual number of staples picked up
1		
5		
10		
20		
40		
60		

Copyright © 2013 Pearson Canada Inc.
The right to reproduce this page is restricted to the purchasing school.

Analysis (What did you learn?)

A. What happened when you used the pencil? What happened when you used the marker?

B. What variables changed the strength of your electromagnet?

C. Compare the data you collected to your hypothesis. What improvements can you now make to your original hypothesis?

Copyright © 2013 Pearson Canada Inc.
The right to reproduce this page is restricted to the purchasing school.

Name: ____________________________

Design Challenge: Build a Motor

The Task

Your friends don't believe that electricity can make something move. It's your job to prove them wrong!

Materials

AA battery
insulated wire with stripped ends (10 cm long)
strong disc Neodymium magnet (rare-earth magnet)
screw

Plan Your Design

Work with a partner. Use what you know about circuits and current electricity to attempt to make the screw spin. Remember: You are trying to prove that electricity can be used to make motion. Draw a diagram and label the parts. Ask your teacher to check your work.

Build Your Design

Try to create a model that will make the screw move independently.

Copyright © 2013 Pearson Canada Inc.
The right to reproduce this page is restricted to the purchasing school.

Test Your Design

Does the electrical circuit create movement? If not, make any necessary changes to your design and try again. Draw any new plans.

Communicate

Compare and contrast your model with what you learned about an electromagnetic motor. The motor you built in this activity is called a homopolar motor. Research the homopolar motor on the Internet to find other models that you can try to recreate.

Copyright © 2013 Pearson Canada Inc.
The right to reproduce this page is restricted to the purchasing school.

Name: ______________________________

Electricity — Use It Safely: Poster Rubric

Student name(s): ______________________________________

Areas of Assessment	1	2	3	4
Basic Concepts The assignment design concerns were understood and followed.	The poster does not meet any of the design concerns.	The poster meets half of the design concerns.	The poster meets more than half of the design concerns.	The poster meets all of the design concerns.
Design and Development The poster is well designed and developed to individual student ability.	The poster is not designed well and is below individual student ability.	The poster is designed fairly well but is below individual student ability.	The poster is well designed and is at individual student ability.	The poster is very well designed and is above individual student ability.
Communication The poster communicates the information required in a way that is appropriate for the intended audience.	The poster does not communicate its message in a clear and precise way and is not appropriate for the intended audience.	The poster communicates its message in a somewhat clear and precise way but is not fully appropriate for the intended audience.	The poster communicates its message in a mostly clear and precise way and is appropriate for the intended audience.	The poster communicates its message in a clear and precise way that is appropriate for the intended audience.

Copyright © 2013 Pearson Canada Inc.
The right to reproduce this page is restricted to the purchasing school.

Name: ______________________________

Interview the Inventor

You have an opportunity to talk to the inventor of one of the items on your timeline. Use the following form to create your interview.

1. What was your life like before you created this invention?

2. What are some interesting facts about your life?

3. What is your invention? How does it work?

4. What interested or prompted you to create this invention?

Copyright © 2013 Pearson Canada Inc.
The right to reproduce this page is restricted to the purchasing school.

5. What was the impact of your invention on the world?

6. How do you think life would be different without your invention?

7. What advice would you give people who have an idea for an invention?

Copyright © 2013 Pearson Canada Inc.
The right to reproduce this page is restricted to the purchasing school.

Name: ________________________________

Conserving Electricity — Action Plan

1. Brainstorm a list of different ways you can save electricity at home and at school.

2. Pick one of your ideas from your list above and create an action plan that you could follow.

Action Plan	
Identify a goal.	
Identify what must be done to meet that goal.	
Determine if anything will prevent or make it difficult for you to meet your goal.	
Describe how you will know when you meet that goal.	
State your completion date.	

I think my action plan will work because ________________________________

____.

One thing that might cause my plan not to work is ________________________

____.

My action plan is important to me because ________________________________

____

____

Copyright © 2013 Pearson Canada Inc.
The right to reproduce this page is restricted to the purchasing school.

Group Members: ______________________________

Design Project Planner: A New Electrical Device

(If you need more space, use the back of this sheet.)

1. The task that the device will do is:

2. The task can be created by:

The materials needed are:

Draw your design. Label all parts.

Copyright © 2013 Pearson Canada Inc.
The right to reproduce this page is restricted to the purchasing school.

3. Build your device.
4. Test your design. Do you need to make any changes to your design? Draw your revised design here.

5. Explain how your device works.

6. Present your device to the class.

Copyright © 2013 Pearson Canada Inc.
The right to reproduce this page is restricted to the purchasing school.

Name: ______________________________

Design Project Rubric: A New Electrical Device

Student name(s): ____________________________________

Areas of Assessment	1	2	3	4
Basic Concepts The three design concerns are understood and followed.	The electrical device does not meet any of the design concerns.	The electrical device meets one of the design concerns.	The electrical device meets two of the three design concerns.	The electrical device meets all three design concerns.
Skills Design, building, and testing of the electrical device	Demonstrates very few of the required skills and strategies for the design, building, and testing of the electrical device.	Demonstrates some of the required skills and strategies for the design, building, and testing of the electrical device.	Demonstrates most of the required skills and strategies for the design, building, and testing of the electrical device.	Demonstrates exceptional use of the required skills and strategies for the design, building, and testing of the electrical device.
Communication The student demonstrates the device and answers questions about it using appropriate vocabulary when presenting the device to the class.	During the presentation, explanation of the device and answers to questions are not very clear or precise.	During the presentation, explanation of the device and answers to questions are somewhat clear and precise.	During the presentation, explanation of the device and answers to questions are mostly clear and precise.	During the presentation, explanation of the device and answers to questions are very clear and precise.
Relating of Science and Technology to Each Other and to the World Outside the School After building and testing the electrical device, the student is able to identify its future use and assess if it is environmentally friendly.	Shows little understanding of the device's future use and whether it is environmentally friendly.	Shows some understanding of the device's future use and whether it is environmentally friendly.	Shows a good understanding of the device's future use and whether it is environmentally friendly.	Shows a complete understanding of the device's future use and whether it is environmentally friendly.

Copyright © 2013 Pearson Canada Inc.
The right to reproduce this page is restricted to the purchasing school.

Name: ______________________________

Unit 2 Test

True/False

1. For the following questions, indicate whether the statement is true (T) or false (F).

a)	T	F	Historically, Saskatchewan used natural energy to get jobs done.
b)	T	F	A photocopier uses the idea of electric currents to create images.
c)	T	F	Fossil fuels are used because they are renewable.
d)	T	F	A current needs a path, a source, and a battery to work.
e)	T	F	A light bulb transforms electrical energy into heat energy.
f)	T	F	Salt water is an insulator of electricity.
g)	T	F	A series circuit can have one light on and one light off at the same time.
h)	T	F	Troubleshooting helps solve electrical problems.
i)	T	F	An electric circuit can make a compass needle move.
j)	T	F	An electromagnet is a permanent magnet.

Multiple Choice

Circle the letter than best answers the question.

2. The ancient Greeks discovered
- a) current electricity
- b) batteries
- c) static electricity
- d) all of the above

3. Luigi Galvani
- a) made the first artificial leg
- b) discovered electricity in a frog's leg
- c) made the first battery
- d) all of the above

4. A battery
- a) is a modern version of a Voltaic pile
- b) is a way to make electricity portable
- c) can be rechargeable
- d) is all of the above

5. Saskatchewan received electricity in
- a) 1890
- b) 1950
- c) 1780
- d) 1920

Copyright © 2013 Pearson Canada Inc.
The right to reproduce this page is restricted to the purchasing school.

Matching

6. Draw an arrow to match the electrical toy in the column on the left to the type of energy transformation in the column on the right.

talking toy parrot	electrical energy to motion
toy racing car	electrical energy to light
toy camera with a flash	electrical energy to sound

Fill in the Blanks

Complete the following sentences.

7. Static electricity will _____________ charges that are the same and _____________ charges that are opposite.

8. Lightning is created when _______________ bump together and build up a charge.

9. A Tesla coil recreates the effects of lightning. An example of an electrical device that uses this technology is __________________.

10. First Nations people respect thunder and lightning. As a sign of respect, they call one of the most important symbols of their spirituality the __________________.

Short Answer

11. What is static electricity? Give two examples in your description.

____

____

____

____

____

12. Name and describe two energy resources. Give one example of a renewable resource and one example of a non-renewable resource.

____

____

____

____

Copyright © 2013 Pearson Canada Inc.
The right to reproduce this page is restricted to the purchasing school.

13. Name one electricity generation plant in Saskatchewan. What kind of power source does it use?

____

____

____

14. What are three concerns about building a new electricity generation plant in a community?

____

____

____

____

____

____

15. Name two things that conduct electricity.

____

____

____

____

Copyright © 2013 Pearson Canada Inc.
The right to reproduce this page is restricted to the purchasing school.

16. Draw the symbols for:

a light bulb	a battery
a closed switch	an LED

17. Use the symbols in question 16 to draw a parallel circuit.

18. Name two types of switches.

____

____

19. In what three fields can people find careers in electricity?

____

____

____

Copyright © 2013 Pearson Canada Inc.
The right to reproduce this page is restricted to the purchasing school.

20. How can you make an electromagnet stronger?

____

____

____

____

21. Check the electrical devices that have an electromagnet in them.

____ crane	____ microphone	____ flashlight
____ car	____ TV remote	____ speaker

22. State an electrical safety tip that your teacher should remember.

____

____

____

____

23. Name two Canadian inventions that use electricity.

____

____

24. Complete these statements:

One way I can conserve electricity is to …

____

____

The thing I would miss most without electricity is ______________________________

because ______________________________

Copyright © 2013 Pearson Canada Inc.
The right to reproduce this page is restricted to the purchasing school.

Answers to Unit 2 Line Masters

LM 2-3: Timeline Template

The following table is an answer key to the timeline. Choose from the table what information you want to display in the timeline. You may choose to include only the dates in the textbook or you may choose to record only the Canadian inventors.

Lesson	Code	Date	Inventor and Invention
1		600 BCE	Ancient Greeks — amber static
1		1752	Benjamin Franklin — kite and lightning
1		1786	Luigi Galvani — electricity in muscles
1		1796	Alessandro Volta — Voltaic pile
12		1821	Hans Christian Oersted — moving compass needles
13		1825	William Sturgeon — first electromagnet
13		1831	Michael Faraday — first electric generator
13		1837	Samuel Morse — first telegraph
10	CAN	1858	John B. Studley — first illuminated glass sign
15	CAN	1876	Alexander Graham Bell — first telephone
15	CAN	1878	Cyril Duquet — modern telephone receiver
6		1879	Thomas Edison — light bulb
4	*	1883	Charles Fritts — first solar cell
2		1891	Nikola Tesla — Tesla coil
13		1898	Reese Hutchinson — first electric hearing aid
15	CAN	1900	Reginald A. Fessenden — first wireless voice message
15		1901	Guglielmo Marconi — first radio transmission across Atlantic
1	*	1913	Fred Wolf — first home electric refrigerator called the Domelre
15	CAN	1924	Sir William Stephenson — sent pictures over a phone line
15	CAN	1927	Edward Samuel Rogers — first plug-in radio
1	*	1929	Clarence Birdeye — first electric freezer
3	*	1937	Chester Carlson — first photocopier
15	CAN	1942	Donald L. Hings — first walkie-talkie
5	*CAN	1965	first CANDU reactor in Ontario
1	CAN	1967	Richard Keefer — garbage battery
15	CAN	1972	Anik 1 — world's first geostationary satellite
15	CAN	1984	SaskTel — installed the longest fibre optic network
15	CAN	1987	Anita Luszszak — pulsating generator
15	CAN	1987	Pierre Couture — developed a version of the electric car
4	*CAN	1995	Hydro-Quebec's James Bay LG 1 dam completed for hydroelectricity
15	CAN	1998	BC inventors were creating a fuel cell for electric cars
4	*CAN	2001	Craik Sustainable Living Project
4	*CAN	2006	Swift Current — Centennial Wind Power Facility
15	CAN	2008	Electric vehicles are travelling the roads of BC

Copyright © 2013 Pearson Canada Inc.
The right to reproduce this page is restricted to the purchasing school.

Codes
CAN – Is a Canadian Inventor
* mentioned in the Teacher's Resource

LM 2-4: The Great Pop Can Race

What Did You Find Out?

The can has an opposite charge to the balloon, so it is attracted to the balloon and will follow it.

LM 2-5: Making Static Electricity Useful — Getting Rid of Static

Some static examples may be:

- Using hand lotion will take away static charges by decreasing friction when you rub your hands together. This will help reduce the amount of static charge you pick up.
- Using an antistatic mat will take away static charges by collecting static charges in the mat. This will help prevent static shock because the mat takes any electric charge that may transfer to a person.
- Not wearing rubber shoes will take away static charges because rubber collects static charges. This will help prevent static shock because the static will not be able to build up on your body.
- Installing wood floors will take away static charges because wood is an insulating material that does not create much static charge when you rub against it. This will help reduce static charge by not creating an environment that will create static shock.

LM 2-7: Design Challenge: Build a Solar Oven

One way to create a solar oven is to line the inside of a pizza box with black construction paper as insulation, then cover the construction paper with aluminum foil. Cut a window at the top of the box and cover it with *clear* plastic wrap.

Copyright © 2013 Pearson Canada Inc.
The right to reproduce this page is restricted to the purchasing school.

LM 2-9: Exploring Energy Transformations

The following are sample answers.

Can you find something that…	Identify the correct transformation.	Draw or describe the device.
… turns on and off?	Light bulb — light Fan — motion	[Answers in this column will vary.]
… you can control the volume of?	Stereo — sound TV — light and sound	
… turns on automatically?	Heater — motion	
… moves in two directions?	Fan — motion	
… gets hot?	Glue gun — heat Oven — heat	
… has a remote switch?	TV— light and sound Data projector — light and sound	
… uses a battery?	Clock — motion Radio — sound	
… produces two different energy transformations?	Overhead projector — light and motion	
… produces three different energy transformations?	Computer — light, sound, motion	

Bonus: Can you find an electrical device that uses magnetic energy?
Anything with a motor has magnetic energy: a computer, phone, microphone, photocopier, and recess bell.

What Did You Find Out?

The energy transformations are light, heat, sound, motion, and magnetism.
A transformation describes what happens to electrical energy when it becomes a different kind of energy in a device that has a specific function.

LM 2-10: Go with the Flow

1. Most materials that turn the LED on have metallic properties.
2. These materials are rubber, plastic, and wood.
3. Students' answers will vary depending on their hypotheses. Answers will likely include the identification of specific conductors, such as metal and salt water, and specific insulators, such as rubber and wood.

Copyright © 2013 Pearson Canada Inc.
The right to reproduce this page is restricted to the purchasing school.

LM 2-11: Lemon Battery

5.

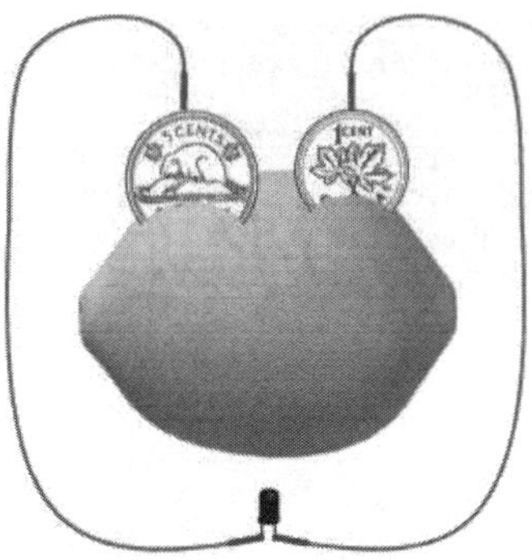

A. The acidic juices in the lemon provide the energy source for lighting the LED.
B. The transformation is from chemical energy to electrical energy to light energy.
C. Most acidic fruits can be used. The higher the acidic content, the more brightly the LED will light up.

What Did You Find Out?

Students should be able to connect this experiment with the discussion about Volta and his battery. The acidic juice acts like the salt solution in his battery and the metals used — nickel and copper — are similar to the zinc and silver used by Volta. This set-up is similar to a modern battery that uses two metallic connectors (electrodes) and an acidic substance. The strength and purpose of the battery depend on the materials used.

LM 2-12: Picture That Circuit

1.

Open Switch	LED	Wire
	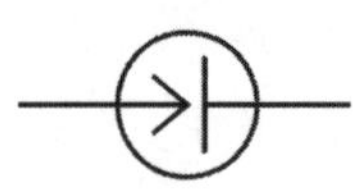	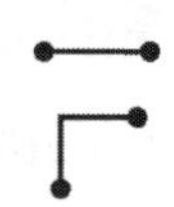

2. Light bulb, closed switch, battery

3.

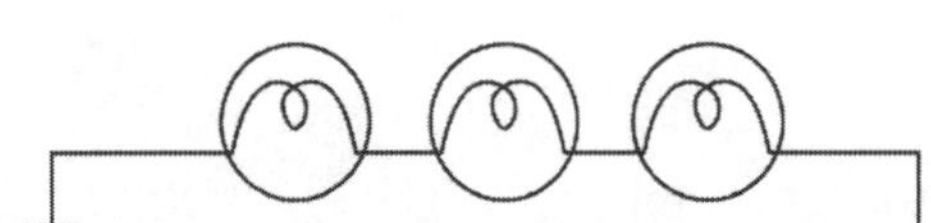

4. When the switch is turned on, the circuit will close. The battery will provide electricity that will flow through the wire to the first light bulb, then to the second light bulb before it returns to the other terminal of the battery.

Copyright © 2013 Pearson Canada Inc.
The right to reproduce this page is restricted to the purchasing school.

LM 2-13: Design Challenge: Design an Alarm System

This alarm will likely need a bell or a light mechanism to replace the radio. The best switch to create this alarm would likely be a reed switch or a photoelectric cell.
Build a reed switch by attaching two pieces of aluminum foil or two paper clips to a clothespin. Pressure needs to be applied in order for the two pieces to touch.

LM 2-14: Design Challenge: Build a Flashlight

With the materials given, the students will likely create a model that looks similar to a real flashlight by using the paper towel tube as the holder for the batteries and wiring. Students can use the aluminum foil or the paper clips to build the switch. Not all the materials need to be used. However, the model should be functioning and repeatable.
Encourage students to use the troubleshooting guide from Lesson 10 to solve this problem.

LM 2-16: Electricity and Magnets

Analysis: (What did you learn?)

A. The pencil should work better than the marker but not as well as the nail in picking up staples.

B. The number of coils that are wrapped around the core material make the electromagnet stronger or weaker. More coils make the electromagnet stronger. A magnetic core material also makes the electromagnet stronger.

C. Students' answers will vary depending on their hypotheses. Answers will likely identify that adding more coils around the core material and using a metal as the core will increase the strength of the electromagnet.

LM 2-17: Design Challenge: Build a Motor

The solution to create this motor is as follows:

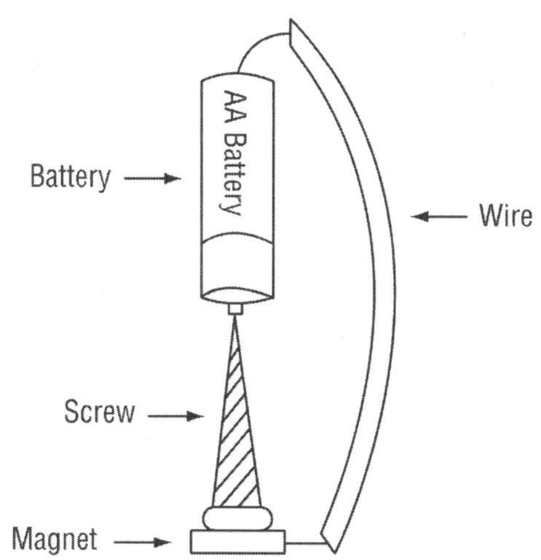

Copyright © 2013 Pearson Canada Inc.
The right to reproduce this page is restricted to the purchasing school.

Communicate

A homopolar motor is the same as an electromagnetic motor because it uses the same materials: a battery, a metallic material, and a magnet to create movement. The difference is that a homopolar motor does not use a wrapped wire to create a magnetic field. The magnetic field in a homopolar motor only produces rotational motion. It cannot be used to pick up objects. Other models, like a homopolar roller and a homopolar spiral wire, use the same concept as the motor model shown above.

LM 2-23: Unit 2 Test

1. **a)** T
b) F
c) F
d) F
e) T
f) F
g) F
h) T
i) T
j) F

2. c)

3. b)

4. d)

5. a)

6. talking toy parrot — electrical energy to sound
toy racing car — electrical energy to motion
toy camera with a flash — electrical energy to light

7. repel, attract

8. clouds

9. a television (also wireless radios, X rays)

10. Thunderbird

11. Static electricity is electrical charges that are found in nature. These charges stay and build up on an object. Some examples of static electricity are lightning, hair that stands up, shocks on doorknobs, or crackles in bed linen.

12. Renewable resources are natural energy sources that do not run out. Examples are hydroelectricity, wind, solar, biomass, and geothermal energy.
Non-renewable resources are natural sources that will eventually be used up. Most non-renewable resources come from fossil fuels. Examples are nuclear fuel, coal, and natural gas.

Copyright © 2013 Pearson Canada Inc.
The right to reproduce this page is restricted to the purchasing school.

13. See Lesson 5 (student book pages 104–107) for a complete list.
Some examples are: Shand, Boundary Dam — coal burning
E.B. Campbell, Athabasca Water Systems — hydroelectric power
Centennial, SunBridge — wind power

14. Some concerns may be damage to animal habitats or heritage sites, the expense of developing or running a new power plant, the amount of space it will use up, or an increase in water or air pollution.

15. Things that conduct electricity include metal (copper, aluminum, nickel, lead), salt water, humans, and plasma.

16.

a light bulb 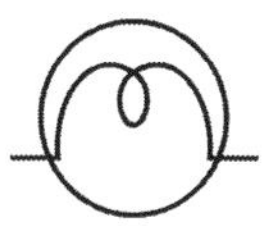	a battery 
a closed switch	an LED 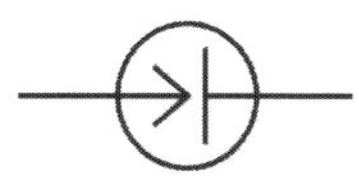

17.

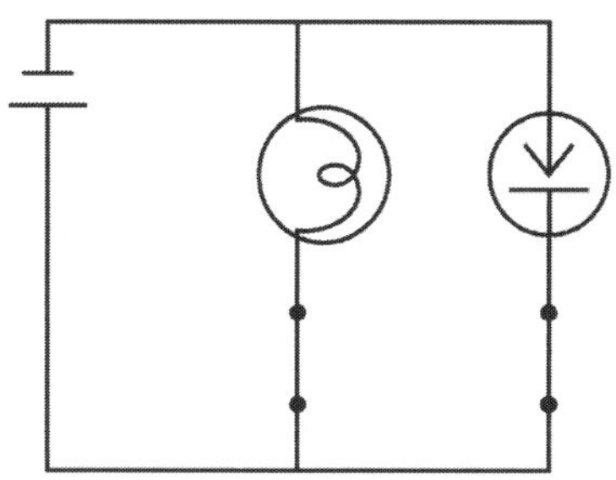

18. Types of switches are toggle, rocker, slide, popper, reed, tilt, and photoelectric cell.

19. The three fields are electricity generation, distribution, and conservation.

20. You can make an electromagnet stronger by increasing the number of coils of wire wrapped around the core and by making sure that the core of the electromagnet is a magnetic material.

Copyright © 2013 Pearson Canada Inc.
The right to reproduce this page is restricted to the purchasing school.

21. __x_ crane __x_ microphone ____ flashlight

__x_ car ____ TV remote __x_ speaker

22. Students should identify a safety tip that is specific to a school or classroom setting. Answers may include tips like making sure electrical equipment is not close to a water source, not overloading an outlet, or not using an electrical cord that is frayed or broken.

23. For a complete list, see Lesson 15 (student book pages 143–146). Answers include the telephone, wireless voice messages, the first plug-in radio, and the walkie-talkie.

24. **One way I can conserve electricity is to …** turn off the lights, limit the amount of time the TV or computer is on, turn down the heat, and unplug unused devices like cellphone chargers.

The thing I would miss most without electricity is … Answers will vary based on experience.

Copyright © 2013 Pearson Canada Inc.
The right to reproduce this page is restricted to the purchasing school.

UNIT 3

Principles of Flight

Table of Contents

Table of Contents *(continued)*

Unit Indicators Correlation Chart

Indicator	Lesson References	Assessment Opportunities
By the end of grade 6, students will be able to:		
FL6.1 Examine connections between human fascination with flight and technologies and careers based on the scientific principles of flight.		
a. Observe and describe physical characteristics and adaptations that enable birds (e.g., ravens, hawks, loons, geese, hummingbirds, sandpipers, cranes, and sparrows), insects (e.g., mosquitoes, dragonflies, grasshoppers, bees, wasps, and butterflies) and bats to fly.	Lesson 1 Unit 3 Review	Work On It, p. 163 Communicate, p. 165, q. 2, 4 Unit 3 Review, p. 221, q. 3, 4
b. Show how First Nations and Métis art and storytelling highlight understanding of and respect for birds.	Lesson 1 Unit 3 Review	Crow Brings the Daylight, pp. 160–161 Unit 3 Review, pp. 221–222, q. 6, 7, 23
c. Examine the role of inspiration and aesthetic design in the development of flying devices (e.g., initial attempts at trying to fly were based on observations of birds).	Lesson 3	Work On It, p. 174
d. Research technological problems that had to be overcome to develop devices that fly (e.g., balloons, kites, gliders, airplanes, helicopters, and rockets) and explain how various creative solutions to those problems have resulted in the development of flying devices with different designs.	Lesson 2 Lesson 3 Lesson 5 Unit 3 Review	Communicate, p. 170, q. 2–4 Work On It, p. 174 Communicate, p. 175, q. 2 Work On It, p. 184 Unit 3 Review, p. 222, q. 24
e. Discuss historical and current contributions of individuals, including Canadians, who have contributed to scientific understanding and technological developments related to flight.	Lesson 3 Lesson 5 Unit 3 Review	Work On It, p. 174 Communicate, p. 175, q. 2 Work On It, p. 184 Communicate, p. 184, q. 1 Unit 3 Review, p. 222, q. 12
f. Describe examples of traditional and modern technologies developed by First Nations, Métis, and other cultures that are based on principles of flight (e.g., atlatl, bow and arrow, slingshot, catapult, boomerang, and trebuchet).	Lesson 2 Unit 3 Review	Communicate, p. 170, q. 1–4 Unit 3 Review, p. 221, q. 5
g. Explain how inventions based on principles of flight have changed the way people work, live, and interact with the environment locally, nationally, and globally (e.g., bush planes in northern Saskatchewan, scheduled airline travel, supply of cargo to remote communities and mine sites, and transoceanic air travel).	Launch Lesson 5 Lesson 12 Unit 3 Review	Work On It, p. 158 Communicate, p. 159, q. 1, 2 Work On It, p. 184 Communicate, p. 214, q. 5 Unit 3 Review, pp. 221–222, q. 2, 21
h. Describe career opportunities in Canada related to the science and technology of flight.	Lesson 12 Unit 3 Review	Communicate, p. 214, q. 5 Unit 3 Review, p. 222, q. 12

Indicator	Lesson References	Assessment Opportunities
FL6.2 Investigate how the forces of thrust, drag, lift, and gravity act on living things and constructed devices that fly through the air.		
a. Diagram how the forces of thrust, drag, lift, and gravity act on living things or devices that fly through the air.	Lesson 1 Lesson 4 Lesson 10 Lesson 11 Lesson 12 Unit 3 Review	Communicate, p. 165, q. 1, 3 Communicate, p. 179, q. 1 Communicate, p. 207, q. 3 Communicate, p. 211, q. 1 Communicate, p. 214, q. 1, 6 Unit 3 Review, p. 221, q. 9, 10
b. Use scientific terminology appropriately (e.g., thrust, drag, lift, and gravity) when communicating ideas about the principles of flight.	Lesson 1 Lesson 2 Lesson 4 Lesson 6 Lesson 7 Lesson 10 Lesson 12 Unit 3 Review	Communicate, p. 165, q. 1–4 Communicate, p. 170, q. 1 Communicate, p. 179, q. 1 Work On It, p. 188 Communicate, p. 192, q. 1, 2 Work On It, p. 195 Communicate, p. 197, q. 1–3 Work On It, p. 206 Communicate, p. 207, q. 1–4 Communicate, p. 214, q. 1, 6 Unit 3 Review, pp. 221–222, q. 1, 8, 11, 22
c. Generate questions related to the principles of flight and rephrase those questions in a testable form (e.g., rephrase a question such as "Why can some gliders travel farther than others?" to "What effect does wing shape have on the distance a glider can travel?").	Lesson 4 Lesson 8 Lesson 10 Lesson 11	Work On It, p. 177 Work On It, p. 198 Communicate, p. 199, q. 1, 2 Communicate, p. 207, q. 2 Work On It, p. 210 Communicate, p. 211, q. 2
d. Describe the role of lift in overcoming gravity and enabling devices or living things to fly.	Lesson 1 Lesson 4 Lesson 6 Lesson 7 Lesson 12 Unit 3 Review	Communicate, p. 165, q. 1, 4 Work On It, p. 177 Communicate, p. 179, q. 1, 2 Work On It, p. 188 Communicate, p. 192, q. 1, 2 Work On It, p. 195 Communicate, p. 197, q. 1–3 Work On It, p. 213 Communicate, p. 214, q. 1 Unit 3 Review, pp. 221–222, q. 1, 13, 17
e. Determine how lift is affected by the shape of a surface by planning and carrying out steps to investigate the effect of wing shape on lift.	Lesson 1 Lesson 6 Lesson 7 Unit 3 Review	Work on It, p. 163 Work On it, p. 188 Work On It, p. 195 Communicate, p. 197, q. 1–3 Unit 3 Review, p. 222, q. 13–18

Indicator	Lesson References	Assessment Opportunities
f. Describe and represent methods for altering drag in flying devices, such as a bird spreading wings or an airplane employing flaps.	Lesson 1	Work on It, p. 163
g. Provide examples of how science and technology have been used to solve problems related to drag in devices that fly.	Lesson 2 Lesson 11 Lesson 12 Unit 3 Review	Communicate, p. 170, q. 2–4 Work On It, p. 210 Communicate, p. 211, q. 3, 4 Communicate, p. 214, q. 3–5 Unit 3 Review, p. 222, q. 22
h. Compare the sources of thrust of various constructed flying devices including the propeller, jet engine, and solid or liquid-fuelled rocket.	Lesson 3 Lesson 10 Lesson 12 Unit 3 Review	Work On It, p. 174 Work On It, p. 206 Communicate, p. 207, q. 4 Communicate, p. 214, q. 4 Unit 3 Review, p. 222, q. 19
FL6.3 Design a working prototype of a flying object that meets specified performance criteria.		
a. Assess the characteristics of flying objects (e.g., balloon, kite, glider, airplane, helicopter, and rocket).	Lesson 1 Lesson 4 Lesson 7 Lesson 8 Lesson 9 Lesson 10 Lesson 11 Lesson 12 Design Project Unit 3 Review	Communicate, p. 165, q. 1 Work On It, p. 177 Communicate, p. 179, q. 1–4 Build On What You Know, p. 179 Communicate, p. 197, q. 1–3 Build On What You Know, p. 197 Work On It, p. 198 Communicate, p. 199, q. 1, 2 Work On It, p. 200 Communicate, p. 203, q. 1, 3, 4 Build On What You Know, p. 203 Work On It, p. 206 Communicate, p. 207, q. 2–4 Build On What You Know, p. 207 Work On It, p. 210 Communicate, p. 211, q. 1–4 Build On What You Know, p. 211 Work On It, p. 213 Communicate, p. 214, q. 1, 2, 3, 6 Work On It, p. 218 Unit 3 Review, pp. 221–222, q. 9, 10, 15, 16, 17, 19, 20, 24
b. Construct a prototype of a flying object that meets student-specified performance and aesthetic criteria.	Lesson 2 Lesson 4 Lesson 8 Lesson 11 Design Project	Work On It, p. 169 Work On It, p. 177 Communicate, p. 179, q. 2 Work on It, p. 198 Communicate, p. 199, q. 1–3 Work On It, p. 210 Communicate, p. 211, q. 2–4 Work On It, p. 218

Indicator	Lesson References	Assessment Opportunities
c. Work collaboratively with classmates to define criteria for judging the performance and aesthetics of a prototype of a flying object.	Lesson 2 Lesson 3 Lesson 4 Lesson 8 Design Project	Work On It, p. 169 Communicate, p. 175, q. 2 Work On It, p. 177 Work On It, p. 198 Communicate, p. 199, q. 1, 2 Work On It, p. 218
d. Select and carefully use appropriate tools in manipulating materials and in building prototypes.	Lesson 2 Lesson 4 Lesson 8 Lesson 11 Lesson 12 Design Project	Work On It, p. 169 Work On It, p. 177 Work On It, p. 198 Communicate, p. 199, q. 3 Work On It, p. 210 Communicate, p. 211, q. 3, 4 Work On It, p. 213 Work On It, p. 218
e. Work collaboratively to collect relevant observations and data to evaluate the performance of a prototype of an object that will fly.	Lesson 2 Lesson 4 Lesson 8 Lesson 9 Lesson 11 Lesson 12 Design Project	Work On It, p. 169 Work On It, p. 177 Work On It, p. 198 Communicate, p. 199, q. 1–3 Work On It, p. 200 Work On It, p. 210 Communicate, p. 211, q. 3, 4 Work On It, p. 213 Communicate, p. 214, q. 2, 3 Work On It, p. 218
f. Demonstrate and explain the importance of selecting appropriate processes for investigating scientific questions and solving technological problems (e.g., explain why it is important to change one variable while keeping others constant in designing and testing prototypes of flying objects).	Lesson 4 Lesson 8 Lesson 9 Lesson 11 Design Project	Work On It, p. 177 Work On It, p. 198 Communicate, p. 199, q. 1, 2 Work On It, p. 200 Work On It, p. 210 Work On It, p. 218
g. Analyze personally collected data and suggest improvements to a prototype design.	Lesson 8 Lesson 11 Lesson 12 Design Project Unit 3 Review	Work On It, p. 198 Communicate, p. 199, q. 1–3 Work On It, p. 210 Communicate, p. 211, q. 4 Work On It, p. 213 Communicate, p. 214, q. 3 Work On It, p. 218 Unit 3 Review, p. 222, q. 20
h. Communicate procedures and results of prototype design, construction, testing, and evaluation in a technical design report.	Launch Lesson 9 Design Project	Build On What You Know, p. 159 Communicate, p. 203, q. 1–4 Communicate, p. 219, q. 1
i. Identify new questions or problems about flight that arise through the prototype design process.	Design Project	Work On It, p. 218

Indicator	Lesson References	Assessment Opportunities
j. Propose designs for futuristic flying devices that meet a particular student-identified need.	Lesson 12 Design Project	Communicate, p. 214, q. 7 Work On It, p. 218

Activity Planning Chart

Note that estimates of class times are based on 40 min per period.

Lesson	Type of Activity	Time (number of classes)	Materials Required (for each group)	Line Masters
Launch: Connecting Flights	discussion	1	chart paper colour markers	LM 3-1 LM 3-2 LM 3-3 LM 3-4
1. Freedom to Fly	guided inquiry	2–3	large piece of cardboard scissors fabric ties cloth tape	LM 3-5
2. Ancient Technologies	open inquiry	2	balloon tape scissors cardboard (Bristol board or cereal box) straws string	LM 3-6
3. Around the World: Fascination with Flight	reading	2–3	Bristol board black markers ruler	LM 3-7
4. Liftoff	guided inquiry	2	lightweight kitchen garbage bags (51 cm × 56 cm) stopwatch or watch with a second hand hair dryer (with variable speeds and temperatures) scissors thread extension cord tape variety of other types and sizes of bags	LM 3-8
5. Flying Canadians	reading	2–3	timeline charts from Lesson 3 red marker green marker ruler	LM 3-9

Lesson	Type of Activity	Time (number of classes)	Materials Required (for each group)	Line Masters
6. Air in Motion	guided inquiry	2–3	3 thin strips of paper (30 cm × 5 cm) 2 index cards (10 cm × 15 cm) 2 thick straws pencil paper compasses scissors glue tape ping pong ball 30 plastic straws 2 empty pop cans ruler	LM 3-10
7. UP Lifting Theories	guided inquiry	2	plastic spoon running water from a tap tape 30-cm wooden ruler or other flat wooden stick	LM 3-11
8. Takeoff	open inquiry	1	scissors tape paper clips paper straws	LM 3-12
9. Moving Faster, Slower, Up, and Down	guided inquiry	2	paper (21.6 cm × 27.9 cm) scissors stapler paper clip	LM 3-13 LM 3-14
10. The Four Forces of Flight	guided inquiry	1	clear plastic film canister Alka-Seltzer® tablet water safety goggles	LM 3-15
11. Payload Liftoff	guided inquiry	1	balloons (variety of shapes and sizes) cardboard or stiff paper fishing line or strong coloured thread plastic drinking straws tape empty drinking boxes with straws modelling clay pennies	LM 3-16

Lesson	Type of Activity	Time (number of classes)	Materials Required (for each group)	Line Masters
12. Flight Just Above the Ground: The Hovercraft	guided inquiry	1–2	old CD or DVD thread spool scissors electrical tape clothespin balloon pennies	LM 3-17
Design Project: Make It Go	open inquiry	3–4	placemat paper glue scissors colour pencils and felt pens scraps of wood cardboard elastic bands various sizes of plastic tubing various sizes of syringes without the needles various types of wire various types of fasteners anything else that may be useful	LM 3-18 LM 3-19 LM 3-20

- If you are fortunate enough to live near an airport, your students will benefit greatly from taking a field trip to visit planes in action. Such a field trip will make a good culminating activity for the unit because it will allow students to consolidate their learning by seeing a variety of airplanes, jet planes, and helicopters in action.
- Invite guest speakers who are involved with flight into the classroom. This will give your students an excellent opportunity to broaden their knowledge and experience as they progress through the unit. You might find pilots, flight engineers, scientists, or navigators who will agree to come and share their experiences with your students.
- Contact a Hovercraft operating company to see if your class could see a Hovercraft in person.
- As you begin to collect materials for the unit, make use of recycled materials as often as possible. You will want to discuss efficient use of materials with your students and set a foundation of respect for the environment throughout their studies. Invite your students to bring in various types of flying toys and commercial kits for building gliders, rubber-band-powered planes, kites, and model rockets. Some students may even have remote-controlled flying toys. This will provide your students with a showcase for demonstrating their knowledge while offering many opportunities to demonstrate properties of air and characteristics of flight in a highly motivating way.

- The Work On It activity in Lesson 10 requires plastic film canisters. With the popularity of digital photography, you may need to approach a photo finishing lab a few weeks prior to the lesson to give people time to collect canisters for you. The film canisters that are most effective for this activity are clear, with lids that fit inside the canister. The black and grey canisters with lids that fit over the sides work less well.
- Throughout the unit, you may want to have the following types of materials on hand so that students may do some free exploration when the opportunity arises: assorted types of paper for gliders, including both stiff bond and softer textured papers such as tissue paper; balloons, straws, small containers such as yogurt packaging, Styrofoam™ deli trays, plastic sheeting and plastic bags, light string and dental floss, sticks and struts.
- You may find that balloons are a requirement for many activities. One possible source for quality balloons is local businesses, banks, or credit unions. When you contact these businesses, you may find them happy to support your classroom by donating balloons.
- Create a materials centre where students can go to do some free exploration and pursue their inquiries. As they progress through the unit, they will need to refer to charts to add to their lists of what they know and answer the questions they are wondering about. You will want to display these charts attractively in an accessible area.
- If you have sufficient room, try to display the flying devices the students create during the unit and any flying devices the students have brought from home. You can assign one student to be curator of the display—a person who can be responsible for the display and who will add labels and names to devices for identification purposes.
- Students will be excited to build their own flying devices in this unit. One norm you may want to develop with your class is when students can build and explore, and where they can store their devices during other instructional times. A suggestion would be to designate an "aeronautics development" time each day. This time period could be during breaks, at the beginning of the day when attendance and other announcements occur, during lunch hour, the first few minutes of science class, etc.

Materials and Equipment Needed for Unit 3

(based on 30 students)

Launch: Connecting Flights	
Materials • 6 pieces of chart paper • 6 colour markers	**Equipment** • no equipment needed
1. Freedom to Fly	
Materials • 15 large pieces of cardboard (from large boxes) • 15 pieces of fabric (to make ties to attach "wings" to arms) • 5 rolls of cloth tape	**Equipment** • 15 pairs of scissors
2. Ancient Technologies	
Materials • 10 balloons • 6 rolls of tape • 6 large pieces of cardboard (Bristol board or cereal boxes) • box of straws • 6 rolls of string	**Equipment** • 15 pairs of scissors
3. Around the World: Fascination with Flight	
Materials • 12 large pieces of Bristol Board • 6 black markers	**Equipment** • 6 rulers
4. Liftoff	
Materials • 7 lightweight kitchen garbage bags • 6 rolls of thread • 6 rolls of tape • variety of other types and sizes of bags	**Equipment** • 6 stopwatches or watches with second hands • 6 hair dryers with variable speeds and temperatures • 6 pairs of scissors • 6 extension cords

Materials and Equipment

(continued)

5. Flying Canadians	
Materials • 6 green markers • 6 red markers • timeline charts from Lesson 3	**Equipment** • 6 rulers
6. Air in Motion	
Materials • 15 strips of paper (30 cm × 5 cm) • 30 index cards (10 cm × 15 cm) • 15 pencils • 450 plastic straws • 50 thick plastic straws • glue • 1 roll of tape	**Equipment** • 1 compass • 1 pair of scissors • 5 ping pong balls • 2 empty pop cans • 15 rulers
7. UP Lifting Theories	
Materials • 8 plastic spoons • 8 rolls of tape	**Equipment** • 8 sinks with running water • 8 rulers or other flat sticks
8. Takeoff	
Materials • 6 rolls of tape • box of paper clips • 30 plastic straws • 60 pieces of paper	**Equipment** • 6 pairs of scissors
9. Moving Faster, Slower, Up, and Down	
Materials • 15 sheets of paper • box of paper clips	**Equipment** • 3 staplers • 15 pairs of scissors
10. The Four Forces of Flight	
Materials • 6 Alka-Seltzer® tablets • 2 L water	**Equipment** • 6 clear plastic film canisters • 30 pairs of safety goggles

Materials and Equipment

(continued)

11. Payload Liftoff	
Materials • 15 balloons (variety of shapes and sizes) • 15 pieces of cardboard or stiff paper • 2 spools of fishing line or strong coloured thread • 15 plastic drinking straws • 5 rolls of tape • 5 empty drinking boxes with straws • 1 package of modelling clay	**Equipment** • 200 pennies
12. Flight Just Above the Ground: The Hovercraft	
Materials • 10 old CDs or DVDs • 10 empty thread spools • 3 rolls of electrical tape • 10 balloons	**Equipment** • 10 pairs of scissors • 10 clothespins • 200 pennies
Design Project: Make it Go	
Materials • 6 pieces of placemat paper • 6 bottles of glue • package of colour pencils or markers • scraps of wood • cardboard • package of elastic bands • various sizes of plastic tubing • various sizes of syringes without needles • various types of wire • various types of fasteners • anything else that may be useful	**Equipment** • 6 pairs of scissors

Materials and Equipment

(continued)

Overall Unit Requirements	
Materials • chart paper • 6 large pieces of cardboard from large boxes • 30 large pieces of Bristol board • 15 pieces of fabric (to make ties to attach "wings" to arms) • 35 balloons • 8 rolls of tape • 3 rolls of electrical tape • 5 rolls of cloth tape • box of straws (thick) • 6 rolls of string • 6 rolls of thread • 2 spools of fishing line • 7 lightweight kitchen garbage bags • variety of other types and sizes of bags • 6 black markers • 6 colour markers • 6 green markers • 6 red markers • package of colour pencils • package of 21.6 cm × 27.9 cm paper • 6 pieces of placemat paper • 30 index cards • pencil • 6 bottles of glue • 8 plastic spoons • box of paper clips • package of elastic bands • 6 Alka-Seltzer® tablets • 2 L of water • 5 empty drinking boxes with straws • 1 package of modelling clay • 10 old CDs or DVDs • 10 empty thread spools • scraps of wood • various sizes of plastic tubing • various sizes of syringes without needles • various types of wire • various types of fasteners	**Equipment** • 15 pairs of scissors • 1 compass • 3 staplers • 8 30-cm rulers • 6 stopwatches or watches with second hands • 6 hair dryers with variable speeds and temperatures • 6 extension cords • 5 ping pong balls • 2 empty pop cans • 8 sinks with running water • 6 clear plastic film canisters • 30 pairs of safety goggles • 200 pennies • 10 clothespins

Addressing Student Preconceptions

Launch: Connecting Flights

Students may not have thought about what life was like before flight. The Launch is important because it gives students an opportunity to identify how flight technology has impacted Saskatchewan in beneficial or harmful ways. Impacts may be both beneficial and harmful — something that 11-12-year-olds may not have explored before.

Lesson 1: Freedom to Fly

One useful activity would be to ask your students what they know (or think they know) about forces, including lift, gravity, drag, and thrust. After this lesson, you could re-visit their initial ideas to correct any false preconceptions.

One preconception that your students may have is thinking of forces in terms of movement, not staying still. When you give a skateboard a push, you are giving it energy. Many students think of pushing as giving the skateboard a force that travels with it and keeps it moving, so it is not surprising that people mistakenly think that things have a "force travelling with them." Students are likely to believe that if something is not moving, there are no forces acting on it. Think of a person trying to push a bicycle with the handbrake on. The bicycle does not move, so no force is evident. Yet scientifically, we know that there are several forces at work.

Students may think that if an object is moving at constant velocity, the force of thrust forward must be greater than the force of drag opposing the force of thrust. Actually, if a plane is moving at constant velocity, these two forces are equal. If the force of thrust is greater, the plane is accelerating (increasing its velocity) forward. Likewise, if the force of lift is greater than the force of gravity, the plane will rise in altitude.

The ultimate goal is for students to understand that when all the forces on an object are balanced (lift up = gravity down, and thrust in the direction of motion = drag opposite to the direction of motion), an object will continue its motion. If initially at rest, it will continue at rest. If initially moving at constant velocity, it will continue moving at constant velocity. So, a plane's engines must supply a thrust at least equal to drag to keep it moving, and the wings must supply a lift at least equal to gravity to maintain altitude.

Lesson 2: Ancient Technologies

Students live in a world filled with technology. They may have an understanding of technologies changing over time to fill a need better than an older technology. If they were to think of cellular phones, they would see that this technology has become smaller, with the ability to take pictures and videos, and has QWERTY keyboards for texting. However, students may not realize that technologies were developed thousands of years ago with the same purpose of filling the needs of society. Spears, atlatl-and-dart systems, and bows and arrows are an excellent example of technologies that changed and became better over time in order for First Nations peoples to hunt more efficiently.

Lesson 3: Around the World: Fascination with Flight

Many people have the preconception that the Wright brothers were the first inventors of flying machines. Lesson 3 shows that people around the world were thinking about, designing, and building flying technologies long before the American Wright Flyer took off at Kitty Hawk.

Lesson 4: Liftoff

The purpose of the introduction to this lesson is to have students think about the questions the Montgolfier brothers, who designed and flew the first hot-air balloon, needed to ask before building their balloon. This introduction gives further insight into the idea that technologies are constantly changing and have not always existed.

Lesson 5: Flying Canadians

Saskatchewan students may not realize the rich history of our province's aviation industry. There are many firsts claimed by the people of Saskatchewan. By adding the Saskatchewan and Canadian contributions to their flight timelines, students will see that many of the contributions by people in Saskatchewan have to do with creating unique uses for air travel.

Lesson 6: Air in Motion

Students may not understand how moving air can have a lower pressure than still air. Students may believe that because wind can put pressure on an object and blow it over, there is more air pressure in an area where air is moving. In fact, there is less air pressure in an area where air is moving at a high velocity. Areas where air is still, or calm, exert higher air pressure. The push from areas of still, or high-pressure, air to areas of fast-moving air can cause objects to move. This idea is a key concept in aerodynamics, so it would be good to thoroughly discuss it with your class.

Lesson 7: UP Lifting Theories

One preconception is that air pressure differences are the sole contributor to lift in airplanes. In fact, the curvature of the wing and angle of attack contribute to lift more than the difference in air pressure.

Students may have the preconception that if gravity and lift are balanced, the object will be at rest. In fact, if gravity and lift are balanced, the object will remain at the same height. If the object is on the ground, it will remain on the ground. If the object is in the air, it will remain in the air. It is only when the forces are unbalanced that the object will move up or down.

Lesson 8: Takeoff

Many students have tried to make and fly paper airplanes. This lesson is their opportunity to learn how the design and structure of paper airplanes affects their flight path, and that you can intentionally build a paper airplane to fly in a certain way.

Lesson 9: Moving Faster, Slower, Up, and Down

Students may have seen a Science Report in the past. This lesson gives them the opportunity to write a Glider Technical Report, which is quite different in structure and content from a Science Report. Their unit Design Project will use a technical report format, so the Glider Technical Report will be useful practice.

Lesson 10: The Four Forces of Flight

One preconception that students have is that rocket propulsion is a result of exhaust gases pushing against something. In fact, rockets can be used in space because they rely on Newton's third law of motion: For every action force, there is an equal and opposite reaction force. To help students understand this law, you can try the medicine ball activity described in the Think Again! section on the bottom of student book page 206.

Lesson 11: Payload Liftoff

Thus far, four forces of flight have been identified in the student book. In rocket flight, there is no lift force. Instead, thrust is a vertical force that acts against both drag and gravity.

Lesson 12: Flight Just Above the Ground: The Hovercraft

Students may not be aware that flight can be achieved only inches above the ground. A Hovercraft achieves this type of flight by creating a cushion of air over which the craft can move.

Design Project: Make It Go

This lesson is an opportunity for students to create their ultimate flying device by using all of their knowledge about the forces of flight and how they can be manipulated. Students may have the preconception that balloon power is the easiest way to manipulate a flying object. By referring to their construction of flying devices in Lessons 2, 4, 8, 9, 11, and 12, students may have a greater variety of ideas for their Design Projects.

Big Ideas

Page 157

The Principles of Flight unit will allow students to explore flight in the natural world, how technologies have been developed over time, the forces acting on objects in flight, and how to design, build, and test their own flying devices. This exploration will occur in the context of Saskatchewan and will examine how flight has impacted and changed our province, and how people from our province have impacted and changed flight technologies.

traditional **KNOWLEDGE**

First Nations and Métis content makes up part of the lessons in this unit. The Principles of Flight unit shows how First Nations and Métis people apply their understanding of flying things to help them survive and live in harmony with Mother Earth. First Nations legends and artwork are presented, as well as a description of changing technologies related to flight, including the spear, atlatl-and-dart system, and the bow and arrow. Words and phrases related to flight in some First Nations languages have been included where appropriate. The Ask an Elder profile highlights Elder Stewart Prosper's observations of bird flight and behaviour.

Once you have determined students' prior knowledge, you may want to hand out LM 3-1 Unit 3 Summary and LM 3-2 Unit 3 Key Terms to help students record their understanding of the unit and key terms.

Connecting Flights

Page 158

Time

1 class period

Key Terms

- technical report
- prototype

Line Masters

- LM 3-1
- LM 3-2
- LM 3-3
- LM 3-4

Assessing Students' Prior Knowledge

- Divide a sheet of chart paper into two columns with the headings Know and Wonder. Explain that you want to find out what students already know about air and flight. Ask, *What do you know about flight?*
- Ask students to work individually at first, writing down everything they think they know about flight. Then ask them to read their responses aloud. Record their statements on the chart paper. If the statement is a factual statement, ask students whether they agree that the statement is true before you add it to the list. If a student questions whether a statement is true, reword the statement as a question and write it in the Wonder column. Finally, ask students if they have any questions or things they would like to learn about flight, and write their responses in the Wonder column.
- By creating this table, you will be able to establish your students' assumptions and preconceptions about the topic. This exercise will also help students to begin the inquiry process.

Introduce the Unit

- Hand out LM 3-2 Unit 3 Key Terms. Ask students to rate their knowledge of each key term on the rating scale given. Ask, *Aside from the questions you have already identified, what topics do you think we will be studying in this unit?*
- Explain to students that they are about to study a unit on flight. Tell them that they will learn about:
  - the characteristics of flight in the natural world
  - the similarities between living things that fly and the technologies that engineers have designed that fly
  - forces that act on all things that fly or glide through the air
  - how to design, build, and test flying devices
- In this unit, students will also come to understand that First Nations and Métis people apply their understanding of flying things to survive in nature and to live in harmony with Mother Earth.
- Hand out LM 3-1 Unit 3 Summary. Ask students to read each statement with a partner and place a checkmark beside the ideas they already know and understand. Students will refer to the Unit 3 Summary throughout the unit.
- Encourage students to bring any materials about air and flight that they may already have at home. These materials could include books, magazines, model airplanes, paper airplanes, rockets, and so on. Other students may know a pilot, navigator, engineer, or scientist who could be a guest speaker for the class.

Ask students for names and permission to contact these people. Alternatively, students could write to these people with their questions about flight.

Introduce the Design Project

- Explain to students that at the end of the unit, they will create a model of their own air-powered vehicle. In groups, students will design a vehicle using the knowledge and skills they will have learned throughout the unit. Based on their final design, they will build a model using a variety of materials.
- Advise students to keep careful records of all their experiments on air and flight to use during this project. Each lesson will include a Build On What You Know section, for which students will write a portion of the technical report they need for their Design Projects. These written summaries should be kept in a separate folder, binder, or section of their notes. Use LM 3-3 Unit Technical Report Table of Contents to help them organize their work.

Get Started ▶

- Project or hand out a map of Saskatchewan, such as the one found at the Canada Maps website (http://www.canada-maps.org/saskatchewan-map.htm).
- Ask students, *How many of you have been to a northern or remote community? What do you remember seeing there? How did the various things you saw get to this community?*
- Refer students to the illustration on student book pages 158 and 159. Ask, *How is the scene in your textbook similar to what you saw on your trip? How is it different?*

Time
30 min
Skills
• classifying • communicating
Grouping
groups
Materials and Equipment
(per group) • chart paper • colour markers
Line Masters
• none

Work On It

- Brainstorming begins as a large class discussion. The results of Procedure steps 1 and 2 can be recorded on the board or overhead transparency.
- Ask students to complete Procedure step 3 in small groups. Each group should use a different colour of marker.
- For Procedure step 4, use the jigsaw procedure, where the travelling group members take their colour marker to add to the next sheet. Each group of travellers should have the opportunity to move through each station to add new thoughts until they return to their original chart.

Communicate

1. Students should do this analysis in small groups. You may choose to have them record their ideas on LM 3-4 Impacts of Flight. Answers will vary. Ideas students identify could include:

Economy	Relationships	Environment
more stores to buy things (+)	people move away from their home communities (+, –)	more garbage from goods brought in (–)
tourists can visit (+)	people move into communities from other places (+, –)	trees cut down to build airstrips (–)
can buy food rather than hunt and grow it (+)	culture is no longer based on hunting and gathering (+, –)	fuel used for planes increases pollution (–)

2. Answers will vary. Ask several students to share their classifications with the class. Include these classifications on a class-generated table. Ask the class if they agree with these students' choices. Help them to see that many changes can be classified as both beneficial (+) and harmful (–).

BUILD ON WHAT YOU KNOW

Students are asked to start thinking about a technical report that they will add to throughout the unit. This report takes the place of a daily journal and gives students a place to record thoughts, try ideas, draw designs and diagrams, and keep a general record of their learning. This report should be placed into a separate section of their notes, binder, or folder. You may choose to use LM 3-3 as the table of contents for the technical report to help students organize their thinking. Students can use this LM as an outline to make sure they have written all the components. To begin their Unit Technical Report, students should create a cover page representing something related to flight.

1 Freedom to Fly

Page 160

Time

2–3 class periods

Key Terms

- force
- gravity
- mass
- lift
- struts
- thrust
- hover
- drag

Line Masters

- LM 3-5

Indicator Assessment Chart

Indicator	Assessment Opportunities
FL6.1 a. Observe and describe physical characteristics and adaptations that enable birds (e.g., ravens, hawks, loons, geese, hummingbirds, sandpipers, cranes, and sparrows), insects (e.g., mosquitoes, dragonflies, grasshoppers, bees, wasps, and butterflies) and bats to fly.	• Work On It, p. 163 • Communicate, p. 165, q. 2, 4
FL6.1 b. Show how First Nations and Métis art and storytelling highlight understanding of and respect for birds.	• Crow Brings the Daylight, pp. 160–161
FL6.2 a. Diagram how the forces of thrust, drag, lift, and gravity act on living things or devices that fly through the air.	• Communicate, p. 165, q. 1, 3
FL6.2 b. Use scientific terminology appropriately (e.g., thrust, drag, lift, and gravity) when communicating ideas about the principles of flight.	• Communicate, p. 165, q. 1–4
FL6.2 d. Describe the role of lift in overcoming gravity and enabling devices or living things to fly.	• Communicate, p. 165, q. 1, 4
FL6.2 e. Determine how lift is affected by the shape of a surface by planning and carrying out steps to investigate the effect of wing shape on lift.	• Work On It, p. 163
FL6.2 f. Describe and represent methods for altering drag in flying devices, such as a bird spreading wings or an airplane employing flaps.	• Work On It, p. 163
FL6.3 a. Assess the characteristics of flying objects (e.g., balloon, kite, glider, airplane, helicopter, and rocket).	• Communicate, p. 165, q. 1

Background Information

The four forces of flight explain how living and non-living things are able to fly. Unbalanced forces work such that the force of lift must overcome the force of gravity. The lighter an object is, the less lift is required to overcome the force of gravity. As well, many living things are shaped to allow them to be caught by wind. For instance, poplar tree seeds are covered in a fuzz to allow them to be carried by wind more easily than if they were smooth like a sunflower seed. A bird's wing shape determines the amount of drag created and the amount of thrust required to move the bird forward, as well as the ease of turning in the air.

traditional ***KNOWLEDGE***

This lesson highlights questions that Aboriginal peoples may ask about the world around them, and the lessons they might learn from Mother Earth. The Thunderbird in the pictograph on student book page 160 is an image of a powerful spirit in the form of a bird. It is believed that lightning flashes from its eyes or beak, and the beating of its wings causes thunder. The story, Crow Brings the Daylight, is an Inuit story that describes how daylight came to the North. The pictograph, the story, and the Ask an Elder profile emphasize the importance of living things in the world.

Get Started ▶

- Draw students' attention to the pictograph of the Thunderbird on student book page 160. Ask students if they have heard about the Thunderbird before. What do students know? Take a moment to explore the significance of the Thunderbird in First Nations and Métis culture.
- Before reading the Crow Brings the Daylight Inuit story, listen to an audio sample of Vince Gassi's "Land of the Midnight Sun," which can be heard at http://www.vincegassi.com/concert_band.html. As noted in the student book, this concert band piece was written for and dedicated to a Canadian high school band, and is based on the story Crow Brings the Daylight. Ask students to visualize which parts of the story the composer was trying to portray during different sections of his music.

! Images on rocks are thought to be paintings of visions that individuals or possibly medicine people may have had. Thunderbird is a common rock painting because of its spiritual importance to the Cree. About 700 rock painting sites have been found across the Canadian Shield, with about 70 of them found in Saskatchewan.

Crow Brings the Daylight

traditional **KNOWLEDGE**

- Scientists might describe a phenomenon such as the six months of darkness as the result of Earth's tilt. First Nations and Métis people and other Aboriginal groups might employ a cultural story, for very different reasons. Differences among explanations don't lessen their value or their validity. A cultural lesson and a respect for a sacred animal such as the crow provide an inherent value to that teaching. Thus, respect for nature and observation of natural phenomena are imparted. If a particular way of understanding the natural world helped the First Nations and Métis people to survive, to define themselves, and to encapsulate their cultural beliefs, then that way of knowing has value and validity in its own right.
- A comparison of a cultural story to a scientific theory examined by Western standards holds little merit. The purpose of these cultural stories was never meant for scientific scrutiny. Indigenous teachings comprise a system of beliefs, long held, which First Nations and Métis and other Aboriginal peoples use to define their place in the natural world. These teachings provide social norms, important lessons, and values that are significant to heritage and culture.
- Traditional stories are vehicles by which cultural teachings are given. Some key points to note are:
  - Traditional First Nations and Métis stories must only be told when there is snow on the ground. Winter is the season of storytelling.
  - The concept of spirit is key to traditional ways of knowing. Teachers should respect that First Nations and Métis people provide a spiritual explanation for a natural phenomenon that is completely valid in their ways of knowing.
  - Stories are given when Tobacco offerings are made. Tobacco is crucial in many First Nations and Métis cultures to show respect for the teaching and for the teacher. Only when the person listening to the story has given Tobacco (or some such gift) to the storyteller can the listener use and tell the story.
  - Cultural stories often impart an important lesson for the listener to discern.
- Students can read this story aloud using the method where one student starts a section and names the next reader when he or she has finished reading.
- After reading the story, ask the questions at the bottom of student book page 161 out loud and ask students to reflect on them. Ask students to summarize their thinking by comparing the questions that an Aboriginal person may ask with the questions that a scientist may ask. How are they the same? How are they different? This summary could be done as a class discussion.

Four Forces in Flight

- This section has many new words that may be unfamiliar to students. One suggestion would be for the teacher to do a Think Aloud approach with this section: The teacher reads the passage aloud and states what ideas or thoughts are going through the teacher's mind as he or she reads. This method is one way of activating and integrating prior knowledge.
- A Think Aloud for the first paragraph could be as follows: "*As I read, I am going to be activating and integrating my prior knowledge.* For scientists, a **force** causes an object's motion to change. *Now, when I think about a force, I think about using my hand to move something. I guess when I push something, I am causing it to change its motion.* It can be a push or a pull. *I haven't thought of a force being a pull before. If I try to think of an example, I guess if I am pulling a wagon with a rope, I am pulling and causing the wagon's motion to stop.* **Gravity** is the force of attraction between two objects that have **mass**. *I have studied about mass before. I know that there is a difference between mass and weight, and that I weigh less on the Moon but have the same mass. Oh, yes, here in the margin it talks about how mass is the amount of matter in an object.* For example, you are pulled toward Earth, and Earth is pulled toward you. *Wow, I had never thought of it that way. I know that Earth pulls down on me, but it is hard to believe that Earth is pulled toward me! I wonder if Earth would move if I jumped really high. Probably not. It must be because my mass is so much smaller than the mass of Earth. I guess I wouldn't notice Earth moving because my mass is so small.*
- Continue the Think Aloud exercise for the entire passage to show text to self and text to world connections. Think Alouds will be suggested throughout this unit, eventually moving to student-led Think Alouds as they make their own connections.

The difference between mass and weight is a common misconception in science. Ensure that students understand that weight is the force of gravity acting on an object in newtons. Mass is the amount of matter an object contains and is usually measured in kilograms.

Since the 1930s, Professor Charles Ellington at Cambridge has studied bee flight and concluded that when a bee takes flight, the air forms a tight circle over the leading edge of its wing. This circle of air creates an area of low pressure, sucking the wing upward. These ideas will be studied in more depth later in this unit.

Origins of words can help students understand the meanings of words. The similarity between "apagin" and "apagiwin" suggests that Aboriginal peoples view the ability to fly and an engine as involving forces.

Time
60 min
Skills
• making models • observing • comparing
Grouping
pairs
Materials and Equipment
(per pair) • large piece of cardboard (from a packing box) to create "wings" • scissors • fabric ties to attach wings to arms • cloth tape
Line Masters
• LM 3-5

CAUTION!

Remind students about knowing where they are running and to be aware of other students running near them, particularly if they are in an enclosed space such as a gymnasium.

Work On It

- Organize student groups before you start, making sure that the expectations for group work are clear. Ask, *What things should you do during an investigation?*
- Read the entire procedure before starting the activity. Make sure all group members understand the procedure. Share the work. Everyone should participate. Be respectful of others and stay focussed on the task.
- Use LM 3-5 Wing Design to show the suggested size and shape for each type of wing.
  - The long wings should be approximately 1.0 m long. The short wings should be approximately half the length of the long wings, or 0.5 m long.
  - The wide wings should be approximately the 0.6 m wide. The narrow wings should be approximately half the width of the wide wings, or 0.3 m wide.
- Students can be arranged into groups of four pairs (8 students). Each pair can be assigned a different shape of wing to create, which will then be shared with other pairs within their larger groups.
- Each student should experience the feel of each pair of wings as they run. Partners help tie the wings on and share ideas. Observations can be recorded on LM 3-5 or in a student-constructed observation table.
- After each person has had an opportunity to be the runner, have a class discussion about the types of observations that students are making. These observations should include their ideas on drag and ease of turning. Remind students to write down observations on their tables. It is important to compare each new set of wings to their previous observations. Words like "more," "less," "easier," and "harder" are important when making these comparisons.
- Students may find that long and wide wings create the most drag and make turning the most difficult. Short and wide wings create a medium amount of drag and make turning easy. Long and narrow wings create a medium amount of drag and make turning difficult. Short and narrow wings create the least amount of drag and make turning easiest.

Think Again! Shaped for Action

- Ask students to reflect on what they learned in the Work On It activity. Ask them to predict which types of wing shapes allow birds to glide or fly faster.
- Make connections between the types of birds mentioned on student book pages 164 and 165 and student observations during the Work On It activity.

Communicate

If students struggle with answering question 1, sketch the diagram from question 1 on the board so that each section of the balloon flight can be discussed. Answer a few of the sections as a class before students try to answer the remainder on their own.

Venn diagrams are used in a number of instances in this unit. If your students are unfamiliar with a Venn diagram, model completing one that compares two ideas they are familiar with before they answer question 2.

1. Section A: Gravity equals lift because the balloon is not yet rising.

   Section B: Gravity is less than lift because the balloon is rising.

   Section C: Gravity equals lift because the balloon is flying at a constant altitude.

   Section D: Gravity equals lift because the balloon is flying at a constant altitude.

   Section E: Gravity is less than lift because the balloon is rising.

   Section F: Gravity equals lift because the balloon is flying at a constant altitude.

   Section G: Gravity is greater than lift because the balloon is coming down.

2. Answers may vary but could be similar to:

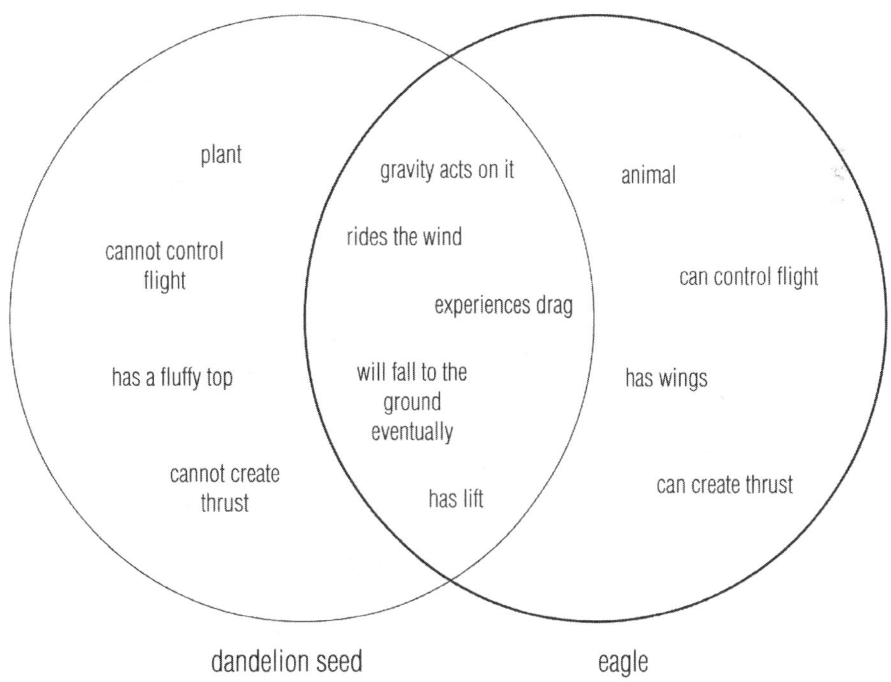

3. Arrow A represents thrust. Arrow B represents drag. Arrow C represents lift. Arrow D represents gravity.

4. **a.** When drag is greater than thrust, the swallow will slow down.
   b. When lift is greater than gravity, the swallow will fly higher.
   c. When drag is equal to thrust, the swallow will fly at a constant speed.

BUILD ON WHAT YOU KNOW

The first section of the students' Unit Technical Report is a summary of the four forces of flight. Students should list, define, and sketch these four forces. A suggestion would be to ask students to hand in their Technical Reports after this lesson so you can assess their work for organization, accuracy, and thoroughness. Written comments will help guide students in future lessons.

For ESL/ELL

Encourage ESL/ELL students to record their thinking with diagrams and sketches in their Unit Technical Reports.

For Reteaching

Ask students to identify the sections on student book pages 162 and 163 that they are having difficulty understanding. Ask them to discuss these ideas with you or with a peer.

For Enrichment

Challenge students to research the ways that different living things achieve flight. Good choices to compare are hummingbirds, ducks, eagles, and insects such as dragonflies. Ask students, *How are the flight techniques of these creatures different? How are they the same?* You may want to organize students into groups to research one type of living thing and then ask them to share their findings with their peers.

Assessment *for* Learning

What to Look For in Student Work	What to Do
Students should be able to distinguish among the four forces of flight, and how they relate to an animal's or object's flight path. Collect students' Technical Reports as a formative assessment. Give comments regarding quality of summaries, organization of work, and general ideas for improvement. As a class, discuss different situations that may exist in a bird's flight. How would a bird's flight look if all forces are equal? The bird could either be at rest or moving at a constant speed in the air at a constant height. What happens when one of the forces is larger or smaller?	• If students are having difficulty determining the results of unbalanced forces, ask them to review Communicate questions 3 and 4 with a partner. If they are still having difficulty, ask them to create their own questions or diagrams showing unbalanced forces, and share them with a partner. • Give suggestions in your teacher comments when assessing student technical reports to help guide their thinking if corrections need to be made.

ASK AN ELDER	Stewart Prosper: The Winged Ones	Page 166

traditional *KNOWLEDGE*

- First Nations and Métis peoples have a strong connection to the natural world. Creative expressions, such as song, dance, prayer, ceremony, crafts, regalia, and clothing reflect symbols of birds, animals, plants, etc. Birds are among the many animals sacred to the First Nations and Métis people of Saskatchewan. Collected for food, for their feathers, and used in ceremony, birds of most kinds are well respected and in some cases revered by the Plains people. Through their depictions and their ceremonies, their awe of the birds and their wonder about flight is evident. Birds hold a central place within the lives and traditions of many First Nations and Métis peoples. Elder Stewart's piece provides a small window, a mere taste of that importance. From food to ceremonies to naming moons in their calendar, birds possess a strong influence.
- Of the many different species in Saskatchewan, the eagle holds a pre-eminent place. For First Nations and Métis peoples, the eagle is a protector, a symbol of strength and courage. At ceremonies such as powwows, eagle feathers and an eagle claw, proudly displayed on the staff, lead the procession. These feather-adorned headdresses are used only at special ceremonies. For their valour and their achievement, the Plains people honour their best with eagle feathers.
- Some Canadians misunderstand the rights of First Nations and Métis peoples to eagle feathers in traditional ceremonies. It is illegal for non-Aboriginal Canadians to possess, buy, trade, or transport feathers without a licence. But under the Canadian Constitution, First Nations and Métis peoples have the right to acquire and possess eagle feathers for ceremonial purposes. For feathers to be taken and collected, a spiritual vision or dream, an interpretation of that dream, a sacred ceremony, and the community's (often an Elder's) permission are needed. Such practices ensure that the legal right is not abused.
- Birds, such as ducks and geese, not only form part of the traditional diet of the First Nations and Métis people of Saskatchewan, they also lend their names to the months of the year. First Nations and Métis peoples have observed for millennia that the migration of birds and their mating seasons occur with a particular frequency. This frequency allows the Plains people to determine times of year.
- Learning the habits of the birds provided traditional First Nations and Métis peoples with ways to survive and to predict where sources of food might be. Through their observations, they practised conservation. *We [the First Nations people] studied the birds to learn their habits, to know when they were nesting, when their feathers were moulting, when to gather eggs. We never took all the eggs for food. We left most of the eggs in the nest. It was in this way we practised conservation [stewardship].* (Source: Delvin Kaniwiykeho and Elder Stewart Prosper).

2 Ancient Technologies

Page 167

Time

2 class periods

Key Terms

- dart
- foreshaft
- atlatl
- fletching
- arrowhead
- flint-napping

Line Masters

- LM 3-6

Indicator Assessment Chart

Indicator	Assessment Opportunities
FL6.1 d. Research technological problems that had to be overcome to develop devices that fly (e.g., balloons, kites, gliders, airplanes, helicopters, and rockets) and explain how various creative solutions to those problems have resulted in the development of flying devices with different designs.	• Communicate, p. 170, q. 2–4
FL6.1 f. Describe examples of traditional and modern technologies developed by First Nations, Métis, and other cultures that are based on principles of flight (e.g., atlatl, bow and arrow, slingshot, catapult, boomerang, and trebuchet).	• Communicate, p. 170, q. 1–4
FL6.2 b. Use scientific terminology appropriately (e.g., thrust, drag, lift, and gravity) when communicating ideas about the principles of flight.	• Communicate, p. 170, q. 1
FL6.2 g. Provide examples of how science and technology have been used to solve problems related to drag in devices that fly.	• Communicate, p. 170, q. 2–4
FL6.3 b. Construct a prototype of a flying object that meets student-specified performance and aesthetic criteria.	• Work On It, p. 169
FL6.3 c. Work collaboratively with classmates to define criteria for judging the performance and aesthetics of a prototype of a flying object.	• Work On It, p. 169
FL6.3 d. Select and carefully use appropriate tools in manipulating materials and in building prototypes.	• Work On It, p. 169
FL6.3 e. Work collaboratively to collect relevant observations and data to evaluate the performance of a prototype of an object that will fly.	• Work On It, p. 169

traditional ***KNOWLEDGE***

Background Information

First Nations peoples' knowledge comes from observing living things in the world. These observations allowed First Nations people to create and change weapon technologies based on their knowledge of bird flight. Over thousands of years, First Nations people developed the spear, the atlatl-and-dart system, and the bow and arrow. Each technology had an improved flight path and allowed hunters to kill prey more efficiently and from greater distances. Over time, ancient technologies have evolved into the modern-day javelin and bow and arrow.

Get Started ▶

traditional ***KNOWLEDGE***

- Compared to modern-day weapons, the atlatl and the bow and arrow may seem primitive, but they were fantastic achievements in technology for their time and remained the weapons of choice for millennia, until steel was introduced. Teachers must avoid the use of language classing these weapons as primitive, which would denigrate the ancient technologies of the First Nations and Métis peoples. Employing what materials they could find from the prairies, First Nations and Métis peoples were able to fashion a composite bow made of bone and wood that could shoot as far as, if not farther than, modern compound bows. That the invention of the bow evolved in North America among the First Nations and Métis peoples, independently from other civilizations such as China, is a testament to the ingenuity of the Plains people.
- A second important point that teachers might need to address is the concept of technology. Technology, loosely defined, consists of tools or techniques that serve a function. Thus, bows and atlatls are technology. Students may have a narrow belief that technology consists only of electronic devices such as cellphones or computers.
- Ask students to think about the technologies they use every day. What is their purpose? Many technologies we have are related to the food we eat, our shelter, communication, and transportation. This was true in the past as well.

The Spear

- A timeline may help students visualize when the spear was prevalent in North America.
- Ask students, *What might Aboriginal people have done to hunt or gather food before the spear was invented? How did the invention of the spear help them?*

Mammoths existed in North America until approximately 4500 years ago, meaning that spears, atlatls and darts, and mammoths existed at the same time. Research the size of a woolly mammoth. Ask students to visualize what it might have been like to face a huge animal with only a spear, and how it may have been easier to face this prey with an atlatl-and-dart.

The Atlatl-and-Dart System

- The atlatl-and-dart system, or more precisely its design, was employed by many different Aboriginal cultures all over the world. Atlatls are hunting tools that use leverage to launch spears or darts. The darts that were employed by ancient migratory people use principles of flight and potential/mechanical energy transfer.
- The ancient weapon cannot be assigned identifiably to any particular language group in Saskatchewan but is believed to have originated 25 000 years ago from Europe and slowly spread across the globe.
- The darts or the spears launched by the atlatl use principles of aerodynamics, lift, and drag. The shape of the spear/dart head deflecting faster-moving air above the spear or dart creates low air pressure above the atlatl. The slower-moving air below the atlatl exerts more pressure, creating a pressure differential that pushes the spear or dart upward. As long as the dart/spear is moving with high speed, the pressure difference is enough to push the spear or dart upward during flight. Then, as the speed of the dart slows, the upward push lessens and the effect of the constant pull of gravity on the spear or dart increases. The fletching of the darts creates a small amount of drag, which stabilizes the dart and prevents it from pitching to either side.
- Some interesting websites for this lesson are (If a given url no longer functions, please search using the website's title.):
  - Kurt Kleiner, "Spear Thrower," New Scientist, 15 May 1999, pp. 40–43, http://www.donsmaps.com/atlatl.html
  - The Royal Saskatchewan Museum has an ancient stone that was used as a weight on the atlatl. The weight that is attached to the atlatl provides a pivot for the dart and apparently muffles the "zip" noise of the dart or spear when it is thrown. http://www.royalsaskmuseum.ca/research/collections/aboriginal_history/neat_stuff_archaeology.shtml
  - "Prehistory, Northern Saskatchewan," *Encyclopedia of Saskatchewan,* http://esask.uregina.ca/entry/prehistory_northern_saskatchewan.html
  - Perkins, William R., "Archeological, Experimental, and Mathematical Evidence Supporting the Use of the Atlatl as a Primary Big Game Procurement Weapon of Prehistoric Americans." *Bulletin of Primitive Technology 20*: 69–72.
  - Thomas J. Elpel, "The Atlatl and Dart: An Ancient Hunting Weapon," http://www.hollowtop.com/atlatlbob.htm
- Lesson plans on how to make and use an atlatl-and-dart system are available.

- Add the atlatl-and-dart to your timeline.
- Ask students, *How did the invention of the atlatl-and-dart system help Aboriginal people?*
- The atlatl-and-dart system is a weapon that students may not be familiar with. There are a number of instructional videos on the Internet that would allow students to see how this system works and how it is different from a bow and arrow. To find these videos, access Google Videos or YouTube and search "atlatl."

The Bow and Arrow

- Bows and arrows supplanted the atlatl-and-dart system as the weapon of choice. It is probably safe to say that bows and arrows were used by all First Nations groups in Saskatchewan. The principles of arrow flight are the same as for the atlatl dart.
- The type of wood used for the shaft, the feathers and their number, and the type of material used for the arrowhead were largely determined by availability of materials in the environment and the purpose for which the arrows were used.
- Research articles suggest that the common number of feathers needed to stabilize an arrow is three, though some arrows had four or more feathers. Feathers that are slightly curved can provide a rotation much as rifling does for bullets and thus increases the accuracy of the projectile.
- Some interesting sites about bows and arrows are (If a given url no longer functions, please search using the website's title.):
  - About the Indian Bow and Arrow, by Saxton Pope: Stories about the origin of the bow and a comparison of weight and distances of bow capability:
    http://www.webdyer.com/artifacts_fossils/assorted_pages/arrows.htm
  - Weapons and Other Tools Used in Pre-European Contact Times (University of Calgary):
    http://www.ucalgary.ca/applied_history/tutor/calgary/weapons.html
- Add the bow and arrow to your timeline.
- Ask students, *How did the invention of the bow and arrow help Aboriginal people?*

(!) Aboriginal peoples took care to use as much of a plant or animal as possible so that there would be little waste. The highbush cranberry tree is a good example. Its leaves, berries, and branches were all used for different aspects of daily life.

Time
30 min
Skills
• making models • experimenting
Grouping
groups
Materials and Equipment
(per group) • balloon • tape • scissors • cardboard (Bristol board or cereal box) • straws • string
Line Masters
none

Work On It

- Organize student groups before you start, making sure that the expectations for group work are clear. Ask, *What things should you do during an investigation?*
- Read the procedure before starting the activity. Everyone should participate. Remind students to share the work, to be respectful of others, and to remain focussed on the task.
- This open inquiry activity will allow students to explore possible ways to control the motion of a balloon.
- Before students begin building, ask the class to brainstorm the criteria for the best flight path. Criteria will vary, but may include distance, straightness, height, and being parallel to the ground.
- One way to measure the flight path distance and straightness is to place a strip of masking tape, approximately 7 m long, on the floor. Students could try to fly their devices along the length of the tape. Measurements can be made from a starting point at the end of the tape for distance, and a measurement can be taken perpendicular from the tape to the landing point to determine the device's straightness.
- Features of balloon-objects that have a good flight path could include being balanced, having a pointed nose, and having control over the air escaping from the back of the balloon.

Communicate

Students could work in pairs to complete these questions. Students may need to do further research if they are unsure of relative sizes of arrows, darts, and spears.

1. Students may use LM 3-6 Ancient Technologies to help answer this question.

Force	Spear	Atlatl-and-dart system	Bow and arrow
Thrust	**Provided by:** person's arm **Size:** small	**Provided by:** atlatl, or throwing board **Size:** medium	**Provided by:** bow string **Size**: large
Drag	**Caused by:** large spear head **Size:** large	**Caused by:** medium-sized dart head and fletching **Size:** medium	**Caused by:** small-sized arrowhead and fletching **Size:** small
Gravity	**Size:** large	**Size:** medium	**Size:** small

2. The problem with the spear was that it had large forces of gravity and drag acting on it, and a relatively small thrust. This meant that the spear could not be thrown a great distance with accuracy. The atlatl-and-dart system decreased both gravity and drag, and increased thrust.
3. The problem with the atlatl-and-dart system is that it still had medium-sized forces of gravity and drag acting on it, with medium-sized thrust. This meant that the atlatl-and-dart system could be used from farther distances with accuracy, but was difficult to use on horseback or from very great distances. The bow and arrow decreased both gravity and drag, and increased thrust.

4. Ancient bows and arrows were still limited in the amount of thrust that the bow could apply to the arrow. As well, ancient arrows were not perfectly straight, which affected their accuracy. Modern bows and arrows are made of strong, flexible materials that allow more thrust to be applied to the arrow, and the arrows are made to be perfectly straight to increase their accuracy.

BUILD ON WHAT YOU KNOW

This section of students' technical reports highlights their knowledge of how to create a projectile that moves in a straight line. The criteria for making a projectile fly in a straight line include balance, a tapered shape, and controlling the thrust being applied to the projectile.

For Reteaching

Videos and pictures of the three weapon types would help students visualize their relative size, weight, and how thrust is applied to them to create flight.

Students may refer to LM 3-1 Unit 3 Summary. Ask, *What ideas have you learned about so far in this unit? Did you learn them in Lesson 1 or 2?*

For Enrichment

Research the different types of bows and arrows used by First Nations people in Canada. Different First Nations groups used different bow sizes and structures, and specific arrows were designed for various purposes and flight paths.

Assessment *for* Learning

What to Look For in Student Work	What to Do
Students should show their understanding of the forces of flight related to hunting technologies in their answers to the Communicate questions. As well, their Technical Report summary should include an understanding of how to create a straight flight path in a projectile.	• If students are having difficulty determining the difference in force sizes acting on hunting technologies, ask them to sketch pictures of the relative sizes of spears, darts, and arrows. Sketches will help them determine the differences in gravity and drag. To help them visualize the amount of thrust provided to each weapon, ask students to examine the mechanism that applies thrust: the arm, throwing stick, and bow.

3 Around the World: Fascination with Flight

Page 171

Time
2–3 class periods
Key Terms
• fuselage • sound barrier • atmosphere • propel
Line Masters
• LM 3-7

Indicator Assessment Chart

Indicator	Assessment Opportunities
FL6 1 c. Examine the role of inspiration and aesthetic design in the development of flying devices (e.g., initial attempts at trying to fly were based on observations of birds).	• Work On It, p. 174
FL6.1 d. Research technological problems that had to be overcome to develop devices that fly (e.g., balloons, kites, gliders, airplanes, helicopters, and rockets) and explain how various creative solutions to those problems have resulted in the development of flying devices with different designs.	• Work On It, p. 174 • Communicate, p. 175, q. 2
FL6.1 e. Discuss historical and current contributions of individuals, including Canadians, who have contributed to scientific understanding and technological developments related to flight.	• Work On It, p. 174 • Communicate, p. 175, q. 2
FL6.2 h. Compare the sources of thrust of various constructed flying devices including the propeller, jet engine, and solid or liquid-fuelled rocket.	• Work On It, p. 174
FL6.3 c. Work collaboratively with classmates to define criteria for judging the performance and aesthetics of a prototype of a flying object.	• Communicate, p. 175, q. 2

Background Information

Early attempts at flight were modelled after flying animals, such as birds and bats. It took many years of experimentation and many aviation catastrophes before inventors finally moved away from the flapping wings to the gliders of Sir George Cayley's design. Flight technologies have changed life on Earth. They have even allowed humans to send technologies beyond Earth's atmosphere.

Get Started ▶

- Ask students to think back to the Work On It activity in Lesson 1. Ask them to reflect on the idea of flapping wings to fly. Do they think this is a possibility? Read the introductory legend about Icarus and Daedalus, which represents peoples' belief that they could fly under their own power.

Ideas, Failures, and Success

- Read student book pages 171–173 orally. Ask a different student to read each time a new date and event is stated. In another form of a Think Aloud exercise, ask another student to respond to the section that was just read with a question he or she may have as a result of the reading. For example:
  Student 1: 1260. Robert Bacon, a Franciscan monk in England, suggested that a person could sit in the middle of an "engine for flying," which would move artificial wings made to beat the air.
  Student 2: I wonder what a Franciscan monk is. I think I know what a monk is, but a Franciscan monk must be something different, because why would a monk be talking about science stuff like engines and flying?
- Ask if anyone knows the answer to the questions raised. It is possible that there will be many unanswered questions that students can choose to find the answers to later. The act of wondering can help students become more actively involved in their reading, regardless of whether the question is answerable or not.

(!) When engines were beginning to replace horses, the term "horsepower" was originally defined as the amount of power that one horse would have to put out to pull a single cart. This definition allowed people to compare the output of steam engines to the power output of draft horses. Since that time, horsepower has been used to measure the output of engines, turbines, electric motors, and other machinery.

Beyond the Atmosphere — Flight into Space

- Ask students to volunteer to read this section orally. Ask another student to respond to the section that was just read with a question, comment, or summary.

(!) Ask students to imagine what it would be like to have your airplane malfunction when you are travelling at twice the speed of sound. Ask them to visualize being ejected from an airplane at this speed and having their suit catch on fire, with their ejector seat getting caught in their parachute. What would students be thinking and feeling? Chuck Yeager survived this situation in 1963.

Time
60 min

Skills
- communicating

Grouping
groups

Materials and Equipment
(per group)
- Bristol board
- black markers
- ruler

Line Masters
- none

Work On It

- Students' timelines will cover 160 years if the final year on their timelines is 2010. This is a very nice number to work with.
- An easy way to divide the Bristol board is to split the total length in half, then half again, then half again, then half again. This will give 16 markings, each 10 years apart.
- Information that should be included on the timeline is the date, the event, and the inventor.
- Having a variety of aviation history books on hand or access to the Internet will make it easier for students to find an additional event to share with their classmates.
- Create a summary table at the front of the room where the additional aviation events can be listed for students to add to their timelines.

Communicate

The purpose of the Communicate questions is for students to realize that in science and technology studies, there are many more failures than successes, and that failures have a huge impact on the advancement of technology. Failures in aviation may be a crash, death, fire, or design that was unsuccessful. There is flexibility with how formal you would like to make student presentations. Students may use LM 3-7 Failure! to help organize their thinking.

1. Answers may vary. Students may initially see failure as a negative thing that makes people feel bad. They may talk about failing an exam, or failing a fitness goal in gym class. When considering whether failure can ever be good, you could talk about having the chance to rewrite a test that they had failed initially. Did they study harder or get help to understand so they could pass the second test? Did their failure help them try to learn what they didn't understand? In science, failure often provides motivation to try harder and figure out a different way to do something. We learn much more when something goes wrong than when our experiments go exactly as predicted.
2. Answers will vary. People or events that students may identify as failures could include Apollo 13, Amelia Earhart, the Hindenburg, or the death of Otto Lilienthal.

For ESL/ELL

Students may benefit from completing a table summary of the important dates, contributions, and people contributing to flight technologies around the world. Table headings could include:

What technology or discovery was created?	When was this technology or discovery made?	Who created this new technology?

For Enrichment

Students can add the failures researched in the Communicate section to their timelines to gain a better understanding of how failures shaped flight technologies.

Assessment *for* Learning

What to Look For in Student Work	What to Do
Students should be able to discuss how failures have helped to improve flight technologies.	• Add the failures to student timelines to show how subsequent discoveries and technologies grew out of the failures that occurred.

4 Liftoff

Page 176

Time
2 class periods
Key Terms
• tether lines • variables
Line Masters
• LM 3-8

Indicator Assessment Chart

Indicator	Assessment Opportunities
FL6.2 a. Diagram how the forces of thrust, drag, lift, and gravity act on living things or devices that fly through the air.	• Communicate, p. 179, q. 1
FL6.2 b. Use scientific terminology appropriately (e.g., thrust, drag, lift, and gravity) when communicating ideas about the principles of flight.	• Communicate, p. 179, q. 1
FL6.2 c. Generate questions related to the principles of flight and rephrase those questions in a testable form (e.g., rephrase a question such as "Why can some gliders travel farther than others?" to "What effect does wing shape have on the distance a glider can travel?").	• Work On It, p. 177
FL6.2 d. Describe the role of lift in overcoming gravity and enabling devices or living things to fly.	• Work On It, p. 177 • Communicate, p. 179, q. 1, 2
FL6.3 a. Assess the characteristics of flying objects (e.g., balloon, kite, glider, airplane, helicopter, and rocket).	• Work On It, p. 177 • Communicate, p. 179, q. 1–4 • Build On What You Know, p. 179
FL6.3 b. Construct a prototype of a flying object that meets student-specified performance and aesthetic criteria.	• Work On It, p.177 • Communicate, p. 179, q. 2
FL6.3 c. Work collaboratively with classmates to define criteria for judging the performance and aesthetics of a prototype of a flying object.	• Work On It, p. 177
FL6.3 d. Select and carefully use appropriate tools in manipulating materials and in building prototypes.	• Work On It, p. 177
FL6.3 e. Work collaboratively to collect relevant observations and data to evaluate the performance of a prototype of an object that will fly.	• Work On It, p. 177
FL6.3 f. Demonstrate and explain the importance of selecting appropriate processes for investigating scientific questions and solving technological problems (e.g., explain why it is important to change one variable while keeping others constant in designing and testing prototypes of flying objects).	• Work On It, p. 177

Background Information

Heated air rises because it takes up more space than cooler air does, and is therefore lighter than cooler air. If a large amount of heated air is contained in a structure such as a plastic bag or balloon, the whole structure will lift. This lift will occur as long as the lift created by the heated air overcomes the force of gravity holding the structure down.

This concept is introduced first because it allows students to look at two simple forces related to air and flight. By building hot-air balloons, lift and gravity can be examined in a simple and engaging way and students will be motivated to explore further.

Get Started ▶

- Ask students if they have ever seen a hot-air balloon. You may wish to have some pictures available. Ask questions such as, *Have you ever seen a hot-air balloon in flight? Was it in a book, on TV, or in real life? Have you ever taken a ride in a hot-air balloon or do you know anyone who has? Where are hot-air balloons usually flown? Why?*
- Read the Get Started section as a class. Pause to allow students time to reflect on the ideas and questions within this section. Ask, *What would it be like to be one of the Montgolfier brothers at a time when hot-air balloons didn't exist? What might they have felt or thought about their invention?*

It is unusual for an invention to be named after its inventor. Exceptions include the Braille alphabet, which was invented by Louis Braille in the early 1800s, and the diesel engine, which was invented by Rudolf Diesel in 1897.

Time

1.5 class periods

Skills

- communicating
- observing
- measuring
- predicting

Grouping

groups of 5

Materials and Equipment

(per group)

- lightweight kitchen garbage bags (51 cm × 56 cm)
- stopwatch or watch with a second hand
- hair dryer (with variable speeds and temperatures)
- scissors
- thread
- extension cord
- tape
- variety of other types and sizes of bags

Line Masters

- LM 3-8

CAUTION!

Be careful when handling the hot hair dryer. Do not let the plastic bag or your fingers touch the heated end of the dryer. Make sure to hold the dryer at least 10 cm from the opening of the bag.

Work On It

- Organize student groups before you start, making sure that the expectations for group work are clear. Ask, *What things should you do during an investigation?*
- Read the procedure before starting the activity. Make sure all group members understand the procedure. Share the work. Everyone should participate. Be respectful of others and stay focussed on the task.
- As a class, read the Safety Caution on student book page 177. Talk to students about launching their balloons. Ensure that they are aware of hazards such as electrical lines, ceiling fans, air ducts, and so on.
- For best results, conduct this activity in a draft-free room with a high ceiling. If weather conditions are favourable (i.e., a cool, windless day) and a long enough extension cord (or cordless hair dryer) is available, consider performing this activity outside, using larger bags (e.g., dry-cleaning bags).
- Prepare a class summary table on chart paper for students to record their flight time data.
- Once students have had one or two successful flights with their balloons, choose the best or longest flight time to share with the class.
- Use LM 3-8 Balloon Flight to guide students in recording their data.
- Ask groups to discuss variables that affect flight times. Students may come up with variables such as the mass of the balloon, the size of the opening of the balloon, the type of material the balloon is made of, the volume of the balloon, and the temperature of the air blown into the balloon.
- Ask each group to choose one of these variables and create a testable question. An example of a testable question is given on page 178 of the student book in Procedure step 6.
- Each group should predict the answer to their testable question.
- Each group needs to create a procedure to test their question. Each group should achieve one or two successful flights with their redesigned balloons and choose their best or longest flight time to share with the class. Groups should compare their results with their predictions.
- As a class, discuss each group's question, prediction, and results. Make a list of variables that a balloonist could adjust to impact the flight path of a hot-air balloon. These variables could include mass (weight), size, material, temperature of air, and size of opening.

! Students can get updated on Michel Fournier's plans at his website, Le Grand Saut (http://www.legrandsaut.org/).

Communicate

Bring the class back together to share their findings. Compare the forces acting on a balloon to the force diagrams drawn in Lesson 1.

1. A force diagram for a hot-air balloon would only include lift (up) and gravity (down). When a hot-air balloon rises, lift is greater than gravity. When a hot-air balloon descends, gravity is greater than lift.
2. **a.** A balloon will fly higher if it is made bigger, if more heat is used, and if it is lighter.
   b. A balloon will stay in the air for a long period of time if it is made bigger, if it is lighter, and if the opening at the bottom is smaller.
3. A balloon will fly higher and longer on a cold day because there is a greater temperature difference between the hot air in the balloon and the cooler surrounding air.
4. Hot-air balloonists carry a supply of propane with them that they can burn as they go. This allows them to reheat the air in the balloon as needed. When they want to land, they let some of the hot air out of the balloon and allow it to sink slowly to the ground.

BUILD ON WHAT YOU KNOW

Students should describe the variables that affect the flight of a hot-air balloon, including mass, volume, air temperature, balloon material, and size of the opening of the balloon. It would be a good time to collect student Technical Reports once again as a formative assessment. Give comments regarding quality of summaries, organization of work, and general ideas for improvement. Doing so will give you a good sense of student understanding of unit concepts.

For ESL/ELL

Create a balloon graphic that would show the features of two different hot-air balloons. One balloon would be designed to fly the longest, and the other balloon would be designed to fly the shortest. Variables to include in these diagrams are:

Longest flight	Shortest flight
small opening	large opening
light balloon material	heavy balloon material
large volume	small volume
hot air temperature inside the balloon	cold air temperature inside the balloon
cold air temperature outside the balloon	warm air temperature outside the balloon
small basket mass	large basket mass

For Enrichment

Students may be interested in organizing a balloon tournament. They could measure the distance from the launch area and total flight time. They could award pilot certificates to the balloons that remain aloft the longest, travel the longest distance, or attain the greatest height.

Assessment *for* Learning

What to Look For in Student Work	What to Do
Students should be able to answer the following questions: – Why do you think your balloon flies? – What do you think makes it stop flying after a while? – Do you think your balloons fly the same way that real hot-air balloons do? – Do you think the air temperature makes any difference to how well your balloon flies? Why or why not?	• If students have difficulty answering the Communicate questions, ask them to review the four forces of flight described in Lesson 1. Another suggestion would be to build the "ideal" balloon as a class demonstration, using the ideas that students have identified in their activity, such as mass (weight), temperature of air, and size of opening.

5 Flying Canadians

Page 180

Time

2–3 class periods

Key Terms

- *Avro Arrow*
- Black Brant
- Alouette-1
- Anik-1
- Canadarm
- Canadarm2

Line Masters

- LM 3-9

Indicator Assessment Chart

Indicator	Assessment Opportunities
FL6.1 d. Research technological problems that had to be overcome to develop devices that fly (e.g., balloons, kites, gliders, airplanes, helicopters, and rockets) and explain how various creative solutions to those problems have resulted in the development of flying devices with different designs.	• Work On It, p. 184
FL6.1 e. Discuss historical and current contributions of individuals, including Canadians, who have contributed to scientific understanding and technological developments related to flight.	• Work On It, p. 184 • Communicate, p. 184, q. 1
FL6.1 g. Explain how inventions based on principles of flight have changed the way people work, live, and interact with the environment locally, nationally, and globally (e.g., bush planes in northern Saskatchewan, scheduled airline travel, supply of cargo to remote communities and mine sites, and transoceanic air travel).	• Work On It, p. 184

Background Information

Canadian aviation history began with a hot-air balloon called the *Star of the East*, which flew over New Brunswick in 1840. This event was exciting and terrifying for thousands of spectators in Saint John, who had never seen a person ascend so high. The balloon's flight lasted for 1 h and 15 min and the balloon descended approximately 30 km east of Saint John. Almost 30 years later, the Aerial Experiment Association was formed in Baddeck, Nova Scotia, led by Alexander Graham Bell. This association was instrumental in the development of many Canadian "firsts" in aviation technology.

To prepare students for Lesson 8, when students will be making their own paper gliders, ask students to investigate different types of paper gliders on their own in advance.

Get Started ▶

- Ask students to reflect on the Work On It activity in the Launch lesson. Ask, *What was Saskatchewan like before flight technologies were invented?*

Canadian "Firsts"

- Ask students to take turns reading sections of the text aloud. Explain that while the passage is being read, it is their responsibility to determine what was important about the passage. Students can either use LM 3-9 Canadian Contributions to Flight or small sticky notes to write dates, events, and inventors as they read each section. This summary can help them complete the Work On It activity in this lesson.

These additional dates, events, and inventors will be added to students' aviation timelines in the Work On It activity for this lesson.

The 1950s to Today

- Continue student reading, paired discussion, and sticky-note summaries throughout this section.
- Ask students to focus on the purpose of aviation inventions, and how those inventions have helped Canadians in the areas of transportation, communication, and defence.

Imagine being only 15 when you earn your pilot's licence. Grade 6 students aren't much younger than Victor Pearson was when he started to fly. Find out what students think is a reasonable age to be able to fly an airplane. In Saskatchewan, you can fly solo at age 14, you can get a recreational pilot permit at age 16, your private pilot licence at age 17, and your commercial pilot licence at age 18.

Time
60 min
Skills
• communicating
Grouping
groups
Materials and Equipment
(per group) • timeline charts from Lesson 3 • red marker • green marker • ruler
Line Masters
• none

Work On It

- Be sure to go over the procedure as a class so that students are clear on which colour markers to use for each piece of data they add to their timelines.
- Students can use the information from their sticky-note summaries, made when they were reading the student book.
- A trend that students may identify regarding contributions by people from Saskatchewan (green) is that many of the contributions occurred between 1910 and 1950, and were in the area of applications or uses for flight technologies, such as aerial spraying or air ambulances.
- A trend that students may identify regarding contributions by people from the rest of Canada (red) is that many of these contributions helped create more efficient, safer, or better flying machines, such as the variable-pitch propeller or crash position indicator. Canadian contributions began as early as 1840 and continue to the present day.

Communicate

You can decide the degree of detail you expect from students' research of the *Avro Arrow*. There are many good websites that students can use to help them fill in the table provided, including one created and maintained by the Saskatchewan Council for Archives and Archivists.

continued →

This site not only gives basic information about the *Avro Arrow* project, but also provides a list of additional links that may be helpful. (http://scaa.usask.ca/gallery/arrow/)

1. Arguments that support the viewpoint that it was a good move to destroy the *Avro Arrow* could include the high costs associated with its development, and the fact that Canada had become part of the United States Aviation Industry from which it could purchase aviation technology at much lower cost than developing its own. Arguments that support the viewpoint that it was a mistake to destroy the *Avro Arrow* could include the number of lost jobs because of the shutdown, the fact that the *Avro Arrow* was much superior to any other airplane at the time, and that the aviation industry around the world didn't create anything equal to the technologies on the *Avro Arrow* until decades later.

For Reteaching

Write the contributions to flight history from Lessons 3 and 5 onto colour paper strips that match the colour coding used in the Work On It activities. Green represents those contributions made by people from Saskatchewan, red represents those contributions made by people from the rest of Canada, and black represents those contributions made by people from the rest of the world. As a class or in small groups, categorize these contributions as new technologies or new uses for technology. This exercise will help students to visualize the nature of the contributions made to flight history by the people of Saskatchewan.

For Enrichment

Ask students to formally debate the question of whether the *Avro Arrow* should have been destroyed or not. They could use their viewpoint table as a planning tool for creating arguments for and against this question. An additional activity could be to ask students to note where major aviation accomplishments occurred in Canada.

Assessment *for* Learning

What to Look For in Student Work	What to Do
After students have successfully completed their timelines and research, they should be able to answer the following questions: - How have Canadians contributed to aviation technology development? - How have people from Saskatchewan contributed to the aviation industry? - How have aviation technologies helped people in Saskatchewan and Canada?	• Ask students to work in pairs and re-examine the significance of the different-colour events on their timelines. Pairs can discuss how they might categorize Saskatchewan contributions and Canadian contributions to aviation technologies. These categories can be shared with the class. • If students are struggling with the effects of aviation technologies in Saskatchewan, they can review their lists from the Unit Launch on student book page 158.

CAREERS and PROFILES | Bob Stallard: Chief Pilot Northern Air Operations *Page 185*

- Model reading the first paragraph out loud and showing the connections you make to your own life. A possible script could look like: *Remember when I read parts of the first lesson to you and made connections to things that I already knew? Today, you are going to have a chance to do this with a partner. Here is what it might look like.* **Bob Stallard began to fly at an early age — around his mom and dad's Creighton, Saskatchewan living room.** *Talk about whether you have ever been to Creighton. Find it on a map to show students where Bob Stallard grew up.* **He used their portable turntable as his flying machine, complete with knobs and dials as his instrument panel.** *Describe what a portable turntable is. Many students would not have heard of a record player before.* **Wanting to be a pilot has been a part of his life for as long as he can remember.** *Talk to your students about when you realized you wanted to be a teacher. How old were you? Are there other jobs you wanted to have?* **"Times were tough and I was the oldest of five boys."** *Relate being the oldest of five boys to your own family and number of siblings. How would the expectations and opportunities for Bob Stallard have been different than they were for you?* **My Mom and Dad didn't have much, but they knew I had a dream, and they helped me make it happen."** *Talk about how moms and dads help their kids realize their dreams. How have you seen parents help their kids achieve something they really want?*
- For the remainder of this Careers and Profiles feature, ask students to work in pairs, alternating reading out loud to each other and making text-to-self and text-to-world connections as they do so.
- As the class completes this reading, ask students to share with the class some of the connections they made between the text and their own lives.

6 Air in Motion

Page 186

Time
2–3 class periods
Key Terms
• aerodynamics • air pressure
Line Masters
• LM 3-10

Indicator Assessment Chart

Indicator	Assessment Opportunities
FL6.2 b. Use scientific terminology appropriately (e.g., thrust, drag, lift, and gravity) when communicating ideas about the principles of flight.	• Work On It, p. 188 • Communicate, p. 192, q. 1, 2
FL6.2 d. Describe the role of lift in overcoming gravity and enabling devices or living things to fly.	• Work On It, p. 188 • Communicate, p. 192, q. 1, 2
FL6.2 e. Determine how lift is affected by the shape of a surface by planning and carrying out steps to investigate the effect of wing shape on lift.	• Work On It, p. 188

Background Information

Bernoulli's principle states that as the speed of a moving fluid increases, the pressure within the fluid decreases. Like all gases, air is considered to be a fluid. When air moves, such as when students blow air, the pressure of the air decreases. The area of stationary air surrounding the moving air has a higher pressure than the moving air does. Objects can be pushed from the area of still air into the area of moving air. This push is often described as a pull into the area of low pressure. This description is incorrect because air pressure pushes objects; it does not pull them.

Get Started ▶

- So far, students have investigated lift caused by expanding air (i.e., hot-air balloons). Most objects that fly move horizontally to give them lift. In this lesson, students will try a number of experiments to demonstrate properties of moving air. Students are asked to make the connection between moving air, air pressure, and movement of objects.

Pressure from the Air

- Begin by asking students to reflect on the inventions that tried to imitate bird flight. Ask, *Were these inventions successful?* These inventions were unsuccessful because they did not correctly imitate the movement of birds' wings in flight.

- Ask students to demonstrate the correct movement of birds' wings with their arms and hands to see how it is different from a simple flapping motion.
- Ask students to read the student book aloud to each other in pairs, making connections much like they did in the Careers and Profiles feature in Lesson 5. Ask students to monitor their comprehension by placing sticky notes in their student books in sections where they need more clarification or explanation. Ask students to share these areas of concern with the class and ask other students to address those concerns, if possible.

!

Many students do not believe that gases are fluids. One of the main features of a fluid is its ability to be poured. A short demonstration you can do to show that a gas can be poured is to put vinegar and baking soda inside an empty pop bottle and quickly close the cap. Explain that the chemical reaction occurring inside the bottle is creating carbon dioxide. In the meantime, light a candle, explaining that a candle flame needs oxygen to burn and that carbon dioxide can put out a flame. Pour the carbon dioxide out of the pop bottle to extinguish the flame.

Time

80 min

Skills

- predicting
- observing
- hypothesizing
- communicating

Grouping

pairs

Materials and Equipment

(per pair)
- 3 thin strips of notepaper (about 30 cm × 5 cm)
- index cards (about 10 cm × 15 cm)
- 3 thick straws, cut in half
- 30 plastic straws
- pencil
- paper
- compasses
- scissors
- glue or tape
- ping pong ball
- 2 empty pop cans
- 30-cm ruler

Line Masters

- LM 3-10

Work On It

- Create Aerodynamic Information Station instruction cards at each station and set out the required materials for each station.
- Put students into groups so that there is one group at each station. If you have a large class, set up two stations of each type.
- If you choose to use LM 3-10 Aerodynamic Information Station Log for this activity, photocopy enough sheets so that each student has a log booklet to record answers.
- After students have completed one activity station, call the class together to discuss the thoroughness of the answers expected at each station. Emphasize that at each station, students are expected to write a prediction, observations, answers to questions, and draw a labelled sketch.

Aerodynamic Information Station 1: Levitating with Lips

- Students may predict that the paper will remain sagging over their chins.
- Students should observe that the paper will move upward as students blow over it.
- Answers to questions:
  - The speed of air above the paper is faster than the speed of air below the paper.
  - The paper moved upward.
  - There was more air pressure below the paper.

Aerodynamic Information Station 2: Moving Air

- Students may predict that the index card will fly up as students blow under it.
- Students should observe that the top of the index card moves downward.

continued →

- Answers to questions:
  - The speed of air above the index card is slower than the speed of air below the index card.
  - The cardboard moved downward.
  - There was more air pressure above the cardboard.
- When students blow under the card with a straw, they should see that the downward movement of the card is more pronounced.

Aerodynamic Information Station 3: Floater Ball

- Students may need to see an example of a pre-made funnel at this information station.
- Students should each make their own funnels.
- Students may predict that the ball will fly out of the funnel.
- Students should observe that the ball remains at the bottom of the funnel.
- Answers to questions:
  - The air was moving fastest at the opening at the bottom of the funnel.
  - The air was moving slowest on the outside, or top, of the funnel.
  - The ball moved toward the bottom of the funnel.
  - The air pressure was highest at the outside, or top, of the funnel.

Aerodynamic Information Station 4: Un-Canny Movements

- Students may predict that the cans will be pushed apart.
- Students should observe that the cans move together over the straws.
- Answers to questions:
  - The air was moving the fastest between the two cans.
  - The cans moved together.
  - The area of high pressure was on the outside of the cans.

Aerodynamic Information Station 5: Temporary Attraction

- Students will try to blow the paper strips together by blowing from one side. They may need direction to blow between the strips.
- Students may predict that they can blow the paper strips together by blowing them from one side.
- Students should observe that blowing between the two paper strips causes them to move toward each other.
- Answers to questions:
  - You need to direct the air between the two paper strips in order to push them together.
  - The air was moving fastest between the two paper strips.
  - The paper strips moved together.
  - The air had the highest air pressure, or ability to push, on the outside of the paper strips.

Before reading this feature, pose the question, *When you pass a semi-trailer truck going in the opposite direction on the highway, why does your car feel like it wants to move toward the truck?* This question is a way to assess students' ability to apply their knowledge from the Aerodynamic Information Stations to examples from their own lives. Read the ! feature and compare student explanations to the explanation in the student book.

Communicate

Allow students to answer question 1 individually, then compare their answers in groups. Finally, share these answers as a class before moving on to answer question 2.

1. All answers should read: **When you blew air into an area, you created an area of *high*-speed air. The object moved *toward* this area. This means the area you blew into had *low* air pressure.**
2. Areas of high-speed air have low air pressure. Areas of low-speed or calm air have high air pressure. Objects can be pushed by high air pressure into areas of low air pressure.

try this at HOME *Changing the Channel*

- This activity is designed to have students explore the change in velocity of a fluid as it moves from a wide to a narrow channel. Students will see that as a channel narrows, the fluid moving through it will speed up.
- Students will see that as their water channel narrows, the pepper particles move faster. This means that the water is also moving faster. It is difficult to see this effect if they use running water from a tap because the water speed is already very fast. For best results, they should pour water from a pitcher.
- If students tilt the cookie sheet too much, the water will move too quickly at the top of the pan and they will not see much difference in speed when the water moves into the narrowed channel.

BUILD ON WHAT YOU KNOW

This section in students' Technical Reports should include their answer to Communicate question 2: Areas of high-speed air have low air pressure. Areas of low-speed or calm air have high air pressure. Objects can be pushed by high air pressure into areas of low air pressure. As well, students should relate these ideas to the force of lift. For an airplane, the area of low pressure must be above a wing, allowing the area of high pressure below the wing to push the wing upward. Students must also choose a sketch from one of their Work On It Aerodynamic Information Stations showing where airspeed is high and low, where air pressure is high and low, and the direction of movement of the object.

For ESL/ELL

Revisit Aerodynamic Information Station 2 or 4. Write the phrases *high airspeed, high air pressure*, and *low air pressure* on sticky notes. Ask a student to demonstrate the procedure at the aerodynamic information station. Ask students to describe what they are observing by first of all placing the sticky notes in the appropriate places. Then ask students to summarize their observation in a full sentence verbally and then in writing.

For Reteaching

After the Work On It activities and Communicate questions have been discussed, do a demonstration with your class. You will need a dime, a countertop or table, and a shallow dish. Place the dime 5–6 cm from the edge of the table, and the shallow dish 3–5 cm away from the dime. Tell students that you will attempt to move the dime into the dish without touching the dime or the dish. Ask them to predict how you might do this. Hopefully, at least one individual will apply what he or she has learned about airspeed and air pressure in this lesson and predict that you could blow across the top of the dime to cause it to jump into the air and into the dish. Try this demonstration. You may want to practise in advance to make sure your dish and dime are an appropriate distance from each other. When you blow across the top of the dime, the dime will jump into the air, join the stream of air you are blowing, and be pushed into the empty dish. Ask students for an explanation of what happens. You may need to lead them by asking, *Where is the air around the dime moving fastest?* Answer: Air above the dime moves fastest. *Where is the air pressure around the dime lowest?* Answer: Air pressure above the dime is the lowest. *Where is the air moving slowest?* Answer: Air below the dime moves slowest. This answer may need some explanation because some students may believe there is no air below the dime. Point out that there is a thin film of air between objects. The air between the table and the dime is still. *Where is the air pressure around the dime highest?* Answer: Air pressure below the dime is highest. From this answer, students should be able to conclude that the air below the dime pushed the dime upward into the stream of air you were blowing.

Assessment *for* Learning

What to Look For in Student Work	What to Do
Students should be able to summarize the relationships among airspeed, air pressure, and movement of an object.	• If students have difficulty with the explanation of these relationships, ask them to review the diagrams they drew. If they continue to have difficulty, you may wish to do a demonstration of the activity from the student book.

7 UP Lifting Theories

Page 194

Time
2 class periods

Key Terms
• angle of attack

Line Masters
• LM 3-11

Indicator Assessment Chart

Indicator	Assessment Opportunities
FL6.2 b. Use scientific terminology appropriately (e.g., thrust, drag, lift, and gravity) when communicating ideas about the principles of flight.	• Work On It, p. 195 • Communicate, p. 197, q. 1–3
FL6.2 d. Describe the role of lift in overcoming gravity and enabling devices or living things to fly.	• Work On It, p. 195 • Communicate, p. 197, q. 1–3
FL6.2 e. Determine how lift is affected by the shape of a surface by planning and carrying out steps to investigate the effect of wing shape on lift.	• Work On It, p. 195 • Communicate, p. 197, q. 1–3
FL6.3 a. Assess the characteristics of flying objects (e.g., balloon, kite, glider, airplane, helicopter, and rocket).	• Communicate, p. 197, q. 1–3 • Build On What You Know, p. 197

Background Information

Lesson 6 highlighted Bernoulli's principle, which is often incorrectly cited as the only contributor to lift in airplanes. Lesson 7 introduces students to two other phenomena that contribute to lift: the Coanda effect and the angle of attack. Bernoulli's principle highlights the push of air from an area of high pressure to an area of low pressure. The Coanda effect highlights the pull of an object into a fluid stream. The angle of attack considers the upward tilt of an airplane, causing air to hit the bottom of the wings and push the airplane upward.

Get Started ▶

- As in Lesson 6, ask students to read the student book in pairs and to monitor their own comprehension by writing any ideas they have difficulty understanding on sticky notes. Ask them to share these ideas with the class and discuss them before moving on to the next section of reading.
- To demonstrate the idea that air moves at different rates above and below an airplane wing, challenge a student to a "race." Begin at the same place. The student's "race track" should be around a desk or object, while your "race track" is straight. Designate a finish line. After the race starts, pace yourself so that you end up at the finish line at the same time your student does. Who had to travel faster?

- Ask students to look at the diagram on student book page 194. They will note that the air above the wing has to travel a longer distance than the air below the wing, meaning that it has to travel faster to get to the other side of the wing at the same time as the air below the wing.

More Lift — Discovery by Chance

- Ask students to continue reading in pairs and to monitor their comprehension by writing ideas they have difficulty understanding on sticky notes.
- Ask students to add the flight of the Coanda to their aviation history timelines.

There are many stories that describe Henri Coanda's single flight with his airplane. One story is that he had not intended to fly that day, but was surprised when the power of his engine caused his airplane to take off. His airplane, the Coanda, left the ground but not for long. His engine caught on fire and he noticed that the flames were travelling along the curved surface of the body of his airplane. He survived the crash and dedicated his life to studying the flow of fluids over curved surfaces.

Time

15 min

Skills

- hypothesizing
- experimenting
- observing

Grouping

groups

Materials and Equipment

(per group)
- plastic spoon
- running water from a tap
- tape
- 30-cm wooden ruler or other flat wooden stick

Line Masters

- none

Work On It

- This activity requires running water rather than water poured from a jug. Water poured from a jug is not moving vertically, and the angle at which it is poured will impact the motion of the spoon.
- Spoons must be taped so that they can move freely with the water.
- When the back of the spoon is under the stream of water, students will see that the stream of water follows the curve of the spoon. It runs off the tip of the bowl and its direction of flow changes slightly after it flows off the spoon. The spoon stays inside the stream of water rather than being pushed out.
- When the front of the spoon is under the stream of water, students will see that the spoon is pushed out of the stream of water.
- When the back of the spoon is in the stream of water again and the spoon is moved away from the stream of water, students will see that the bowl of the spoon is kept inside the stream of water. Eventually, the spoon will be pulled out of the stream of water as the handle is moved farther away.
- When the flow rate of the water is increased over the back of the spoon, students can move the handle farther away from the tap before the spoon is released from the stream of water.
- After completing the experiment, ask students to share their observations and thoughts, and to answer the questions in the middle of student book page 196, which guide students to connect their observations with lift in an airplane.
- The upper side of an airplane wing must be curved so that the air moving over it pulls the wing upward.
- The amount of lift increases as the wing is angled downward because the wing is pulled upward even more into the stream of air.
- If the downward angle of the wing is too great, the air can no longer pull the wing up.

Think Again! How Tilt Affects Lift

- The angle of attack also contributes to lift in airplanes. To show how, you could launch a paper airplane horizontally and then launch the paper airplane with its nose pointing up. Which launch provides more lift? The student book explains that the angled nose launch provides more lift because the air hits the bottom of the wings to push the airplane upward.
- The student book states that the angle of attack is most obvious when a plane takes off or lands. The paper airplane demonstration shows why the angle of attack is important when a plane takes off. Ask students why. The answer is that the nose up position is more obvious during takeoff and landing because when an airplane is slowing down, the other two contributors to lift — air pressure and air moving over a curved surface — are not very large. This is because the air is not moving as quickly around the wings. So, another form of lift is needed so that the plane does not suddenly fall out of the sky.

Communicate

These questions challenge students to apply their knowledge from both Lesson 6 and Lesson 7 to wing design. When answering questions 1 and 3, the students may need to be reminded that a heavier object requires more lift than a lighter object does.

1. The largest amount of lift would be created by the jet wings because they are large and are angled downward slightly. Also, the jet is the heaviest object shown, so it needs the greatest amount of lift to fly. The smallest amount of lift would be created by the hang glider wings because they are the smallest and completely straight (not angled). Also, the hang glider is the lightest object shown, so it needs the smallest amount of lift to fly. The amount of lift generated by the glider wings would be between that generated by the jet wings and the hang glider wings.
2. The wing in the middle diagram would create the most lift, the wing in the top diagram would create the next highest amount of lift, and the wing in the bottom diagram would create the least amount of lift. This is because a wing at an angle experiences the most lift unless the angle is so great that the air flow can no longer travel along its surface.
3. The "ultimate" airplane wing would be large to create the greatest amount of lift, light to ensure the smallest amount of gravity, curved on its upper surface to allow the pull of air upward, and angled downward at its tip to increase the angle of attack.

BUILD ON WHAT YOU KNOW

Student summaries of how fluids move along curved surfaces would include a discussion that fluid moves in a straight line or it follows the curve of a surface. If the surface is angled away from the stream of fluid, there is a larger amount of lift. If the angle is too great, the fluid will no longer be able to follow the surface and there will be no lift generated. So, airplane wings must be curved and angled downward to generate the greatest amount of lift. Including a sketch will help students understand and remember this effect.

For Reteaching

To reteach all of the factors that contribute to lift, use LM 3-11 Exploration Guide: The Forces of Flight. Copy the line master onto an overhead transparency and answer the questions with students. It is important that students understand that there are many contributing factors to the force of lift, including high temperatures causing air to expand, the push of air from high pressure to low pressure, the pull of air as it moves over a curved surface, and the angle of attack, which causes air to hit the bottom of the wings and push the flying device upward.

For Enrichment

Ask students to compare airplane wing shapes before and after Henri Coanda's discovery. When were wings with a curved upper surface first built? How did Coanda's research affect airplane design?

Assessment *for* Learning

What to Look For in Student Work	What to Do
Ask students if they understand the four different contributors to lift. Student answers to Communicate question 3 will help you to assess many of these ideas.	• Use LM 3-11 to summarize and clarify all ideas related to lift from Lessons 4, 6, and 7. • Collect students' Technical Reports as a formative assessment. Give comments regarding quality of summaries, organization of work, and general ideas for improvement.

8 Takeoff

Page 198

Time
1 class period
Key Terms
none
Line Masters
• LM 3-12

Indicator Assessment Chart

Indicator	Assessment Opportunities
FL6.2 c. Generate questions related to the principles of flight and rephrase those questions in a testable form (e.g., rephrase a question such as "Why can some gliders travel farther than others?" to "What effect does wing shape have on the distance a glider can travel?").	• Work On It, p. 198 • Communicate, p. 199, q. 1, 2
FL6.3 a. Assess the characteristics of flying objects (e.g., balloon, kite, glider, airplane, helicopter, and rocket).	• Work On It, p. 198 • Communicate, p. 199, q. 1, 2
FL6.3 b. Construct a prototype of a flying object that meets student-specified performance and aesthetic criteria.	• Work on It, p. 198 • Communicate, p. 199, q. 1–3
FL6.3 c. Work collaboratively with classmates to define criteria for judging the performance and aesthetics of a prototype of a flying object.	• Work on It, p. 198 • Communicate, p. 199, q. 1, 2
FL6.3 d. Select and carefully use appropriate tools in manipulating materials and in building prototypes.	• Work On It, p. 198 • Communicate, p. 199, q. 3
FL6.3 e. Work collaboratively to collect relevant observations and data to evaluate the performance of a prototype of an object that will fly.	• Work on It, p. 198 • Communicate, p. 199, q. 1–3
FL6.3 f. Demonstrate and explain the importance of selecting appropriate processes for investigating scientific questions and solving technological problems (e.g., explain why it is important to change one variable while keeping others constant in designing and testing prototypes of flying objects).	• Work On It, p. 198 • Communicate, p. 199, q. 1, 2
FL6.3 g. Analyze personally collected data and suggest improvements to a prototype design.	• Work On It, p. 198 • Communicate, p. 199, q. 1–3

Background Information

This lesson allows students to apply what they know about wing and airplane design to create their own flying devices. A suggestion would be to let them know a few weeks before this lesson that they will be creating their own paper gliders, so that they can learn about different types of paper gliders on their own beforehand. Students will need time to design, build, test, redesign, and rebuild their gliders. Students may share their knowledge with each other throughout the activity.

Get Started ▶

- As a class, discuss students' answers to the questions posed at the top of page 198.

Background Information for Designers

- Read and discuss the Background Information for Designers section to review what students have learned thus far about flight.

Time

40 min

Skills

- communicating
- experimenting
- making models
- inferring

Grouping

individuals

Materials and Equipment

(per group)
- scissors
- tape
- paper clips
- paper
- straws

Line Masters

- LM 3-12

CAUTION!
Make sure students direct their flying devices away from classmates to prevent injury.

Work On It

- Have a pile of scrap paper on hand for students to use freely for this activity.
- Remind students that they may share their knowledge of paper glider building with others, but the intent of sharing is not for the entire class to build the same type of paper glider.
- Emphasize to students that the airports are not competitions among students, but rather a way to determine which task each airplane performs best. This evaluation will be highly subjective, and students will need to use their own judgment to determine which task their airplane performs the best.
- Choose open spaces for your three airports. Set up airport labels that include a description of the flight path expected, as shown on student book page 199.
- To measure the distance from a target in Airport 3, tape a piece of string to the middle of the target. Ask students to stick a piece of masking tape with their initials on it onto the string at the distance their airplane landed from the target.
- Allow time at the end of the period for students to place their paper planes at the airport where their device performed the task the best. Review the airplane designs at each airport and look for similarities. Record these similarities on a table for students to refer to later. Students can use LM 3-12 Airport Analysis to make notes on the airplane designs.

Communicate

Students can answer Communicate questions 1, 2, and 3 individually as the class reviews design features of airplanes at each airport. Students can use LM 3-12 Airport Analysis to make notes on the airplane designs.

1. Airplanes that do well at Airport 1 will fly straight for a long distance. Design features may include tight folds and a narrow body. Airplanes that do well at Airport 2 will turn, loop, or have a curved flight path. Design features may include loose folds, a wide body, and unbalanced wings. Airplanes that do well at Airport 3 will be very accurate. Design features may include a weighted nose and small, balanced wings.
2. Students should be able to describe differences such as mass, wingspan, size, materials used, tightness of folds, nose weight, etc.
3. Answers will vary. Students may make suggestions such as using larger, smaller, lighter, or stiffer paper. They may choose to add mass (weight) to the nose or tail. Students could suggest folding the paper in a different way, making the wings bigger or smaller, or making a more aerodynamic design.
4. Answers will vary. Safety measures may include acting responsibly, not having sharp objects protrude from the airplane, throwing the device away from their peers, waiting their turn to test their device, or calling out warnings when they are ready to launch their airplanes.
5. Answers will vary. Students may have used scrap paper and recycled materials to build their devices, they may have recycled their devices after they finished testing them, and they may have conserved materials by using parts of one device to create a new one.

For ESL/ELL

To assist students in summarizing their ideas, ask them to sketch the design features common at each airport as part of their answers to Communicate question 1.

For Reteaching

Challenge students to build a paper glider that has a specific purpose, such as being able to hit a target accurately. Ask students to build and sketch this paper glider, labelling the key features that allow it to exhibit the flight path specified.

Assessment *for* Learning

What to Look For in Student Work	What to Do
Students should be able to look for patterns in design that exist at each airport, as shown by their answers to Communicate question 1.	• Ask students to build each of the three types of airplanes using the features listed in Communicate question 1. Test the airplanes to see if they match the flight path required at each airport.

9 Moving Faster, Slower, Up, and Down

Page 200

Time

2 class periods

Key Terms

none

Line Masters

- LM 3-13
- LM 3-14

Indicator Assessment Chart

Indicator	Assessment Opportunities
FL6.3 a. Assess the characteristics of flying objects (e.g., balloon, kite, glider, airplane, helicopter, and rocket).	• Work On It, p. 200 • Communicate, p. 203, q. 1, 3, 4 • Build On What You Know, p. 203
FL6.3 e. Work collaboratively to collect relevant observations and data to evaluate the performance of a prototype of an object that will fly.	• Work On It, p. 200
FL6.3 f. Demonstrate and explain the importance of selecting appropriate processes for investigating scientific questions and solving technological problems (e.g., explain why it is important to change one variable while keeping others constant in designing and testing prototypes of flying objects).	• Work On It, p. 200
FL6.3 h. Communicate procedures and results of prototype design, construction, testing, and evaluation in a technical design report.	• Communicate, p. 203, q. 1–4

Background Information

Students will find that anything on their gliders that causes drag can change the direction of flight. Adjusting flaps on the wings of their gliders will allow them to control flight patterns. Raising both flaps on the wings will force the rear of the plane down and into a climbing angle. By raising the flaps sufficiently, the plane will continue to climb until it flips over, completing a loop. Raising the flap on one wing only will cause the plane to turn in the direction of that wing.

Get Started ▶

- In this lesson, students will build stunt flyers to learn more about how adjustments to wings affect flight performance. They will follow directions to build model gliders that will be used for experimental flights focussed on variables that affect the duration and direction of flight. They are asked to write a Glider Technical Report on the results of these experimental flights. This report is an important practice before they write their Unit Technical Reports at the end of the unit.

- Ask students, *As a plane travels through the air, what makes it change direction? How does it turn? How does it climb or dive? How does it slow down or speed up?*
- Students may be aware that the small flaps and ailerons on the plane's wings are adjustable. Moving these parts causes different types of drag on the plane and makes it change direction. Explain to students that this lesson will let them try these adjustments on their own planes.

Time

50 min

Skills

- experimenting
- making models

Grouping

pairs

Materials and Equipment

(per pair)

- paper 21.6 cm × 27.9 cm (8 1/2 × 11)
- scissors
- stapler
- paper clip

Line Masters

- none

CAUTION!

Remind students about safety rules for launching their gliders. Ensure that students direct their gliders away from themselves and their classmates.

Work On It

- Ask students to work in pairs to construct their gliders following the steps shown on student book page 201. You may need to help some students fold or cut their gliders. It is important that they build their gliders carefully so that there is uniformity of design. They will then be able to compare adjustments and results fairly.
- If possible, allow students to use the gymnasium or other large space to test-fly their creations. This will help lessen the chance that students will be hit by other airplanes.
- Student should observe that:
  - When both flaps are up, the glider's nose moves up.
  - When both flaps are down, the glider's nose moves down.
  - When the left flap is up and the right flap is down, the glider will corkscrew toward the left side, or counterclockwise.
  - When the right flap is up and the left flap is down, the glider will corkscrew toward the right side, or clockwise.
- Additional adjustments may include placing weight on the tip, wing, or rear of the plane, adjusting the shape of the nose, or changing the shape of the flaps.

While students are flying their gliders, they can experiment with angle of attack. Ask, *What is the ideal angle to launch your glider?*

Think Again! Reporting on Research

- Review work that students have already done on their Unit Technical Reports. The Build On What You Know assignments at the end of each lesson are part of the body of students' Unit Technical Reports.
- A cover page states the research topic. Students' "mini" technical reports can be titled the "Glider Technical Report."

- Go through the outline of a technical report and the purpose of each section. If students have previously written science reports, discuss how technical reports are similar to and different from science reports.

Communicate

Ask students to share the results of their investigations as a class. Ask, *How are flight patterns adjusted on real airplanes? How is the way you adjusted the flight patterns of your gliders similar to the way flight patterns are adjusted on airplanes?*

Use LM 3-13 Glider Technical Report Planning Sheet to help students organize their thinking in order to write their Glider Technical Reports. Use LM 3-14 Glider Technical Report Assessment Rubric to help you assess these "mini" technical reports.

1. Answers will vary. The summary is a short overview of the report and the key findings of student research. A sample summary is: *Paper gliders and airplanes use flaps to control the direction of flight. Flight trials were done to discover that raising or lowering wing flaps changes the path of a paper glider.*
2. Answers will vary. The introduction is the section in which students describe the purpose of their research, the methods they used, and why their research is important for the reader to read. A sample introduction is: *Controlling the flight path of an airplane is very important when you are trying to design or fly one. Flaps affect the amount of drag acting on an airplane. In our research, we observed the flight path of a paper glider as its flaps were raised and lowered to find out how to control the flight path of an airplane.*
3. Answers will vary. The body is the section in which students describe the theory behind their work, their research methods, observations, results, and interpretations of results. The body of the report should include: *a definition of drag, an outline of the procedure, results of experiments, how drag and the experimental results are related, and how a pilot can control the flight of an airplane. Sketches may help students make sense of their ideas.*
4. Answers will vary. The conclusion is the section in which students write an overview of their research, methods, and results. A sample conclusion is: *We wanted to discover how a pilot could use flaps to control the flight of an airplane. By testing a paper glider, we observed that the drag was greater above the airplane when both flaps were up, causing the nose of the airplane to go up. We also observed that the drag was greater below the airplane when the flaps were both down, causing the nose of the airplane to go down. When one flap was up and the other was down, we observed that the airplane corkscrewed toward the flap that was up. A pilot steers an airplane using these techniques.*

BUILD ON WHAT YOU KNOW

Students are asked to summarize their learning by explaining how they would modify their gliders to perform specific manoeuvres. As well, students are asked to go back to their results from Lesson 8 and note the impact of different design features on flight path. These summaries may be done in written form or with labelled sketches.

For ESL/ELL

Create a graphic organizer that summarizes the effects of different flap positions on the flight path of a paper glider. For example:

Ask students to read from their graphic organizers in full sentences.

For Enrichment

Research the wing structure of a modern airplane. How do pilots control the direction of flight and altitude of the airplane using flaps and ailerons?

Assessment *for* Learning

What to Look For in Student Work	What to Do
Students should understand how flaps are used to adjust drag on a wing and change the direction of flight.	• Retest a glider as a class. Ask the class to predict the flight path when each flap adjustment is made, and then test the prediction in front of the class. Using the idea of drag, ask students to explain the connection between flight path and flap position.

10 The Four Forces of Flight

Page 204

Time

1 class period

Key Terms

- internal combustion engine
- propeller
- jet engine
- rocket engines

Line Masters

- LM 3-15

Indicator Assessment Chart

Indicator	Assessment Opportunities
FL6.2 a. Diagram how the forces of thrust, drag, lift, and gravity act on living things or devices that fly through the air.	• Communicate, p. 207, q. 3
FL6.2 b. Use scientific terminology appropriately (e.g., thrust, drag, lift, and gravity) when communicating ideas about the principles of flight.	• Work On It, p. 206 • Communicate, p. 207, q. 1–4
FL6.2 c. Generate questions related to the principles of flight and rephrase those questions in a testable form (e.g., rephrase a question such as "Why can some gliders travel farther than others?" to "What effect does wing shape have on the distance a glider can travel?").	• Communicate, p. 207, q. 2
FL6.2 h. Compare the sources of thrust of various constructed flying devices including the propeller, jet engine, and solid or liquid-fuelled rocket.	• Work On It, p. 206 • Communicate, p. 207, q. 4
FL6.3 a. Assess the characteristics of flying objects (e.g., balloon, kite, glider, airplane, helicopter, and rocket).	• Work On It, p. 206 • Communicate, p. 207, q. 2–4 • Build On What You Know, p. 207

Background Information

The purpose of this student book section is to have students review the four forces of flight, and to introduce ideas about different forms of engines that provide thrust in flying machines. Students will have the opportunity to explore expanding gases as a form of thrust in the Work On It activity in this lesson.

Get Started ▶

- Read the introduction as a class. This section is a review of Lesson 1.
- Discuss what happens to an airplane when there is no thrust. Relate the slowing airplane to the other forces at work, such as drag and lift.
- Students may make statements such as, "There is more gravity as the plane descends." If this comment arises, be sure to point out that there is less lift, but the same amount of gravity as long as nothing has been thrown out of the airplane.

Thrust and Drag — Opposing Forces

- There are many technical terms in the reading on student book page 205. To address these terms, ask students to scan the page and monitor their comprehension by making a list of difficult or technical words. Terms students might list are words like "combustion," "efficiency," "igniting," and "exhaust." Make up a class list of words that need to be explored. Assign an equal number of words to each student. Ask them to find the meaning of each word by using a dictionary, either print or on-line.
- Go back to the beginning of student book page 205 and ask students to take turns reading aloud. When a student comes to one of the difficult words identified, ask the student who researched that word to share its meaning with the class. Reread the sentence with the definition of the difficult word in mind. Ask, *Does that sentence make sense now that you know the definition of this word?*
- Ask students to continue reading the section aloud. Monitor students' comprehension of this new material.

Time
20 min
Skills
• observing • inferring
Grouping
groups
Materials and Equipment
(per group) • clear plastic film canister • Alka-Seltzer® tablet • water • safety goggles
Line Masters
• none

CAUTION!

Remind students not to stand directly over their canister rockets. Students may be tempted to approach their canisters if they take a few moments to launch. Also remind students that they must wear their safety goggles even if their group has completed the procedure because a rocket from another group may cause them injury.

Work On It

- You can find film canisters at photofinishing labs. With the popularity of digital photography, you may need to put in a request a few weeks prior to this activity so that a lab can gather these canisters for you.
- The film canisters that work best for this activity are clear with lids that fit inside the canister. The black and grey canisters with lids that fit over the sides work less well.
- Students can often use one tablet to launch their rocket several times.
- The thrust for the rocket is created by the gas that is produced when the tablet reacts with water.

Think Again! Check Out Thrust and Engines

- If students ride scooters or skateboards to school, try doing the activity suggested in the first paragraph at the bottom of student book page 206. This activity will demonstrate Newton's third law of motion: For every action force, there is an equal and opposite reaction force. Relate this law to how a jet engine creates thrust.
- Ask, *Have you ever put your fingers over the end of a water hose when there is water coming out of it? What happens?* Relate this activity to how a rocket engine creates thrust.

Communicate

The web that students create in question 1 could be done either as a class activity or as an individual reflection. Students may use LM 3-15 The Web of Flight to brainstorm a list of words and ideas they have learned so far in this unit. Students can then create categories that they can use to sort these terms, followed by a mind map that summarizes how these ideas are related. Students can continue to add to this mind map throughout the rest of the unit and use it as a review tool.

1. Answers will vary. Categories of words or ideas may include inventions, uses, forces, parts of flying devices, people, airplane design, and flight path.
2. Answers will vary. One way to change the drag on an airplane is to change its shape by changing its design, using flaps, or using a parachute. If the shape of an airplane is more aerodynamic (narrower, smaller), then the airplane will have less drag and fly faster. If the shape of an airplane is less aerodynamic (wider, larger), then the airplane will have more drag and fly slower.
3. **a.** In this diagram, all of the forces are equal, so the airplane will move at a constant speed and at a constant altitude.
   b. In this diagram, the thrust and drag forces are equal, but the force of lift is greater than the force of gravity. So, the airplane will move at a constant speed horizontally but will be rising vertically.
4.

	Internal combustion engines and propellers	**Jet engines**	**Rockets**
Source of thrust	the spinning propeller causes air pressure changes that push the airplane forward	release of exhaust gases from the rear of the airplane	exhaust gases that are accelerated out the back of a craft through a narrow nozzle

BUILD ON WHAT YOU KNOW

This section of students' Unit Technical Reports summarizes what they know about the different sources of thrust, as they noted in Communication question 4.

For ESL/ELL

Create a cloze procedure for Communicate question 3. For example:

Because lift and gravity are ____________________, the plane will ______________________________. Because drag and thrust are ____________________, the plane will ______________________________.

Ask students to read their responses out loud to help make connections between oral and written language.

For Reteaching

Ask students to perform the medicine ball demonstration described on the bottom of student book page 206. Ask students, *How is this demonstration related to how a jet flies?* Ask students to perform the garden hose demonstration described on the bottom of student book page 206. Ask students, *How is this demonstration related to how a rocket flies?*

For Enrichment

Research the drag-reducing technologies being created for athletes who compete in speed-related sports such as speed skating, alpine skiing, and running. These technologies might be in the areas of clothing or equipment. How might these technologies reduce drag? Why is reducing drag important?

Assessment *for* Learning

What to Look For in Student Work	What to Do
Students should demonstrate an understanding of the different sources of thrust, as shown by their answers to Communication question 4.	• Students can reread student book pages 205 and 206, and attempt the Newton's third law of motion activity (throwing a heavy object while on a skateboard) suggested at the bottom of page 206.

CAREERS AND PROFILES — Heather Knox: First Officer

Page 208

- Ask students to read this Careers and Profiles section to each other in pairs. A suggestion would be for one student to be the interviewer and one student to be the interviewee.
- Ask pairs of students to brainstorm a list of questions that they would like to ask Heather if they could meet her.
- Invite a pilot to come to your classroom to talk to your class. Encourage students to ask some of the questions they brainstormed to ask Heather.

11 Payload Liftoff

Page 209

Time
1 class period
Key Terms
• payload
Line Masters
• LM 3-16

Indicator Assessment Chart

Indicator	Assessment Opportunities
FL6.2 a. Diagram how the forces of thrust, drag, lift, and gravity act on living things or devices that fly through the air.	• Communicate, p. 211, q. 1
FL6.2 c. Generate questions related to the principles of flight and rephrase those questions in a testable form (e.g., rephrase a question such as "Why can some gliders travel farther than others?" to "What effect does wing shape have on the distance a glider can travel?").	• Work On It, p. 210 • Communicate, p. 211, q. 2
FL6.2 g. Provide examples of how science and technology have been used to solve problems related to drag in devices that fly.	• Work On It, p. 210 • Communicate, p. 211, q. 3, 4
FL6.3 a. Assess the characteristics of flying objects (e.g., balloon, kite, glider, airplane, helicopter, and rocket).	• Work On It, p. 210 • Communicate, p. 211, q. 1–4 • Build On What You Know, p. 211
FL6.3 b. Construct a prototype of a flying object that meets student-specified performance and aesthetic criteria.	• Work On It, p. 210 • Communicate, p. 211, q. 2–4
FL6.3 d. Select and carefully use appropriate tools in manipulating materials and in building prototypes.	• Work On It, p. 210 • Communicate, p. 211, q. 3, 4
FL6.3 e. Work collaboratively to collect relevant observations and data to evaluate the performance of a prototype of an object that will fly.	• Work On It, p. 210 • Communicate, p. 211, q. 3, 4
FL6.3 f. Demonstrate and explain the importance of selecting appropriate processes for investigating scientific questions and solving technological problems (e.g., explain why it is important to change one variable while keeping others constant in designing and testing prototypes of flying objects).	• Work On It, p. 210
FL6.3 g. Analyze personally collected data and suggest improvements to a prototype design.	• Work On It, p. 210 • Communicate, p. 211, q. 4

Background Information

In Lessons 1 to 10, much of student learning has been focussed on the generation of lift in flying objects. This lesson highlights rockets, which do not generate lift. Rather, thrust is the upward force that moves the rocket against gravity. Students will pay attention to payload distribution, and attempt to raise the highest amount of payload.

Get Started ▶

- Pique student interest by telling them about the 2009 world record holder for the largest model rocket, Steve Eves, from Ohio. A video and article can be found on the *National Geographic* website: http://news.nationalgeographic.com/news/2009/04/090427-worlds-largest-model-rocket.html
- Read the first paragraph on student book page 209 out loud. Ask students to brainstorm what types of things would need to be included in a space shuttle's payload. What do astronauts require in order to live in outer space?
- Read the second paragraph on student book page 209. Ask students to predict how the force diagram on a rocket might be different than the force diagram on an airplane. Sketch these diagrams on the board. You may also want to sketch the force diagram for a hot-air balloon and ask students to compare the forces acting on all three flying devices.
- After students have read the third paragraph on student book page 209, ask them to reflect on their lift review worksheet from Lesson 7. Can any of these contributors to lift help a rocket fly? The answer is no, so there is no force of lift present during a rocket's flight.

Time
30 min
Skills
• experimenting • building models
Grouping
pairs
Materials and Equipment
(per group) • balloons (variety of shapes and sizes) • cardboard or stiff paper • fishing line or strong coloured thread • plastic drinking straws • tape • empty drinking boxes with straws • modelling clay • pennies
Line Masters
• none

Work On It

- Having a variety of balloon shapes and sizes available will allow students to explore the advantages and disadvantages of long versus wide or large versus small balloons.
- Students should do a test flight with their rocket designs before attempting to attach payloads.
- Students may find it easier to inflate the balloons before attaching them to their rockets.
- Once student pairs have found the maximum payload their rockets can hold, ask them to report their results to the class. As a class, try to determine the characteristics of those rockets that were able to carry the heaviest payloads.

Communicate

Ask students to share their answers after they have had an opportunity to answer questions on their own or in pairs.

1. Answers will vary. One answer may be that rockets work due to thrust provided by escaping air from the balloon. The direction is controlled because the straws move along strings. Gravity is relatively constant because the mass of the rocket only decreases slightly due to loss of air from the balloon. Drag is reduced as the rocket rises because the size of the balloon gets smaller as it loses air.
2. The shape of the balloon will affect the rocket's flight. A wider balloon will experience more drag than a narrower balloon.
3. Answers will vary. In general, a narrower, larger balloon will carry the most payload because a narrower balloon will create the least amount of drag, and a larger balloon will create the most thrust.
4. Answers will vary. Ideas may include changing the shape of the balloon, attaching wings or fletching to the straw to help control flight, and putting straws into the neck of the balloon to help air escape in a more controlled way.

BUILD ON WHAT YOU KNOW

Student summaries will include ideas such as the even distribution of payload, using lightweight materials to secure the payload, decreasing the amount of drag by reducing the size of the rocket, and increasing the amount of thrust by increasing the amount of air in the balloon.

For Reteaching

Sketch a force diagram for a rocket, an airplane, and a hot-air balloon. Ask students, *How are these force diagrams the same? How are they different?*

For Enrichment

In 2004, the da Vinci Project proposed to launch a manned rocket from Kindersley, Saskatchewan. This project would have been the first privately funded manned rocket ever to have been launched. Ask students to research what this project was, and what prevented the launch from occurring.

Create juice box rockets as described in LM 3-16 Juice Box Rockets. In this activity, air is being used to provide thrust to an object.

Assessment *for* Learning

What to Look For in Student Work	What to Do
Students should be able to identify the forces present in a rocket and how they do or do not change during rocket flight. The force of gravity remains constant, the force of drag decreases because the balloon size decreases, and the force of thrust decreases because the amount of air escaping from the balloon decreases.	• Show the flight of a rocket by demonstrating a balloon rocket similar to the ones used in the Work On It activity. Sketch the balloon rocket before the launch. Launch the rocket. Ask students to observe its flight. Sketch the balloon rocket at the height of its flight path. Ask students to identify the factors contributing to gravity, drag, and thrust. Identify how those factors changed during flight, and relate those factors to the changes in gravity, drag, and thrust.

12 Flight Just Above the Ground: The Hovercraft

Page 212

Time
1–2 class periods
Key Terms
• Hovercraft
Line Masters
• LM 3-17

Indicator Assessment Chart

Indicator	Assessment Opportunities
FL6.1 g. Explain how inventions based on principles of flight have changed the way people work, live, and interact with the environment locally, nationally, and globally (e.g., bush planes in northern Saskatchewan, scheduled airline travel, supply of cargo to remote communities and mine sites, and transoceanic air travel).	• Communicate, p. 214, q. 5
FL6.1 h. Describe career opportunities in Canada related to the science and technology of flight.	• Communicate, p. 214, q. 5
FL6.2 a. Diagram how the forces of thrust, drag, lift, and gravity act on living things or devices that fly through the air.	• Communicate, p. 214, q. 1, 6
FL6.2 b. Use scientific terminology appropriately (e.g., thrust, drag, lift, and gravity) when communicating ideas about the principles of flight.	• Communicate, p. 214, q. 1, 6
FL6.2 d. Describe the role of lift in overcoming gravity and enabling devices or living things to fly.	• Work On It, p. 213 • Communicate, p. 214, q. 1
FL6.2 g. Provide examples of how science and technology have been used to solve problems related to drag in devices that fly.	• Communicate, p. 214, q. 3–5
FL6.2 h. Compare the sources of thrust of various constructed flying devices including the propeller, jet engine, and solid or liquid-fuelled rocket.	• Communicate, p. 214, q. 4
FL6.3 a. Assess the characteristics of flying objects (e.g., balloon, kite, glider, airplane, helicopter, and rocket).	• Work On It, p. 213 • Communicate, p. 214, q. 1, 2, 3, 6
FL6.3 d. Select and carefully use appropriate tools in manipulating materials and in building prototypes.	• Work On It, p. 213
FL6.3 e. Work collaboratively to collect relevant observations and data to evaluate the performance of a prototype of an object that will fly.	• Work On It, p. 213 • Communicate, p. 214, q. 2, 3

Indicator	Assessment Opportunities
FL6.3 g. Analyze personally collected data and suggest improvements to a prototype design.	• Work On It, p. 213 • Communicate, p. 214, q. 3
FL6.3 j. Propose designs for futuristic flying devices that meet a particular student-identified need.	• Communicate, p. 214, q. 7

Background Information

Hovercraft are vehicles that use an engine to create both thrust and lift. Air is pushed out of the back of the vehicle in order to move it forward. A rudder helps to control the direction of flight. Air pushed out of the bottom of the craft is held in by skirting to create a cushion of air, allowing the vehicle to hover slightly above the ground. This air cushion creates a virtually friction-free surface for the Hovercraft to ride on.

Hovercraft are becoming more prevalent in western Canada because search and rescue teams have begun using them for their missions. They are relatively easy to launch and are able to travel over a multitude of surfaces, making them an ideal vehicle for travel in wilderness areas.

Get Started ▶

- Generate interest in studying about Hovercraft by showing a video such as those posted on the HovPod website under the "video" link: http://www.hovpod.com/
- Ask students, *If a Hovercraft is only hovering a few centimetres above the ground, is it really flying?* Students should look at the forces acting on a Hovercraft in order to try to answer this question.

Lift and Thrust

- Ask students to read this section in pairs. They can use sticky notes to jot down pieces of information.
- Students should draw a diagram showing the forces acting on a Hovercraft.
- Ask students, *What creates the force of thrust and the force of lift in a Hovercraft?*

Time
30 min
Skills
• building models
Grouping
groups
Materials and Equipment
(per group) • old CD or DVD • thread spool • scissors • electrical tape (or duct tape) • clothespin • balloon • pennies
Line Masters
• none

Work On It

- Thread spools could be collected from homes, home economics labs, tailors, quilting clubs, church groups, and sewing services.
- CDs and/or DVDs are consumable in this activity. It is unlikely that CDs can be used more than once because they wear out and become weak if the metal film is removed. Ask your school's computer teacher, your division IT personnel, or students to bring in used CDs or DVDs.
- Students may think back to what they learned about payload in Lesson 11 to help them load their payload onto their Hovercraft.

! The paper covering over the end of the spool forces the air to travel through the centre hole in the spool, which is then directed through the hole in the CD or DVD. If the paper is missing, students can cover the ends of their spools with electrical or duct tape.

Think Again! Hovercraft in Canada

- Ask students, *Why would some Hovercraft be able to carry larger payloads than others?*
- Read this section out loud. Ask students to brainstorm the different uses for Hovercraft in Saskatchewan.

If Time Allows

These questions will help students to change variables to try to influence the performance of their Hovercraft. Answers will vary.

- One idea for making their Hovercraft fly for a longer time would be to control the flow of air out of the balloon using a clothespin.
- One idea for making their Hovercraft fly over different surfaces would be to create a flexible skirt around its edge to help keep the cushion of air from escaping.
- One idea for causing a Hovercraft to move in a particular direction would be to place a rudder on the Hovercraft.

Communicate

Ask students to share their answers after they have answered the questions individually. Use LM 3-17 A Vehicle of the Future to guide student thinking for question 7.

1. The force diagram will include all four forces of flight. Thrust points forward, drag points backward, lift points upward, and gravity points downward.
2. Answers will vary. Students may have found that their Hovercraft did not travel over rough surfaces or surfaces that were at an angle.
3. Answers will vary. Ideas may include a larger source of lift, which would be from a larger balloon, or a flexible skirt that would hold the air cushion underneath the Hovercraft.
4. The model created is similar to a real Hovercraft because air pushed underneath the Hovercraft is used to create lift.
5. Search and rescue teams would use Hovercraft because Hovercraft do not require a road to travel on and they can move over a variety of surfaces, including water, ice, and snow. Teams can launch a Hovercraft quickly and leave very little mark on the environment.
6. **a.** Unique features of flying devices:

Hovercraft	Hot-air balloon	Airplane
-four forces of flight -engine and propeller create thrust -forced air creates lift	-only lift and gravity -no force of thrust -hot expanding air creates lift	-four forces of flight -engine and propeller create thrust -air movement over wings, changes in air pressure, and angle of attack create lift

   b. Answers will vary. Look for connections between the circumstances and the appropriate flying device being used.
7. Answers will vary. Students should choose one flying device on which to model their future vehicle and explain why they have made this choice.

For Reteaching

Create word strips with the words *lift, thrust, drag,* and *gravity* on different-colour pieces of paper. Create a sorting mat with the column headings *Hovercraft, airplane,* and *hot-air balloon.* As a class or in small groups, place the force words in the appropriate columns of the sorting mat. Use sticky notes to identify what contributes to each of these forces in each type of flying device.

For Enrichment

Learn more about Hovercraft in Canada by looking at James Rolston's River Rider™ Hovercraft Corp. website: http://www.riverrider.ca/. This site links to videos, pictures, and a 360° virtual look at a personal Hovercraft.

Assessment *for* Learning

What to Look For in Student Work	What to Do
Students should be able to identify the forces of flight acting on a Hovercraft and the source of these forces.	• If students have difficulty identifying the four forces of flight acting on a Hovercraft, they can look back at Lesson 1 and Lesson 10 to help identify the forces and the source of each force.

ASK AN EXPERT James Rolston: Hovercraft Operator

Page 215

- Ask students to work in pairs to do a Think Aloud session with this section. They should take turns reading out loud and commenting on the connections they make to their own lives or knowledge.
- You may want to model a Think Aloud session once again by reading the first paragraph to the class. A sample script could be: "**James Rolston, Jr. from Delisle, Saskatchewan loves fun and adventure.** *I have been to Delisle before. It is just outside of Saskatoon. I think it is on the highway to Rosetown.* **He pilots and sells personal Hovercrafts.** *Hmmm ... I had no idea that people could actually buy a Hovercraft right here in Saskatchewan.* **Unlike a boat or a snowmobile, a Hovercraft is not "stuck" on one surface.** *I guess you could travel on water or land or snow in a Hovercraft. In Saskatchewan, that would be a really good idea because you could use it all year round.* **It moves easily over water, land, ice, or snow.** *Yes, a personal Hovercraft would definitely be a good idea in Saskatchewan.*"

DESIGN PROJECT

Make It Go

Page 216

Time

3–4 classes

Skills

- making models
- experimenting
- controlling variables
- comparing

Grouping

groups of two or more

Materials and Equipment

(per group)

- placemat paper
- glue
- scissors
- scraps of wood
- cardboard
- elastic bands
- colour pencils and felt pens
- various sizes of plastic tubing
- various sizes of syringes without the needles
- various types of wire
- various types of fasteners
- additional materials as required

Line Masters

- LM 3-18
- LM 3-19
- LM 3-20

Learning Expectations

Indicators Met in Unit Project

FL6.3 a. Assess the characteristics of flying objects (e.g., balloon, kite, glider, airplane, helicopter, and rocket).
FL6.3 b. Construct a prototype of a flying object that meets student-specified performance and aesthetic criteria.
FL6.3 c. Work collaboratively with classmates to define criteria for judging the performance and aesthetics of a prototype of a flying object.
FL6.3 d. Select and carefully use appropriate tools in manipulating materials and in building prototypes.
FL6.3 e. Work collaboratively to collect relevant observations and data to evaluate the performance of a prototype of an object that will fly.
FL6.3 f. Demonstrate and explain the importance of selecting appropriate processes for investigating scientific questions and solving technological problems (e.g., explain why it is important to change one variable while keeping others constant in designing and testing prototypes of flying objects).
FL6.3 g. Analyze personally collected data and suggest improvements to a prototype design.
FL6.3 h. Communicate procedures and results of prototype design, construction, testing, and evaluation in a technical design report.
FL6.3 i. Identify new questions or problems about flight that arise through the prototype design process.
FL6.3 j. Propose designs for futuristic flying devices that meet a particular student-identified need.

Background Information

Many factors will come into play as students design their air vehicles. The forces of lift, thrust, gravity, and drag will need to be balanced for a stable design. The mass of the vehicle will need to be light enough in relation to the amount of thrust that is generated. Ways to generate thrust include throwing, harnessing air escaping from balloons, or using propellers attached to rubber bands. Ways to generate lift include heating air, using balloons, or curving wing shape.

Get Started ▶

- Students are challenged to apply what they have learned about air and flight to design an air vehicle. They work in groups to follow a design process, including brainstorming, planning, designing, and construction. They will present their models to their classmates.

- Discuss as a class how the placemat activity will work. This process is described on student book pages 216 and 218. Students will work in engineering teams. Read this process as a class. Allow three minutes for each student to brainstorm ideas for their model. After three minutes, allow students time to compare their ideas within their groups. As a group, students will summarize their ideas in the centre of their placemats and then share these ideas with the class.

CAUTION!

For safety reasons, students may wish to demonstrate their flying designs in the gymnasium. Remind students to fly their models away from people.

Work On It

- Use LM 3-18 Design Project Planner: Make It Go to help structure student thinking, and LM 3-19 Design Project Reflection Sheet: Make It Go to help students reflect on their planning.
- Ask students to suggest criteria for what the class will decide is a good design. These criteria can be used to guide the student design process.
- To begin thinking about what design each engineering team will pursue, ask students to list all of the flying devices they have built during the unit. Ask:
  - Could you combine two or more models you have already built?
  - What changes can you make to the design or materials?
  - How could you modify one of your models so that it does new or different things?
  - What new methods could you design to launch your flying device?
- Advise students that there is no one way to do this activity.
- Students should apply a design, build, test, observe, evaluate, redesign, rebuild, test, observe, re-evaluate cycle. Each trial must be written down and will become part of the body of students' Unit Technical Reports.
- Visit groups as they work and ask them to explain how they are planning their air-powered vehicles. If several groups have similar plans, encourage them to share ideas and question each other.

Communicate

The Unit Technical Report will include the summaries written for the Build On What You Know sections at the end of each lesson, as well as the design cycle that students recorded in the Design Project Work On It section. Remind students of the parts of their Technical Reports by referring to their work in Lesson 9. Once students are satisfied with the flying models they have developed, bring the class back together. Using the class-created criteria, ask students to assess the performance of each prototype as groups present. Use LM 3-20 Unit Technical Report Assessment Rubric to assess students' Technical Reports.

1. Answers will vary. The Unit Technical Report should summarize the theory, knowledge, and procedures from the unit and Make It Go activity.
2. Answers will vary. Each presentation should include a thorough and accurate description of the flying device, a demonstration, and an explanation of any connection of special features to the theory in the unit.

For Reteaching

Show exemplars of student work from the Glider Technical Report from Lesson 9. Go through each of the four parts of the technical report, showing excellent and good work. Discuss as a class how a good response could be made into an excellent response.

For Enrichment

The Skycar, invented by Canadian Paul Moller, is described as the world's only personal vertical takeoff and landing (VTOL) vehicle. A complete description, videos, and other information about this futuristic vehicle can be found at http://www.moller.com/.

Assessment *for* Learning

What to Look For in Student Work	What to Do
Use questions such as the following to help you to assess students' problem-solving skills: • Can students construct hypotheses about flight and test them experimentally? • Can students develop fair ways to compare the performance of test models? • How do students incorporate new knowledge from test flights into their designs? • Can students explain why they made a particular alteration to a design? • Do students demonstrate flexibility in adapting a chosen design? • Are students willing to take risks and consider new ideas?	• If students are having difficulty designing and communicating their ideas, work as a large group to complete LM 3-13 with an example prototype. Reteach students what a hypothesis is, and model how to communicate observations and explanations for design changes.

Unit 3 Summary

Page 220

Students may wish to use this unit summary as a study guide. The Unit Summary is available on LM 3-1.

Unit 3 Review

Page 221

Explain Your Stuff

- The short-answer questions provided on this page could be used as part of an end-of-unit test or an in-class review of the unit, among other possibilities. Examples of the types of answers you may expect are presented below.

1. An object that is falling has a larger force of gravity than lift. An object that is flying has an equal or larger force of lift than gravity.
2. Answers will vary. Some ideas could include the ability to transport people and goods to northern areas, as well as to provide services such as air ambulances and fire fighting.
3. Three special adaptations that allow a bird to fly are hollow bones, muscles that can be used to turn one wing slightly up and the other wing slightly down like flaps to control direction, and wings shaped to glide, flap quickly, or turn easily.
4. The four forces of flight acting on a puffin would all be smaller than the forces of flight acting on an eagle. Lift is smaller due to the puffin's smaller wing size, gravity is smaller due to its smaller mass, drag is smaller due to its smaller body size, and thrust is smaller due to the fact that its muscles are not as powerful as an eagle's to push the puffin's body forward.
5. The bow and arrow is an improvement over the atlatl-and-dart system because it creates more thrust with the string of the bow than the atlatl launching stick, and the arrow is lighter and smaller, so it is less affected by drag and gravity.
6. Aboriginal Elders learn about and understand nature by observing the world around them, and noting how things affect each other. They would have created things that fly by observing the balance of a flying animal and using feathers to balance the darts and arrows they made. They may also have noted that smaller, lighter flying animals are able to fly quickly. This observation may have led them to think about the weight and size of the spear, dart, and arrow, causing them to design smaller, lighter flying weapons.

7. Answers will vary. All moon calendars were a way to predict and track the change of seasons according to the 13 moon cycles that exist in a calendar year. First Nations people know the appropriate times to move, plant, or gather food according to their calendars. They observed winged animals' migration and could predict when they would see certain types of birds and other animals according to their moon calendars.
8. The four forces of flight are lift, gravity, drag, and thrust. Lift is the force that moves an object upward, and can be generated by expanding air, air movement, and fluids moving over a curve. Gravity is the force that attracts anything with mass toward Earth. Thrust is the force that moves a flying device forward. Drag is the force that resists forward motion.

9.

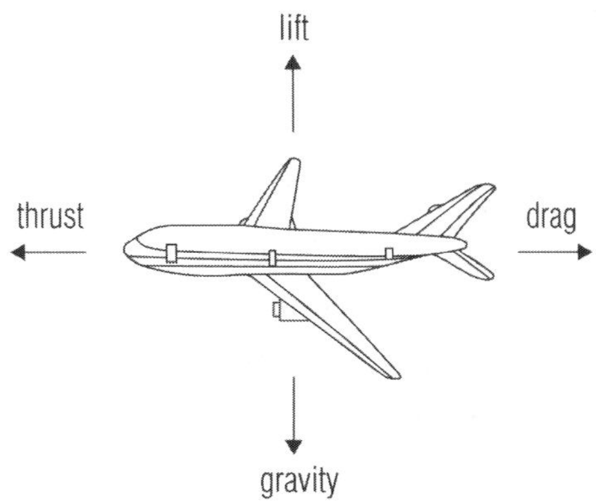

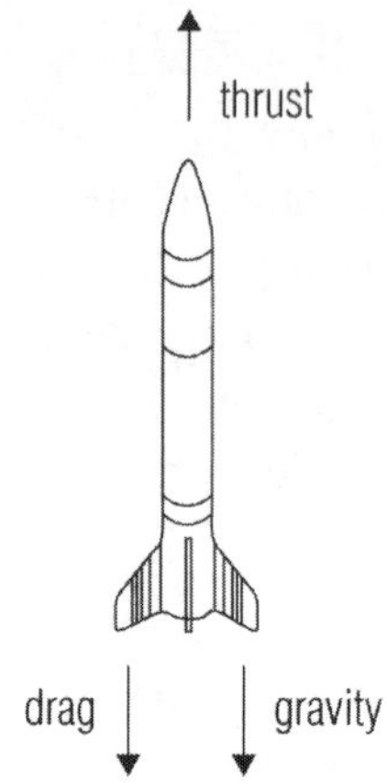

10.

	Airplane	Rocket	Hot-air balloon
Forces that are the same	gravity		
Forces that are different	lift, drag, thrust	drag, thrust	lift

11. A flying device rises when the force of *lift* is greater than the force of *gravity*.

12. Answers will vary. Students may have chosen someone from Lesson 5, a career profile, an Elder profile, or other knowledge they have from other sources.

13. The paper would move upward because the air above the paper would be moving quickly, causing an area of low air pressure. The air below the paper would be still, so the air pressure below the paper would be high. The air pressure below the paper would push the paper into the area of low pressure above.

14. An undertow is an area of quickly moving water, causing an area of low pressure. A swimmer in an area of calm water would be in an area of high pressure. The swimmer could be pushed from this area of high pressure into the area of low pressure, causing the swimmer to be caught in the current.

15. Fast airspeed above a wing causes an area of low pressure. Slower airspeed below the wing is an area of high pressure. The air below the wing will push the wing upward into the area of low pressure, causing lift.

16. Air, like all fluids, tends to follow a curved surface. When air meets the top of a wing, it follows the curve of the wing. This motion causes the wing to be pulled upward into the airstream.

17. Answers will vary. Some ideas may include large, angled wings with curved upper surfaces, and light construction to decrease gravity.

18. When a gull is flying on a calm day, it creates thrust by flapping its wings. Thrust moves the gull forwa rd, creating lift as air moves over its wings. On a windy day, a gull can simply spread its wings and allow the air to move over its wings to create lift.

19. An internal combustion engine creates lift by turning a propeller. The shape of a propeller is similar to a wing in that it produces different areas of air pressure. The area of low pressure is in front of the propeller. The area of high pressure behind the propeller moves the plane forward. A jet engine gives off hot exhaust gases behind the plane, creating thrust. In a rocket, gases are accelerated through small nozzles, creating thrust.
20. For most flying devices, including airplanes, hot-air balloons, and Hovercraft, the amount of payload the flying device can carry is determined by the balance of payload on the device and the ratio of lift versus gravity. For a rocket, the amount of payload is determined by the balance of payload and the ratio of thrust versus gravity and drag.
21. Canada developed flight technologies that go into space to research the aurora borealis, or Northern Lights, because they interfere with telecommunications, and to build a communications satellite that would provide service for the entire country.
22. Sports chosen may include running, skiing, or speed skating. To decrease drag, an athlete could wear tight-fitting clothing and make his or her body outline as aerodynamic (smooth) as possible.
23. Answers will vary. Legends, pictographs, dances, or ceremonies may be included as answers.
24. Answers will vary. One example would be:

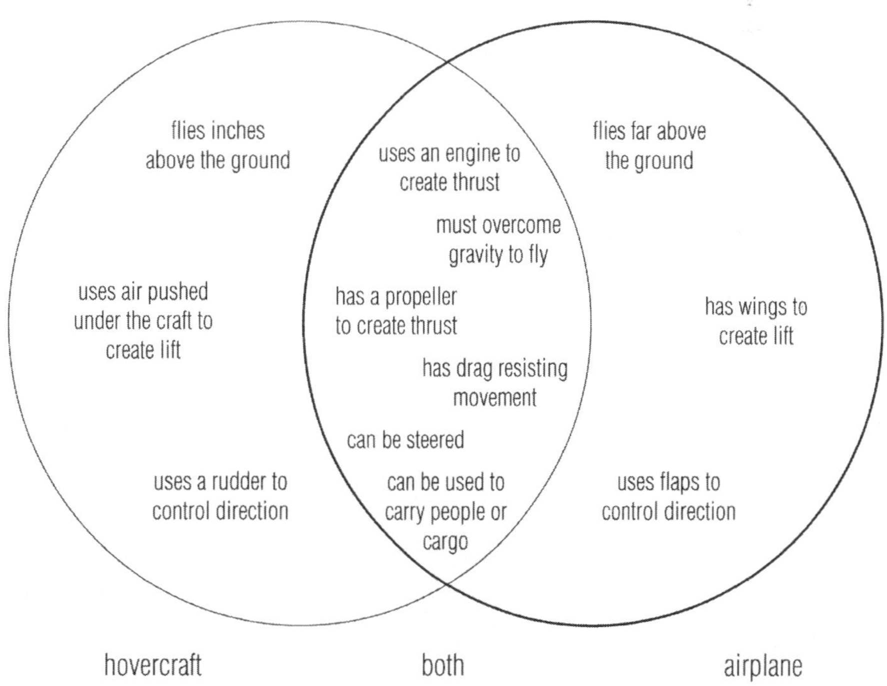

How Did You Do?

Self-evaluation allows students to communicate their learning and their feelings about it. Seeing how students view their learning can give you insight and information on which to base your programming decisions.

Ask students to answer these questions individually, then to share their answers with the class. Some students will likely find some areas of this unit easier than other areas. This exercise may help students identify who can give them assistance to understand difficult concepts.

Unit 3 Line Masters

Table of Contents

Table of Contents *(continued)*

Name: ______________________________

Unit 3 Summary

Here are some of the things you will learn about flight.

Something I know and understand before starting the Principles of Flight Unit.	Lesson(s) where I learned about this idea or learned more about this idea.	Important Points about Principles of Flight
		First Nations and Métis honour living things that fly, by including them in their sacred art and storytelling.
		To learn the knowledge of flight from First Nations and Métis Elders, you would need to learn how to make and use things that fly. Aboriginal peoples' knowledge is expressed in a design of some technology, such as a bow and arrow. It is also expressed in art forms, such as dance.
		Flight technologies have changed from an attempt to imitate the flight of living things to technologies that use an understanding of the four forces of flight as described by scientists: drag, gravity, thrust, and lift.
		Canadians have played an important role in the development of flight technologies. People from Saskatchewan have played an important role in the development of unique uses for flight technologies.

Copyright © 2013 Pearson Canada Inc.
The right to reproduce this page is restricted to the purchasing school.

Something I know and understand before starting the Principles of Flight Unit.	Lesson(s) where I learned about this idea or learned more about this idea.	Important Points about Principles of Flight
		A device can fly if lift is greater than gravity.
		Air that is moving at a higher speed will create an area of low pressure. This can create lift, as an object is pushed into that area of low pressure.
		Air will tend to follow the surface of a curved object. This creates lift if an airplane wing has a curved upper surface.
		Flying devices with different features will have different flight patterns.
		Flaps on wings allow a pilot to control the direction of an airplane's flight by adjusting the drag on an airplane.
		There are many different types of engines that provide thrust to an aircraft, including internal combustion, jet, and rocket engines.
		Rocket flight is affected by thrust, drag, and gravity.
		Hovercraft are flying machines designed to travel over water or land, only centimetres above the ground.

Copyright © 2013 Pearson Canada Inc.
The right to reproduce this page is restricted to the purchasing school.

Name: ______________________________

Unit 3 Key Terms

Word	I know nothing about this word.	I can spell this word correctly.	I have seen/heard it before.	I can define it as it relates to science.
aerodynamics				
air pressure				
Alouette-1				
angle of attack				
Anik-1				
arrowhead				
atlatl				
atmosphere				
Avro Arrow				
Black Brant				
Canadarm				
Canadarm2				
dart				
drag				
fletching				
flint-napping				
force				
foreshaft				
fuselage				
gravity				
hover				
Hovercraft				
internal combustion engine				
jet engine				
lift				
mass				
payload				
propel				
propeller				
prototype				
rocket engines				

Copyright © 2013 Pearson Canada Inc.
The right to reproduce this page is restricted to the purchasing school.

Word	I know nothing about this word.	I can spell this word correctly.	I have seen/heard it before.	I can define it as it relates to science.
sound barrier				
struts				
technical report				
tether lines				
thrust				
variables				

Copyright © 2013 Pearson Canada Inc.
The right to reproduce this page is restricted to the purchasing school.

Name: ______________________________

Unit Technical Report Table of Contents

Use this Table of Contents as an outline to make sure you have written all the components of your technical report.

Unit Technical Report Table of Contents **Page**

Summary	

Introduction	

Body:	Build On What You Know	
Lesson 1:	The Four Forces of Flight	
Lesson 2:	Controlling a Projectile	
Lesson 4:	Lift in a Hot-Air Balloon	
Lesson 6:	Lift due to Air Pressure Changes	
Lesson 7:	Lift due to Air Flow	
Lesson 9:	Controlling Flight with Glider Design	
Lesson 10:	Source of Thrust	
Lesson 11:	Carrying a Payload	
Body:	Design Project	
Prototype:	Design and Testing	

Conclusion	

Copyright © 2013 Pearson Canada Inc.
The right to reproduce this page is restricted to the purchasing school.

Name: ____________________________________

Impacts of Flight

- Categorize the changes you and your group listed as something that affects the economy, relationships, or the environment. If you think a change affects more than one category, write it in every column in which you think it should be placed.
- Decide if a change is beneficial (+) or harmful (–) to a community. If you think a change is both beneficial and harmful, note it as (+, –).

Economy	Relationships	Environment

Copyright © 2013 Pearson Canada Inc.
The right to reproduce this page is restricted to the purchasing school.

Name: ______________________________

Wing Design

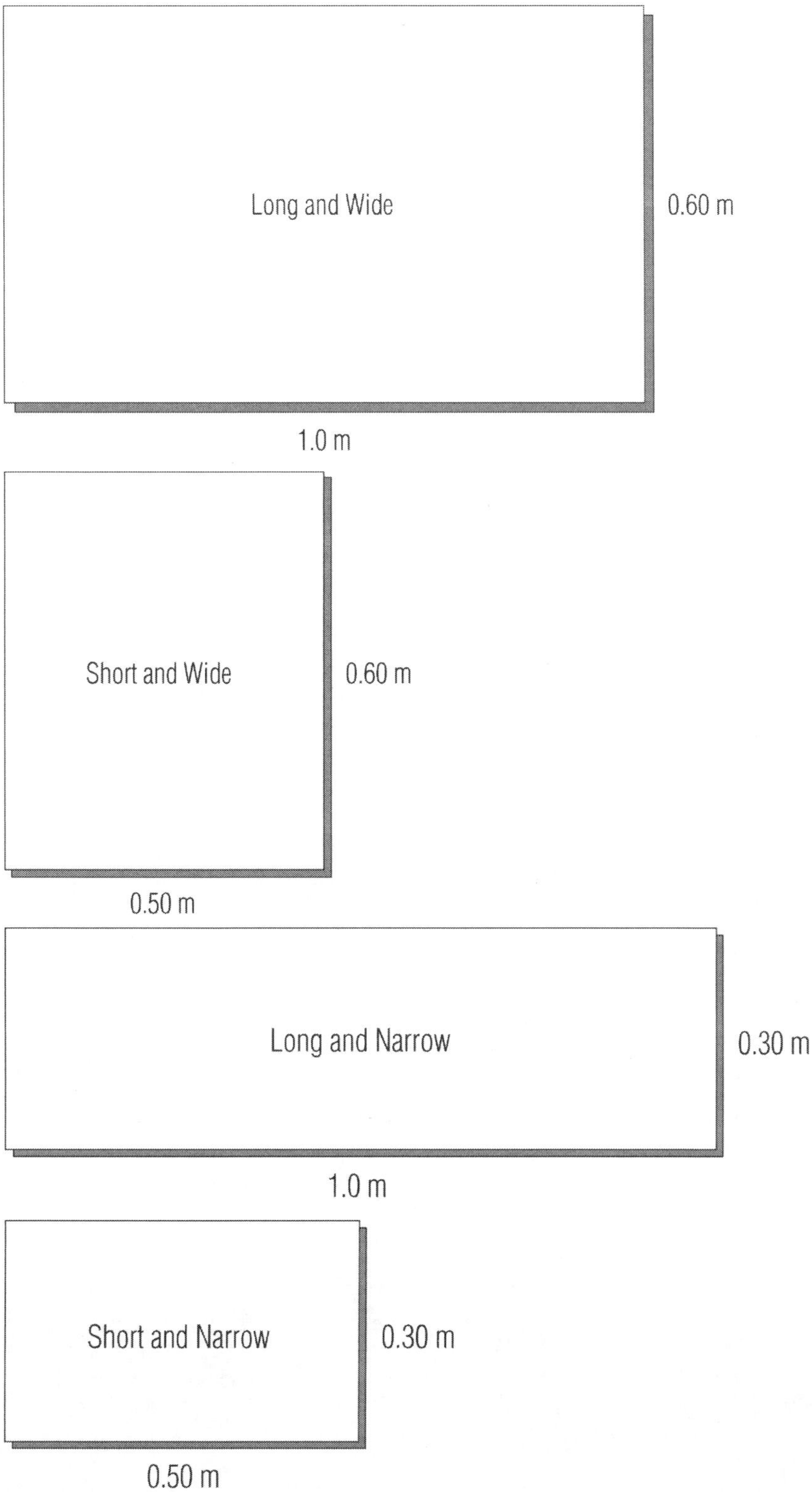

Copyright © 2013 Pearson Canada Inc.
The right to reproduce this page is restricted to the purchasing school.

Observations

Wing type	Drag	Ease of turning
long and wide		
short and wide		
long and narrow		
short and narrow		

Copyright © 2013 Pearson Canada Inc.
The right to reproduce this page is restricted to the purchasing school.

Name: ______________________________

Ancient Technologies

Fill in the following table to help you understand the forces of flight acting on the spear, the atlatl-and-dart system, and the bow and arrow.
To determine the size of the force, compare it to the force in the other technologies and rate it as small, medium, or large.

Force	Spear	Atlatl-and-dart system	Bow and arrow
Thrust	Provided by: Size:	Provided by: Size:	Provided by: Size:
Drag	Caused by: Size:	Caused by: Size:	Caused by: Size:
Gravity	Size:	Size:	Size:

Think about the evolution of the three weapons. Fill in the flow chart below.

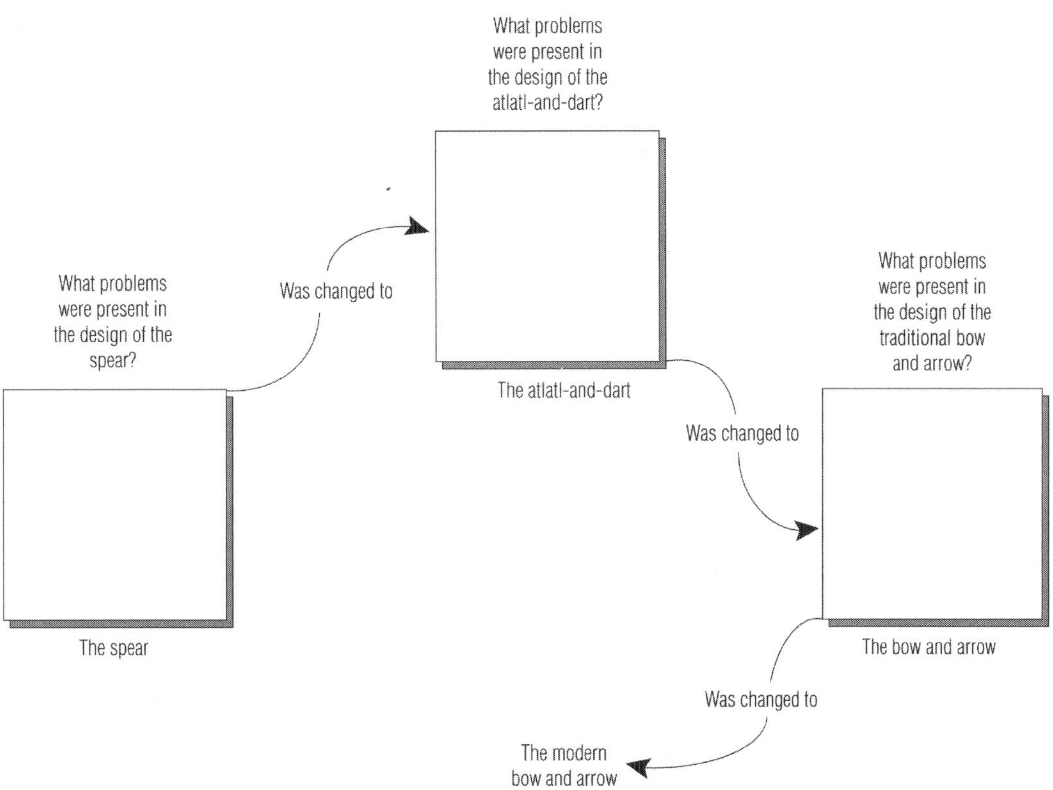

Copyright © 2013 Pearson Canada Inc.
The right to reproduce this page is restricted to the purchasing school.

Name: ______________________________

Failure!

Partners: ____

WHOM have you chosen to research? ________________________

HOW did they fail?

What happened after they failed?

What did THEY do?

What did OTHERS do?

HOW did this failure change the development of new flight technologies?

Copyright © 2013 Pearson Canada Inc.
The right to reproduce this page is restricted to the purchasing school.

Name: ________________________________

Balloon Flight

Record your data from Flight Trial 1.

Trial	Temperature of hair dryer	Fan speed of hair dryer	Length of tether lines	Mass of balloon	Balloon material	Size of balloon	Time
1							

What factors could change your flight time? Create testable questions that are related to at least three of these factors.

Factors	Testable Questions

Put a star beside the testable question that your group will be investigating. Write a procedure in the space below that will allow you to test this question. Be sure to control variables.

1.

2.

3.

4.

Copyright © 2013 Pearson Canada Inc.
The right to reproduce this page is restricted to the purchasing school.

Prediction

Record your data from Flight Trial 2.

Trial	Temperature of hair dryer	Fan speed of hair dryer	Length of tether lines	Mass of balloon	Balloon material	Size of balloon	Time
2							

Share your question, prediction, and results with your class.

Copyright © 2013 Pearson Canada Inc.
The right to reproduce this page is restricted to the purchasing school.

Name: ____________________

Canadian Contributions to Flight

Use the following table to help you organize information about the contributions Canadians have made to flight technologies (You may need to use more than one copy!). You may not be able to complete every column for each technology.

Technology/Use	When?	Who?	Where?

Copyright © 2013 Pearson Canada Inc.
The right to reproduce this page is restricted to the purchasing school.

Name: ______________________________

Aerodynamic Information Station Log

Aerodynamic Information Station 1: Levitating with Lips

Prediction

Observations

Questions

What was the speed of the air above the paper compared to the speed of the air below the paper?

How did the paper move?

Where was there more air pressure?

Sketch

Copyright © 2013 Pearson Canada Inc.
The right to reproduce this page is restricted to the purchasing school.

Aerodynamic Information Station 2: Moving Air

Prediction

Observations

Questions

In step 2, what was the speed of the air above the index card compared to the speed of the air below the index card?

What direction did the cardboard move when you blew under it?

Where was there more air pressure?

Sketch

Copyright © 2013 Pearson Canada Inc.
The right to reproduce this page is restricted to the purchasing school.

Aerodynamic Information Station 3: Floater Ball

Prediction

Observations

Questions

Where was the air moving the fastest?

Where was the air moving the slowest?

In what direction did the ball move?

Where did the air have the most push, or air pressure?

Sketch

Copyright © 2013 Pearson Canada Inc.
The right to reproduce this page is restricted to the purchasing school.

Aerodynamic Information Station 4: Un-Canny Movements

Prediction

Observations

Questions

Where was the air moving the fastest?

Which direction did the cans move toward?

Where was there an area of high pressure?

Sketch

Copyright © 2013 Pearson Canada Inc.
The right to reproduce this page is restricted to the purchasing school.

Aerodynamic Information Station 5: Temporary Attraction

Prediction

Observations

Questions
Where do you need to direct the air?

Where was the air moving the fastest?

How did the paper move?

Where did the air have the most push, or air pressure?

Repeat step 2 using the thick straw to blow the air.
Compare the results of steps 2 and 3.

Sketch

Copyright © 2013 Pearson Canada Inc.
The right to reproduce this page is restricted to the purchasing school.

Communicate

1. Look back at the diagrams you created to describe your observations. In your notebook, fill in the following summary table.

Activity	When you blew air into an area, you created an area of _______-speed air.	The object moved _________ this area.	This means the area you blew into had _______ air pressure.
1	high low	toward away from	high low
2	high low	toward away from	high low
3	high low	toward away from	high low
4	high low	toward away from	high low
5	high low	toward away from	high low

2. Write a sentence that summarizes what you discovered about the relationships among airspeed, air pressure, and movement of an object.

Copyright © 2013 Pearson Canada Inc.
The right to reproduce this page is restricted to the purchasing school.

Name: ____________________________________

Exploration Guide: The Forces of Flight

Critical Question: What causes the force of lift in flying objects?

What are the key terms and their definitions?

air pressure —

fluid —

angle of attack —

additional term —

additional term —

What are the supporting questions and answers?

How is lift created in a hot-air balloon?

How can air pressure create lift on an airplane wing?

How can fluid moving over a wing create lift in an airplane wing?

How does the angle of attack create lift?

Copyright © 2013 Pearson Canada Inc.
The right to reproduce this page is restricted to the purchasing school.

What is the main idea in the answer?

How can we use the main idea?

Is there an overall idea? Is there a real-world use for the overall idea?

Copyright © 2013 Pearson Canada Inc.
The right to reproduce this page is restricted to the purchasing school.

Name: ____________________________________

Airport Analysis

Which task did your flying device perform best?

Look at the flying devices at each airport. What similarities in design made different devices perform a task particularly well?

Airport 1: Fly over a desk 5 m away and land on the other side.	Airport 2: Complete one air trick, such as a loop, a sharp turn left or right, or your choice.	Airport 3: Fly as close as possible to a target on a desk.

What differences in design exist among gliders at each airport?

Airport 1: Fly over a desk 5 m away and land on the other side.	Airport 2: Complete one air trick, such as a loop, a sharp turn left or right, or your choice.	Airport 3: Fly as close as possible to a target on a desk.

Copyright © 2013 Pearson Canada Inc.
The right to reproduce this page is restricted to the purchasing school.

Name: ____________________

Glider Technical Report Planning Sheet

Summary

- 1–2 sentences

- topic of report

- key findings

Introduction

- importance of research

- research question

- how research is linked to other unit knowledge

Body

- detailed theory: define drag

- experiments done: outline procedure

- results of testing

- interpretation: how drag and results are related, how a pilot could control airplane flight

Conclusion

- why research was done

- how research was done

- what was discovered

Copyright © 2013 Pearson Canada Inc.
The right to reproduce this page is restricted to the purchasing school.

Name: ________________________________

Glider Technical Report Assessment Rubric

Category	1	2	3	4
Summary statement	Summary does not describe either the topic of the report or key findings.	Either the topic of the report or key findings is missing.	The summary describes the main components of the report, including the topic of the report and key findings.	The summary is well written and describes the main components of the report, including the topic of the report and key findings.
Introduction	The purpose of the research and report, the research question, and a connection between the research and unit information are either incorrect or missing.	The purpose of the research and report, the research question, and a connection between the research and unit information are partially identified, but are not stated clearly.	The purpose of the research and report, the research question, and a connection between the research and unit information are identified, but are not stated clearly.	The purpose of the research and report, the research question, and a connection between the research and unit information were clearly identified.
Body	Significant key components are either missing or inaccurate.	Key components are missing.	All of the theory related to drag, the procedure, the results, and the interpretation of the results are accurately described.	All of the theory related to drag, the procedure, the results, and the interpretation of the results are thoroughly and accurately described.
Conclusion	The conclusion does not describe the most important components.	The conclusion includes some of the most important components.	The conclusion includes why, how, and what research was conducted.	The conclusion is well written and includes why, how, and what research was conducted.

Copyright © 2013 Pearson Canada Inc.
The right to reproduce this page is restricted to the purchasing school.

Name: ________________________________

The Web of Flight

STEP 1: Brainstorm all the new words you have learned so far in your flight unit.

STEP 2: Look at the words you brainstormed in step 1. What categories could you use to sort these words? Choose four categories and write them inside the bubbles in the diagram below. Colour each bubble with a different colour. Sort the words you brainstormed in step 1 into each of the categories below by underlining each word in the same colour as its category. Rewrite and link each word to the category bubbles below.

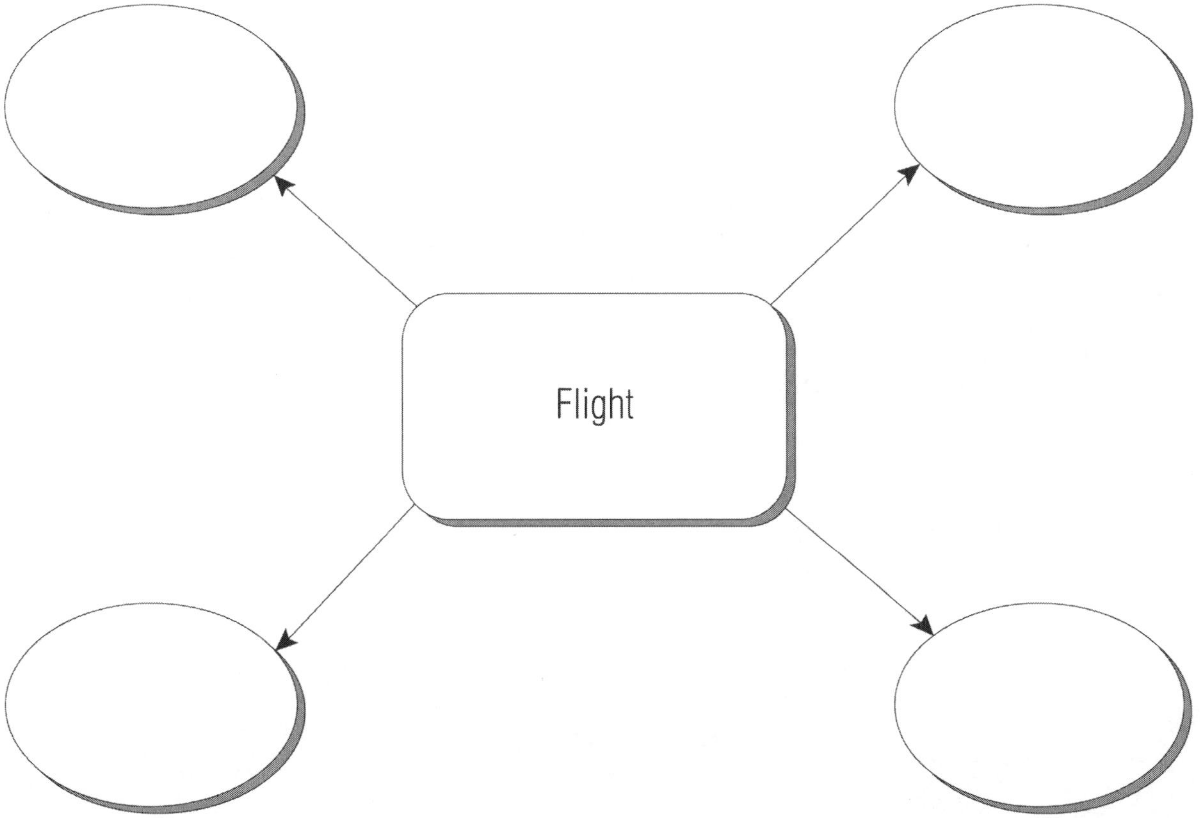

Copyright © 2013 Pearson Canada Inc.
The right to reproduce this page is restricted to the purchasing school.

Name: ______________________________

Juice Box Rockets

Did you know that a juice box can be made into a rocket? Complete this activity to build your own juice box rocket.

Materials
empty juice boxes with straws (clean and dry)
modelling clay
tape
thin cardboard

Procedure
1. Seal one end of the straw closed with tape or cover it with a piece of modelling clay. Either of these methods will seal the straw and add a little weight. The weighted end of the straw will become the nose of the rocket.
2. Push the straw into the drinking box.
3. Squeeze the box hard to launch the straw rocket.

CAUTION: Be sure to direct your rockets away from people.

4. Retrieve your rocket and inflate the box by blowing in the straw hole. You are ready for another flight.
5. You may wish to add small cardboard tabs or fins to the weighted end of the straw rocket and observe their effect on its flight.

What Did You Find Out?
A. What caused your rocket to lift off?

B. How did adding tabs or fins to your rocket affect its flight?

Copyright © 2013 Pearson Canada Inc.
The right to reproduce this page is restricted to the purchasing school.

Name: ________________________________

A Vehicle of the Future

Imagine that you are designing a flying vehicle of the future that could be used by people every day. You need to think about traffic issues, environmental issues, and distances that people will travel regularly.

What type of flying device would your design of a vehicle of the future resemble?

a) Hovercraft

b) hot-air balloon

c) airplane

d) other: ________________________

Sketch your design on a separate piece of paper.

What is one issue of the future that your vehicle design would address?

How would your vehicle design address this issue?

What would provide the following in your design?

Thrust

Lift

How would you control the direction of flight in your design?

Copyright © 2013 Pearson Canada Inc.
The right to reproduce this page is restricted to the purchasing school.

Name: ______________________________

Design Project Planner: Make It Go

Group members: ________________________ Trial no.: ______________

The Technology Design Cycle:

A. What type of flying device will your design be based on?

____

Materials needed	How you are going to gather them

B. Sketch your design.

C. Build and test your design.
Observations:

Copyright © 2013 Pearson Canada Inc.
The right to reproduce this page is restricted to the purchasing school.

Class criteria met by prototype	Class criteria not met by prototype

What changes could you make to your design?

Describe your new design. Once you are satisfied with your prototype, answer the questions on the LM 3-19 Design Project Reflection Sheet: Make It Go.

Copyright © 2013 Pearson Canada Inc.
The right to reproduce this page is restricted to the purchasing school.

Name: ______________________________

Design Project Reflection Sheet: Make It Go

My final design is the best design I created because

My design still does not meet these criteria well:

My design uses ____________________________________ to create lift, and

____ to create thrust.

If I were to start this design project again, I would

Materials I wish I had access to for my project are

The most difficult part of the Design Project was

When our class decided on the criteria to judge a good design, I wish we had included

Copyright © 2013 Pearson Canada Inc.
The right to reproduce this page is restricted to the purchasing school.

Name: ______________________________

Unit Technical Report Assessment Rubric

CATEGORY	1	2	3	4
Cover Page	Not a relevant representation.	Representation of a flying object, being, or device.	Creative representation of a flying object, being, or device.	Creative, well-done representation of a flying object, being, or device.
Summary Statement	Summary does not describe the key components.	Not all of the components are mentioned.	Summary describes the three main components.	The well-written summary describes the main components of the report, including theory basics.
Introduction	The purpose of the research and report is incorrect or irrelevant.	The purpose of the research and report is partially identified, and is stated in a somewhat unclear manner.	The purpose of the research and report is identified, but is stated in a somewhat unclear manner.	The purpose of the research and report is clearly identified and stated.
Body (Lesson 2 —Four Forces)	The forces of flight are not included or are inaccurately described.	The forces of flight that are included are accurately described with the aid of a diagram.	All four forces of flight are accurately described with the aid of a diagram.	All four forces of flight are thoroughly and accurately described with the aid of a diagram.
Body (Lesson 3 —Controlling the Projectile)	Ways to control the path of a projectile (thrust, balance, direction, and drag) are not included or are inaccurately described.	Ways to control the path of a projectile (thrust, balance, direction, and drag) that are included are described accurately.	Ways to control the path of a projectile (thrust, balance, direction, and drag) are accurately described.	Ways to control the path of a projectile (thrust, balance, direction, and drag) are thoroughly and accurately described.
Body (Lesson 4 —Controlling Lift in a Balloon)	Ways to create lift in a hot-air balloon (hot air, small opening, and light material) are not included or are inaccurately described.	Ways to create lift in a hot-air balloon (hot air, small opening, and light material) that are included are described accurately.	Ways to create lift in a hot-air balloon (hot air, small opening, and light material) are accurately described.	Ways to create lift in a hot-air balloon (hot air, small opening, and light material) are thoroughly and accurately described.

Copyright © 2013 Pearson Canada Inc.
The right to reproduce this page is restricted to the purchasing school.

CATEGORY	1	2	3	4
Body (Lesson 6 —Speed and Air Pressure)	The effect of air-speed on air pressure and the generation of lift are described inaccurately.	The effect of air-speed on air pressure and the generation of lift are described accurately.	The relationship between speed and air pressure and how this effect creates lift is accurately described.	The relationship among speed, air pressure, and lift (high speed = low pressure, push) are thoroughly and accurately described.
Body (Lesson 7 —Coanda Effect)	The Coanda effect and how it generates lift is described inaccurately.	The Coanda effect is described accurately.	The Coanda effect and how it generates lift is accurately described.	The Coanda effect and how it generates lift (curved wing, pull) is thoroughly and accurately described.
Body (Lessons 8, 9 — Design)	The design features are not included or are inaccurately described.	The design features that are included are accurately described.	All design features are accurately described.	All design features to create different flight paths (accurate, flies a long distance, can perform tricks) are thoroughly and accurately described.
Body (Lessons 8, 9 — Flaps)	The effects of flaps have not been included or are inaccurately described.	The effects of flaps that have been included are accurately described.	All of the effects of flaps with respect to flight path (up, down, corkscrew) are accurately described.	All of the effects of flaps with respect to flight path (up, down, corkscrew) are thoroughly and accurately described.
Body (Lesson 10 — Thrust)	The sources of thrust are not included or are inaccurately described.	The sources of thrust that are included are accurately described.	The sources of thrust are accurately described.	The sources of thrust (propeller, gases, acceleration of fluid) are thoroughly and accurately described.
Body (Lesson 11 — Payload)	The design features are not included or are inaccurately described.	The design features that are included are accurately described.	The design features needed to carry a large payload are accurately described.	The design features needed to carry a large payload are thoroughly and accurately described.

Copyright © 2013 Pearson Canada Inc.
The right to reproduce this page is restricted to the purchasing school.

CATEGORY	1	2	3	4
Body (Prototype Design)	The prototype design has not been included or is inaccurately described.	The prototype design has been accurately described.	The prototype design has been accurately described with the aid of a sketch.	The prototype design has been thoroughly and accurately described (design features) with the aid of a sketch.
Body (Prototype Testing)	The test results and observations have not been included or are inaccurate.	The test results that have been reported have been accurately described.	The observations made during prototype testing have been accurately described.	The observations made during prototype testing have been thoroughly and accurately described.
Conclusion	The conclusion does not describe the most important findings.	The conclusion includes some of the most important findings.	The conclusion includes most of the important findings.	The conclusion is well written and includes the most important findings: design, shape/size, and flaps.
Flight Criteria	The prototype meets none of the criteria determined by the class to describe a good flying device.	The prototype meets some of the criteria determined by the class to describe a good flying device.	The prototype meets almost all of the criteria determined by the class to describe a good flying device.	The prototype meets all of the criteria determined by the class to describe a good flying device.
Presentation Criteria	The presentation is missing key features or includes inaccurate information.	The presentation is missing one key element, but the elements presented are accurate.	The presentation includes an accurate description of the flying device, demonstration, and connection of special features to theory.	The presentation includes a thorough and accurate description of the flying device, demonstration, and connection of special features to theory.

Copyright © 2013 Pearson Canada Inc.
The right to reproduce this page is restricted to the purchasing school.

Name: ___________________________________

Unit 3 Test

Modified True/False

1. For the following questions, indicate whether the statement is true (T) or false (F). Rewrite false statements to make them true.

a) T F If drag and thrust are equal, a flying device will stop.

b) T F An atlatl-and-dart system uses a small board to apply thrust.

c) T F Humans are able to imitate a bird in flight because we can build large wings.

d) T F A larger airplane wing creates more lift.

e) T F A rocket only has three forces of flight acting on it.

f) T F Drag causes a flying object to move backward.

g) T F A short, narrow wing allows a bird to turn easily.

h) T F Thrust must be greater than drag in order for an object to move forward.

i) T F Lift must be greater than gravity in order for an object to remain in flight.

j) T F When a bird stops flying and lands on the ground, the force of gravity acting on the bird decreases.

Copyright © 2013 Pearson Canada Inc.
The right to reproduce this page is restricted to the purchasing school.

Multiple Choice

Circle the letter that best answers the question.

2. The first flying device that carried a person was
  a) a monoplane glider created by Sir George Cayley
  b) an ornithoptor designed by Leonardo da Vinci
  c) a hot-air balloon created by Joseph and Jacques Montgolfier
  d) the American *Wright Flyer* created by Orville and Wilbur Wright

3. In a Hovercraft, the engine contributes to the force of
  a) thrust
  b) lift
  c) gravity
  d) thrust, lift, and gravity

4. When you compare the wings of a puffin to the wings of an eagle, an advantage of puffin wings is the ability to
  a) create more lift
  b) create more thrust
  c) turn more quickly
  d) create more gravity

5. Flaps on an airplane affect the force of
  a) thrust
  b) drag
  c) lift
  d) gravity

6. Consider the following airplane.

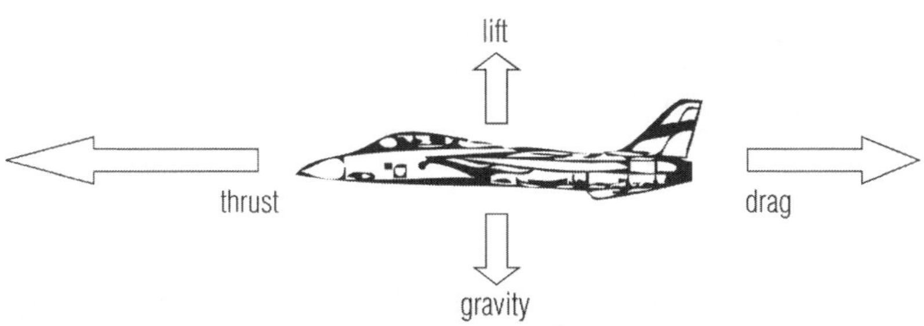

From the diagram, the plane is
  a) moving forward at a constant speed
  b) moving upward and speeding up
  c) staying at the same height and speeding up
  d) moving downward and slowing down

Copyright © 2013 Pearson Canada Inc.
The right to reproduce this page is restricted to the purchasing school.

7. Consider the following airplane.

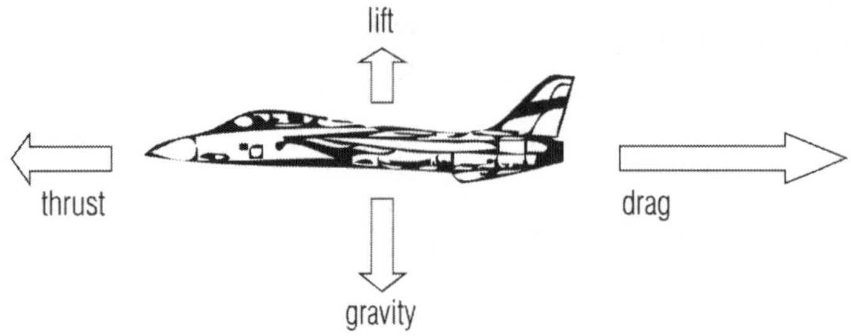

From the diagram, the plane is
a) moving upward at a constant speed
b) moving upward and speeding up
c) staying at the same height and speeding up
d) moving downward and slowing down

8. Consider the following airplane.

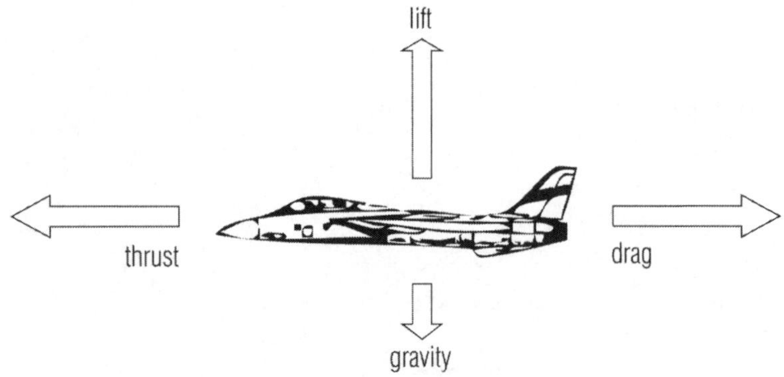

From the diagram, the plane is
a) moving upward at a constant speed
b) moving upward and speeding up
c) staying at the same height and speeding up
d) moving downward and slowing down

9. Something that does not contribute to the force of drag acting on an object is
a) the size of the object
b) the weight of the object
c) the shape of the object
d) the smoothness of an object's surface

Copyright © 2013 Pearson Canada Inc.
The right to reproduce this page is restricted to the purchasing school.

10. Which type of engine can be used to provide thrust outside the atmosphere?
a) internal combustion
b) propeller
c) rocket
d) jet

Matching

11. Match the term on the left with the correct description on the right.

gravity	A. the force that moves an object forward
thrust	B. the force that slows down or prevents motion
lift	C. the force that attracts an object to the ground
drag	D. the force that causes something to rise

Fill in the Blanks

Complete the following sentences.

12. ______________________________ is the study of air in motion.

13. The cargo carried by an airplane or rocket is called its ______________________________.

14. The throwing stick used to launch a dart is called a(n) ______________________________.

15. Higher airspeed has ______________________________ air pressure.

16. The tilt of an airplane that provides lift when taking off or landing is known as the

______________________________.

17. ______________________________ is the constant push of air.

Short Answer

18. In your opinion, what is the most important contribution to flight technology or uses made by a person from Saskatchewan? Give reasons for your answer.

____

____

____

____

____

Copyright © 2013 Pearson Canada Inc.
The right to reproduce this page is restricted to the purchasing school.

19. How did First Nations cultures show their understanding and respect for birds?

20. Explain how curved wings create lift in an airplane. You may use a sketch to help with your explanation.

21. Compare the atlatl-and-dart system and the bow and arrow using the following Venn diagram. How are they the same? How are they different?

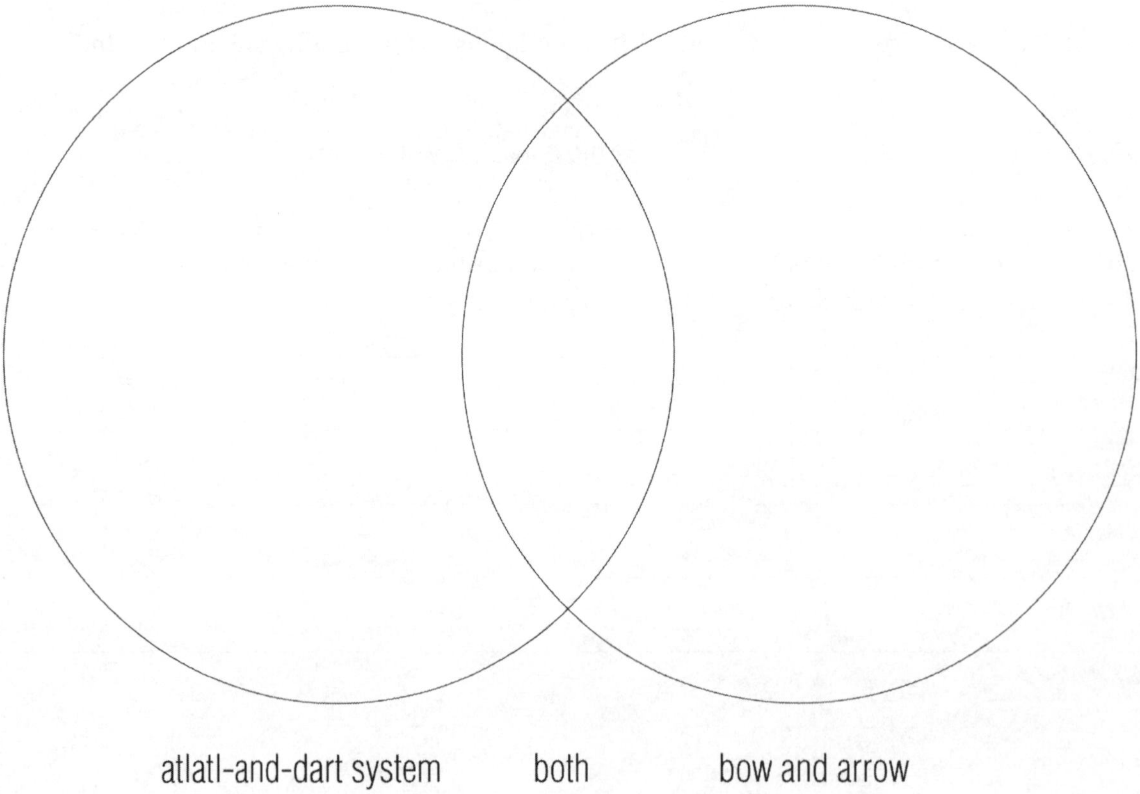

Copyright © 2013 Pearson Canada Inc.
The right to reproduce this page is restricted to the purchasing school.

22. What is the role of failure in the creation of new technologies? Explain.

23. How might you build the best hot-air balloon? What characteristics would it have?

24. How has flight changed life in Saskatchewan? Describe at least three changes and state whether you think they are beneficial or harmful.

Copyright © 2013 Pearson Canada Inc.
The right to reproduce this page is restricted to the purchasing school.

Answers to Unit 3 Line Masters

LM 3-4 Impacts of Flight

Economy	Relationships	Environment
Answers will vary, but could include: There are more stores to buy things. (+) Tourists can visit. (+) People can buy food rather than hunt and grow it. (+)	*Answers will vary, but could include:* People move away from their home communities. (+, –) People move into communities from other places. (+, –) Culture is no longer based on hunting and gathering. (+, –)	*Answers will vary, but could include:* More garbage is created from goods brought to the North. (–) Trees are cut down to build airstrips. (–) Fuel used for planes increases pollution. (–)

LM 3-5 Wing Design

Wing type	Drag	Ease of turning
long and wide	most drag	most difficulty turning
short and wide	medium amount of drag	easy turning
long and narrow	medium amount of drag	difficult turning
short and narrow	least amount of drag	easiest turning

LM 3-6 Ancient Technologies

Force	Spear	Atlatl-and-dart system	Bow and arrow
Thrust	provided by: person's arm size: small	provided by: atlatl (throwing board) size: medium	provided by: bow string size: large
Drag	caused by: large spear head size: large	caused by: medium-sized dart head and fletching size: medium	caused by: small-sized arrowhead and fletching size: small
Gravity	size: large	size: medium	size: small

Copyright © 2013 Pearson Canada Inc.
The right to reproduce this page is restricted to the purchasing school.

LM 3-9 Canadian Contributions to Flight

Technology/Use	When?	Who?	Where?
Star of the East Hot-Air Balloon Flight	August 10, 1840	Professor L. A. Lauriat	Saint John, New Brunswick
Flying Sausage Engine-Powered Dirigible	July 13, 1906	Charles Hamilton	Dominion Park, Montreal
First Canadian Pilot flying *Red Wing*	March, 1908	Casey Baldwin	
June Bug first to fly 1 km in North America		Aerial Experiment Association	
Silver Dart, first powered flight in Canada	February 23, 1909	John McCurdy	Near Baddeck, Nova Scotia
First successful Canadian aircraft engine	September 10, 1910	William Wallace Gibson	Victoria, British Columbia
First flight from Saskatoon to Regina	1919	Roland Groome and Robert McCombie	Saskatoon to Regina
First licensed aerodrome in Canada	1919	Roland Groome, Robert McCombie, Edward Clarke	Regina
First registered aircraft in Canada	April 20, 1920	Roland Groome	Saskatchewan
First Canadian to earn an Air Engineer's Certificate	April 20, 1920	Robert McCombie	Saskatchewan
First commercial flying licence in Canada	July 20, 1920	Roland Groome	Saskatchewan
Aerial photography surveys	1924	Royal Canadian Air Force	Northern Saskatchewan
First civilian air ambulance service in North America	1946	Saskatchewan Air Ambulance Service	Saskatchewan
Smoke jumpers used to fight fires	1947		Saskatchewan
Aerial crop spraying	1951	Hugh McPhail	Saskatchewan
Variable-pitch propeller	1927	Wallace R. Turnbull	Rothesay, New Brunswick
G-suit	1940	Wilbur R. Franks	Toronto, Ontario
Propeller de-icer	1941	John L. Orr and T. R. Griffith	Ottawa, Ontario
Crash Position Indicator	1957	Harry Stevinson	Carleton Place, Ontario

Copyright © 2013 Pearson Canada Inc.
The right to reproduce this page is restricted to the purchasing school.

Technology/Use	When?	Who?	Where?
Avro Arrow developed	1950s	Government of Canada	
Youngest and oldest active flyer in Canada	1930–1995	Victor Pearson	Luseland, Saskatchewan
Black Brant rocket	1959	Albert Fia	
Alouette-1 satellite launched	September 29, 1962		
Anik-1 satellite launched	November 9, 1972		
Canadarm	November 13, 1981		
First Canadian in space	October 5, 1984	Dr. Marc Garneau	Space Shuttle Challenger
Canadarm2	2001		International Space Station

LM 3-10 Aerodynamic Information Station Log

Aerodynamic Information Station 1: Levitating with Lips

Prediction: Students' answers will vary.

Observations: *When you blow above the paper, it lifts up.*

Answers to Questions:

The speed of the air above the paper is faster than the speed of the air below the paper.

The paper moved up.

There was more air pressure below the paper.

Sketch

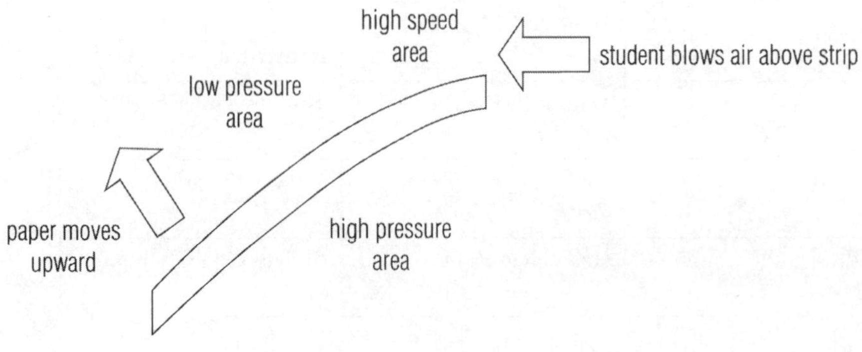

Copyright © 2013 Pearson Canada Inc.
The right to reproduce this page is restricted to the purchasing school.

Aerodynamic Information Station 2: Moving Air

Prediction: Students' answers will vary.

Observations: *When you blow below the index card, the top of the card moves downward.*

Answers to Questions:
The speed of the air above the index card is slower than the speed of air below the index card.

The cardboard moved downward.

There was more air pressure above the cardboard.

Sketch

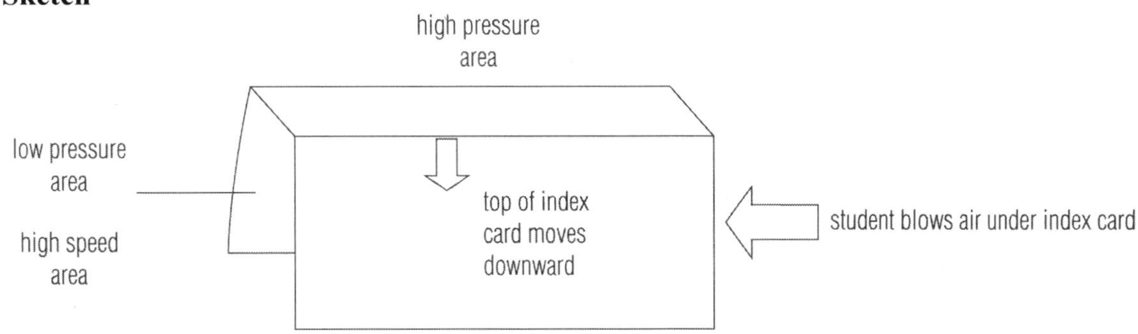

Aerodynamic Information Station 3: Floater Ball

Prediction: Students' answers will vary.

Observations: *The ball remains at the bottom of the funnel.*

Answers to Questions:

The air was moving the fastest at the bottom of the funnel.

The air was moving the slowest on the outside, or top, of the funnel.

The ball moved toward the bottom of the funnel.

The air pressure was highest on the outside, or top, of the funnel.

Copyright © 2013 Pearson Canada Inc.
The right to reproduce this page is restricted to the purchasing school.

Sketch

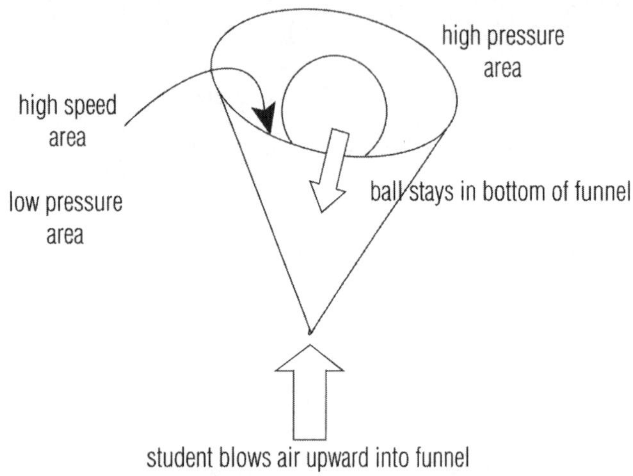

Aerodynamic Information Station 4: Un-Canny Movements

Prediction: Students' answers will vary.

Observations: *The cans move together over the straws.*

Answers to Questions:

The air was moving fastest between the two cans.

The cans moved toward each other.

The area of high pressure was on the outside of the cans.

Sketch

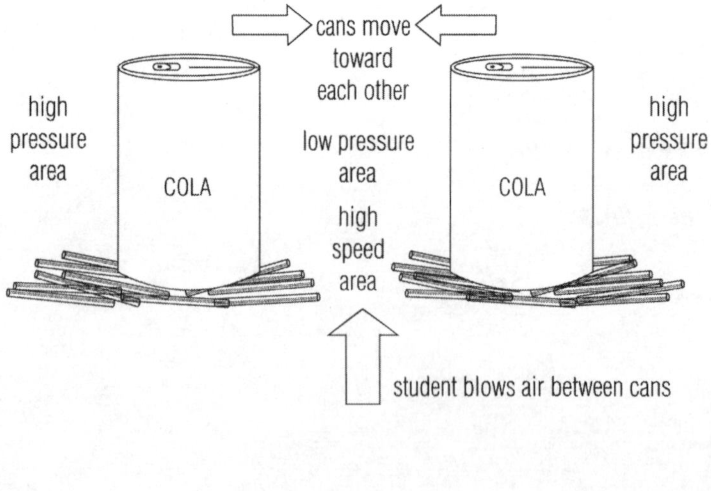

Copyright © 2013 Pearson Canada Inc.
The right to reproduce this page is restricted to the purchasing school.

Aerodynamic Information Station 5: Temporary Attraction

Prediction: Students' answers will vary.

Observations: *Blowing between the two paper strips causes them to move toward each other.*

Answers to Questions:

You need to direct the air between the two paper strips in order to push them together.

The air was moving the fastest between the two paper strips.

The paper strips moved together.

The air had the highest air pressure, or ability to push, on the outside of the paper strips.

The strips move closer together when you blow using the straw.

Sketch

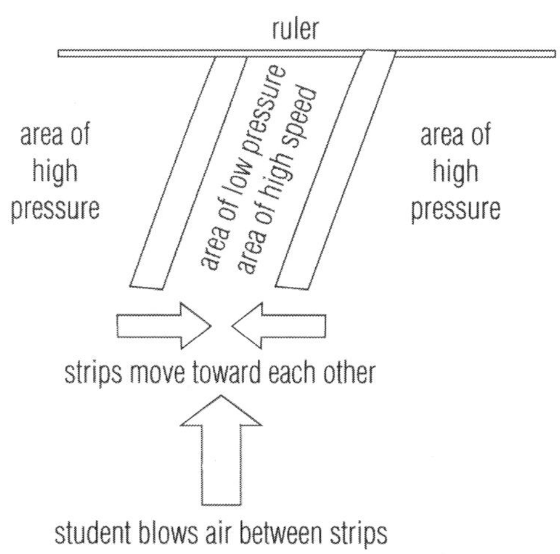

Copyright © 2013 Pearson Canada Inc.
The right to reproduce this page is restricted to the purchasing school.

Communicate

1.

Activity	When you blew air into an area, you created an area of ______-speed air.	The object moved ________ this area.	This means the area you blew into had ______ air pressure.
1 Levitating with Lips	high	toward	Low
2 Moving Air	high	toward	Low
3 Floater Ball	high	toward	Low
4 Un-Canny Movements	high	toward	Low
5 Temporary Attraction	high	toward	Low

2. Areas of high-speed air have low air pressure. Areas of low-speed or calm air have high air pressure. Objects can be pushed by high air pressure into areas of low air pressure.

LM 3-11 Exploration Guide: The Forces of Flight

air pressure — the constant push of air

fluid — any liquid or gas that flows

angle of attack — the tilted position of an aircraft as it moves through the air

additional term — Terms may vary. An additional term may be thrust — the force that pushes any object forward.

additional term — Terms may vary. An additional term may be lift — a force that causes something to rise, or overcome gravity.

How is lift created in a hot-air balloon?
Lift is created in a hot-air balloon because hot air expands and so is less dense than cool air. This difference will provide the balloon with a lift force.

How can air pressure create lift on an airplane wing?
When air moves with a higher speed, it creates an area of low pressure. When air above a wing has lower pressure, and the air below a wing has high pressure, the wing is pushed upward into the area of low pressure.

How can fluid moving over a wing create lift in an airplane wing?
When air, a fluid, moves over a wing, it moves along the curved surface. At the same time, a fluid moves in a straight line. This effect causes the air to pull the wing upward.

Copyright © 2013 Pearson Canada Inc.
The right to reproduce this page is restricted to the purchasing school.

How does the angle of attack create lift?
When the nose of an airplane is pointed upward, air hits the bottom of the wings, pushing the aircraft upward.

What is the main idea in the answer?
Lift is caused by many different things in flying devices. In a hot-air balloon, the difference in density between hot and cold air provides lift. In an airplane, the thrust of an airplane allows air to move around the wings. When an airplane is taking off, the nose is pointed up, allowing air to move beneath the wings, pushing them up. As well, air moves more quickly above a curved wing than below it, creating an area of low air pressure above the wings. The area of high pressure below the wings pushes the wings up. Air is also a fluid, which will move along a curved surface, but at the same time air travels in a straight line. This effect pulls the wing upward.

How can we use the main idea?
This idea can be used when designing flying devices. When creating a hot-air balloon, it would be best to have a large balloon with a small opening to let very little warm air escape. As well, it might be best to fly a hot-air balloon on a cool day so there would be a bigger temperature difference between the inside and outside of the balloon.

When creating an airplane to have the most lift, you could design one with large, curved wings to catch the greatest amount of air on takeoff, and the curve would give you the most push from air below and pull from air above.

Is there an overall idea? Is there a real-world use for the overall idea?
Answers will vary. In the real world, new flight technology would include creating the biggest, lightest wings to save on fuel. Large, light wings would use less fuel because they would provide the most lift with the same amount of thrust. Using less fuel would protect the environment, and airplanes would be safer and have the greatest amount of lift.

LM 3-12 Airport Analysis

Airport 1: Fly over a desk 5 m away and land on the other side.	Airport 2: Complete one air trick, such as a loop, a sharp turn left or right, or your choice.	Airport 3: Fly as close as possible to a target on a desk.
Design features may include: - tight folds - narrow body	Design features may include: - loose folds - wide body - unbalanced wings	Design features may include: - weighted nose - small wings - balanced wings

Copyright © 2013 Pearson Canada Inc.
The right to reproduce this page is restricted to the purchasing school.

Airport 1: Fly over a desk 5 m away and land on the other side.	Airport 2: Complete one air trick, such as a loop, a sharp turn left or right, or your choice.	Airport 3: Fly as close as possible to a target on a desk.
Answers will vary, but could include: - mass - wingspan - size - materials used - tightness of folds - nose weight - weight distribution		

LM 3-21 Unit 3 Test

1. a) False — If drag and thrust are equal, a flying device will move at a constant speed.
b) True
c) False — Humans are not able to imitate a bird in flight.
d) True
e) True
f) False — Drag causes a flying object to slow down.
g) True
h) False — Thrust must be greater than or equal to drag in order for an object to move forward.
i) False — Lift must be greater than or equal to gravity in order for an object to remain in flight.
j) False — When a bird stops flying and lands on the ground, the force of gravity acting on the bird stays the same.

2. c)
3. d)
4. c)
5. b)
6. c)
7. d)
8. a)
9. b)
10. c)
11. gravity — C
thrust — A
lift — D
drag — B
12. aerodynamics
13. payload
14. atlatl
15. lower

Copyright © 2013 Pearson Canada Inc.
The right to reproduce this page is restricted to the purchasing school.

16. angle of attack
17. air pressure
18. Answers will vary.
19. First Nations cultures showed their understanding and respect for birds by representing them in their artwork and storytelling, by observing and conserving bird populations, and by naming the moons and months using bird names.
20. Curved wings contribute to both the push and pull of air on a wing. The curved wing causes air to travel faster above the wing. This creates an area of low pressure above the wing, allowing the area of high pressure below the wing to push the wing upward. As well, air travels along the curve on the top of the wing. Air also tends to travel in a straight line, resulting in the air pulling the wing upward.

21.

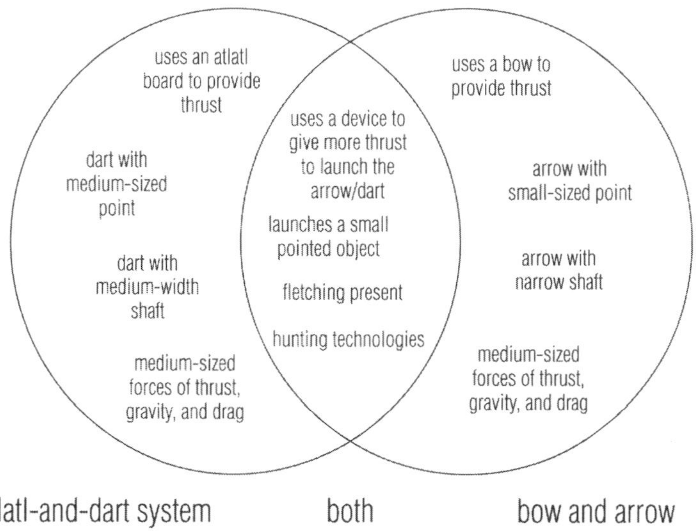

22. Failure helps in the creation of new technologies. It reveals flaws in thinking or design. Failure can motivate people to try harder to figure out a problem. People learn a lot more from an experiment that did not work than they do from an experiment that goes exactly as planned.
23. The best hot-air balloon would be large, made of lightweight material that can hold air in, and have a small opening.
24. Answers will vary, but could include increased movement of people moving to and from the North (beneficial and harmful), increased environmental damage to the North (harmful), and easier access to health care (benefit).

Copyright © 2013 Pearson Canada Inc.
The right to reproduce this page is restricted to the purchasing school.

UNIT 4

Our Solar System

Table of Contents

Table of Contents *(continued)*

Unit Indicators Correlation Chart

Indicator	Lesson References	Assessment Opportunities
By the end of grade 6, students will be able to:		
SS6.1 Research and represent the physical characteristics of the major components of the solar system, including the sun, planets, moons, asteroids, and comets.		
a. Use a variety of sources and technologies to gather and compile pertinent information about the physical characteristics of the major components of the solar system.	Launch Lesson 1 Lesson 2 Lesson 3 Lesson 6 Lesson 7 Lesson 8 Lesson 10 Lesson 11 Lesson 12 Design Project Unit 4 Review	Work On It, p. 224 Work On It, p. 228 Build On What You Know, p. 229 Work On It, p. 232 Communicate, p. 233, q. 1 Build On What You Know, p. 236 Work On It, p. 246 Communicate, p. 248, q. 1, 2, 4 Work On It, p. 250 Communicate, p. 251, q. 1–5 Build On What You Know, p. 251 Work On It, p. 254 Communicate, p. 254, q. 1 Work On It, p. 262 Communicate, p. 262, q. 1–4 Work On It, p. 266 Think Again!, p. 267, q. 1–4 Work On It, p. 270 Work On It, p. 287 Unit 4 Review, pp. 291–292, q. 1–3, 15–18, 20, 21
b. Analyze historical and current technological developments that have enabled human observation of the major components of the solar system.	Lesson 5 Lesson 14 Unit 4 Review	Work On It, p. 244 Work On It, p. 279 Communicate, p. 280, q. 2 Unit 4 Review, pp. 291–292, q. 13, 23–28
c. Construct a timeline of Canadian and worldwide research efforts related to understanding the major components of the solar system.	Lesson 14	Work On It, p. 279 Communicate, p. 280, q. 1–3
d. Evaluate the validity and usefulness of different sources of information about the physical characteristics of the solar system.	Lesson 2 Lesson 10 Lesson 11 Lesson 12 Design Project Unit 4 Review	Communicate, p. 233, q. 1, 2 Work On It, p. 262 Communicate, p. 267, q. 1–3 Work On It, p. 270 Work On It, p. 287 Unit 4 Review, p. 292, q. 21

Indicator	Lesson References	Assessment Opportunities
e. Use star charts and astronomy guides to investigate the night sky, including constellations, and record observations using notes in point form, data tables, simple diagrams, and/or charts.	Launch Lesson 7 Lesson 13 Unit 4 Review	Work On It, p. 224 Work On It, p. 250 Work On It, p. 275 Communicate, p. 276, q. 3 try this at HOME, p. 276 Unit 4 Review, p. 291, q. 8
f. Describe objects in the heavens, as indicated through First Nations and Métis art and stories or by Elders or Traditional Knowledge Keepers.	Lesson 5 Lesson 13 Unit 4 Review	Work On It, p. 244 Work On It, p. 275 Communicate, p. 276, q. 3 Unit 4 Review, p. 291, q. 6, 7, 10, 12
g. Create scale-distance and/or scale-size models of the major components of the solar system.	Lesson 2 Lesson 6 Lesson 8 Lesson 11 Lesson 12 Lesson 13	Work On It, p. 232 Work On It, p. 246 Work On It, p. 254 Communicate, p. 254, q. 3 Communicate, p. 267, q. 3 Work On It, p. 270 Work On It, p. 275
h. Evaluate the usefulness and accuracy of scale-distance and/or scale-size models of the major components of the solar system.	Lesson 2 Lesson 6 Lesson 8	Communicate, p. 233, q. 2 Communicate, p. 248, q. 6 Communicate, p. 254, q. 3
i. Explain how evidence is continually questioned in order to validate scientific knowledge about the solar system.	Unit 4 Review	Unit 4 Review, p. 292, q. 23, 26, 27
SS6.2 Assess the efficacy of various methods of representing and interpreting astronomical phenomena, including phases, eclipses, and seasons.		
a. Examine how people of different cultures, including First Nations, have recorded (e.g., medicine wheel, Mayan calendar, Stonehenge, pyramids) and used understandings of astronomical phenomena (e.g., positions of the stars and/or planets) to solve practical problems such as the appropriate time to plant and harvest crops, to support navigation on land and water, or to foretell significant events through stories and legends.	Lesson 5 Unit 4 Review	Work On It, p. 244 Unit 4 Review, p. 291, q. 10, 12
b. Examine ways in which humans have represented understanding of or interest in astronomical phenomena through music, dance, drama, visual art, or stories.	Lesson 5 Unit 4 Review	Work On It, p. 244 Unit 4 Review, p. 291, q. 6–8, 10, 12
c. Demonstrate the importance of selecting appropriate processes for investigating scientific questions and solving technological problems by explaining why astronomy is considered a part of science but astrology is not.	Lesson 13 Unit 4 Review	Communicate, p. 276, q. 5 Unit 4 Review, p. 292, q. 23

Indicator	Lesson References	Assessment Opportunities
d. Propose personal explanations for the causes of seasons, phases, and eclipses.	Lesson 4 Lesson 5 Lesson 9 Unit 4 Review	Communicate, p. 241, q. 6 Communicate, p. 244, q. 3 Communicate, p. 257, q. 1, 2 Unit 4 Review, p. 291, q. 6, 11, 12, 14
e. Demonstrate how Earth's rotation causes the day and night cycle and how Earth's 23.5° tilt and revolution around the sun causes the yearly cycle of seasons.	Lesson 3 Lesson 4 Unit 4 Review	Work On It, p. 235 Work On It, p. 237 Build On What You Know, p. 241 Unit 4 Review, p. 291, q. 4, 5
f. Propose explanations for how the yearly cycle of seasons might differ if Earth's axis were not tilted.	Lesson 4	Communicate, p. 241, q. 5
g. Consider alternate models of seasons and explanations for those models (e.g., the six-season model of the Woodland Cree, the rainy and dry seasons of some tropical and subtropical regions).	Lesson 5 Unit 4 Review	Work On It, p. 244 Unit 4 Review, p. 291, q. 12
h. Model the relative positions of the sun, Earth, and moon to demonstrate moon phases and lunar and solar eclipses.	Lesson 6 Lesson 9 Unit 4 Review	Work On It, p. 246 Work On It, p. 256 Unit 4 Review, pp. 291–292, q. 14, 19, 29, 30
i. Propose questions related to astronomical phenomena to investigate using models and simulations, such as "Do other planets exhibit phases?", "How would seasons on Earth differ if Earth were not tilted?", "How would patterns of eclipses change if the sun, Earth, or moon were different diameters or positioned at different locations?"	Lesson 4 Lesson 6 Lesson 9 Unit 4 Review	Communicate, p. 241, q. 5 Communicate, p. 248, q. 5 Communicate, p. 258, q. 8 Unit 4 Review, pp. 291–292, q. 14, 21, 30
SS6.3 Evaluate past, current, and possible future contributions of space exploration programs including space probes and human spaceflight, which support living and working in the inner solar system.		
a. Construct a timeline of Canadian and worldwide space exploration programs related to living and working in space, including collaborative efforts among countries.	Lesson 14 Unit 4 Review	Work On It, p. 279 Unit 4 Review, p. 292, q. 23
b. Analyze how astronauts are able to meet their basic needs (e.g., food, water, shelter, and waste elimination) while living and working in space.	Lesson 15 Unit 4 Review	Work On It, p. 283 Unit 4 Review, p. 292, q. 28
c. Research the various work roles and worldwide locations required to support human spaceflight programs.	Lesson 14 Unit 4 Review	Work On It, p. 279 Communicate, p. 280, q. 1–3 Unit 4 Review, p. 292, q. 23–27

Indicator	Lesson References	Assessment Opportunities
d. Describe instances where scientific ideas and discoveries have led to new inventions and applications (e.g., lunar buggy, space shuttle, Canadarm, Dextre, and the International Space Station) that support human exploration of space and which have extended scientific knowledge related to living and working in space.	Lesson 14 Unit 4 Review	Work On It, p. 279 Unit 4 Review, p. 292, q. 23–25, 27
e. Identify potential personal, societal, technological, and environmental barriers to living and working in space.	Lesson 14 Lesson 15 Unit 4 Review	Work On It, p. 279 Work On It, p. 283 Communicate, p. 284, q. 2 Unit 4 Review, p. 292, q. 28
f. Design a model of a habitable space vehicle that can travel to and return from a student-selected location in the inner solar system.	Design Project	Work On It, p. 287
g. Investigate the work being done in preparation for future space travel and make predictions about future achievements related to living and working in space.	Lesson 15 Unit 4 Review	Communicate, p. 284, q. 4 Unit 4 Review, p. 292, q. 27, 28

Activity Planning Chart

Note that estimates of class times are based on 40 min per period.

Lesson	Type of Activity	Time (number of classes)	Materials Required (for each group)	Line Masters
Launch: Cosmic Journeys	discussion open inquiry	1	notebook pencil poster paper research materials	LM 4-3
1. Tracking Our Nearest Star	guided inquiry	1	small mirror or mirror chip masking tape mural paper (1 sheet for the class) colour pencils Optional activity: Bristol board binoculars tripod	LM 4-4
2. That Glorious Old Sun	reading guided inquiry	1	216 mm × 279 mm (8 ½ × 11-inch) sheets of paper metre sticks tape pencils index cards straight pins calculator	LM 4-5
3. Patterns of Light and Darkness	guided inquiry	1	globe pin or toothpick Plasticine or modelling clay compass (optional)	LM 4-6
4. And the Seasons Go Round and Round	guided inquiry	1	flashlight light large and small sheets of paper globe Plasticine or modelling clay pin or toothpick pencil, tape, or chalk	LM 4-7
5. Worldviews of the Seasons	reading open inquiry	2	computers with Internet access reference books	none
6. The Moon's Changing Face	guided inquiry	1	light source Styrofoam™ ball painted black or a small dark-colour play ball pencil or knitting needle darkened room	LM 4-8
7. The Moon on the Move	guided inquiry	1	table for recording	LM 4-9

Activity Planning Chart *(continued)*

Lesson	Type of Activity	Time (number of classes)	Materials Required (for each group)	Line Masters
8. Earth's Companion	open inquiry	1	Plasticine or modelling clay section of lunar map/photograph sculpting tools (plastic knives, craft sticks, etc.) tray or shallow boxes toothpicks	LM 4-10
9. Blackout!	reading guided inquiry	1	marble flashlight large ball small ball	LM 4-11
10. The Inner Planets of Our Solar System	reading	2	paper crayons, markers, colour pencils	LM 4-12
11. The Outer Planets of Our Solar System	reading	2	Planet Comparison Tables 1 and 2 chart paper poster paper (optional) modelling materials	LM 4-13
12. Comets, Meteoroids, and Asteroids: Oh My!	reading guided inquiry	2	flour cocoa powder shallow pans rocks of similar shape varying in sizes (1–4 cm in diameter) ruler or tape measure	LM 4-14
13. Sky Pictures	reading guided inquiry	2	sky map coffee tin black paper shoebox	LM 4-15
14. What's Happening in Space?	reading	2	paper appropriate for presentation reference materials crayons/markers/colour pencils	LM 4-16
15. Living in Space, the New Frontier	reading guided inquiry	2	paper and pencil reference materials	LM 4-17

Lesson	Type of Activity	Time (number of classes)	Materials Required (for each group)	Line Masters
Design Project: Space Vehicle	open inquiry	3	paper pencil construction paper Styrofoam™ balls plastic cardboard boxes markers string elastic bands mini-lights tape glue computer (optional) scissors	LM 4-18 LM 4-19

- Field trips could include going to a local observatory. The University of Saskatchewan has an observatory that allows field trips.
  http://physics.usask.ca/observatory/

The observatory also organizes viewings on clear Saturday nights. You may wish to see if organizing an after-hours trip for interested students (and parents!) is possible.

- The Saskatchewan Science Centre in Regina runs camps. You may want to see if there is a space camp that can be organized for students.
- Guest speakers may include members of local astronomy clubs and Traditional Knowledge Keepers to tell legends (only during the winter months).
- The Canadian Space Agency and NASA often have podcasts featuring astronauts and other space scientists.
- Some useful websites are:
  NASA
  http://www.nasa.gov/
  Canadian Space Agency
  http://www.asc-csa.gc.ca/eng/default.asp
  Astronomy Magazine
  http://www.astronomy.com/asy/default.aspx
  (Note: If any of these urls no longer function, please try searching the title given for each url using a search engine such as Google.)
- There are thousands of websites related to space and the solar system. A quick Google search using the terms "solar system" or "space" will reveal many sites with useful information and interesting photos for you to use with your class.

Materials and Equipment Needed For Unit 4

(based on 30 students)

Launch: Cosmic Journeys	
Materials • notebook • pencil • poster paper	**Equipment** • research materials
1. Tracking Our Nearest Star	
Materials • masking tape • mural paper (1 sheet for the class) • Optional activity: Bristol board tape	**Equipment** • small mirror or mirror chip • Optional activity: binoculars tripod
2. That Glorious Old Sun	
Materials • 216 × 279 mm (8 ½ × 11-inch) sheets of paper • tape • pencils • index cards	**Equipment** • metre sticks • straight pins • calculator
3. Patterns of Light and Darkness	
Materials • Plasticine or modelling clay	**Equipment** • globe • pin or toothpick • compass (optional)
4. And the Seasons Go Round and Round	
Materials • large and small sheets of paper • pencil, tape, or chalk • Plasticine or modelling clay	**Equipment** • flashlight • light • globe • pin or toothpick
5. Worldviews of the Seasons	
Materials • notebook • pen or pencil	**Equipment** • computers with Internet access • reference books
6. The Moon's Changing Face	
Materials • no materials needed	**Equipment** • light source • Styrofoam™ ball painted black or a small, dark-colour play ball • pencil or knitting needle

Materials and Equipment

(continued)

7. The Moon on the Move	
Materials • table for recording • pen or pencil	**Equipment** • no equipment needed
8. Earth's Companion	
Materials • Plasticine or modelling clay	**Equipment** • section of lunar map/photograph • sculpting tools (plastic knives, craft sticks, etc.) • tray or shallow boxes • toothpicks
9. Blackout!	
Materials • notebook • pen or pencil	**Equipment** • marble • flashlight • large ball • small ball
10. The Inner Planets of Our Solar System	
Materials • paper • crayons, markers, colour pencils	**Equipment** • no equipment needed
11. The Outer Planets of Our Solar System	
Materials • chart paper • poster paper (optional) • modelling materials • 216 × 279 mm (8 ½ × 11-inch) sheets of paper (optional)	**Equipment** • no equipment needed
12. Comets, Meteoroids, and Asteroids: Oh My!	
Materials • flour • cocoa powder	**Equipment** • shallow pans • rocks of similar shape varying in sizes (1–4 cm in diameter) • ruler or tape measure
13. Sky Pictures	
Materials • sky map • coffee tin or shoebox • black paper	**Equipment** • no equipment needed

Materials and Equipment

(continued)

14. What's Happening in Space?	
Materials • paper appropriate for presentation • crayons, markers, colour pencils	**Equipment** • reference materials
15. Living in Space, the New Frontier	
Materials • paper • pencils	**Equipment** • reference materials
Design Project: Space Vehicle	
Materials • paper • pencil • construction paper • Styrofoam™ balls • plastic • markers • cardboard boxes • string • elastic bands • mini-lights • tape • glue	**Equipment** • computer (optional) • scissors

Materials and Equipment

(continued)

Overall Unit Requirements	
Materials • masking tape • mural paper (for class) • Optional activity: Bristol board • 216 × 279 mm (8 ½ × 11-inch) sheets of paper • pencils • index cards • table for recording • section of lunar map/photograph • crayons, markers, colour pencils • chart paper • poster paper (optional) • flour • cocoa powder • sky map • coffee tin or shoebox • black paper • construction paper • Styrofoam™ balls • plastic • cardboard boxes • string • elastic bands • mini-lights • glue • tape	**Equipment** • small mirror or mirror chip • Optional activity: binoculars tripod • metre sticks • straight pins • globe • pin or toothpick • Plasticine or modelling clay • compass (optional) • flashlight or light source • Styrofoam™ ball painted black or a small, dark-colour play ball • pencil or knitting needle • sculpting tools (plastic knives, craft sticks, etc.) • tray or shallow boxes • marble • large ball • small ball • shallow pans • rocks of various shapes (1–4 cm in diameter) • ruler or tape measure • reference materials • computer (optional) • scissors • calculator

Addressing Student Preconceptions

Launch: Cosmic Journeys

Most students will have noticed the Sun, Moon, and stars since they were quite young. They also will have experienced day and night and the seasons of the year. So, by Grade 6, they will have formed ideas about how things in the sky move and function. The Launch gives them the opportunity to discuss their ideas and explore them further.

Students may have the preconception that they are unable to identify astronomical bodies without the use of equipment. Teachers should emphasize that students will be able to observe a lot by just using their eyes.

Lesson 1: Tracking Our Nearest Star

Students sometimes think that shadows are reflections of an object on the ground. Therefore, you may want to review shadows with them, using simple demonstrations or investigations with light sources in the classroom. It is important to elicit students' views on shadows, and then help them to restructure these views to properly explain shadows caused by light sources. If students first understand how objects block the light from a simple light source held in various locations in the classroom, they will more easily understand how objects like a stick or our bodies block the light from the Sun as it moves across the sky.

Lesson 2: That Glorious Old Sun

Some Grade 6 students may think that Earth is the same size or even bigger than the Sun. Earth is actually 100 times smaller in diameter than the Sun. Some students may also think of the Sun's shape as a disk rather than a sphere. Therefore, you may wish to have a discussion about the Sun's size and shape to elicit students' preconceptions.

Lesson 3: Patterns of Light and Darkness

The pattern of day and night is a result of Earth's daily rotation on its axis. The side of Earth that faces the Sun experiences day, and the side of Earth that faces away from the Sun experiences night. However, research studies have shown that as many as 50 percent of 11- and 12-year-old students don't know this cause of day and night.

Lesson 4: And the Seasons Go Round and Round

Most people think that Earth's seasons are caused by its changing distance from the Sun, that is, in the summer it is hotter because Earth is closer to the Sun. However, the opposite is true. Earth is closest to the Sun in the winter. The diagram and photo on student book page 239 clearly show this concept. It is important to allow students time to reflect on their new understanding of the seasons, and to apply it to situations and other celestial objects. This is exactly what the Communicate questions at the end of this lesson encourage students to do.

Lesson 5: Worldviews of the Seasons

Many students believe that only the Western scientific explanation of how the seasons change is valid. Just as Western science has developed explanations through observation, other ways of knowing have also developed over time as a result of human observation. Students should not be quick to dismiss these ways of knowing.

Lesson 6: The Moon's Changing Face

Few students in elementary school understand the Moon's phases. Most students think that the Moon's phases are caused by Earth's shadow being cast on the Moon as it moves. Others think that the Moon's phases are caused by clouds coming between us and the Moon. Some students think that all the phases occur every night. It will be a challenge to help students understand that phases of the Moon are the illuminated portion of the Moon as it is viewed from Earth, when the Moon and Earth are in different positions relative to the Sun. The Communicate questions at the end of this lesson will help students restructure their concepts, so students should be given sufficient time to complete them.

Lesson 7: The Moon on the Move

It might be helpful to ask each student to create a drawing of the Sun–Moon–Earth positions to match the four phases of the Moon. Be prepared to accept that even after Lesson 6, many students will still have trouble with this concept.

Lesson 8: Earth's Companion

You may wish to elicit your students' ideas about the surface of the Moon before doing this activity. Get Started (on student book page 252) can lead into a class discussion on this topic. Some students may have preconceptions about the relative size of the Moon compared to Earth. In a recent study of Grade 6 students, 15 percent of them thought that the Moon was larger than Earth.

Lesson 9: Blackout!

Once students are accustomed to simulating the motion of the Sun, Moon, and Earth in the classroom, they will be better prepared to understand eclipses. The scale of the Sun, Moon, and Earth is important. The Moon's diameter is one-quarter the size of Earth's diameter. So, a tennis ball and a basketball accurately represent the relative sizes of the Moon and Earth, respectively. The Sun's diameter is 100 times Earth's diameter, and very far away. So, when students use a flashlight to model the Sun, they should be aware that they are only modelling the Sun's rays reaching one side of either the Earth or Moon models, not from the Sun itself.

Lesson 10: The Inner Planets of Our Solar System

Many students have little idea of relative sizes of and distances between the Sun, Moon, and Earth, let alone the sizes of and distances between the planets. So, you may want to introduce this lesson by listing the following celestial objects in order of their size: the Sun, Mercury, the Moon, Earth, and Jupiter. This demonstration will serve as a review, as well as alerting you to what students may already know about the planets.

Lesson 11: The Outer Planets of Our Solar System

As in Lesson 10, students will learn about the sizes of and distances between the outer planets. Students often think of the outer planets as only having rings (Saturn) or a giant spot (Jupiter). However, with more and more information constantly being gathered, scientists now know that the outer planets are much more interesting than that. As well, many students still consider Pluto to be a planet, which is no longer the case.

Lesson 12: Comets, Meteoroids, and Asteroids: Oh My!

You may wish to elicit your students' ideas about craters and what causes them, before doing the activity in this lesson. Get Started (on student book pages 268 and 269) can lead into a class discussion on this topic. Some students may have preconceptions about what is a planet, an asteroid, a comet, or a meteor/meteorite.

Lesson 13: Sky Pictures

Most people don't realize that the stars in a constellation only appear to form a group. If you could view the same constellation from another position in our galaxy, the stars would not appear together in one clump.

Lesson 14: What's Happening in Space?

Most people believe that most space science is done solely by NASA. In Canada, we often don't know about the contributions of Canadian space scientists. Many people don't even know that there is a Canadian Space Agency.

Lesson 15: Living in Space, the New Frontier

Many students believe that astronauts just float around and eat freeze-dried food. In this lesson, students will gain a better understanding of the challenges astronauts face living in microgravity, and how these astronauts conduct their research.

Design Project: Space Vehicle

Students may think that there is a "one size fits all" vehicle that would work on all planets. Each of the planets in our solar system has a unique environment, which needs to be considered when students are designing their vehicles for their chosen planets.

Big Ideas

Page 223

Our solar system is much more than just the planets, which include Earth, and the Sun. There are many other celestial bodies that comprise our solar system.

Most of science is based upon the observations of predictable patterns. This is also the case in space science. Big Ideas 2 and 3 focus on the idea of cycles and patterns. It is through the observations of the natural world that First Nations and Métis people were able to survive in harmony with nature. This alternative way of knowing has validity in explaining many of the phenomena that occur around us.

We have learnt about our solar system through observations and patterns of movement of the celestial bodies that make up the system. Through advances in technology, Big Idea 4, we have gained knowledge about these objects. In fact, we have changed our minds about the classification of those objects. Canada has been a quiet leader in these advancements.

Once you have determined students' prior knowledge, you may want to hand out LM 4-1 Unit 4 Summary and LM 4-2 Unit 4 Key Terms.

Cosmic Journeys

Page 224

Time
1 class
Key Terms
• astronomers
Line Masters
• LM 4-3

Assessing Prior Knowledge

- Divide students into groups of three or four and ask them to brainstorm the following question: *What is an astronomer?*
- After students have had time to create their definitions, discuss as a class the definitions that students have developed.
- Ask students, *Why is it important for astronomers, or any scientist, to be able to fill in tables and collect data? Where does the data, or information that scientists collect, come from?* Discussion should lead students to suggest the ability of scientists to recognize patterns in nature, and to draw conclusions from their observations. This discussion is a great way to include the idea that First Nations people developed their traditional knowledge through the observations of patterns in the natural world. The conclusions that were made from these observations helped First Nations and Métis people to survive.

Introduce the Unit

- Making observations is an important part of this unit. Students will be able to observe the Moon, stars, and planets. They will be able to see Mercury, Venus, Mars, Jupiter, and Saturn.
- Many people confuse planets and stars. You could start a discussion about the difference between planets and stars by asking, *When you are looking at the night sky, how can you tell the difference between a planet and a star?* Write students' suggestions on the board.
- You can tell the difference between a star and a planet by following a simple rule of thumb: If it twinkles, it is a star. Unlike stars, planets are reflecting light and not making their own sources of light. If you find an object in the night sky, observe it for a few minutes. If it does not twinkle, then there is a good chance you are observing a planet.
- Students will have many questions about the solar system and this is the perfect opportunity for them to do some self-directed research.

Introduce the Design Project

- At the end of this unit, students will create a space vehicle. The purpose of the space vehicle will be to visit and explore one of the planets that the students will learn about during this unit. Students will also be using what they have learned from the lessons on space exploration. Explain to students that these lessons are directly related to the Design Project and that they should be thinking about their projects throughout the unit. They may want to jot down ideas and drawings in their space portfolios throughout the unit.

Get Started ▶

- You may want to start the students thinking about the unit by asking them to write down some questions that they have about our solar system. They can share their questions in small or large groups.
- Once the students have written their lists of questions, you may want to ask students to create a bulletin board or a poster of those questions that can be displayed in the classroom.

Time

50 min

Skills

- observing
- interpreting
- comparing
- communicating

Grouping

groups of 2 or 3

Materials and Equipment

(per group)
- poster paper (optional)
- research materials

Line Masters

- none

Work On It

- You may want to group the students based on similar interests. This would lead students to create research projects that keep them engaged.
- You may want to have books available or computer access for your students to complete this activity.

Communicate

Student answers may vary but should include a reason why they are sure of their answers. A sample answer is:

- **Can you ever see the Moon in the daytime sky?** Yes, I often see the Moon when I am coming home from school and the Sun is still shining.
- **Is it possible to see the planet Jupiter in the night sky without a telescope?** Yes! Jupiter is the second brightest planet in the sky after Venus. You can see 99 percent of the objects that make up the mass of the solar system (Sun, Moon, Earth, Venus, Jupiter, Mars, Mercury, and Saturn) with your unaided eyes.
- **Can we see the same stars any time of the year?** No, because the view of the stars we see is always changing. Earth orbits the Sun and since Earth is tilted on an axis, we get different views depending on the time of year. This is why we have summer and winter constellations.
- **Is there ever really a Blue Moon?** Yes, but certain conditions are necessary. The Moon will appear to be blue when there are particles, usually of sulfur, in the air that are wider than the bandwidth of red light (0.7 μm) and only particles of this size are present. These particles appear when some volcanoes erupt and sometimes during forest fires. In the 1950s, a forest fire in British Columbia sent sulfur particles into the atmosphere. When the Moon was viewed in England, it appeared blue! People started using the phrase "once in a blue moon" in popular culture in the 1930s after it appeared in a farmer's almanac. The almanac defined a blue moon to be the fourth full moon in a season. Usually, there are three full moons per season. The definition was misquoted in the 1940s to mean that two full moons appear in the same month. This definition is the current accepted definition.
- If students are planning on observing the night sky, go over the sky-watching tips listed on student book page 225. When watching the night sky, students should use a method of record keeping, such as that presented in LM 4-3 Record Keeping. The following is an example of a record a student might make (see top of next page):

Date: Sept. 15
weather conditions: clear and warm
equipment: binoculars
who was there: me and my dad
sketches

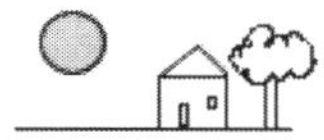

Notes: When we went to look at the Moon, it was low in the sky, very big, and orange. My dad said it was a Harvest Moon. Using the binoculars, we could see the surface much better.

BUILD ON WHAT YOU KNOW

The Build On What You Know section is similar to a notebook or portfolio. The purpose of this activity is to be a self-guided discovery where students can record their observations of the night sky. Some students will prefer to draw their observations, whereas other students will prefer to write down what they observe.

1 Tracking Our Nearest Star

Page 226

Time
1 class period for set-up plus additional time if needed

Key Terms
• vapour • sunspots

Line Masters
• LM 4-4

Indicator Assessment Chart

Indicator	Assessment Opportunities
SS6.1 a. Use a variety of sources and technologies to gather and compile pertinent information about the physical characteristics of the major components of the solar system.	• Work On It, p. 228 • Build On What You Know, p. 229

Background Information

The nearest star to Earth is 145 million kilometres (or one astronomical unit (1 AU)) away. The next closest star is 300 000 times farther away. In terms of stars, our Sun is pretty typical of the over 200 billion stars in the Milky Way galaxy. What makes the Sun so special, at least to us, is that without it, there would be no life on Earth. Earth's proximity to the Sun is what allows Earth to support life. It affects our seasons, climate, weather, ocean and air currents, and provides energy so plants can make food.

Scientists estimate that the Sun is about 5 billion years old. It contains 99.86 percent of the mass of the entire solar system. This mass is made up of ionized gases. These gases, held in place by gravitational attraction, produce the energy that comes from the Sun. This energy is in the form of light and heat.

The heat of the Sun is enough to create and maintain thermonuclear fusion reactions. At the Sun's core, the reactions generate about 383 billion trillion kilowatts per second of energy. This amount of energy is the same as 100 billion tonnes of TNT exploding every second. The Sun's surface isn't quite as hot. The core has an estimated temperature of about 8 million Kelvin, whereas the surface is a "cool" 7000 K.

The 500-km-thick surface, or photosphere, of the Sun is made up of escaping radiation, light, and "sunspots." During a total eclipse, the reddish rim we can observe is known as the chromosphere. The chromosphere is made of hot, highly energized hydrogen atoms. Beyond the chromosphere is the corona, which creates the solar winds. The solar winds help send the Sun's charged particles to the edges of the solar system.

traditional *KNOWLEDGE*

Some First Nations, including the Saulteaux, believe that the Sun moves around Earth, not that Earth moves around the Sun. The Lakota people traditionally harmonized their movements through the Black Hills to the movement of the Sun. They moved in an elliptical pattern, which mimics the movement of certain constellations in relation to the Sun.

Get Started ▶

- To help students start thinking about the Sun, ask them to create a web about what they observe about the Sun.
- Often students will become very excited about space science, especially when they have the opportunity to make their own observations. Be sure to go over the importance of the safety precautions that should be taken when observing the Sun.

Sunny Facts

- The Sun appears to move from east to west in the sky. The apparent motion of the Sun is caused by Earth rotating counterclockwise. Earth turns toward the east as it rotates on its axis once every 24 h (approximately). Because Earth is tilted, the Sun rises due east and sets due west only during the spring and fall equinoxes (about March 21 and September 21). In the summer months, the Sun rises in the northeast and sets in the northwest, whereas during the winter months the Sun rises in the southeast and sets in the southwest.
- Through a discussion, ask students if they know what would happen if the Sun were directed onto a piece of paper using a magnifying lens. The paper soon begins to smoulder and eventually bursts into flame.
- Ask students if they know why using a magnifying lens causes the paper to burn. What would happen if they left a sheet of paper in the Sun without a magnifying lens? Help students understand that the lens focusses the Sun's light to a concentrated area, making it more powerful and thus burning the paper. Explain that the same thing could happen to the retinas in their eyes if they looked through a lens at the Sun. Ask, *What would be a safe way to look at the Sun? How have you made your observations about the Sun? How would you go about studying it in greater detail?* Some students may have seen the Sun projected via a pinhole-projected image, binoculars projecting its image onto a sheet of paper, a telescope projecting its image onto a sheet of paper, or by a mirror reflecting the image of the Sun.

Time

20 min to set up, entire day to make measurements

Skills

- observing
- interpreting
- experimenting
- hypothesizing
- measuring
- communicating
- controlling variables

Grouping

groups

Materials and Equipment

(per group)
- small mirror or mirror chip
- masking tape
- mural paper (1 sheet for the entire class)
- colour pencils

Line Masters

- LM 4-4

CAUTION!

Be sure not to look directly at the Sun. It can cause damage to the retinas of the eyes.

If you are using mirror chips, advise caution because the sides of the mirror chips can be sharp. To avoid cuts, be sure to tape the edges of the mirror chips.

Work On It

- You will need a sunny day to do this project successfully. As well, students will need to be able to make markings on the mural paper throughout the day to show that the Sun moves. This activity works very well if you take measurements on a number of sunny days, not just on the first day.
- Students' eyes can be irritated if a bright light is shone into them. Be sure that the reflection of light by the mirror occurs on the mural paper.
- If it is possible to find a pair of binoculars or a scope that can be mounted on a tripod, try the activity described at the bottom of student book page 227. It will allow the students to observe the Sun in a safe manner.
- Set rules for level of noise and respect for others. Point out to students that they do not all have to go to the window sill to conduct the inquiry. Allow students time to explore with the mirrors, investigating the sharpness, size, and positioning of the Sun's image. Encourage them to project the image at varying distances and angles.
- Once students have the method established, discuss where to set the mirror to get the sharpest image while tracking the Sun. Do a trial run of reflecting the image onto the mural paper, tracing the Sun's disk, and recording the date and time of observation. Discuss how students will be responsible for tracking the Sun's path for the next while. Suggest that they look for patterns of movement.
- You may wish to set up a schedule of pairs of students so as to involve all class members in collecting the data. By collecting data over a long period of time and/or collecting it on the same date at various monthly or seasonal intervals, students can begin to make valuable comparisons and conclusions about the apparent movement of the Sun.
- The activity on LM 4-4 Sun and Moon Finder will allow students to make a model to help them observe that Earth revolves around the Sun. If we were to use only the observations of the Sun in the sky, we would incorrectly assume that the Sun orbits Earth. This activity can also be used to illustrate the rising and setting of the Moon.

Communicate

The Communicate questions are to be used as a student reflection on the Work On It activity.

1. Students' responses should indicate that the apparent path of movement is opposite to the real path of movement. In the morning, the Sun's projected image tracks downward as the Sun rises higher in the sky. In the afternoon, when the Sun dips lower in the sky, the projected image will be seen to track higher on the wall or mural paper.
2. The path of the Sun's movement will track upward or downward, and will move from west to east on the sheet. It will be reversed from the Sun's apparent motion because of the mirror image.

BUILD ON WHAT YOU KNOW

This exercise is a continuation of the previous Build On What You Know activity. Students should continue to add to their observations throughout the unit. As they progress, they should show a development in observation skills, as well as in identification skills.

This section asks the question, "How do you think the apparent movement of objects in the sky could be useful to people in some way?" Many students will respond that the motion of objects helps to indicate the passage of time. Many First Nations and Métis people looked for the appearance of certain stars and even changes in the Moon to determine what time of the year it was. Knowing the time of the year was essential to their survival.

For ESL/ELL

Ask students to complete the activity in the For Reteaching section.

For Reteaching

A simple activity to show how the Sun appears to move through the sky is to use the concept of shadows.

1. Early in the morning, ask the students go out into the playground. Ask a few students to volunteer casting shadows. Trace the footprints of these volunteers in the playground to mark where they are standing. Then trace an outline of each volunteer's shadow.
2. Throughout the day, ask the volunteers to stand in their traced footprints. Compare the location of the shadow to the original shadow. Do a second tracing of the shadow.
3. Continue making tracings throughout the day.

The shadow will move and many students will assume that it is the Sun that is moving, especially because it appears that the Sun moves across the sky. Many people forget that it is Earth that is moving, not the Sun. Earth's movement in relation to the Sun is why the shadows move.

For Enrichment

To build concepts of time related to astronomy, ask students to draw a line perpendicular to the path of movement of the Sun. Then ask them to predict how long it will take for the whole disk of the Sun to cross the line. Try this activity on different days throughout the year using the same mural paper to record observations. Students will be able to see how the altitude of the Sun changes with the seasons.

Assessment *for* Learning

What to Look For in Student Work	What to Do
Look at students' written work in the Communicate questions. Students should realize that the Sun appears to move across the sky, but it is really Earth that is moving.	• If students are still having difficulty, you can do the For Reteaching activity.

2 That Glorious Old Sun

Page 230

Time

1 class period

Key Terms

- atmosphere
- photosphere
- chromosphere
- corona

Line Masters

- LM 4-5

Indicator Assessment Chart

Indicator	Assessment Opportunities
SS6.1 a. Use a variety of sources and technologies to gather and compile pertinent information about the physical characteristics of the major components of the solar system.	• Work On It, p. 232 • Communicate, p. 233, q. 1
SS6.1 d. Evaluate the validity and usefulness of different sources of information about the physical characteristics of the solar system.	• Communicate, p. 233, q. 1, 2
SS6.1 g. Create scale-distance and/or scale-size models to represent the major components of the solar system.	• Work On It, p. 232
SS6.1 h. Evaluate the usefulness and accuracy of scale-distance and/or scale-size models of the major components of the solar system.	• Communicate, p. 233, q. 2

Background Information

The Sun is made up of mostly hydrogen and helium, with trace amounts of other gases that together amount to less than one percent.

Sunspots are impermanent features that result from a tear in the Sun's photosphere (surface). They are associated with powerful magnetic fields that block some of the outward radiation from the Sun's core. The affected region is several thousand degrees cooler, so the sunspots appear darker by contrast. Each sunspot has a black core, called the umbra, and a lighter surrounding ring, called the penumbra. Sunspots range in size from hundreds to hundreds of thousands of kilometres in diameter. Very large sunspots may be seen with the naked eye, but usually magnification is necessary. The number of sunspots fluctuates over an 11-year cycle. Toward the maximum of a cycle, there may be over 100 visible sunspots. A sunspot maximum occurred in 2001–2002.

traditional *KNOWLEDGE*

The Sun Dance is an important yearly event for most First Nations people. It was a time to celebrate the renewal of life on Earth and in the tribe. This was a sacred time that had not only religious implications, but social and legal consequences as well. Many of the important decisions involving the people would be decided at this time because it was a gathering of many tribes.

Get Started ▶

- Students know that sunlight is essential to making plants grow. Because Saskatchewan receives so much sunshine, traditionally it has been an agricultural province.

Sun Science

- The distances in space are enormous. To make it easier for scientists and non-scientists to discuss our solar system, scientists have developed the idea of astronomical units (AU). One astronomical unit is the distance from Earth to the Sun. We use astronomical units to discuss how far apart the different objects in our solar system are.
- Students can build an edible model of the Sun. Ask students to cover a cookie (Sun) with white frosting. Shake red and yellow sprinkles on the frosted cookie. The sprinkles represent the photosphere, which has a granular appearance. Chocolate chips can represent sunspots. Students should know that sunspots appear in pairs, so two chips should be placed side by side. Licorice can represent prominences, which tend to be near sunspots because the area is much more active and tends to have a stronger magnetic field. The prominences can be straight up or on their sides.
- Nuclear reactors use the process of nuclear fission to generate power. Fission is the splitting of a large radioactive nucleus into smaller nuclei, which releases a great deal of energy that is used to make steam to power generators. Nuclear fusion is the process that occurs in stars to generate energy (see Unit 2, Lesson 5). Fusion involves two smaller nuclei combining to form one larger nucleus. This process generates even more energy than fission, but scientists have yet to discover how to replicate it here on Earth for generating power.
- Given that the Sun is about 150 million kilometres away from Earth, ask students to imagine how hot it must be on the Sun's surface if a mere 35°C of heat on Earth makes us feel hot.

! Because the distances in the solar system are so large, astronomers have developed the astronomical unit, or AU. It is the distance from Earth to the Sun. Astronomers have calculated this distance to be $1.495\ 978\ 706\ 91 \times 10^{11}$ m, or about 150 million kilometres. They use this system so that when they discuss distances within our solar system, they don't get overwhelmed by large numbers.

A red giant refers to a large, bright star that may range in size from 0.5–10 solar masses (1 solar mass = the mass of our Sun). It is in the later stages of its lifetime. It is believed that our Sun may become a red giant at some point in its lifetime.
Blue giants are large and extremely bright stars. When they are observed, they appear blue. It is believed that at the end of their very short lifetimes, these stars become supernovae.
White dwarfs are very small and dense stars. They emit stored heat, which gives them a very faint luminosity. It is believed that they are no longer undergoing nuclear fusion reactions and are at the very end of their life cycle.
Red dwarfs are also very small and dense stars. They tend to have a solar mass of 0.5 or less. They have a very slow rate of nuclear fusion and so tend to emit very little light and heat.
Our Sun is the best example of a yellow dwarf star. Yellow dwarfs tend to have solar masses in the range of 0.8–1.0.
An infrared star is a star that has a low temperature or a dense environment caused by dust. Infrared stars emit no visible light. They only emit infrared wavelengths (heat).
A neutron star is what is left over when a star collapses (after a supernova). It has a lot of heat (energy). These stars tend to have a solar mass of 1.35–2.1.

We often think of seismology as being only related to Earth and the study of earthquakes (seismic waves). There is a branch of astronomy, called stellar seismology, which studies the observed vibrations on the surface of the Sun in order to help astronomers know more about the interior of the Sun. The same basic principles that guide the seismology we use on Earth guide stellar seismologists.

Work On It

In Procedure step 1, students will determine the diameter of the image. In step 4, students will determine the distance to the image. The distance to the Sun is given as 149 600 000 km on student book page 230. The diameter of the Sun is the unknown variable that students need to isolate and calculate using the equation given on student book page 232.

- You may have to review the concept of ratios with your class in order for them to be successful in this activity.
- Be sure that the students draw parallel lines. You may have to review the term "parallel."
- Check that the students have built the apparatus correctly and that the pinprick of light is between their parallel lines.

Time

30 min

Skills

- inferring
- interpreting
- experimenting
- comparing
- measuring

Grouping

pairs or small groups

Materials and Equipment

(per group)
- 216 × 279 mm (8 ½ × 11-inch) sheets of paper
- tape
- pencils
- index cards
- metre sticks
- straight pins
- calculator

Line Masters

- none

CAUTION!

Because students are working to determine the size of the Sun, be sure that they never look directly into the Sun because doing so could cause permanent damage to their eyes.

Think Again! What Else Have We Learned About the Largest Object in Our Solar System?

- Students often wonder why the planets and other objects in our solar system orbit the Sun.
- Gravity is the pull of one object on another. If two objects are of similar mass, the effects of gravity are not very noticeable. If there is a big difference in the two masses, for example, Earth and the average grade 6 student, the object with the larger mass will pull the object with the smaller mass toward itself. That is why we stay on the surface of Earth. Earth's mass is so much greater than ours that it pulls us toward its centre. This is also the reason why planets orbit the Sun. The larger mass of the Sun pulls the planets (and other objects) toward it.

Communicate

These questions allow students to reflect on and process the information they gathered in the Work On It activity.

1. Answers will vary. Most students can't comprehend how large the Sun is compared to Earth.
2. Answers may vary. Many students may find using ratios difficult if the concept is relatively new. Students may use the following as real-life examples of using ratios: cooking (making a recipe bigger or smaller) and determining the amount of seed/fertilizer/chemical on a field.

For ESL/ELL

It may be easier for the students to attempt the For Reteaching activity in order to understand the size of the Sun.

As there is a lot of new terminology in this unit, you may want students to start a visual dictionary or list of key terms that they can refer to throughout this unit. Terms that they could add in this section include atmosphere, photosphere, chromosphere, and corona.

For Reteaching

You will need LM 4-5 Sun–Earth Ratio and two students for this activity.

1. Show the students the image of the Sun on LM 4-5. Discuss how big Earth should be relative to the size of the Sun on this LM.
2. Show students the cutout of Earth's image at the bottom of LM 4-5. Ask students how far apart the Sun's image and the Earth cutout should be so their relative distance apart is correct. You could ask one student to walk what he or she thinks is the correct distance.
3. The correct distance is about 20 m. Students should look back to the Sun image from this distance. This model correctly represents the distance and size of the Sun relative to Earth.

For Enrichment

Students can research current and past missions to the Sun. They should find out the names of the spacecraft, the objectives of the missions, and the results of the missions.

Assessment *for* Learning

What to Look For in Student Work	What to Do
Observe the students working during the Work On It activity. You may want to clarify their understanding informally during the activity by asking them how they have determined their ratios. Also, be sure that they understand how much bigger the Sun is compared to Earth through the use of the ratios.	• Students may have difficulty with the math in this lesson. Some students have difficulty understanding how ratios work. You may have to teach ratios to the entire class or to individual students. • If understanding the size of the Sun is still difficult, see the For Reteaching activity for further reinforcement. • This informal formative discussion and understanding can be confirmed through the summative written Communicate questions.

3 Patterns of Light and Darkness

Page 234

Time

1 class period

Key Terms

- rotates
- axis
- revolves

Line Masters

- LM 4-6

Indicator Assessment Chart

Indicator	Assessment Opportunities
SS6.1 a. Use a variety of sources and technologies to gather and compile pertinent information about the physical characteristics of the major components of the solar system.	• Build On What You Know, p. 236
SS6.2 e. Demonstrate how Earth's rotation causes the day and night cycle and how Earth's 23.5° tilt and revolution around the Sun causes the yearly cycle of seasons.	• Work On It, p. 235

Background Information

While Earth travels through space around the Sun, it also spins (rotates) on its axis. We call the length of time it takes Earth to spin around once, with respect to the Sun, a day (solar day), or 24 h. Astronomers use a term called the *sidereal day.* It is based on the period of Earth's rotation as measured by fixed stars. For Earth, this day equals 23 h, 56 min, and about 4 s of mean solar time.

For about 357 days of the year, there is some place on Earth where the Sun never rises at any time during the 24-h day. These places are located approximately between the latitudes 67°N to 90°N and from 67°S to 90°S. There are, however, two very brief periods (about four days each) when the Sun rises or is above the horizon everywhere on Earth for all or part of each day. The two periods are approximately between March 18 and 22, and between September 21 and 24. During these days, the Sun is above the horizon at all locations from pole to pole.

At the North Pole (latitude 90°N), the Sun is above the horizon continuously from March 19 to September 24. When the Sun sets September 24, it does not rise again until March 19. By the end of October, twilight disappears from the sky and dawn does not glow significantly until about mid-February.

Get Started ▶

- Ask the students, *What do you know about the position and motion of Earth in relation to the Sun?* Ask students to demonstrate, using their bodies to represent Earth and the Sun, or to make a quick sketch. Most students will indicate a Sun-centred system.
- Read the opening paragraph on student book page 234. Call students' attention to the picture and invite students to offer comments about it. Continue reading. Check for understanding of the terms "axis" and "apparent movement." "Axis" is likely to be a new word for most students. You may wish to use a spinning top or a basketball to demonstrate the concept of something spinning on its axis.
- If possible, show a picture of the Ptolemaic model of the solar system, in which Earth is fixed at the centre of the solar system. Explain how, in Europe, views different from an Earth-centred one were controversial long after Copernicus's time. Copernicus faced a lot of opposition for his Sun-centred view of the solar system. Sometimes it takes a long time for new scientific theories to be accepted.
- To help students understand the concept of Earth revolving around the Sun while rotating on its axis, have one student, representing the Sun, stand still, while another student, representing Earth, spins (rotates) and, at the same time, revolves (turns) in a circle around the first student.
- To demonstrate the meaning of a horizon, place a round pizza pan against a globe. If a student were to stand in the middle of the pan, the student would see only the edge (horizon) and the sky above it. This would be similar to a horizon one would see at the ocean. If you take your students outside, they will realize that horizons look different depending on where they are looking.

Time
40 min
Skills
• making models • inferring • observing • interpreting • comparing
Grouping
groups
Materials and Equipment
(per group) • globe • pin or toothpick • Plasticine or modelling clay • compass (optional)
Line Masters
• none

Work On It

- Develop the idea that, until recently, astronomers have not been able to travel to space to find answers to questions. Thus, they set up models using items to represent space objects to find answers to questions.
- Help students become familiar with how to orient the globe so that the North Pole points north and the shaded part remains shaded with as little light falling on it as possible. Once students understand how the globe must be oriented (Procedure steps 1, 2, and 3), then you may wish to divide the class into groups so they can perform the activity themselves.
- Answers to questions:
  a. If we were to compare the ratios of the shadow of the toothpick to the shadows cast on the ground, we would find that they are similar.
  b. Students should identify that the side opposite to where the light source illuminates the globe is the dark side of the globe. Students may also identify the region on the globe. The continents of Asia, Australia, and parts of Africa will be in darkness.

c. Depending on the time of day during this experiment, students should identify that the Sun would be rising on the Pacific Rim of Asia. Again, depending on the time of day, they may say that the Sun is setting in the Middle East, Russia, East Africa, and possibly eastern Europe.

d. Students' answers will depend on what time of day the activity occurs. If it is morning in Saskatchewan, it will be morning along western North America. As the day goes on, the area where morning occurs moves farther west of the Pacific Rim. Where it is midnight will also depend on what time the activity takes place. If it is 10 a.m. in Saskatchewan, then it will be midnight in Beijing, China. As our day goes on, the location where it is midnight will move farther west, through mainland Asia and toward Europe.

Communicate

To summarize, ask, *How do shadows help us judge when the Sun is directly overhead? How can we test for this in our model?*

1. It depends on the time of year. When Earth has moved in its orbit so that the North Pole is tilted away from the Sun at an angle of 23.5°, the Sun cannot reach it. So, the North Pole will be in some degree of darkness 24 h a day during this time.
2. It depends on the season. When Earth has moved in its orbit so that the South Pole is tilted toward the Sun, the South Pole experiences 24 h of daylight while the North Pole has 24 h of darkness. Conversely, when Earth moves in its orbit so that the North Pole is tilted toward the Sun, then the North Pole experiences 24 h of light. On the first day of spring or fall, all places on Earth should get equal hours of light and dark.
3. Answers may vary. Some students will give an approximate time (for example, evening, afternoon, morning). Some students may realize that Earth turns 360° in about 24 h, thus about 15° in an hour and 1° in four minutes. If they can determine how many degrees east or west the place is from where they are located, they may be able to tell time more precisely.
4. When Earth rotates on its axis, it turns in and out of the Sun's light, which causes day and night.

BUILD ON WHAT YOU KNOW

Students should recognize that the Sun appears to move from east to west in the sky. Some students may deduce that the apparent motion of the Sun is caused by Earth rotating counterclockwise. Earth turns toward the east as it rotates on its axis approximately once every 24 h. Because Earth is tilted on its axis, the Sun rises due east and sets due west only during the spring and fall equinoxes (about March 21 and September 21). In summer, the Sun rises in the northeast and sets in the northwest, whereas during winter, the Sun rises in the southeast and sets in the southwest.

Students should also be making some kind of recording of where they have been observing the setting of the Sun. They can use LM 4-6 Observing the Sunset to record their observations either in words or drawings.

For ESL/ELL

If the playground has a merry-go-round, ask the majority of students to sit on it facing outward. The merry-go-round represents Earth. Ask one student to stand approximately 2 m from the merry-go-round. This student represents the Sun.

Slowly spin the merry-go-round counterclockwise, just as Earth rotates on its axis.

Ask students, *Who is in the "daylight"? Who is in the "darkness"? Who is seeing the sunrise? Who is seeing the sunset? For whom is it noon? For whom is it midnight?*

For Reteaching

You may set up another model of Earth and the Sun to teach students about day and night. Use the globe to represent Earth and a flashlight or projector light to represent the Sun. In a slightly darkened room, shine the light on the globe. Which side has light, or day? Which side is in darkness? Why? Rotate the globe counterclockwise slowly. Where is it light now? Where is it dark now? Ask students to put a bit of Plasticine on their location on the globe and imagine that the Plasticine is a person. Is it night or day for that person? Turn the globe a little counterclockwise. Is the Sun getting low or high in the sky? Is it about to get dark or light? Tie in the terms "sunrise" and "sunset." Place two or three figures on the globe in various places. Who is getting the most light? Who is getting the least light?

For Enrichment

Ask students to learn about the different time zones. They should learn about the International Date Line and what purpose this line serves.

Assessment *for* Learning

What to Look For in Student Work	What to Do
Check with the students during the Work On It activity informally to make sure they understand how the position of Earth relative to the Sun affects the periods of night and day and the seasons. You will be able to gauge students' understanding based on their answers to the Communicate questions.	• If students are still having difficulty, see the For Reteaching or For ESL/ELL sections for further reinforcement.

4 And the Seasons Go Round and Round

Page 237

Time
1 class period
Key Terms
• none
Line Masters
• LM 4-7

Indicator Assessment Chart

Indicator	Assessment Opportunities
SS6.2 d. Propose personal explanations for the causes of seasons, phases, and eclipses.	• Communicate, p. 241, q. 6
SS6.2 e. Demonstrate how Earth's rotation causes the day and night cycle and how Earth's 23.5° tilt and revolution around the Sun causes the yearly cycle of seasons.	• Work On It, p. 237 • Build On What You Know, p. 241
SS6.2 f. Propose explanations for how the yearly cycle of seasons might differ if Earth's axis were not tilted.	• Communicate, p. 241, q. 5
SS6.2 i. Propose questions related to astronomical phenomena to investigate using models and simulations, such as "Do other planets exhibit phases?", "How would seasons on Earth differ if Earth were not tilted?", "How would patterns of eclipses change if the Sun, Earth, or Moon were different diameters or positioned at different locations?"	• Communicate, p. 241, q. 5

Background Information

Seasons are caused by the tilt of Earth's axis of rotation with respect to the plane of its orbit around the Sun. The angle of Earth's axis is fixed in space as it orbits the Sun. Most of the time, the northern point of Earth's axis is pointed toward Polaris, the North Star. Earth is just slightly closer to the Sun in the winter than in summer (by about five million kilometres, or 3.3 percent).

In winter, because the North Pole is tilted away from the Sun, the northern hemisphere receives less concentrated sunlight than in summer. Sunlight hits Earth at a low angle, from below the equator, so the energy from sunlight is spread out over larger areas, which reduces its effectiveness in heating the land. When combined with fewer hours of daylight, temperatures stay cooler in winter. In summer, as the North Pole tilts toward the Sun, the number of sunlight hours increases and sunlight hits Earth at a higher angle, from above the equator, giving more concentrated light and thus increasing the amount of solar energy the ground receives.

continued →

traditional ***KNOWLEDGE***

In the northern hemisphere, the longest day of the year on Earth is the summer solstice, around June 21, when the Sun is at its highest point in the sky. The shortest day of the year is the winter solstice, around December 21, when the Sun is at its lowest point in the sky.

Some First Nations people, such as the Cree, believed that you could tell the type of winter (long or short, warm or cold) it would be from the visible markings on the Moon in the fall.

Since Earth is in orbit around the Sun at a tilt, certain constellations are visible at certain times of the year. Often, the appearance of these constellations would signal times for ceremonies or even ritual tasks. For example, the Lakota would look for the appearance of the constellation Cansasa Ipusye, or Dried Willow, to signal the time in the winter months to collect red willow. The inner bark was used as part of the Tobacco in the sacred pipe. Spiritually, the appearance of this constellation let the Lakota know that the circle of the teachings of the sacred pipe would begin anew.

Get Started ▶

- Discuss with students the patterns they have noticed in their observations of the night sky. Encourage students to share their notes, sketches, or photos to support their observations. Also review what is happening in their tracking of the Sun. Encourage them to discuss any patterns or cycles they are noting with respect to tracking the Sun on their large sheet of paper. Ask, *What is happening to cause patterns in the sky?* Record their thoughts on the board or on a KWL chart. Revisit what students have previously recorded. Is there anything they want to change? Ask students to indicate what they would like to know about seasons, and add these questions to the KWL chart.
- Ask students to look at the photos on student book page 237. For each photo, ask, *What season is represented in each photo? How do you know? How long does it take to go through a cycle of seasons? Is Earth closer to the Sun in summer or in winter?* Invite them to read the paragraph to find the answers to some of these questions.

Time
30 min
Skills
• making models • inferring • observing • interpreting • comparing
Grouping
pairs or groups
Materials and Equipment
(per group) • large and small sheets of paper • pencil, tape, or chalk • flashlight • light • globe • Plasticine or modelling clay • pin or toothpick
Line Masters
• LM 4-7

Work On It

- Be sure that students understand the concept of the tilt of Earth's axis of rotation with respect to the plane of its orbit around the Sun. The angle of Earth's axis of rotation is fixed in space as it moves around the Sun. The axis is pointed toward Polaris, the North Star. Allow students time to explore with a globe and see that it is tilted on its axis at an angle of 23.5°.
- To help students understand how Earth keeps spinning on its axis without tipping over, spin a top on a slight angle. The gravity of Earth is trying to pull the top down while the top is trying to remain upright. While Earth spins, its gravity is trying to keep it upright while the gravity (pull) of the Sun and the Moon is trying to pull it over. These constant opposite pulls keep Earth spinning at the same angle.
- When taking the globe through its orbit, be sure it is always held or placed so that its axis is tilted toward the north. Be sure that students have the opportunity to observe that, as Earth rotates counterclockwise on its axis while it orbits the Sun, there are more hours of daylight in the northern hemisphere when the North Pole is tilted toward the Sun (i.e., in summer). Conversely, there are fewer hours of daylight when the North Pole is pointed away from the Sun in winter. Students also should observe their stick person carefully for:
  - when it reaches sunrise and when it reaches sunset
  - how long it is in sunlight
  - the length of the shadows
- Leave this station set up so that as many students as possible can have an opportunity to walk the globe through its orbit and learn through hands-on experience. As they do so, they can complete LM 4-7 The Seasons Go Round and Round.

Think Again! The Full Story of Summer Heat

- If students are having trouble understanding this concept, use a light bulb and shine it on an object, such as a piece of black construction paper, for five minutes. Ask students to feel the paper for warmth. Continue heating that same piece of paper for another five minutes (double the time) and ask students to feel the paper once again. Students should notice that when the paper is heated for a longer period of time, it is much warmer. The same idea applies to heating Earth.

Communicate

1. The light became either more or less intense, causing the shadow to become longer and less sharp or shorter and sharper.
2. Answers may vary, but students should name a place in the southern hemisphere.
3. This answer will depend on the season when the activity is done, but should name the season opposite to what students are experiencing.
4. The seasons are caused by the tilt of Earth's axis of rotation with respect to the plane of its orbit around the Sun. As Earth tilts toward the Sun in summer, it is warmer because the Sun is visible for more hours each day, providing us with more total heat energy. Also, in summer, sunlight strikes Earth's surface more directly, increasing the amount of solar energy the land receives.
5. Students may not be able to accurately answer this question, but should understand that the change in seasons on Earth depends on the tilt of Earth's axis of rotation. If Earth were not tilted, seasons on Earth would be less pronounced. Other factors that affect the changing of the seasons include a planet's distance from the Sun, its period of rotation, and its atmosphere. All of these factors together affect the changing of the seasons. You may want to discuss how certain parts of Earth, such as areas near the equator, experience very little change from season to season because the tilt of Earth's axis with respect to the Sun is less pronounced at these locations.
6. Mars is the planet that would have seasons most similar to those on Earth. It has a tilt very similar to Earth's tilt, an atmosphere, a similar period of rotation (about 24 h), and it is similarly close to the Sun. Venus has an atmosphere of very thick heavy clouds that hold in its heat, a greater tilt, and a unique rotation—it keeps almost the same face to the Sun, just as the Moon does, but rotates opposite to most bodies in the solar system. Seasons on Uranus would not be comparable to Earth's seasons because Uranus is tilted at 90° to its orbit.

BUILD ON WHAT YOU KNOW

Provide opportunities for students to share their observations with each other. The sky will change in that constellations will shift from east to west by a noticeable amount within a 45-min period. Students should choose one particular constellation to observe (for example, Orion). They can observe it at a particular time each evening and keep a record of it over several months. What shifts do students note in its position during that time? Stars in the north appear to revolve slowly around the sky's pivot point, the north celestial pole, not far from Polaris (the North Star, which hardly moves at all). They will see these constellations all year. The most familiar one will probably be Ursa Major (the Big Dipper). Students will notice how its position changes over time: Is it upright? Is it pouring water out?

For ESL/ELL

See the For Reteaching section.

For Reteaching

There are many great mini clips that can be found on the Internet. These mini clips may help students visualize the concepts of axis and orbit in conjunction with the model activity that they have done.

For Enrichment

Ask students, *What would the seasons be like on a planet where the tilt of the axis is different?* Ask students to choose a planet and research this question on the Internet or in the library. Encourage them to work in groups and to present their findings to the class as creatively as possible.

Assessment *for* Learning

What to Look For in Student Work	What to Do
Check students during the Work On It activity informally to see if they understand the concept of how Earth's rotation about its axis and about the Sun affects the seasons. You will be able to gauge students' understanding based on their answers to the Communicate questions.	• Students may have difficulty with the idea of tilt of axis. Since they have already used models, you may want to use diagrams of the angles and areas of Earth covered by sunlight at various times of the year. You may want to use a basketball (representing Earth) and different sizes of cones (cone size will depend on whether it is winter or summer) to show how much of the Sun's energy reaches and covers Earth. • If students are still having difficulty, see the For Reteaching activity for further reinforcement.

5 Worldviews of the Seasons

Page 242

Time
2 class periods

Key Terms
• equinoxes • solstices • Moose Mountain circle

Line Masters
• none

Indicator Assessment Chart

Indicator	Assessment Opportunities
SS6.1 b. Analyze historical and current technological developments that have enabled human observation of the major components of the solar system.	• Work On It, p. 244
SS6.1 f. Describe objects in the heavens, as indicated through First Nations and Métis art and stories or by Elders or Traditional Knowledge Keepers.	• Work On It, p. 244
SS6.2 a. Examine how people of different cultures, including First Nations, have recorded (e.g., medicine wheel, Mayan calendar, Stonehenge, pyramids) and used understandings of astronomical phenomena (e.g., positions of the stars and/or planets) to solve practical problems such as the appropriate time to plant and harvest crops, to support navigation on land and water, or to foretell significant events through stories and legends.	• Work On It, p. 244
SS6.2 b. Examine ways in which humans have represented understanding of or interest in astronomical phenomena through music, dance, drama, visual art, or stories.	• Work On It, p. 244
SS6.2 d. Propose personal explanations for the causes of seasons, phases, and eclipses.	• Communicate, p. 244, q. 3
SS6.2 g. Consider alternate models of seasons and explanations for those models (e.g., the six-season model of the Woodland Cree, the rainy and dry seasons of some tropical and subtropical regions).	• Work On It, p. 244

Background Information

Throughout history, it has been important all over the world to know when the seasons are about to change. Knowledge of the timing of these changes was based upon observations of the natural world. Sometimes, through these observations, technologies were created to help different people know when the changes of the seasons were about to occur. For many people, this information was important because it would signal when to plant crops, when to harvest, and even when the flood season was approaching.

Students may be familiar with some of the technologies that were built to signal changes in the seasons, such as Stonehenge in England, the pyramids of Giza in Egypt, and Chichen Itza in Mexico. Other structures are not as familiar, such as the Sun Dagger petroglyphs in Chaco Canyon, New Mexico. Scientists and archaeologists are still trying to decode some of the mysteries of these structures.

Get Started ▶

- Ask students if any of them are familiar with ways that their families know the seasons are about to change. Depending on their cultural backgrounds, they may have new information to share with their classmates.
- It is important to stress that much can be learned about the world around us by observing nature and the interactions that occur in the natural world.

Legends, Observations, and Astronomy

traditional ***KNOWLEDGE***

- Many ancient cultures, such as the Chinese and the Mayans, as well as First Nations and Métis people, use a lunar calendar. Greek and Roman civilizations later adopted a solar calendar. For the First Nations and Métis people of Saskatchewan, a lunar calendar, which has thirteen months, had survival value and practical implications. The months in the FNM lunar calendar borrow their names from natural phenomena. For example, the sixth month, called pâskâwihowipîsim in Cree, or egg hatching moon, describes the month when birds hatch.

- Teachers should be aware that the spelling of the names of months may vary depending on the particular Cree dialect being used. Knowing the name of the month taught survival and respect for the land. For example, a traditional hunter would avoid killing hatchlings and female birds during the month of pâskâwihowipîsim. Eggs collected during this month were limited in number to ensure the future viability of a flock.
  Source:http://www3.edu.gov.mb.ca/cn/support/aboriginal/moonnames.html
  originally from the unit "The Night Sky", by Shaun Nagy, La Loche, appendix A, page 2, in the project *Rekindling Traditions*: http://www.usask.ca/education/ccstu/units/night_sky.html
- Other natural phenomena, such as freeze-up and break-up of ice, were signs of changing seasons. The Woodland Cree divided the year into six seasons instead of four: spring, summer, fall, freeze-up, winter, and break-up. Thawing and freezing of ice brought its challenges, took a certain amount of time, and thus influenced the lives of these people. Adapting to these changes meant acknowledging a changing time or season for survival.
- First Nations cultural life had seasonal cycles. The people lived in particular ways using particular technologies based on the seasons. Seasonal calendars vary across cultures.
- This lesson provides an excellent opportunity to introduce First Nations and Métis ways of knowing. Most people recognize the importance of the circle in First Nations cultures. It is a symbol of interconnectedness, equality, and continuity. The seasons are also a kind of circle. No season is more important than the others, and they flow into each other.
  - The Saulteaux, who speak Nakawē, recognize four seasons: winter (pipōn), spring (sīgwan), summer (nīpin), and fall (tagwāgin).
  - The Lakota also recognize four seasons: winter (waniyetu), spring (wetu), summer (bloketu), and fall (ptanyetu).
  - The Plains Cree recognize six seasons: winter (pipon), break-up (mīyoskamin), spring (sīkwan), summer (nīpin), fall (takwākin), and freeze-up (ēkaskatik).
  - The Dené also recognize six seasons: winter (hhaiy é), break-up (holuk'é), spring (nasot'a), summer (sine), fall (t'ą̨haiye naįtti), and freeze-up (hhaiye t'az é).
- Ask students, *Does geographical location influence the number of seasons that First Nations recognize? Why would some First Nations recognize six seasons and others recognize only four?* Ask students to brainstorm how different First Nations may have to prepare for the different seasons.

As was shown in the previous lesson, the equinoxes occur twice a year: on the first day of spring (around March 21) and the first day of fall (around September 22). Due to Earth's position in its orbit around the Sun and the angle of Earth's axis, the equinoxes have equal hours of day and night. The term "equinox" comes from the Latin words *aequus* (equal) and *nox* (night).

The Sun is at its highest position at noon on the longest day of the year, the summer solstice (around June 21 in the northern hemisphere and around December 21 in the southern hemisphere). The Sun is at its lowest position on the shortest day of the year, the winter solstice (around December 21 in the northern hemisphere and around June 21 in the southern hemisphere). Because of Earth's tilt, the northern and southern hemispheres experience opposite seasons. The term "solstice" comes from the Latin words *sol* (sun) and *sistere* (to stand still) because at the solstices, the apparent north or south movement of the Sun stops before it reverses direction.

The circle is an important spiritual symbol for First Nations people. You will see the use of the circle in many different explanations. It is often used in astronomy in the circle of the seasons and in the circles of the Sun and Moon.

Circles of stones dot the continent of North America. Author Murray Smith offers, "In Alberta and Saskatchewan, there is evidence that native peoples studied the stars and planets, for in these areas there are huge circular rock formations called 'medicine wheels.' It has been suggested that these were used to track the changing seasonal star patterns. " (Smith, 1982)

There is much controversy that surrounds these sites and no one can say for certain who constructed them. For many First Nations and Métis people of Saskatchewan, the sacred circles were constructed by early ancestors, a Plains people, who may have employed circles to divine important seasonal phenomena like the solstices or equinoxes. In Saskatchewan, ancient cairns and stone circles may be found at Moose Mountain and in Big Muddy.

The medicine wheel is a fairly new concept. However, the circle symbolism is used in many cultures around the world to express the interconnectedness of all life. The medicine wheel is a physical manifestation of this consciousness of interconnectedness.

In First Nations and Métis spirituality, everything in the physical world has a counterpart in the spiritual world, whether it be a plant, animal, human, or even a rock. It is this connection that makes many First Nations people protective of the environment.

Time
70 min
Skills
• communicating • researching
Grouping
individuals, pairs, or groups
Materials and Equipment
(per group) • computers with Internet access • reference books
Line Masters
• none

Work On It

- Depending on the time frame and availability of resources, you may want students to work in partners or small groups.
- Allow students to be creative.
- You could use this opportunity to ask some students to focus on First Nations peoples in North America and how they observed, explained, and/or celebrated the changing seasons.

Communicate

1. Answers will vary. For example, students may not have known that a site called Buena Vista, in the Peruvian Andes, is home to the oldest known observatory, which is 4200 years old. This observatory marks the start of the summer and winter solstices.
2. Answers will vary. For example, students may find it interesting that the Chinese developed the science of astronomy for almost 2000 years. They recorded a solar eclipse in 2137 BCE.
3. Answers may vary. For example, for some students the appearance of a robin may signal the start of spring.

For ESL/ELL

This lesson may provide ESL students with the opportunity to share aspects of their own cultures with their classmates about how seasons are celebrated and/or observed.

For Enrichment

Some ancient cultures built impressive structures that indicated when the seasons were changing. These structures include: Chaco Canyon Sun Dagger petroglyph, Stonehenge, Chichen Itza, and some, but not all, medicine wheels. Ask students to build a model of one of these structures that illustrates how the structure indicates the changing of the seasons.

Assessment *for* Learning

What to Look For in Student Work	What to Do
Students should demonstrate an ability to research. Depending on the situation, they may have to work in groups, so look for ability to work in groups. Students will also be demonstrating presentation skills.	• If students are having difficulty with this section, they may have to choose a simpler culture to investigate and/or simplify their projects.

Ken Goodwill: A Lesson from the Stars and the Moon

Page 245

- The cosmos was a means by which the ancient people forecast their fortunes, predicted the seasons, navigated at night, and related to the beliefs about the great beyond. Only through careful observation did they arrive at knowledge of the cosmos. Even though the student text highlights the star knowledge of the Dakota people, other First Nations groups also had star knowledge.
- The Lakota and Nakota (who use dialects of the same Siouan language as the Dakota) share very similar star knowledge as the Dakota. Three generalizations that can be made among these three dialect groups are that star knowledge is sacred, only certain types of knowledge can be given to the general public, and star knowledge guides communal ceremonies and rites. For more information about Siouan star knowledge, teachers are encouraged to examine the following links (Note: If any of the following urls are broken, use the titles as the basis for an Internet search using a search engine like Google):

  Lakota Ethnoastronomy by Dr. Steven Mizrach (Florida International University) (http://www.fiu.edu/~mizrachs/lakota.htm)

  Aboriginal Star Knowledge Home Page by Paula Giese (http://www.kstrom.net/isk/stars/starmenu.html)

  Lakota star map (http://geometryofplace.com/images/sitepdf/starknow.pdf)

  NASA and Lakota Sioux Join Together to Reach the Stars— Press release (http://www.tahtonka.com/stars.html)

  Lakota star and constellation names (http://faculty.normandale.edu/~physics/Hollabaugh/Lakota/Lakota%20Star%20Names.pdf)

  Lakota sundial (NASA website) (http://genesismission.jpl.nasa.gov/product/genesis_kids/sunwatchers/sunwatchers2.html)
- The Cree possessed different beliefs about nighttime phenomena. Some believed that northern lights were spirits that danced to the afterlife. Any who called down these spirits might find them to be benevolent or malicious.

- This belief is akin to one found in Dené culture. Other knowledge about the nighttime sky includes a lore surrounding the stars. For example, the Cree call the Milky Way Cheepahi Meskanaw, or spirit road, because they believe it is a path that spirits follow to the next world. The Cree have names for many stars. For example, *Kisci-Okima-Achak*, or the Great Chief Star, is the star that we know as Vega. For the Cree, *Kisci-Okima-Achak* directs the destiny of all the other stars. Names for the constellations exist also in Cree, though many of these constellations may not have an equivalent in the Western zodiac constellations. *Ochakatakos-iskewew,* or the Little Fisher, is the Cree term for Ursa Minor.
  Source: Names for the constellations in Cree and Anishinabe (http://www.virtualmuseum.ca/Exhibitions/Cosmos/english/html/ways oflooking.html)
- The Dené people of northern Saskatchewan also possessed wisdom about the cosmos. They used the stars and Moon to travel at night. They kept track of the passing of time using the stars, especially when there is no Sun in the winter months. They named their constellations. Through careful observation of the phases of the Moon, they derived a calendar for determining the cycle of the six seasons. Knowledge about the stars allowed them to make weather predictions. The northern lights in Dené teachings comprise an entity that must be respected. They believed that the northern lights consume clouds and as a result bring cold weather. One could die if one inhaled a breath of the northern lights. Each Dené dialect group had similar but unique beliefs about the northern lights. For example, when the northern lights are reddish in colour, for the Dehcho Dené people, it signifies war. The Dogrib Dené, like their counterparts the Sahtu, believe one should never whistle at the lights lest one attract their unwanted attention. Most of these teachings, derived through observation and imparted through oral tradition, are meant to convey lessons on heritage, communal values, and survival.
- For more information on Dené star knowledge, see *Dene Kede-Dene Traditional Knowledge about the Moon and the Stars* (http://www.ece.gov.nt.ca/Divisions/kindergarten_g12/curriculum/Den e%20Kede%20Curriculum%20Document/The_Land_and_the_Sky/Mo on_Stars.htm)

6 The Moon's Changing Face

Page 246

Time
1 class period

Key Terms
• laser beam

Line Masters
• LM 4-8

Indicator Assessment Chart

Indicator	Assessment Opportunities
SS6.1 a. Use a variety of sources and technologies to gather and compile pertinent information about the physical characteristics of the major components of the solar system.	• Work On It, p. 246 • Communicate, p. 248, q. 1, 2, 4
SS6.1 g. Create scale-distance and/or scale-size models of the major components of the solar system.	• Work On It, p. 246
SS6.1 h. Evaluate the usefulness and accuracy of scale-distance and scale-size models of the major components of the solar system.	• Communicate, p. 248, q. 6
SS6.2 h. Model the relative positions of the sun, Earth, and Moon to demonstrate Moon phases and lunar and solar eclipses.	• Work On It, p. 246
SS6.2 i. Propose questions related to astronomical phenomena to investigate using models and simulations, such as "Do other planets exhibit phases?", "How would seasons on Earth differ if Earth were not tilted?", "How would patterns of eclipses change if the Sun, Earth, or Moon were different diameters or positioned at different locations?"	• Communicate, p. 248, q. 5

Background Information

To understand the motion of the Moon, you need to remember the following:

- When you are looking at the Moon and the stars behind it, the Moon will appear to move eastward.
- The Moon shows the same "face" to Earth regardless of which phase it is in.
- The Moon has an elliptical counterclockwise orbit around Earth. This orbit takes 7.3 days, which is known as the sidereal period or sidereal month.

As the Moon goes through its phases, its light, which is a reflection of the Sun's light, changes because different amounts of the Moon's surface are illuminated. The amount of illumination the Moon receives from the Sun depends on Earth's location relative to the Sun. The figure below illustrates how the Moon's position around Earth affects how much light it reflects from the Sun.

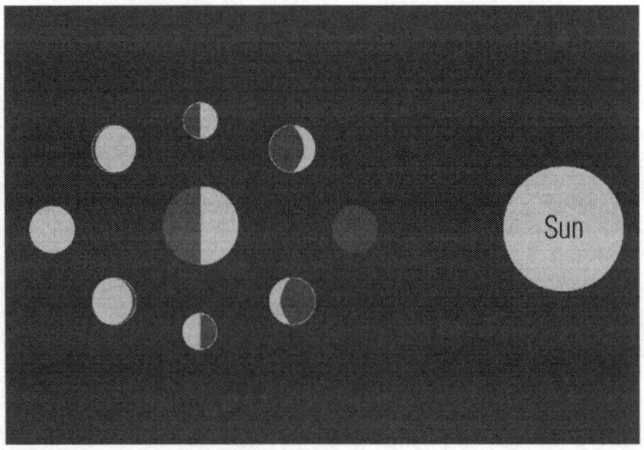

Get Started ▶

- Review with students the difference between objects emitting light and objects reflecting light. Ask students to brainstorm objects that either reflect or emit light. As a class, classify these objects according to whether they emit or reflect light, and whether these objects are natural or human made.
- Ask students, *Does the Moon emit or reflect light? How far away is the Moon from Earth? Does it always look like a lighted round ball? What causes the apparent change in its shape?*

Time

30 min

Skills

- making models
- observing
- comparing
- measuring

Grouping

pairs or small groups

Materials and Equipment

(per group)
- light source
- Styrofoam™ ball painted black or a small, dark-coloured play ball
- pencil or knitting needle

Line Masters

- none

Work On It

- You may wish to demonstrate this activity for the whole class before students experiment in pairs. It is important that each student has the opportunity to be Earth and revolve the ball (Moon) in its cycle around Earth.
- Facilitate students as they work. It is important that students revolve the ball around their heads only once during a cycle. Keeping the "x" on the ball facing them will help them understand that the Moon rotates once as it revolves once around Earth.
- If students find that their own shadow covers the ball (the Moon) when it is opposite the light source (the Sun), ask them to hold the ball above their heads.
- Allow time for manipulation, exploration, and discussion of how light reflects from a three-dimensional sphere. It is very important that students see first-hand that a single source of light can light only half of a sphere (such as a ball) at one time, no matter which way the ball is turned. Take time to help students achieve this understanding.

Communicate

1. The half of the Moon that faces the Sun is always lit, but all of the lit side of the Moon does not always face Earth. The Moon appears to change its shape over the course of a month because of its movement around Earth. As it moves, the Moon changes position both in relation to Earth and to the Sun. The observed phase of the Moon is determined by its position relative to Earth and the Sun.
2. The scientific names for each of the degrees of the Moon's orbit, or Moon phases, are:

   45° waxing crescent Moon
   90° first quarter Moon
   135° waxing gibbous Moon
   180° full Moon
   225° waning gibbous Moon
   270° last quarter Moon
   315° waning crescent Moon
   360° new Moon
   See also the illustration on page 249 of the student book.
3. The changing shape or phase of the Moon follows a pattern. Students might cite a growing (waxing) shape from a sliver or crescent to a half Moon to an almost full Moon to a full Moon. Then it decreases to less than a full Moon, down to a half Moon, to a sliver, and finally to no lighted phase. Then the cycle begins again.
4. When the Moon is directly between Earth and the Sun, the side facing the Sun is illuminated but the side facing Earth is in shadow. During this phase, the Moon cannot reflect light toward Earth, so we cannot see it from Earth. If students think back to their explorations in the Work On It activity with how balls reflect light, they will more easily understand why we do not see a lighted phase at this position of the Moon in relation to Earth and the Sun.

continued →

5. Phases of Earth can be seen from the Moon. They are the complements of the phases of the Moon we see on Earth. For example, when we see a crescent Moon on Earth, someone on the Moon would see an almost full Earth. Students' sketches should be based on the Sun-Earth-Moon model they used in the Work On It activity.
6. It is important to use a model of a ball and light to show the different phases of the Moon because we can see what is going on without going into space. Students should learn that the lit area on the Moon's surface increases until the surface showing is entirely lit. Then the lit surface decreases until there is no light being reflected from the surface of the Moon that faces Earth. Students' answers to the second part of this question may vary, but may include answers such as "If the Moon is rotating, why do we always see the same face?"

For ESL/ELL

Refer to the For Reteaching section of this lesson.

For Reteaching

Hand out copies of LM 4-8 Moon Phases so students can create their own Moon phases.

For Enrichment

Students can conduct a research investigation to demonstrate that the Moon's apparent change in size is an optical illusion. Ask, "*Why does the Moon appear much larger when it rises or sets compared to when it is at a higher altitude?*" Students should discover through research that this phenomenon is an optical illusion. You can conduct an experiment to show that the size of the Moon doesn't change. By using a paper clip bent so that it lines up with the bottom and top of the Moon, like a caliper, students will find that the Moon is always the same size, no matter where it happens to be in the sky. Ask students to use this caliper to determine if the size of the Moon actually changes.

Assessment *for* Learning

What to Look For in Student Work	What to Do
Check with students during the Work On It activity to ensure that they understand that the Moon's appearance changes throughout the month. You may want to do this orally.	• If students are having difficulty with the Work On It activity, ask them to do the activity in the For Reteaching section for reinforcement.

7 The Moon on the Move

Page 249

Time
1 class period
Key Terms
• phases • altitude • satellite
Line Masters
• LM 4-9

Indicator Assessment Chart

Indicator	Assessment Opportunities
SS6.1 a. Use a variety of sources and technologies to gather and compile pertinent information about the physical characteristics of the major components of the solar system.	• Work On It, p. 250 • Communicate, p. 251, q. 1–5 • Build On What You Know, p. 251
SS6.1 e. Use star charts and astronomy guides to investigate the night sky, including constellations, and record observations using notes in point form, data tables, simple diagrams, and/or charts.	• Work On It, p. 250

Background Information

The first quarter of the Moon occurs on the seventh day of the lunar cycle, the full Moon occurs on the fourteenth or fifteenth day, and the last quarter occurs on the twenty-second day. A full cycle of the Moon around Earth represents about a month, or 29.53 days. The movement of the Moon from a crescent to the full-Moon phase models the two-week period when the Moon can be seen in the evening sky.

The times when the Moon is visible to us follow an orderly pattern or cycle (see the diagram on student book page 249).

- A full Moon rises at about sunset and sets at about sunrise.
- The Moon rises and sets about 50 minutes later each day.
- A first-quarter (waxing) Moon rises at about noon and sets at about midnight. It can often be spotted in the afternoon sky.
- A third-quarter (waning) Moon rises at about midnight, sets at about noon, and can be seen in the morning sky.
- A crescent Moon just after a new Moon can be seen around sunset and may be seen for a couple of hours after sunset.
- All crescent Moons are just before or just after a new Moon.
- The new Moon phase is not visible to us on Earth.

traditional ***KNOWLEDGE***

The Dené used the phases of the Moon for the measurement of time. They observed the world around them and recognized that the Moon would have a certain appearance at certain times of the year. (See below for examples of the names of the Moons according to the Cree and Dené people.) These changes in the Moon let them know when to go to the hunting grounds and different camps.

continued →

The Dené people also used the Moon as a measurement of distance — how long it took to get somewhere. For example, it might take two days or nights to get to a camp, or someone may return in two moons.

Moon	Cree	Translation		Dené	Translation
1	kisêpîsim	Elder Moon or Great Moon		edzahi zaghë	Cold Moon
2	mikisowipîsim	Eagle Moon		dët'anichogh zaghë	Eagle Moon
3	niskipîsim	Goose Moon		hah zaghë	Goose Moon
4	ayîkipîsim	Frog Moon		ts' ëli zaghë	Frog Moon
5	sâkipakâwipîsim	Leaf Budding Moon		ëghézë zaghë	Egg Moon
6	pâskâwihowipîsim opâskâwihopîsim	Egg Hatching Moon		ëghéz yëhóli zaghë	Egg Hatching Moon
7	paskowipîsim	Moulting Moon		?idélza zaghë	Moulting Moon
8	ohpahowipîsim	Flying Up Moon		?echëth zaghë	Bird Moon
9	takwâkipîsim	Autumn Moon		na?idéli zaghë	Birds Going Back Moon
10	nôcihitowipîsim	Mating Moon		dëní ëlk' ënádíhi zaghë	Moose Breeding Moon
11	pinâskowipîsim	Migrating Moon		eyunë dzinë zaghë	Crazy Day Moon
12	ihkopiwipîsim	Frosty Moon		hayë zaghë	Winter Moon
13	pawâcakinasîsipîsim	Frost Exploding Moon		tëtleghë yati zaghë	Praying Night Moon

Get Started ▶

- Ask students to draw a picture of the Moon as they visualize it. Line up the various pictures on the wall, noting the many differences. Challenge students to try to order the pictures as they occur in reality.
- Refer students to the photos on student book page 249, showing the various shapes (phases) of the Moon. Ask students to consider if the phases of the Moon pictured here occur in this particular order. Ask them to look at the details on each photo of the Moon to help them to determine if the photos are oriented the same way. Then ask them to work in pairs to compare opinions and gain consensus as to whether this series of photos is in the correct sequence.

The names and phases of the Moon have often indicated different events. The Chinese would start a new month at sunrise after the New Moon. Many people believe that the Moon affects human cycles and rhythms and so they pay close attention to the different phases of the Moon.

Measuring the Altitude of the Moon

- Altitude is the height or angle of an object above the horizon (the line at which Earth and the sky appear to meet). The horizon is at 0°. Ninety degrees is straight up. Each fist (with the thumb flat) is approximately 10°. Knuckles on an index finger can also be used to measure degrees. Between the tip of the finger and the first knuckle is 2°, between the first and second knuckle is 3°, and between the second knuckle and the last is 4°.
- Another measure that students may be interested in is the azimuth. Azimuth is how far something is from north, along the horizon. Zero degrees is north, 90° is east, 180° is south, and 270° is west. Hands/fists can be placed side by side to determine the azimuth. First, use a compass to determine north. A hand with fingers splayed is approximately 20°, a closed fist is 10°, and a finger width is about 1°.
- Both altitude and azimuth are used together to describe the position of an object at a particular time.
- Before students do the Work On It activity to determine the altitude of the Moon, they may want to practise finding the positions and heights of trees or buildings near their school or homes using altitude and azimuth measurements.

The first artificial satellite was *Sputnik*, launched on October 4, 1957. Since then, humans have been launching satellites for a multitude of uses (GPS, communications, and television). There is real concern about the number of satellites now orbiting Earth. One of the problems, other than the concern that this space junk may crash to Earth, is that it is orbiting Earth at a speed of 7.5 km/s. If even a speck of debris from this space junk hits an important satellite or space shuttle, it could do serious damage.

Time

20 min

Skills

- observing
- interpreting
- data collection

Grouping

individuals

Materials and Equipment

(per group)
- table for recording (LM 4-9)

Line Masters

- LM 4-9

Work On It

- In this lesson, students predict changes within the monthly cycle of the Moon, then seek to affirm these predictions through first-hand observations. They learn the names of the phases of the Moon and a strategy for measuring the altitudes of objects in the sky.
- Note that this activity requires out-of-class observation time over a period of a couple of weeks (this can be extended to a month if you want). If possible, begin the activity when the sky is fairly clear and the Moon is in its first or third quarter and can be seen in the sky at least during part of the school day. Give students copies of LM 4-9 Moon Observations for recording their observations. If there are too many cloudy days and nights for the patterns to become apparent, you may want to extend the time you allot for this activity.

continued →

- Periodically hold "Cosmic Circle" sessions so students can share what they are observing about the Moon. These sessions will allow them to pose questions to clarify misunderstandings, and will provide a springboard for further observations. They will also allow you an opportunity to assess students' progress in learning about Earth's nearest neighbour, the Moon.
- Help students to understand that changes in the Moon's shape (phases) take place very gradually, and that the Moon is not only seen in the night sky but in the day sky as well, near the first and last quarters.
- Determine students' level of understanding of angles, and degrees as units of measurement for angles. You may wish to spend time talking about degrees as units of measurement, showing how even opening a door creates an angle to the door frame. Ask students to practise the fist method for estimating altitude in the sky, pictured on student book page 250.
- If the Moon is in its first or last quarter, take students outside to search for it. Caution them to avoid looking at the Sun. Ask,
  - *How would you describe the Moon's location?*
  - *How would you describe its altitude? What strategy can you use to estimate its altitude?*
  - *How would you explain the direction in which you should look to see the Moon?*
  - *How would you describe to someone else the shape of the Moon at this time or phase?*
- When you return to the classroom, establish with students a method of keeping records of their observations of the Moon. Ask students to make an ongoing attempt to observe the Moon and to record the dates and times of their observations as well as the Moon's direction and height above the horizon.
- After observing for a period of time, ask students to look again at the photos under Get Started on student book page 249, and ask if they feel these photos are correctly sequenced based on what they have been observing.

Communicate

1. The Moon grows gradually from a crescent (sliver) to a full disk and then decreases from a full disk back to a sliver to nothing seen (a new Moon is not visible to us on Earth).
2. Students may not be able to accurately answer this question, but will have some creative ideas. The Moon seems to be larger when rising and setting than when it is high in the sky because of an optical illusion, possibly due to our brains perceiving the horizon to be more distant than the point overhead.
3. Students may see many light-grey patches and a few dark patches on the Moon's face. Most of these patches are the Moon's seas — flat areas formed from molten lava from the Moon's interior. Some of the lighter patches viewed are mountainous areas pockmarked with craters, believed to have been formed either by meteorites or by volcanic eruptions. Students may be able to infer that, because these features remain the same, the same side of the Moon is always facing Earth. These light and dark regions have given rise to many interpretations over the years and have been the basis of myths. Some people see a face on the Moon; others see a rabbit or a lion. Ask students what they imagine is on the Moon's face.

4. The Moon appears to move across the sky from an easterly to a westerly direction.
5. Students should be able to predict that the Moon will rise about 50 min later than it did the previous day, and that it will rise in the eastern sky. About six hours later, it will be in the south. Six hours after that, it will be in the west, and six hours later, it will set.

BUILD ON WHAT YOU KNOW

Students should be aware that the Moon may rise at a slightly different time than the daily newspaper states. Such references usually state times for sea level horizons. A hill or a mountain will block the Moon until it has risen higher than the sea level horizon given in the newspaper. Published Moon rising times will also be different if the newspaper is published at a different longitude than students' observation locations.

For Enrichment

Ask students to investigate the phases of moons of other planets in the solar system.

Assessment *for* Learning

What to Look For in Student Work	What to Do
The main activity in this lesson is data collection. Look for neat data collection, and also for students' ability to report orally on their observations of the changes in the Moon's phases. You can also look at students' answers to the Communicate questions to see if students understand that the Moon goes through cyclic phases.	• To reinforce students' understanding of the cyclic nature of the Moon's phases, you may want them to draw the phases of the Moon to create a flipbook.

8 Earth's Companion

Page 252

Time

1 class period

Key Terms

- maria
- terrae
- rills
- craters
- revolution
- synchronous rotation
- space probes

Line Masters

- LM 4-10

Indicator Assessment Chart

Indicator	Assessment Opportunities
SS6.1 a. Use a variety of sources and technologies to gather and compile pertinent information about the physical characteristics of the major components of the solar system.	• Work On It, p. 254 • Communicate, p. 254, q. 1
SS6.1 g. Create scale-distance and/or scale-size models to represent the major components of the solar system.	• Work On It, p. 254 • Communicate, p. 254, q. 3
SS6.1 h. Evaluate the usefulness and accuracy of scale-distance and scale-size models of the major components of the solar system.	• Communicate, p. 254, q. 3

Background Information

In 1609, Galileo made the first known sketch of the Moon from his telescope. In 1647, Johannes Hevelius made the first lunar map. In 1840, John William Draper made the first daguerreotype (an early type of photograph) of the Moon. In October 1959, a Soviet space probe sent back the first photograph of the dark side of the Moon. From 1969 to 1972, a total of 12 astronauts of the Apollo space program visited the Moon and gathered lunar material. Three remote-operated Soviet crafts also landed and returned with samples.

The Moon has no atmosphere or any traces of water on its surface. The crust of the Moon appears to be thicker than Earth's. It is covered with craters, mountains, plains, and valleys. There are two primary types of terrain on the Moon: the heavily cratered and very old highlands, and the younger *maria*. The maria, which comprise about 16 percent of the Moon's surface, are huge impact craters that were later flooded by molten lava. They are concentrated on the near side of the Moon (the side facing Earth). Most of the surface is covered with *regolith*, a mixture of fine dust and rocky debris produced by meteorite impacts. On the far side of the Moon is the largest impact crater in the solar system, Pole-Aitkin, which is 2250 km in diameter and 12 km deep.

Even with its unique terrain, the Moon's composition is much like Earth's. Some scientists believe that when Earth was first forming, a large object (about the size of Mars) crashed into Earth. This impact sent a part of the still-forming Earth into space. As the various pieces collected together and cooled, they became the Moon.

Get Started ▶

- During their observations of the Moon, students will have noted many features that can be seen with the naked eye. Ask students to draw their own maps of the Moon. Revisit the Build On What You Know entry from Lesson 7 in the students' Space Portfolios. Add to the Space Portfolio or modify it with information and questions about the Moon.
- Indicate to students that, until the 1960s, we only had pictures of one side of the Moon. Why do they think this was so? Students should be able to relate that the Moon's rotation and its revolution around Earth are synchronized such that the Moon keeps the same face to Earth. Therefore, we only saw one side of the Moon until flights to the Moon enabled humans to take photographs of the other side of the Moon.

Moon Facts

- Refer students to student book page 253 to examine the photo. Ask, *How does the surface of the Moon compare with that of Earth?* Ask students to imagine they are astronauts on the Moon communicating with Earth. How would they describe the Moon's surface to people on Earth? Record descriptive words on the board.
- Invite students to read the student book to find out further information about the physical aspects of the Moon. Review the terms "rills" and "craters." Help students to grasp how far 1000 km is by comparing it to a meaningful distance. For example, driving to Winnipeg from Regina and back is a distance of 1142 km — just over 1000 km.

There are three sources of Moon rocks: those collected by Apollo missions, those collected by the Soviet Union Luna missions, and those naturally ejected from the Moon, usually by some type of impact, which fall to Earth as meteoroids.

Time
30 min
Skills
• making models • interpreting • comparing
Grouping
individuals or pairs
Materials and Equipment
(per group) • Plasticine or modelling clay • sculpting tools (plastic knives, craft sticks, etc.) • tray or shallow boxes • section of lunar map/photograph • toothpicks
Line Masters
• LM 4-10

Work On It

- There are three ways that work with this activity: Ask the class to re-create the entire surface of the Moon by giving the students different sections or asking them to draw a lunar surface freestyle. They can use LM 4-10 Surface of the Moon as a reference. If this LM is not detailed enough, there are lots of good images of the Moon on the Internet that you can show students. One example is http://www.controleng.com/blog/11800318/post/480020048.html Simply search "Moon" using a search engine to find good photos to share with students.
- Students should be able to identify the various geological formations of the Moon and their parts. You may want them to make "flags" out of toothpicks and paper to identify the parts.
- The ideal colour to use for this activity is off-white or grey, but any colour or mixture of colours will work.

Communicate

1. All the Moon's surface features were created billions of years ago. Student answers may vary but students should recognize that the craters were formed when large objects hit the Moon. The rays seen from the crater are caused by materials thrown out of the crater at impact. Some of the crater impacts caused mini craters to form around the large craters. The maria, or seas, were once thought to be old oceans, but these "seas" formed from ancient pools of lava that have hardened. The mountains are lava formations.
2. Answers may vary. Students should choose an area that is flat for their landing site.
3. Students' answers may vary. The answer may depend upon what section of the map is assigned and if all students replicated the same section.

For Enrichment

Students could research myths about the appearance of the Moon and its features, such as the Man in the Moon. Students could also research the appearance of the dark side of the Moon.

For ESL/ELL

ESL students may need help with some of the terminology in this section. You may wish to pair them with students whose first language is English. You may also have ESL students add terms such as maria, terrae, rills, revolution, and synchronous rotation to their visual dictionaries.

Assessment *for* Learning

What to Look For in Student Work	What to Do
Check for students' understanding of the different features of the Moon while they are doing the Work On It activity. Students should show an understanding of the concept of what the surface of the Moon is like through their Communicate responses. These questions will reinforce the creation of the Moon surface model.	• If students are having difficulty understanding the surface and composition of the Moon, you may have to explain how the features were created.

9 Blackout!

Page 255

Time
1 class period

Key Terms
- umbra
- penumbra
- lunar eclipse
- solar eclipse

Line Masters
- LM 4-11

Indicator Assessment Chart

Indicator	Assessment Opportunities
SS6.2 d. Propose personal explanations for the causes of seasons, phases, and eclipses.	• Communicate, p. 257, q. 1, 2
SS6.2 h. Model the relative positions of the Sun, Earth, and Moon to demonstrate Moon phases and lunar and solar eclipses.	• Work On It, p. 256
SS6.2 i. Propose questions related to astronomical phenomena to investigate using models and simulations, such as "Do other planets exhibit phases?", "How would seasons on Earth differ if Earth were not tilted?", "How would patterns of eclipses change if the Sun, Earth, or Moon were different diameters or positioned at different locations?"	• Communicate, p. 258, q. 8

Background Information

An eclipse occurs when there is a lining up of the Sun, Moon, and Earth. The angular size (the angle of the sky the object seems to cover) and the optical illusion of small objects that are near appearing larger than larger objects far away helps to explain how an object as large as the Sun can be "blocked out" by an object the size of the Moon. The diagram below illustrates how a smaller object (the Moon) can completely block our view of a much larger object (the Sun) under the right conditions.

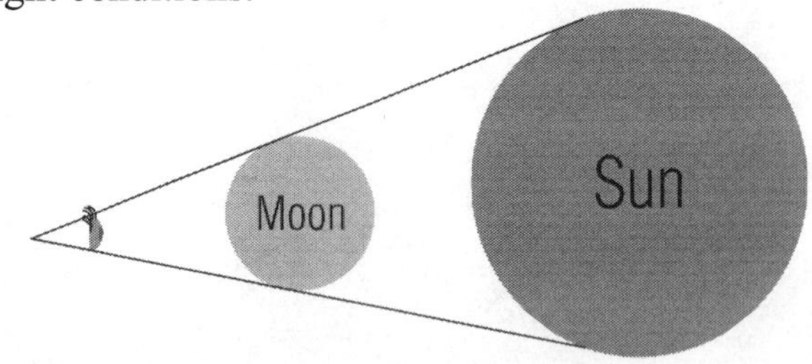

If the angular size of the Moon and Sun are the same, an eclipse may occur. An eclipse may be total (all of the object is blocked) or partial (only a part of the object is blocked).

A small light source shining on an object produces a dark shadow called an *umbra* because the object stops all the light falling behind it. A large light source produces a dark umbra and a lighter shadow called a *penumbra*, where some of the light shines past the object into the shadow and lightens it. During an eclipse, observers in the lighter shaded area (penumbra) view a partial eclipse, while those in the total shaded area (umbra) view a total eclipse. During a total eclipse, a bright ring of sunlight — the *annulus* — sometimes remains visible.

Even though the Moon moves around Earth once a month, a solar eclipse does not occur monthly. The reason is because the Moon's orbit is not parallel to Earth's orbit around the Sun. For a total solar eclipse to occur, there must be an exact alignment of Earth, the Moon, and the Sun, with the Moon casting its shadow on Earth. The same idea applies to a lunar eclipse. An eclipse of the Moon occurs at the full Moon phase, whereas an eclipse of the Sun occurs at the new Moon phase.

Not everyone on Earth may observe an eclipse, especially a solar eclipse, because the size of the Moon's shadow will only touch part of Earth's surface.

A lunar eclipse may be viewed directly with the naked eye. A solar eclipse should only be viewed indirectly by projecting the image of the Sun onto a surface to avoid eye damage.

Get Started ▶

- Before students can understand eclipses, they need to have an understanding of shadows. Begin by asking, *What is a shadow*? Record students' thoughts on the board.
- Hold up a rectangular object and ask, *What will the shadow of this object be like?* Record students' predictions (for example, rectangular, all black, flat on the floor surface, fuzzy, sharp). Give each small group an opaque ruler or rectangular object to stand upright and make it cast a shadow. Note that you may need to darken the room somewhat so that light is coming from one direction only. Ask students to draw the ruler and its shadow and make observations about them. Students should try this activity in several settings so that light hits the ruler from different directions, and compare their observations. Guide them in observing that the shadow has a light part and a dark part.
- When students have finished investigating, ask,
  - *What did you observe about shadows?*
  - *How is the Sun related to the formation of shadows?*
  - *When you looked carefully at the shadow, was it the same colour throughout? How would you describe what you saw?*
  - *What do you think happens to cause a shadow to have a darker and a lighter part? How did the size of each part compare?*

- Refer students to the first paragraph of student book page 255. Invite them to read the paragraph, and to explore making shadows using their pencils or other objects. Guide them to discovering the following:
  - a shadow is cast opposite the light
  - a shadow likely has a dark part and a lighter part
  - the lighter part of a shadow can be very small or quite large, as during an eclipse
  - the shadow extends into space — it is three-dimensional, not two-dimensional
- Students often think of shadows as being two-dimensional rather than three-dimensional. Before students read the remaining paragraphs on student book page 255, ask, *Do you think objects in space cast shadows? Why or why not?* After a discussion, demonstrate that shadows extend in space by inviting students to place their hands in the air above the shadow cast on the ground.
- Next, ask students to brainstorm what they think of when they hear the word "eclipse." Introduce the concept of solar and lunar eclipses by reading and examining the diagrams at the bottom of student book page 255. Note the dark and light parts of the shadows. Can they deduce which diagram illustrates a lunar eclipse (top) and which one illustrates a solar eclipse (bottom)? Can they apply from prior learning what phase the Moon must be in for each of these eclipses to occur? The Moon must be in the new Moon phase for a solar eclipse and in the full Moon phase for a lunar eclipse.
- After reading Get Started, ask students how it is possible for the Moon, which is much smaller than the Sun, to block the Sun's light. Record their ideas and then ask them to do the Work On It activity to find out. After the activity, ask them to answer this question based on their observations. Although the Sun is 400 times bigger than the Moon, it is also 400 times farther away from Earth.
- Ask students to perform a webquest to learn more about eclipses. See LM 4-11 Eclipse Webquest.

Time
30 min
Skills
• inferring • observing • interpreting • comparing
Grouping
individuals, pairs, or small groups
Materials and Equipment
(per group) • marble • flashlight • large ball • small ball
Line Masters
• none

Work On It

- Emphasize again that, because we do not commonly have the opportunity to travel to space, we use models and simulations to understand natural events such as eclipses. Explain that this activity will allow students to simulate eclipses using common objects.
- When simulating the lunar eclipse, darken the room and guide students as they do the activity. As they work in their groups, ask, *What do you notice?*
- After students have simulated the lunar eclipse, challenge them to use the balls and light for simulating a solar eclipse. Ask, *How would you have to change the position of the Moon to create a solar eclipse?* Help them to set up and simulate a solar eclipse using the balls and light. Refer them to the diagram of the solar eclipse on student book page 255, and allow sufficient time for students to explore the relative positions of the Sun, Earth, and Moon.
- When simulating the solar eclipse, be sure that students hold the marble with their arms stretched out straight in front of them. Ask, *What do you notice?*
- When students are working on their Communicate questions, they may need to return to their simulations of a solar and a lunar eclipse to answer some of the questions.

Communicate

1. For a total solar eclipse to occur, there must be an exact alignment of Earth, the Moon, and the Sun, with the Moon casting its shadow on Earth. Total solar eclipses do not happen every month because the plane of the Moon's orbit is not parallel to the plane of Earth's orbit around the Sun. In students' drawings, the correct positioning of the Moon is in the new Moon phase. The Moon should be positioned so that its shadow falls on Earth.
2. For a total lunar eclipse to occur, there must be an exact alignment of Earth, Moon, and Sun, with Earth casting its shadow on the Moon. In students' drawings, the correct positioning of the Moon is in the full Moon phase. The Moon should be positioned so that Earth's shadow falls on it.
3. A solar eclipse is less noticeable than a lunar eclipse because:
   - the Sun is so bright that even though a large part of it is covered by the Moon, its brightness may not be diminished enough to be noticeable
   - the cone of the Moon's shadow traces such a small path across Earth that only people in that pathway get to see the eclipse
4. An eclipse of the Sun could occur during the new Moon phase.
5. An eclipse of the Moon could occur during the full Moon phase.

continued →

6. The drawing should include a dark, fuzzy, disk-like shadow crossing Earth.
7. A lunar eclipse is longer than a solar eclipse because the shadow Earth casts on the Moon during a lunar eclipse is larger than the shadow the Moon casts on Earth during a solar eclipse. A larger shadow takes a longer time to pass.
8. The Moon, Earth, and Sun have to be in specific positions for an eclipse to occur. So, if they were in different positions, there would be no eclipse. If the diameters of the Sun, Earth, and Moon were different, an eclipse could occur as long as the three bodies were aligned correctly.

Remind students that they must never look at an eclipse of the Sun with the naked eye or through smoked glass, negatives, binoculars, or telescopes, even when there is only a small sliver showing. Review with students how they can project an image of the Sun so they can safely view a solar eclipse.

BUILD ON WHAT YOU KNOW

Help students recognize their location on the map using longitude and latitude, and check whether or not they will be in the path of totality. If not, what will be the closest place to which they might travel? Share with students how amateur and professional astronomers "go all out" to view the rare spectacle of a solar eclipse, even if it means travelling long distances. Despite all efforts, there is no guarantee that the weather will co-operate and bring a clear day to permit viewing the eclipse under optimum conditions.

For ESL/ELL

See the activity in the For Reteaching section for possible ideas for teaching this concept to ESL learners.

For Reteaching

Students can get a sense of the various stages of an eclipse by simply drawing a circle and using a coin to represent the shadow that passes over the circle. They will see that the Sun looks as if someone had taken a bite out of it in the early stages of an eclipse.

For Enrichment

Invite students to simulate the following model and answer the question as to why there are not eclipses during every full and new Moon phase. The plane of the Moon's orbit is slightly tilted (about 5°) with respect to the plane of Earth's orbit. The point of intersection of the two planes is called a *node*. Use two Hula Hoops® — one to represent the ecliptic (path of the Sun and Earth) and one to represent the orbit of the Moon — to demonstrate and solve why sometimes there are eclipses at the new and full Moon phases but at other times there are not. Your head may represent Earth.

Assessment *for* Learning

What to Look For in Student Work	What to Do
Check for student understanding of what creates shadow and what creates eclipses while they are doing the Work On It activity. When writing answers to the Communicate questions, students should show an understanding that the Sun, Earth, and Moon need to be properly aligned in order for an eclipse to occur.	• If students are having difficulty with understanding how eclipses occur during the Work On It activity, you may have to repeat the procedure together. • You may also refer to the For Reteaching activity.

10 The Inner Planets of Our Solar System

Page 259

Time

2 class periods

Key Terms

- Mercury
- Venus
- retrograde motion
- Earth
- meteoroid
- meteor
- Mars
- meteorites

Line Masters

- LM 4-12

Indicator Assessment Chart

Indicator	Assessment Opportunities
SS6.1 a. Use a variety of sources and technologies to gather and compile pertinent information about the physical characteristics of the major components of the solar system.	• Work On It, p. 262 • Communicate, p. 262, q. 1–4
SS6.1 d. Evaluate the validity and usefulness of different sources of information about the physical characteristics of the solar system.	• Work On It, p. 262

Background Information

Mercury is now considered the smallest planet because Pluto has been reclassified as a dwarf planet. Mercury was named after the messenger of the Greek gods because of the speed at which it orbits the Sun. Mercury was first observed by Galileo Galilei in 1610.

Because it is so close to the Sun, Mercury is difficult to observe. It is only during the daylight hours, ideally at sunrise or sunset, when the best images of Mercury can be seen. Even the Hubble Space Telescope cannot be used to observe Mercury directly because of interference from solar rays that can damage its instrumentation.

Very little was known about the closest planet to the Sun until the 1960s, when astronomers began to study Mercury using radar imaging. Most of the information we now have about Mercury was gathered by the *Mariner 10* probe in 1974–1975. What we know is that Mercury has an iron core that makes up 75 percent of its mass. This iron core is covered with a rocky mantle and crust only 600 m thick. It is this core that gives Mercury its magnetic field. There is only one other planet in the solar system that has a magnetic field: Earth.

Due to its extremely slow rotation, it was first believed that Mercury had one side that never faced the Sun. We now know this is not true. This slow rotation on its axis is responsible for Mercury's having some of the most extreme temperatures in the solar system, from 467°C during the day to –183°C at night.

Venus is the hottest planet in the solar system. It has a thick layer of atmospheric gases that trap heat, creating a "greenhouse effect." The temperature at the surface therefore averages around 484°C. There is also a lot of pressure on this planet, enough to crush rocks on its surface.

When astronomers have been able to see through Venus's thick atmosphere, they have seen two surprises. First, there are few craters and these craters are not very old. Astronomers currently believe that the lack of craters is due to volcanic eruptions that may "resurface" the planet. In fact, probes have indicated that 85 percent of the rocks that are on the surface of Venus are volcanic. Second, Venus rotates on its axis in the opposite direction to Earth, and this rotation is very slow. One day (time it takes for a rotation) on Venus (243 Earth days) lasts longer than a year (time it takes for Venus to orbit the Sun) of Venus (225 Earth days).

Earth is the only planet in the solar system capable of supporting life. Everything about Earth makes this possible, from its distance from the Sun (not too close and not too far), all the way to the chemical compositions that can be found here.

Only a small amount of Earth makes up the mantle. The mantle is the layer just below the crust of a planet and above the outer core (centre). Most of Earth's mass is in its liquid mantle, and the rest makes up the outer and inner cores. Earth has a magnetic field, which is what orients our compasses.

Mars is the most visited planet in our solar system. We have been fascinated by the red planet for centuries. Astronomers have held many theories about this planet, such as that it may have been inhabited by other life forms because of the presence of canals, or that it is a dust-covered wasteland.

Mars is covered with a fine dust-like substance, which settles out of its atmosphere. This dust not only reflects light, but it can also trap chemicals that help to create Mars' icy caps. Just like Earth, Mars' surface has changed over time. There are craters, volcanoes, mountains, and valleys. Mars has the largest known volcano in the solar system, Olympus Mons, and there are so many large volcanoes that they have changed the round shape of the planet.

In the years to come, we will learn much more about Mars because there are planned expeditions, both robotic and human-led, in the future.

Get Started ▶

- Direct students' attention to the picture on page 259 of the student book. Ask them to describe what they see. They may say:
  - planets circling the Sun (smaller ones closer to the Sun)
  - a belt of something (asteroids) between the inner planets and the outer planets
- Point out that up to this point, most discussions have focussed on Earth, the Moon, and the Sun. Ask students to name other natural bodies in space. Most students will know that there are other planets in the solar system that orbit the Sun.

- Share with students that the word "planet" comes from the ancient Greeks. These people noticed that some points of light in the sky moved while others appeared fixed. They called these moving points of light planets, meaning wanderers.

The Inner Planets

- Read this section with the students. There is a lot of information here, but they may want to find more information.
- Alternatively, have students work individually or in small groups with a structured approach to reading and taking notes. Emphasize that the point of this lesson (and Lesson 11) is not to memorize the information, but to use it to make comparisons.
- You might want to ask students to start a table in which they can record information about the planets. Have them create the table with eight rows for information so that they can add the outer planets to the table once they read Lesson 11.

Many people mistakenly believe that the solar system is only composed of the planets and the Sun. There is so much more to a solar system, and with advancing technologies we are finding out more about what makes up our solar system.

It sometimes appears as though the planets are moving in a backward direction. Sometimes we see artificial satellites undergo this type of motion in the night sky because they are orbiting Earth faster than Earth is spinning on its axis. When the inner planets show retrograde motion, it is because they are orbiting the Sun faster than the outer planets are. Earth is playing hurry up and catch up. The apparent backward motion of the inner planets, Mercury and Venus, occurs because their orbits around the Sun are smaller than Earth's orbit. There are some great simulations of this on the Internet—use "retrograde motion" as the term for a search engine.

Time

40 min

Skills

- comparing
- communicating
- researching

Grouping

individuals

Materials and Equipment

(per group)
- paper
- crayons, markers, colour pencils

Line Masters

- LM 4-12

Work On It

- This activity is best done individually. Students can use LM 4-12 Research Organizer to help them with their research.
- Make sure that students are including facts and not creative information about their planet (so no spas on Mars).
- Be sure to give the students some time to share their work with others.
- If students create their own brochures, it may help to avoid the dreaded "cut and paste" that many students use.

Communicate

The answers to these questions are found in the student book.

1. Because Mercury is so close to the Sun, the light from the Sun makes it difficult to see this planet. The best times to see Mercury are when the Sun's light is minimized at sunset and sunrise.
2. Venus's atmosphere is made up of a thick cloud of gases. This cloud traps heat near the planet, just like a greenhouse. The trapped heat directly affects its weather, causing intense winds, for example. As well, this cloud of gases reflects some of the Sun's light, making Venus one of the brightest objects in the sky.
3. When meteorites enter Earth's atmosphere, there is friction between the meteorites and the gas particles in the atmosphere. Friction causes heat, and the meteorites may burn up in the atmosphere before reaching Earth's surface.
4. Mars is known as the red planet. Its colour is caused by its iron-rich soil, which is rusting. This rusting (oxidation) creates its unique red colour.

For ESL/ELL

You could ask students to create a mobile of the planets. If possible, make the planets to scale.

For Reteaching

See the ESL activity above. In addition, you may have students write basic facts about the planets on one side of the planet picture (where appropriate).

Assessment *for* Learning

What to Look For in Student Work	What to Do
You should look for students' developing research skills. Students should be able to state what they have learned in this section in their own words to show that they have understood the lesson.	• If students are overwhelmed by the choices they have for research, limit their choices to a couple. • If students are having difficulty with the wording of their project, they can use illustrations to convey their information.

11 The Outer Planets of Our Solar System

Page 263

Time
2 class periods

Key Terms
• Jupiter • Saturn • Uranus • Neptune

Line Masters
• LM 4-13

Indicator Assessment Chart

Indicator	Assessment Opportunities
SS6.1 a. Use a variety of sources and technologies to gather and compile pertinent information about the physical characteristics of the major components of the solar system.	• Work On It, p. 266 • Think Again!, p. 267, q. 1–4
SS6.1 d. Evaluate the validity and usefulness of different sources of information about the physical characteristics of the solar system.	• Communicate, p. 267, q. 1–3
SS6.1 g. Create scale-distance and/or scale-size models to represent the major components of the solar system.	• Communicate, p. 267, q. 3

Background Information

Jupiter was the planet that Galileo Galilei turned his newly developed telescope to in 1610. He discovered four of Jupiter's moons. What Galileo could not see is that Jupiter has a very small rocky core that is surrounded by liquid metallic hydrogen. Because Jupiter is so large, the pressure from the planet itself has compressed the liquid hydrogen into a more metallic form. This "metal" layer is surrounded by another layer of liquid hydrogen and helium.

Because of its large size, some astronomers believe that Jupiter could have become a star. They estimate that if it were just 50 times larger than its present size, its core would have collapsed upon itself, generating nuclear fusion. The process of nuclear fusion gives stars their energy.

The bands of colour we see on Jupiter are caused by the gases that make up its atmosphere. These gases spread out because of the speed at which Jupiter rotates on its axis. Jupiter has the fastest rotation of any planet in our solar system. Around Jupiter, there are 63 moons and three sets of rings. The rings are 5920 km in width and only 1 km thick! They weren't discovered until the *Voyager 1* probe beamed back images in the 1970s.

Saturn spins so quickly that it bulges at the equator, giving it a sort of squashed-football shape. Saturn is similar to Jupiter in many ways. It is believed that it has the same type of core and layers, and even their atmospheres are similar. Saturn's cloud layer is thicker and its atmosphere tends to be cooler than Jupiter's.

Saturn's most famous feature is its rings, which were discovered by Galileo in 1610. He thought they were attached to the planet, but in 1659, astronomer Christiaan Huygens showed that they are not. Saturn also has numerous moons. The one that scientists are most interested in is the moon Titan. It is larger than the planet Mercury, and it may be the only moon in our solar system to have an atmosphere. Scientists want to study this moon because it may be similar to what Earth may have been like millions of years ago.

Uranus is named after the Greek god of the sky. This planet was first discovered by William Herschel in 1781. It was the first planet to be discovered using a telescope. Herschel had seen this planet many times but had originally dismissed it as a star. Made of rock and ice, this planet's axis of rotation is on its side. It is believed that this drastic tilt was caused by a large object colliding with this planet early in its formation. Like the other gas giants, Uranus has many moons and a thin set of rings surrounding it.

Neptune is now the farthest planet from the Sun. Neptune was discovered on the basis of mathematical calculations. (See the !feature on student book page 265.) It has been difficult to observe in the past because of the interference of Earth's atmosphere, but with advancing technologies of Earth-based telescopes and the Hubble Space Telescope, much more has been and will continue to be learned about this planet. Neptune has rings, multiple moons, and two spots similar to Jupiter's Great Red Spot.

In 2006, the International Astronomical Union (IAU) adopted an official definition of a planet. According to this definition, to be considered a planet, an object must

- orbit the Sun
- be massive enough so that its own gravitational force shapes it into a sphere (hydrostatic equilibrium)
- have cleared the neighbourhood around its orbit

According to this new definition, Pluto is no longer considered a planet because it does not meet the third criterion: it is part of a "sea" of other celestial objects that occupy the same region of space. This definition has not been accepted by all astronomers. Some still think that Pluto should be considered a planet. This example can be used to illustrate that science evolves and theories change based on new information.

Get Started ▶

- Read this section in the student book with students. There is a lot of information here, but they may want to find more information.

- Alternatively, have students work individually or in small groups with a structured approach to reading and taking notes. Emphasize that the point of this lesson (and Lesson 10) is not to memorize the information, but to use it to make comparisons.

The Gas Giants

- You could ask students to use the library or the Internet to research the names of the gas giants in Greek and Roman mythology. Ask them to research the myths associated with these names and to present their findings to the class. Then ask students why they think these names were chosen for these planets. Do they think these names are appropriate?
- Many people make the mistake of mispronouncing "Uranus." It is pronounced "YOOR-a-nus," not "your-anus" or "urine-us."
- Ask students to add information about the Gas Giants to the table that they created during Lesson 10. Put students into groups and then challenge them to create questions for playing a trivia game using the tables that they have created. Students can then trade their questions with another group to play the game. Alternatively, create the questions yourself to play the game as a class.
- To help students understand the distances between all of the planets, try the following activity.
  - You will need nine students to complete this activity. Each student will have a sign indicating that he or she is part of the solar system: Sun and planets. If you choose, you can ask students to read some information about the part of the solar system they represent.
  - The set of distances listed in the second column is for a solar system model with a diameter of just over 300 m. The set of numbers listed in the third column can be used if space is limited, and is based upon a 30-m model.

Student	Distance from origin (300-m model solar system)	Distance from origin (30-m model solar system)	Planet/Sun
1	0 m	0 m	Sun
2	4.1 m	0.30 m	Mercury
3	7.6 m	0.56 m	Venus
4	10.5 m	0.77 m	Earth
5	16.0 m	1.17 m	Mars
6	54.5 m	4.01 m	Jupiter
7	100 m	7.35 m	Saturn
8	201 m	14.79 m	Uranus
9	315 m	23.18 m	Neptune

The Discovery of a New Planet

- Neptune was discovered because the orbit of Uranus was slightly different than what it should be. Astronomers hypothesized that there must be another planet nearby that affects the orbit of Uranus by its gravitational pull. Based on the location of Uranus, astronomers calculated the location of Neptune. Neptune was finally observed through a telescope by Johann Galle in 1846.
- The discovery of Neptune is a good opportunity to discuss the nature and progress of science. If a hypothesis is unable to adequately explain observations, a new hypothesis may be suggested, and experiments, observations, and calculations are made to verify the new hypothesis. In this way, scientists continually add to what was done in the past, and we gain more and more detailed knowledge about the universe we live in.
- Ask students to summarize information from this lesson and Lesson 10. Ask students:
  - Which planets rotate most slowly? most quickly?
  - Which planets revolve around the Sun most slowly? most quickly?
  - What is the relationship between the distance from the Sun and the speed of revolution around the Sun? To answer this question, ask students to think of or use a tetherball. The shorter the string, and the closer the ball is to the pole, the faster the ball goes around the pole.

John Couch Adams was born in 1819 in Cornwall, England. His extraordinary math skills amazed his farming family and teachers from an early age. At university, he learned what he could about the planet Uranus's orbit. He hypothesized that there could be a planet beyond Uranus. To demonstrate this possibility, he started doing mathematical calculations to validate his hypothesis. He did these calculations in this head, without writing them down. He eventually wrote them down and submitted them, but he was not taken seriously until the planet Neptune was discovered. The discovery of Neptune occurred based upon the mathematical calculations of Urbain Le Verrier. Le Verrier's calculations were very similar to Adams's. It was decided that Le Verrier and Adams would share the credit for the discovery of Neptune.

Time

40 min

Skills

- comparing
- communicating
- researching

Grouping

pairs or groups

Materials and Equipment

(per group)

- chart paper
- poster paper (optional)
- modelling materials
- 216 × 279 mm (8 ½ × 11-inch) sheets of paper (optional)
- Planet Comparison Tables 1 and 2

Line Masters

- LM 4-13

Work On It

- Use LM 4-13 Planet Comparison Chart to help students organize their information during the Work On It activity.
- There is room at the bottom of LM 4-13 to add any additional comparisons that you may want the students to make.
- Be sure that the students include information about all of the solar system in this activity, not just the outer planets

Think Again! Ask, Discuss, and Review

Answers to the Think Again! questions are given below.

1. The bands of colour on Jupiter are created by the gases on Jupiter and in its atmosphere. Because Jupiter spins so quickly, the clouds of gases are stretched out into bands. Jupiter's Great Red Spot is actually a storm cloud, which is similar to a hurricane.
2. Although Saturn is an enormous planet, it is actually so light that it could float like a cork on water. Saturn does not have a solid surface.
3. Uranus has a unique spin. It appears to have retrograde motion and it spins on its axis at an angle of just under 90° to the Sun. It is believed that a large object collided with the planet and changed its axis of rotation.
4. Neptune is known as the big blue Popsicle because it has a core of melted rock that is surrounded by extremely cold water/ice. This planet gets its blue colour from the gas methane.

To calculate how long it would take a cellphone call to go from Earth to Jupiter, first determine the distance from Earth to Jupiter. If the distance between Earth and the Sun is 1.0 AU and the distance from the Sun to Jupiter is 5.2 AU, then the distance from Earth to Jupiter is 4.2 AU. If a cellphone call takes 8.3 min to travel 1.0 AU (from Earth to the Sun), then it takes 8.3 min/AU × 4.2 AU or about 35 min to travel from Earth to Jupiter.

Communicate

1. Answers will vary, but should include information about one of the outer planets.
2. Answers will vary, but should include information about one of the outer planets.
3. Answers will vary, but the model should contain all the parts of the solar system.

   An example of the scale size of the bodies of the solar system might look like the following:

Body	Body diameter (mm)
Sun	500
Mercury	1.7
Venus	4.3
Earth	4.5
Mars	2.4
Jupiter	50.1
Saturn	41.8
Uranus	16.8
Neptune	16.3

try this at HOME

- The purpose of this activity is for students to think about the planets as part of a whole system, not just as inner and outer planets.
- Students need to recall the information they learned in Lessons 10 and 11.

  Students will need to justify why they chose a particular planet and think about the challenges of visiting this planet. This activity sets the stage for the Design Project.

For Reteaching

To help reinforce the lesson, be sure to ask students to read information cards about the planets.

For Enrichment

Ask students to research how their weight will change on the outer planets. They can also calculate their actual weight on Earth.

Assessment *for* Learning

What to Look For in Student Work	What to Do
Students should know the basic facts about the outer planets, including atmosphere, rings, surface temperature, etc. They should also demonstrate an understanding that the planets are part of the solar system. They should be able to name the planets in order, starting from the Sun.	• If students are having difficulty with this lesson, complete the activity described in the Gas Giants section in which students model the solar system and give facts about the individual planets. Another alternative is to create and play Planet Jeopardy to reinforce students' understanding of basic facts about the planets.

12 Comets, Meteoroids, and Asteroids: Oh My!

Page 268

Time

2 class periods

Key Terms

- planet
- dwarf planet
- consensus
- asteroids
- asteroid belt
- comets
- fireballs
- meteorites
- variable
- fair test

Line Masters

- LM 4-14

Indicator Assessment Chart

Indicator	Assessment Opportunities
SS6.1 a. Use a variety of sources and technologies to gather and compile pertinent information about the physical characteristics of the major components of the solar system.	• Work On It, p. 270
SS6.1 d. Evaluate the validity and usefulness of different sources of information about the physical characteristics of the solar system.	• Work On It, p. 270
SS6.1 g. Create scale-distance and/or scale-size models to represent the major components of the solar system.	• Work On It, p. 270

Background Information

Comets are believed to be the remains from when our solar system was formed over 4.6 billion years ago. They are often called "dirty snowballs" because they contain a mixture of ice (water and frozen gases) and dust.

Every year, new comets are being discovered. Some of these comets, called long-period comets, have enormous orbits around the Sun (about 30 million years), whereas other comets, called short-period comets, have relatively short orbits (on average around 200 years). We don't see a comet until it comes close to the Sun. As the Sun heats up the comet, its distinct parts become visible.

The parts of a comet include the nucleus, coma, hydrogen envelope, dust tail, and ion tail. The nucleus is the main part of the snowball. It is the solid part of the comet and its size can range from 1 km to 100 km in diameter. As the comet comes closer to the Sun, the coma begins to appear. The coma surrounds the nucleus with a mixture of evaporated gases: water vapour, ammonia, and carbon dioxide. It can be 1000 times larger than the nucleus. The hydrogen envelope surrounds the coma. It becomes larger as the comet approaches the Sun. Its shape tends to be irregular because solar winds affect it.

The dust tail always points away from the Sun. It is made up of dust particles from the comet's nucleus. The pressure from solar winds pushes the dust backward so that it trails the comet. The dust tail is the part of the comet that is usually seen because the dust reflects sunlight.

continued →

The tail spreads out from the nucleus just like water from a garden hose because the comet itself is moving at the same speed at which the dust is moving away. The ion tail is made up of electrically charged gas particles of carbon dioxide, water vapour, and/or nitrogen.

Asteroids: The first known record of an asteroid was in 1801, when Giuseppe Piazzi believed he had found a new comet. What he found was an asteroid. There are thousands of asteroids in our solar system. Some of the largest are 200 km in diameter. However, if we put all the known asteroids together, their combined mass would be less than that of the Moon.

There are three basic types of asteroids:

- C-type asteroids are very dark and carbon based. They account for 75 percent of all asteroids.
- S-type asteroids tend to be fairly bright and made of a nickel and iron mixture with magnesium silicates. This type accounts for 17 percent of all asteroids.
- M-type asteroids are bright, and made up of pure nickel and iron. Almost 8 percent account for this type.

Asteroids are also classified according to their locations:

- The Main Belt is located 2–4 AU from the Sun, in the area between Mars and Jupiter.
- Near Earth asteroids come close to Earth (0.983–1.3 AU).
- Trojans are located closer to Jupiter and away from the Main Belt.
- Centaurs are located in outer parts of our solar system.

Meteors are often seen as streaks of light across the night sky. The most common name for them is "falling stars." They occur when chunks of rocky or metallic matter, called meteoroids, enter Earth's atmosphere. A meteoroid is called a meteor when it enters Earth's atmosphere. The friction between the meteor and Earth's atmosphere causes the meteor to heat up and glow. Usually this glow is short lived and can only be seen as a streak. The majority of these glowing meteors burn up in the atmosphere 50–95 km above Earth's surface, but some reach Earth. Meteors that reach Earth are known as meteorites.

Meteorites are usually one of three types:

- Stony, usually consisting of silicon and oxygen, along with small amounts of iron, magnesium, and other elements. Stony meteorites are classified as chondrites (pieces of the same materials that formed the planets) or achondrites (pieces from a larger parent body such as an asteroid).
- Iron meteorites are believed to come from metal cores. They usually consist of iron and nickel.

- Stony-iron meteorites come from the inner crust of a "parent" body. They tend to have equal amounts of iron and stone.

The largest known meteorite to fall to Earth weighed 60 t and landed in what is today Namibia an estimated 80 000 years ago. In November 2008, a meteor lit up the sky across Saskatchewan. Pieces of the meteorite were discovered in the west central area of the province, near Lloydminster, but the streak of light from it was seen even in Manitoba!

Many people are confused by the terms meteors, meteoroids, and meteorites. Each term has a specific meaning.

- Meteoroids are pieces of cosmic debris in the solar system.
- Meteoroids are called meteors when they enter Earth's atmosphere and begin to glow brightly.
- Meteorites are meteors that fall to Earth's surface.

traditional KNOWLEDGE

Many people call meteoroids falling stars. Many of the important stories of the Lakota involve "Fallen Star." To learn more about "Fallen Star," you may wish to find the book *Lakota Star Knowledge: Studies in Lakota Stellar Theology* by Ronald Goodman.

Get Started ▶

- You may want to open the lesson with a discussion with your students about how many of them have seen a "falling star." Ask, *How many students observe the meteor showers in August, the annual Perseid meteor shower?*
- You may want to find more legends that involve comets, meteors, and asteroids. There are many from all over the world.
- Many people confuse asteroids, comets, and meteors. Be sure to clarify the definitions of each of these bodies for students.
- Be sure to clarify for students the differences between meteoroids, meteors, and meteorites (see the Background Information section).
- You may want to ask students to research other dwarf planets in the solar system—Ceres, Haumea, Eris, and Makemake.
- Interested students could research the Kuiper Belt or the Oort Cloud. The Kuiper Belt is a disk-shaped area past Neptune. Pluto is part of the Kuiper Belt. Many short-period comets are thought to come from the Kuiper Belt. The Oort Cloud is a cloud of comets that lies at the outer region of the solar system. Long-period comets are thought to come from the Oort Cloud.

Chasing Comets

- You may wish to ask students to research other Canadians who have discovered comets. Ask them to bring in photos or draw pictures of space objects to create a space collage to post in the classroom.
- There are many "recipes" on the Internet for making your own "comet." They all require access to dry ice.
- You may wish to ask students to research the times during which the most notable meteor showers occur, namely, the Perseids and Leonids. The Perseids peak on August 12 every year. The Leonids peak around November 17 every year and produce a meteor storm about every 33 years. Students could be reminded to watch for these meteor showers when they are scheduled to occur.
- Students may also be interested in researching how common meteorites are. How likely is it that one will ever fall into their backyards, creating a large crater?

A Dark-Sky Preserve (DSP), sometimes called a Dark-Sky Reserve, is an area that has been set aside and has eliminated or controlled the amount of light pollution. Astronomers have noticed that light pollution has begun to interfere with their observations. The first DSP was established in 1999, in Torrance Barrens, Ontario. Saskatchewan established the Cypress Hills Preserve in 2004, which is currently the largest one in Canada. Canada, with the work of the Royal Astronomical Society, has established one of the world's highest standards for the establishment and maintenance of these areas. There are now DSPs all over the world.

Time

30 min

Skills

- making models
- inferring
- interpreting
- experimenting
- comparing
- measuring
- controlling variables

Grouping

pairs or small groups

Materials and Equipment

(per group)

- shallow pans
- rocks of similar shape varying in sizes (1–4 cm in diameter)
- ruler or tape measure
- flour
- cocoa powder

Line Masters

- LM 4-14

CAUTION!

The flour and cocoa powder can become slippery on the floor. Students should be careful not to spill flour and cocoa powder on the floor.

Be careful when dropping the rocks. Make sure everyone is behind the student dropping the rock.

Work On It

- Brainstorm with students as to what could have caused craters on the Moon. List these ideas on the board or chart paper for future reference.
- Ask, *If the impact of meteoroids causes craters, what determines the size of the craters?* Students might suggest the meteoroids' size, shape, force, and so on. Help students understand that scientists set up simulations to test theories. Refer them to the simulation on student book page 270 to test the theory that meteoroids could have caused craters on the Moon. Help them to understand that, in an investigation, a step is often repeated in order to verify results. Remind students that, to ensure a fair test, only one variable may be changed at a time. Ask students what variables could make a difference to the size of the crater. Ask them to test each variable separately and record their observations in a table like the one on page 271 of the student book.
- Students can record their observations on LM 4-14 Creating Craters.
- This activity can be extremely messy. Be sure to have the necessary tools to help clean up afterward.
- If possible, and for easy clean-up, you may want to do this activity outside. You will need a day when it is not windy.
- If you don't want the mess and can't go outside, you can complete this activity with plaster instead of flour and cocoa. However, it may be more difficult to see the rills that are formed.

Communicate

Discuss the simulation. Ask, *Was there anything about your results that surprised you? Did your results match your predictions? What did you find most challenging?*

1. Students' sketches should be clearly and accurately labelled. Advise them that they may have difficulty in seeing rays. Even rays in craters on the Moon and rocky planets are difficult to see.
2. The larger the rock, the larger is the crater. Astronomers have discovered that meteoroids cause craters about 20 times their size.
3. Usually the higher the drop, the larger the crater.
4. Although students may not have discovered this result during their experiments, all meteoroids, regardless of shape, create round craters.
5. Answers may vary. Add any questions to the KWL chart and ask for volunteers to research answers to them. Students might use the Internet or print resources to answer them, or consult with a professional or amateur astronomer.

For Reteaching

You may want to review the parts of a crater created by the impact of meteoroids by drawing a diagram with the students.

For Enrichment

Ask students to research the orbits of different comets. Ask them to predict when different comets will make their next appearance near Earth.

Assessment *for* Learning

What to Look For in Student Work	What to Do
Using oral questions, determine if students understand the differences between asteroids, comets, and meteors. Examine students' results and diagrams from the Work On It activity to determine if they know the different parts of a crater. You can re-evaluate, using the Communicate questions.	• Create a Venn diagram showing the similarities and differences between asteroids, comets, and meteors. • Make a two-dimensional drawing of a crater, and show and label the different parts.

ASK AN EXPERT Dr. Stéphanie Côté: Astronomer

Page 272

- This feature would be a great lead-in piece before visiting an observatory or having an expert guest speaker come to talk to the class.
- If neither of these resources is available or accessible, you may ask students to research the type of education needed to become a professional astronomer, or conduct a career exploration to find out career opportunities for astronomers.
- You may also ask students to research the space science done by the National Research Council and/or the Royal Astronomical Society.

13 Sky Pictures

Page 273

Time
2 class periods

Key Terms
• constellations • Leo • Orion • Cassiopeia • Cepheus • circumpolar stars

Line Masters
• LM 4-15

Indicator Assessment Chart

Indicator	Assessment Opportunities
SS6.1 e. Use star charts and astronomy guides to investigate the night sky, including constellations, and record observations using notes in point form, data tables, simple diagrams, and/or charts.	• Work On It, p. 275 • Communicate, p. 276, q. 3 • try this at HOME, p. 276
SS6.1 f. Describe objects in the heavens, as indicated through First Nations and Métis art and stories or by Elders or Traditional Knowledge Keepers.	• Work On It, p. 275 • Communicate, p. 276, q. 3
SS6.1 g. Create scale-distance and/or scale-size models to represent the major components of the solar system.	• Work On It, p. 275
SS6.2 c. Demonstrate the importance of selecting appropriate processes for investigating scientific questions and solving technological problems by explaining why astronomy is considered a part of science but astrology is not.	• Communicate, p. 276, q. 5

Background Information

Stars move tens of kilometres per second, but their relative motion seen from Earth is so slight that the constellations remain stable for thousands of years. However, the sky as a whole has an apparent motion caused by Earth spinning on its axis and by Earth's yearly orbit around the Sun. The daily axis rotation means that at different times of the night, any one point on Earth faces a different direction. This motion can be observed on a clear night by standing so that a bright star is above a marker object such as a pole or building. Viewed again 15–45 min later, the star will seem to have moved a noticeable amount. The stars seem to shift from east to west just as the Sun does each day. Stars in the north slowly rotate around the sky's pivot point, the north celestial pole, not far from Polaris (the North Star), which hardly moves at all. Because of Earth's orbit around the Sun, different constellations are prominent during different seasons.

continued →

traditional KNOWLEDGE

There are five First Nations language groups in Saskatchewan. Each language has its own unique names and legends for the constellations that can be seen in Saskatchewan's night skies. Refer to the table below for some of the names that are traditionally used by the Cree.

English	Cree	Translation	Other
Gemini	Amisk Achak	Beaver stars	
Gamma Aquila (first to rise) and Altair (second to rise)	Petapun Achak	Coming Dawn Stars	The Coming Dawn Stars are the children of the Morning Star. They rise before her, and are lined up so that they point to where the Morning Star will appear.
Pleiades	Pakone-Kisik	Hole in the Sky	This is how the Sky Woman came to Earth. The Sky Woman gave birth to mankind.
Milky Way (westward)	Cheepahi Meskanaw	Spirit Road	When a person dies, the person's spirit goes to the star world. The person dances along this path to the place of eternal happiness in the west.
Vega	Kisci-Okima-Achak	Great Chief Star or King Star	This star controls all the other stars and gives them a role as a ruling spirit or star for all living things on Earth. He also causes water to be taken from the rivers and lakes into the heavens, which he later returns as snowfall.
Venus	Kisikaw Achak or Wapan Achak	Day Star	
Polaris	Kewatino Achak	North Star	
Capella	Mikinaw	Turtle Star	The turtle acts as a teacher and interpreter of the Shaking Tent ceremony. The turtle interprets the language of spirits to the people.
Corona Borealis, or Northern Crown	Matootsan	Sweat Lodge	
Big Dipper, or Ursa Major	Ochekatak	The Fisher	

English	Cree	Translation	Other
Little Dipper, or Ursa Minor	Ochakatakos-iskewew	Little Fisher Stars or Little Fisher	
Sun	Pisim		
Jupiter	Sawanachak	Southern Star	
Moon	Tipiskawi Pisim		

The Lakota people were one of the few First Nations that made a written record of the star maps. The constellations were painted on a hide. The Lakota call the stars "the holy breath of the Great Spirit." It is by observing these stars, in the form of constellations, that the Lakota people know when to perform sacred ceremonies. They believe that when ceremonies are performed on Earth at the same time as they are occurring in the spirit world, as indicated by the appearance of specific constellations, sacred power can be drawn down to Earth from the spirit world.

The Lakota use the appearance of the constellations to move to various sites. Ceremonies are performed at these sites.

Get Started ▶

- As a class, revisit and update the KWL chart. Ask, *What can we add to the Learned column? What new questions do you have for the Wonder column?*
- Provide an opportunity for students to share their Space Portfolios with the class or in a small group. What have they been seeing and learning as they have observed the sky? While they have been mainly observing the phases of the Moon, some may have sightings of stars or planets to share. Ask them what these patterns of stars looked like to them. Did anyone else see the same patterns? Show a dot-to-dot pattern of stars and ask what pictures students see in the dots. Share with them how people have been looking to the sky for ages and seeing pictures. To the early shepherds out in the field, they were a source of comfort and familiarity, something to watch during their long nights in the field.
- Ask students to work in groups or pairs to read the first three lines on student book page 273 and share their reflections on the points raised. They should then carefully view the pictures on this page and consider if they have ever seen any of these patterns of stars. If so, during what season? Brainstorm as a class how patterns of stars (constellations) or certain stars have been of benefit to humans over time, for example, in navigation, monitoring the passage of time, a source of comfort, or an inspiration for myths and stories.
- Ask students to read the various stories connected to the constellations illustrated on student book page 273. Explain to the class that many constellations have had different names in various cultures and at different times.

Finding Constellations

- Review with students that, just as we have models of Earth (globes), we have models of the sky. These models are called star maps. Explain that the constellations we can see are different from season to season and depend on what part of the planet we are viewing the sky from. Refer students to the polar map on student book page 274, which shows circumpolar stars that can be seen during any season in the northern hemisphere.

Time
60 min
Skills
• making models • observing
Grouping
individuals, pairs
Materials and Equipment
(per group) • sky map • coffee tin or shoebox • black paper
Line Masters
• none

Work On It

- Give students an opportunity to examine the polar constellations (star patterns). Comment that even though Polaris is bright compared to the other stars of the Little Dipper, it is fairly faint compared to other bright stars and visible planets such as Venus and Jupiter.
- Constellation Pictures: Ask students, *How can you create a model of stars?* Facilitate students as they work in their groups to design and build their models.

Communicate

1. Answers may vary. Post some of the questions to motivate students to look for answers.
2. Students should have an opportunity to share their work. Post the stories and pictures on the wall, or combine them into a class book.
3. Encourage students to research constellations that can be seen from their latitude. Be sure students include some of these constellations in their Space Portfolios.
4. Some students may already be familiar with using Polaris, or the North Star, to find other stars.
5. Students' answers may vary. Astronomy is based upon the scientific method, which uses observations and measurements to study celestial bodies. From these quantitative measurements, we see patterns about which we develop hypotheses, theories, and laws.

   Although it uses stars as a basis, astrology makes predictions based upon the positions of planets and stars. These predictions are open to interpretation, or are qualitative. Interestingly, most astrologers don't look up into the sky or make observations. Instead, they use charts that were created hundreds of years ago. Because astrology does not use the scientific method, it is not considered a science, whereas astronomy is.

try this at HOME

- The purpose of this activity is to allow students to use the knowledge they have gained in this unit in a real-life situation.
- You will need to provide students with an appropriate star chart.
- Be sure to review tips on how to make observations with students (see the Launch section).
- Students will have to make notes about the location, time, and date of their constellation observations.
- There are great plans on making a planisphere (portable star chart) and viewer at the National Research Council website (http://www.nrc-cnrc.gc.ca/eng/education/astronomy/constellations/index.html)

For ESL/ELL

ESL students should be able to complete the For Reteaching activity. You can expand this activity as a way to give insight and connection to students' cultural backgrounds. For example, they can discuss/write/illustrate a legend/story related to a constellation from their own culture.

Ask students to add new words to their visual dictionaries—constellation, circumpolar, navigation.

For Reteaching

If students are having difficulty with the idea of how constellations are formed, try the following:

- Give the students a copy of Line Master 4-15 Making Your Own Constellations.
- Ask students to join stars with lines, a lot like a connect-the-dots picture.
- Once their figure is made, ask them to name and/or describe their picture. Remind the students that the picture they have made is known as a constellation.

For Enrichment

The constellations we see in Saskatchewan may not be seen in all places in the world, especially in the southern hemisphere. Ask students to research which constellations are unique to the northern hemisphere and/or which constellations are unique to the southern hemisphere.

Assessment *for* Learning

What to Look For in Student Work	What to Do
Students should be able to recognize patterns in the constellations they see and make.	• If students are having difficulty, refer to the For Reteaching section and/or star chart, which include lines between the stars to show the stars that make up constellations.

14 What's Happening in Space?

Page 277

Time

2 class periods

Key Terms

- Canadarm
- payloads
- Canadarm2
- Hubble Space Telescope
- James Webb Space Telescope
- Radar
- Radarsat
- microgravity

Line Masters

- LM 4-16

Indicator Assessment Chart

Indicator	Assessment Opportunities
SS6.1 b. Analyze historical and current technological developments that have enabled human observation of the major components of the solar system.	• Work On It, p. 279 • Communicate, p. 280, q. 2
SS6.1 c. Construct a timeline of Canadian and worldwide research efforts related to understanding the major components of the solar system.	• Work On It, p. 279 • Communicate, p. 280, q. 1–3
SS6.3 a. Construct a timeline of Canadian and worldwide space exploration programs related to living and working in space, including collaborative efforts among countries.	• Work On It, p. 279
SS6.3 c. Research the various work roles and worldwide locations required to support human spaceflight programs.	• Work On It, p. 279 • Communicate, p. 280, q. 1–3
SS6.3 d. Describe instances where scientific ideas and discoveries have led to new inventions and applications (e.g., lunar buggy, space shuttle, Canadarm, Dextre, and the International Space Station) that support human exploration of space and which have extended scientific knowledge related to living and working in space.	• Work On It, p. 279
SS6.3 e. Identify potential personal, societal, technological, and environmental barriers to living and working in space.	• Work On It, p. 279

Background Information

Canadarm — Its proper name is the Shuttle Remote Manipulator System, but with its recognizable Canada logo, it has become better known as the Canadarm. In 1975, NASA gave Canada the important task of developing a device that could assist astronauts with a multitude of tasks. The device that was created has been on more than 50 missions and has never malfunctioned. It has been used in shuttle operations, helped to fix the Hubble Space Telescope, and is currently being used in the construction of the International Space Station (ISS). The Canadarm has been used as a workhorse for space walks, as an "eye in the sky" for visual inspections of the shuttle, a portable light source, for public relations activities (IMAX movie cameras have been mounted on it), and as a platform to do experiments on micrometeorites.

Canadarm2 was developed with the purpose of working on the International Space Station. It was installed in 2001 on the ISS, with the help of Canadian astronaut Chris Hadfield, as a key component to the building of the station. Canadarm2 can make its way around the ISS like an inchworm, and is equipped with four cameras to help it see.

Hubble Space Telescope— Positioned above our atmosphere is the Hubble Space Telescope (HST). It is above our atmosphere so that light from distant stars and galaxies that is often distorted by the atmosphere when viewed from Earth is no longer a factor in observing celestial objects. This astronomical tool was launched in 1990 from the space shuttle *Discovery*, and has sent back hundreds of thousands of images for scientists to study.

The HST orbits once around Earth every 97 min. As it travels, the HST gathers light, in fact more light than is possible for the human eye to detect. Just as with our eyes, the more light the HST can capture, the better the image it can produce. Think about how your vision works in the middle of the night when you are trying to focus on something in the dark.

The HST had a problem that was discovered after it was launched: The images it was sending back were blurry. The primary mirror had a spherical aberration, which means that it was slightly the wrong shape. The flaw was only 1/50 of the thickness of a sheet of paper, but it caused the mirror to focus the light in a different place, creating the distortion. The solution was to fit the HST with "glasses." A series of small mirrors, called the Corrective Optics Space Telescope Axial Replacement (COSTAR), were installed on the telescope.

continued →

James Webb Space Telescope — The success of the Hubble Space Telescope prompted NASA, the European Space Agency (ESA), and the Canadian Space Agency (CSA) to collaborate and start building another space telescope, the James Webb Space Telescope (JWST), scheduled for launch in 2013. Astronomers from all over the world will be using this telescope for four main areas of study: first light and reionization, the assembly of galaxies, the birth of stars and protoplanetary systems, and planetary systems and the origins of life.

The James Webb and Hubble Space telescopes will both be positioned outside of Earth's atmosphere and will be used to look at distant celestial events, but there are differences between them, outlined in the table below.

Hubble Space Telescope	James Webb Space Telescope
uses mostly optical and ultraviolet wavelengths to examine the universe	uses mostly infrared wavelengths to examine the universe
mirror size: 2.4 m in diameter	larger mirror: 6.5 m in diameter
close orbit around Earth: ~ 570 km above Earth's surface	1.5 million km from Earth: Earth is also 1.5 million km from the Sun. Earth will be between the JWST and the Sun.
1.2 m long with a maximum diameter of 4.2 m	the Sun shield measures 22 m x 12 m
launched by the space shuttle	to be launched by *Ariane 5* rocket

Radarsat —On November 4, 1995, Canada launched Radarsat, a remote-sensing satellite. This satellite is equipped with Synthetic Aperture Radar (SAR). This radar uses microwaves, which can transmit information or images through clouds, smoke, darkness, and any type of weather conditions. A unique feature of Radarsat is that users can select different types of beams. The swath of the beam can be 35–500 km, with a resolution of 10–100 m. It has an orbit of 24 days and gives views of the Arctic daily and views of any part of Canada within three days. If the 500-km swath beam is used, it can give a view of the equatorial latitudes every six days. During an orbit, Radarsat can collect images spanning up to 1.1 million km^2 of Earth's surface. Information from Radarsat is downlinked to receiving stations in Prince Albert, SK, Gatineau, QC, or Fairbanks, AK. The downloaded information can be given to users within a few hours of when it was captured by the satellite.

Radarsat has a Sun synchronous orbit, which has a few advantages:

- the same view at the same time on different days
- it is always exposed to sunlight, so it can operate on solar rather than battery power

- it can downlink information at different times than other remote-sensing satellites can. Other satellites tend to transmit information only during mid-morning. Radarsat allows individuals to receive information throughout the day, not just at a certain time.

Because Canada is the second largest country in the world, it has diverse landscapes and climates. Radarsat was originally developed to monitor environmental change and help with making decisions about resource sustainability. It has been used for so much more:

- for monitoring the spring ice break-up in the Mackenzie Delta (1999)
- for monitoring the flooding of the Red River in Manitoba
- for monitoring crop information in Canada, Argentina, and China (rice)
- for monitoring glaciers in Antarctica
- for monitoring the *Sea Empress* oil spill off the coast of Wales (1996)
- for detecting forest cover changes in South America
- for monitoring the Guagua Pichincha Volcano in Ecuador

Get Started ▶

- Begin with a brainstorming session in which you ask, *What do you know about space?* In talking about space, students will likely focus on the components of the solar system. Encourage them to link the concept of exploration with the need for technology for carrying out space missions. Some students may have seen science fiction movies or television programs, so you may need to guide them in distinguishing between fact and fiction. At the same time, explain that some of our present-day technologies, such as the submarine in the novel *20 000 Leagues Under the Sea,* by Jules Verne, was once science fiction. Continue the discussion by asking students to list things they have seen in space movies and on TV. Ask, *What have you seen that you think might be possible in your lifetime? in 200 years?*
- Begin by viewing the photo on student book page 277. Ask students, *Do you recognize this piece of technology? What do you know about it?* Ask students to individually read the first paragraph on this page and answer the question.

Canada in Space

- Continue by discussing the importance of technology in the exploration of space.
- Ask students to create a 30-s commercial highlighting the achievements of Canadians and the Canadian Space Agency. Students should highlight four Canadian facts related to space.

- Websites such as NASA and the CSA provide a history of space exploration as well as the current happenings in space. News releases from the CSA indicate Canada's role and contributions to space exploration. You may want to encourage students to visit these sites to learn more about current "events" in space.
- Students might be interested in searching the Canadian Space Agency website to learn how Canadarm, Canadarm2, and Radarsat were built. Who built them? Where were they built? What kinds of educational background do the people involved in these projects have?
- Canada has three different types of satellites in space. Ask students to search on the Canadian Space Agency website to find out the purpose of each type of satellite. Students can then choose one satellite to research in greater depth and write a paragraph about what it does.
- You may wish to conduct the following demonstration to model the properties of microgravity.
  1. Make a small hole in the side of a paper cup toward the bottom.
  2. With your finger over the hole, fill the cup halfway with water.
  3. Remove your finger from the hole for a second and note what happens. (Water flows out.)
  4. With your finger on the hole, drop the cup from a height toward a container. Observe what happens when the cup is in free fall. What happens to the water when it hits the container? (While the cup is falling, the water doesn't stream out of the hole because the water and cup are falling at the same rate.)

  If you have a video camera, try taping this demonstration. Then play the tape using slow motion or pause to see the different stages of free fall.
- Ask students to research how astronauts train to prepare for being in a microgravity environment (Vomit Comet). Ask how many of them would enjoy having this kind of experience.

Time

60 min

Skills

- communicating
- researching

Grouping

individuals

Materials and Equipment

(per group)

- paper appropriate for presentation
- crayons, markers, colour pencils
- reference materials

Line Masters

- LM 4-16

Work On It

- Help students to understand that a remarkable series of spacecraft have explored our Moon and all but one of the planets during the last half of the twentieth century. These explorations are significant not only for what they have revealed about our solar system, but also for the technological progress they represent.
- Recognize the important contributions that Canadians have made to space science.
- Students can use LM 4-16 Canadian Milestones in Space Exploration to help organize their research.

Think Again! Positive or Negative?

- The International Space Station is the most heavily shielded space vehicle ever made. Despite this protection, in the International Space Station's first 10 years, it has been moved a total of eight times because of the threat of collision with space debris.
- Currently, the United States is tracking 18 000 major pieces of space debris, but most estimates state that there are over 1.8 million kg of human-made materials orbiting Earth. One of the problems of all this garbage is that some of the debris travels at incredible speeds. If the space debris is orbiting Earth at an altitude of 2000 km, it could have an impact speed of 36 000 km/h. At this speed, a 1-mm-long metal chip can do the same damage as a .22-calibre rifle bullet, and a piece of metal the size of a tennis ball will do the same amount of damage as 25 sticks of dynamite!
- Some space debris falls to Earth, appearing to be a meteor as it burns up in the atmosphere. Other pieces have the potential to do incredible damage to satellites, space telescopes, the ISS, and even astronauts on space walks. On February 10, 2009, a deactivated Russian communications satellite, *Kosmos-2251*, collided with an American communications satellite, *Iridium 33*. This collision, above northern Siberia, not only destroyed both satellites, but now poses an even greater threat because of the debris that was created.

(!) These websites provide a vast array of information and teaching suggestions. They are frequently updated.

Communicate

Communicate questions can be used to see if all students understand the information that was presented in this lesson.

1. Answers may vary. Students may identify with Julie Payette, a recent astronaut. In debriefing students' findings, challenge them to reflect on what all of the astronauts have in common, such as commitment, drive, initiative, an appreciation for the natural environment, and technological abilities.
2. Answers may vary. There are new tools, devices, and strategies being planned and implemented continually. NASA and the CSA have links that present challenges to students to solve make-believe technology problems in space.
3. Answers may vary and may include:
   - Radarsat with respect to GPS (global positioning systems) to track locations or positions on Earth; used in peacekeeping missions to monitor displacement of refugees and to aid in airlifts and other military support operations
   - satellite imaging for monitoring aspects of Earth's environment: seasonal changes on Earth, tracking temperatures of oceans and ocean currents, tracking ice and snow cover, tracking weather patterns, mapping vegetation and natural resources, such as deforestation
   - common items such as Velcro®, Gore-Tex®, and Mylar®, first used for astronauts' clothing, have become standard for clothing worn on Earth. Mylar is used for solar filters and camping gear.
   - freeze-dried foods
   - satellite communication systems for transmitting TV images around the world
   - microelectronics and medical imaging are technologies that have developed and surged due to the rush for space exploration

For ESL/ELL

See the activity in the For Reteaching section.

For Reteaching

Ask students to create a memory map. Be sure that students explain its construction. Another suggestion is to create flash cards, with the Canadian accomplishment or astronaut on one side and a description on the other side.

For Enrichment

Students could research the causes and effects of space debris.

Assessment *for* Learning

What to Look For in Student Work	What to Do
Students should be able to demonstrate their knowledge of Canadian accomplishments in space science through their presentations, Communicate questions, and oral answers.	• This lesson is heavy with specific facts. Some students may have difficulty memorizing the material. Use a concept map (see Toolkit 5, student book page 312) to help them learn about Canadian accomplishments in space science. You could create Canadian Achievements in Space flash cards to help students with this lesson.

CAREERS AND PROFILES Dr. Dafydd Rhys Williams: Astronaut and Physician

Page 281

- You may want to ask students to create an information poster about a Canadian astronaut.
- On the CSA website, there are podcasts involving our astronauts. There are often opportunities for students to interact live with astronauts through the CSA and NASA websites. Check the websites for these opportunities.
- It's important for students to know that astronauts come from diverse backgrounds. Ask students to find out about the requirements for becoming an astronaut.

15 Living in Space, the New Frontier

Page 282

Time
2 class periods
Line Masters
• LM 4-17

Indicator Assessment Chart

Indicator	Assessment Opportunities
SS6.3 b. Analyze how astronauts are able to meet their basic needs (e.g., food, water, shelter, and waste elimination) while living and working in space.	• Work On It, p. 283
SS6.3 e. Identify potential personal, societal, technological, and environmental barriers to living and working in space.	• Work On It, p. 283 • Communicate, p. 284, q. 2
SS6.3 g. Investigate the work being done in preparation for future space travel and make predictions about future achievements related to living and working in space.	• Communicate, p. 284, q. 4

Background Information

There is much planning that occurs before astronauts go into space. They must take everything they need for survival with them. There isn't a store just around the corner. It takes three days to get to the International Space Station. What requirements need to be met before a mission can be launched?

Food — Just like on Earth, astronauts eat three meals a day. But because of physical space considerations, there is no refrigerator and food needs to be heated differently. So, to prevent spoilage, food must be properly prepared and stored. Food is stored in disposable packages, which need to be flexible and easy to use. Space food comes in five formats:

- Rehydrated: Water is removed from certain foods and beverages, which helps to conserve weight.
- Thermostabilized foods are heat processed to destroy enzymes and harmful micro-organisms. We are familiar with these foods because there are similar foods available on our grocery shelves: canned fish and fruits and pudding cups. These foods are ready to eat and some only require reheating.
- Irradiated food has been exposed to radiation to destroy harmful micro-organisms. It is similar to thermostabilized food and comes in flexible packages.

- Frozen foods are only available on the ISS, which has a freezer in the galley.
- Natural-form foods include fresh fruits and vegetables, and some nuts. Usually these foods need to be consumed during the first few days of a mission to prevent spoilage.

Astronauts select their menus in advance (8–9 months in advance on the ISS) so that nutritionists can ensure that the astronauts will get all the vitamins, minerals, and calories they will need. Nutritionists allow the astronauts to choose their own meals because it is often difficult to get astronauts to eat. Because of microgravity, astronauts' stomachs "float" upward, which makes them feel full even though they have not eaten. Astronauts often have to make an effort to eat their meals. In addition, many astronauts' tastes change when they are in space. What was appealing on Earth is not appealing in space.

There are some limitations to what astronauts can select. Bread is not permitted because it crumbles, so tortillas are used instead. Salt and pepper are in liquid form. Some foods would just float away, which can clog equipment or get in astronauts' eyes, mouth, or nose, such as cracker crumbs, potato chip crumbs, and popcorn.

Many people may think that astronauts eat their food from tubes. Some astronaut food does come in tubes, but astronauts eat most of their meals off trays. The trays are magnetized so that utensils will stick to them and not float away. The trays also have Velcro®, which not only holds the tray to the table, but also secures the food packages. When the meal is over, astronauts clean their trays with special disposable wipes.

Rest —There is no set day and night in space, but just like on Earth, it's important for astronauts to get proper rest to stay healthy. They are scheduled for eight hours of sleep each night. Astronauts often don't sleep for eight hours straight because they are often excited to be in space, and on the ISS, there is a lot of noise with all the machinery needed to support the station.

Each astronaut has his or her own sleeping space. On the ISS, this space includes a drawer the size of a suitcase that can hold personal belongings. Astronauts on the ISS and in the space shuttle sleep in sleeping bags. Because of microgravity, there is no up or down in space. This state can make for some interesting sleeping arrangements. Astronauts can sleep in any orientation, but they must be attached to a solid structure using a "sleeping restraint" so they don't float and bump into something, thus hurting themselves or damaging equipment. They also need to make sure that their heads are secured with straps so that they don't move during the night.

continued →

Exercise — When we are on Earth, we know the importance of exercise. It is even more important in space. Exercise helps lessen the effects of microgravity. Our muscles have to work against gravity, even when we are just sitting on the couch. Without gravity, muscles atrophy (lose mass, tone, and strength). Bones become weaker because gravity is no longer holding the matrix of bone material together, causing mineral loss similar to osteoporosis. The heart doesn't have to pump blood against the effects of gravity to get blood to the brain. The heart is a muscle, so it also can atrophy, a state similar to cardiovascular disease.

Astronauts are scheduled to exercise two hours a day on stationary bicycles and/or treadmills. They are strapped to the exercise equipment, which gives some additional resistance (more exercise), and allows them to use it more effectively.

Hygiene — Bacteria multiply much quicker in space than on Earth, so it is very important that astronauts keep clean to remain healthy. This isn't as easy as it is on Earth because of the limited water supply in space. The ISS is equipped with a shower. To use it, an astronaut holds a water hose in one hand and a vacuum for the water in the other hand. Most astronauts don't use the shower because it uses about 4 L of water. Instead, they use a pre-moistened cloth, which is disposed of after use, and have a sponge bath. They use special soaps and shampoos from tubes like toothpaste, which don't create bubbles. When they brush their teeth, astronauts use special toothpaste that can be swallowed, which eliminates the need for water. When astronauts need to use the toilet, there is a seal formed between their bottom and the toilet. A gentle vacuum disposes of the waste. Solids are compressed and stored for removal, whereas liquid wastes are usually recycled into water.

Get Started ▶

- With the class, begin a word web on the word "explore." Point out that the desire to explore is part of the curious nature of humans. Ask students to suggest books, television shows, or movies that depict space exploration.
- Ask students to read the second paragraph on student book page 282. Discuss the photo and ask, *What is happening here?* Weightlessness. *Is weightlessness fact or fantasy?*
- Ask students if they have ever experienced a feeling of weightlessness. They may describe the effect of being in an elevator, on a roller coaster, or in a pool of water. Ask, *What are the advantages of weightlessness? What are the disadvantages of weightlessness?*

- Be sure students clearly understand that the weightlessness experienced by astronauts is not zero gravity, but actually very low gravity or *microgravity*.

Time
80 min
Skills
• inferring • communicating • predicting • researching
Grouping
pairs or small groups
Materials and Equipment
(per group) • paper • pencils • reference materials
Line Masters
• LM 4-17

Work On It

- Assist students as they plan their investigations by helping them identify the resources they will need. During the first class period, students should be able to divide the research, plan how they will record the information, and decide how to present the information to the class.
- Students can use LM 4-17 Living in Space Presentation Rubric to help plan their presentations.

Communicate

To motivate students to answer these questions, ask them to pretend that they are applying to become astronauts. In order to apply, they must fill out a form or attend an interview during which they will be asked these and other questions.

1. Answers will vary, but should include the reasons for wanting to travel in space or why they are not interested.
2. Answers will vary, and could include sparser living conditions, absence from family and friends, little choice in recreation and food, and potential risks to physical and mental health.
3. Answers may vary, depending on students' interests.
4. Students may already know, or will have found out through their research, what is currently happening on the ISS. Their answers on whether or not they would like to travel to the ISS may vary, but should include reasons why or why not.

For Reteaching

If students are having difficulty with the content of this lesson, ask them to create a graphic organizer of a human's needs in space. Their organizer should include food, water, oxygen, sleep, exercise, comfortable temperature, protection, morale, and recreation.

For Enrichment

Challenge students to research answers to these questions:
- What problems or disadvantages are there to space exploration?
- How might these problems be handled?

Assessment *for* Learning

What to Look For in Student Work	What to Do
Students should understand that there are many factors involved in working and living in space. Their presentations should demonstrate an understanding of the adaptations that need to be made.	• Ask students to create a graphic organizer or mind map to show their understanding of this lesson.

CAREERS AND PROFILES

Dr. Nicole Buckley: Space Scientist

Page 285

- This profile provides an excellent opportunity for students to examine the contributions made by Canadians to space science, and the technologies that have been developed by Canadians and non-Canadians that make our lives easier.
- Check the Canadian Space Agency for opportunities to learn more about the contributions it has made to many fields of study as a result of its work in space.

DESIGN PROJECT

Space Vehicle

Page 286

Time

120 min

Skills

- making models
- inferring
- observing
- interpreting
- experimenting
- hypothesizing
- communicating

Grouping

pairs or small groups

Materials and Equipment

(per group)
- paper
- pencil
- computer (optional)
- construction paper
- Styrofoam™ balls
- plastic
- cardboard boxes
- markers
- string
- elastic bands
- mini-lights
- tape
- glue
- scissors
- reference materials

Line Masters

- LM 4-18
- LM 4-19

Learning Expectations

Indicators Met in Unit Project

SS6.1 a. Use a variety of sources and technologies to gather and compile pertinent information about the physical characteristics of the major components of the solar system.
SS6.1 d. Evaluate the validity and usefulness of different sources of information about the physical characteristics of the solar system.
SS6.3 f. Design a model of a habitable space vehicle that can travel to and return from a student-selected location in the inner solar system.

Background Information

The Mars Exploration Rovers were launched toward Mars on June 10 and July 7, 2003. These Rovers have specific designs that enabled them not only to meet the challenges of landing on the planet Mars, but also to perform their specific mission: to explore the surface and geology of Mars.

The Rovers had to be small enough to fit in the nose of a *Delta II* rocket — about the size of a golf cart. Even with this small size, the Rovers had to do big things. Some of design specifications of the Rovers are:

- body made of a lightweight material (aluminum)
- equipped with solar panels — 600 W of power near Earth and 300 W on Mars
- many layers of insulation to protect the instruments from cold temperatures
- equipped with Sun sensors and star scanners so they can determine their orientation
- equipped with hydrazine propellant, used in pulses and burns for a proper landing
- communications systems to send images and data back to Earth
- airbags to lessen the impact of landing
- a six-wheel-drive system on a rocker bogie suspension, which ensures that all six wheels are on the rough terrain at all times. Each wheel has cleats and its own motor. The maximum speed is 5 cm/s.
- nine cameras: six for navigation, three for exploration
- an arm equipped with a RAT (Rock Abrasion Tool) for taking rock samples

Get Started/Work On It

- Discuss with the students the challenges that engineers had to consider when they designed the Rovers.
- Remind students that not all missions go as smoothly as planned, which is why testing their vehicles is important.
- Also remind students that their vehicles must be adapted for the planet that they choose to visit. They must research the challenges of visiting that planet, and brainstorm possible solutions.
- Students can use LM 4-18 Design Project Planner: Space Vehicle and LM 4-19 Design Project Rubric: Space Vehicle to help plan their vehicles.

Communicate

These questions are meant to be used as a reflective tool for the work done by the students.

1. Questions should reflect the projects done by the students and should have a logical foundation.
2. Answers will vary, but should reflect the work the students have done. Every project will have its challenges, from finding the proper materials to working with certain group members.
3. Answers will vary, but should reflect the projects done by other students. Some groups may have come up with solutions that other groups may not have thought of.
4. Answers will vary, but should show that students have reflected on the work they did for their projects.

For Enrichment

Students can research actual space vehicles. They can look at what was used in the past, and what is planned for the future.

Assessment *for* Learning

What to Look For in Student Work	What to Do
Students should demonstrate an understanding that specific planetary environments must be taken into consideration when designing their space vehicles. Students can demonstrate this knowledge formally within the design and informally throughout the project. Be sure to ask the students throughout the project to explain the choices they have made in their designs and how their decisions relate to the planet they have chosen to explore. Students should work as a team to create their space vehicles.	• If students are not taking their planet's environment into consideration, be sure to reinforce the importance of their vehicles' adaptations to their design. • If they are unsure of what adaptations need to be made, be sure to review their chosen planet's unique features. Then, through directed brainstorming, ask students to redesign their vehicles.

Unit 4 Summary

Page 290

Students may wish to use this unit summary as a study guide. The Unit 4 Summary is available as a line master (LM 4-1).

Unit 4 Review

Page 291

Explain Your Stuff

You may want to use these questions as summative evaluation, and the Communicate questions throughout the unit as formative evaluation.

1. Ways to observe the Sun safely include:
   - use a mirror chip to catch the Sun's light and project it onto another surface
   - use a telescope or a pair of binoculars pointed toward the Sun, with the lens casting the image onto a sheet of paper
   - use a pinhole apparatus that casts the image onto the back of a large box or container
2. Sunspots are cooler spots on the Sun's surface. They occur when the surface tears a bit because magnetic fields block out the heat of the Sun. Some sunspots are larger than Earth.
3. The Sun affects Earth in the following ways:
   - it warms water, which evaporates, rises into the atmosphere, condenses, and falls back to Earth as rain
   - air becomes warmed, begins to move (hot air rises), causing wind
   - just like air, water moves when it is warmed, creating ocean currents
   - sunlight provides energy for plants to make their own food. Plants are at the base of the food pyramid, so essentially the Sun provides energy for all life forms.
4. If it is daylight where you are, then generally it will be dark 180° longitude from where you are, bearing in mind differences in latitude and the number of daylight versus dark hours.
5. Because Earth's axis is tilted, in the summer we receive more direct, concentrated light, so the ground gets more solar energy.
6. Answers may vary, but may include the solstices (Chichen Itza or Stonehenge) or the appearance of comets. Most cultures considered comets to be bad signs. For example, the Aztec ruler Montezuma II saw the appearance of a comet as a sign that his rule was over. It is believed that he surrendered to Cortes without much of a fight for this reason. The !Kung people of Namibia saw the appearance of comets as a good sign that heralded good fortune coming to the people.

7. It is human nature to try to explain what is going on around us. Often these stories are based on spiritual beliefs. Because there are so many different beliefs, each set of beliefs offers different explanations for star patterns.
8. Answers will vary depending on the constellations students studied during the unit.
9. Seasons are caused by the tilt of Earth's axis of rotation. In winter, when the North Pole is tilted away from the Sun, the northern hemisphere receives fewer hours of sunlight. The sunlight is less concentrated and comes in at a low angle. In summer, when the North Pole is titled toward the Sun, the northern hemisphere receives more hours of sunlight and more concentrated sunlight comes in at a higher angle.
10. First Nations and Métis people used constellations for:
    - determining the time of the year (appearance of certain constellations at specific times)
    - navigation at night
    - spiritual rituals
11. In order, the lunar phases are: new Moon, waxing crescent, first quarter, waxing gibbous, full Moon, waning gibbous, third or last quarter, and waning crescent. Any of these phases can occur at the beginning of a month, depending on when a calendar month begins in relation to the lunar cycle. Student sketches should resemble those on page 249 of the student book.
12. The passage of time was indicated by the cycles of the Moon. The names of the Moon cycles vary among different First Nations tribes.
13. Astronomers estimate altitude, or height, in the sky by using a fist held vertically at arm's length, with the thumb lying flat on the top of the fist. The height of the four fingers and thumb in the fist counts as 10° (each finger and thumb counts as 2°). To use this method, line up your fist with the horizon, and then place one fist on top of the other until they are lined up with the Moon, star, or planet.
14. **a.** A lunar eclipse occurs when the Moon passes into the shadow cast by Earth in space. It occurs at the full Moon phase.
    b. An eclipse of the Sun occurs at the new Moon phase, when the Moon passes between the Sun and Earth and blocks the Sun's light. During a total solar eclipse, Earth, the Moon, and the Sun are exactly aligned.

    For diagrams, refer to page 255 of the student book.
15. The surface of the Moon has been affected by meteors and comets hitting its surface, creating craters. The Moon has craters within craters, craters on top of craters, and even connecting craters. They vary in size from a few metres to 1000 km wide. One recently discovered crater on the Moon's dark side is filled with ice. The crater is so deep that you could fit Mount Everest inside it!

16. The inner planets are Mercury, Venus, Earth, and Mars. The outer planets are Jupiter, Saturn, Uranus, and Neptune.

17. Mercury has a very thin atmosphere that can't slow down meteors, so its iron-and-rock surface is pockmarked with craters.

    Venus's atmosphere is much like a thick cloud. The brightness of Venus, which is often mistaken for a star, is caused by the reflection of sunlight from this thick cloud. Not only does the cloud reflect light, it also traps heat on the planet, just like a greenhouse. The planet's temperature can reach 484°C — hot enough to melt lead. The "greenhouse effect" also affects the weather on the planet. Winds on Venus have been estimated to be 380 km/h. That's faster than most tornadoes!

    Earth's gases in its atmosphere are important. They help to absorb some of the Sun's harmful radiation before it reaches the surface of Earth. The atmosphere also protects us from meteoroids. Our atmosphere also regulates heat and water circulation to support life.

    Mars' atmosphere is thinner than that of Earth and gives less protection. The surface of Mars has been affected by the impact of meteorites, creating many craters.

18. The outer planets are called the Gas Giants because they are the largest planets in our solar system and are made up of mostly gases that surround a core of rock and metal in layers, just like the layers of an onion.

19. **A:** penumbra
    B: umbra

20. Meteors are fragments of rock and dust. They are visible only if they enter our atmosphere and begin to burn.

    Asteroids have an elliptical (or squished-circle) orbit around the Sun. Most of them are found between Mars and Jupiter in the asteroid belt. They are made up of the same materials as the inner planets. Some astronomers believe that they are the leftovers from when the planets formed.

    Comets are a mixture of frozen water, frozen gases, and dust that didn't get incorporated when the solar system was formed. Comets orbit the Sun in unusual orbits, but until they get near the Sun, comets are invisible.

21. The faster the speed of a meteor, the more energy will be involved in the making of the crater. A small meteor could make a large crater if it has enough speed (energy) to displace (move) enough material.

22. **A:** ray
    B: rim
    C: basin

23. Answers may vary and could include Radarsat, Canadarm, the Hubble Space Telescope, freeze-dried food, microchips, and artificial satellites.

24. Its proper name is the Shuttle Remote Manipulator System, but with its recognizable Canada logo, it has become better known as the Canadarm. It is a device that assists astronauts with a multitude of tasks. It has been used in shuttle operations, it has helped to fix the Hubble Space Telescope, and it is currently being used in the construction of the International Space Station. It is a workhorse for space walks, an "eye in the sky" for visual inspections of the shuttle, a portable light source, and it has been used for public relations activities (IMAX movie cameras were mounted on it) and as a platform to do experiments on micrometeorites.

25. Answers may vary, and could include Gore-Tex®, Velcro®, freeze-dried food, and microchips.

26. Answers may vary, but can include Roberta Bondar, the first Canadian woman in space, who studied the effects of microgravity on the human body, and Dafydd Williams, who has more space walk hours than any other Canadian and has studied the human brain. Robert Thirsk stayed on the ISS for six months in May 2009 — a record for time spent in space by a Canadian.

27. The ISS, or the International Space Station, is an international research facility being constructed in space. Canada's contributions to the ISS include personnel as well as the creation of the Mobile Servicing System (MSS), which includes Canadarm2.

28. Basic needs of astronauts include:

    - Sleep: Astronauts must have a darkened area or wear eye shields to block out the Sun. They can use earplugs and cover themselves with a sound-suppressing blanket to block out noise.
    - Exercise: Scientifically planned exercise is included in the schedule of activities of all astronauts to counter the effects of the microgravity environment.
    - Food: Food is prepared in special packages to prevent crumbs floating around and fouling up the machinery. Much of the food is dried on Earth so it will last longer. The food is packed in plastic bags and is reconstituted with water. Liquids are drunk from special plastic containers with straws attached, similar to the drink boxes we have on Earth.
    - Hygiene: Astronauts brush their teeth as they do at home, only they can swallow the toothpaste. There is no shower on the space shuttle so astronauts take sponge baths. Waste water is released into space although future systems may recycle it.

29. The differences between a solar and a lunar eclipse include:

    - A lunar eclipse happens when Earth is directly between the Sun and the Moon. A solar eclipse happens when the Moon is between Earth and the Sun.
    - A lunar eclipse can only occur during a full Moon, when the Moon is directly opposite the Sun. A solar eclipse can occur at specific times. If there was additional teaching on this topic, students may have learnt that eclipses can be partial or annular (total).

- It is quite safe to watch a lunar eclipse with the naked eye, whereas watching a solar eclipse without eye protection can seriously damage your eyesight.

30. In order for a solar eclipse to occur, the Moon's inner, or umbral, shadow must pass across Earth's surface. The Moon's shadow that sweeps across Earth is known as the Path of Totality. It only covers 1 % of Earth's surface. The Moon, Sun, and Earth must be lined up in the same plane and in the correct order for a solar eclipse to occur. Because this specific alignment occurs infrequently, solar eclipses are rare.

How Did You Do?

Self-evaluation allows students to communicate their learning and their feelings about it. Seeing how students view their learning can give you insight and information on which to base your programming decisions.

Ask students to answer these questions individually, then to share their answers with the class. Some students will likely find some areas of this unit easier than other areas. This exercise may help students identify who can give them assistance to understand difficult concepts.

Unit 4 Line Masters

Table of Contents

Table of Contents *(continued)*

Name: ______________________________

Unit 4 Summary

Here are some of the things you will learn about the solar system.

Something I know and understand before starting the Our Solar System unit.	Lesson(s) where I learned about this idea or learned more about this idea.	Important Points about Our Solar System
		The word solar means "sun." In our solar system each of the eight planets moves in its orbit around the Sun, which is at the centre. Other components of the solar system include comets, asteroids, and meteoroids.
		The Sun is a star and, like other stars, emits its own light. Other objects in space, such as planets, moons, comets, meteoroids, and asteroids, reflect light from the Sun.
		Your vision can be harmed by looking directly at the Sun with the naked eye. There are various ways to project the Sun's image onto a surface so as to safely view its image.
		The Sun provides the energy for life on Earth.
		Earth's tilt and movement around the Sun causes the change of seasons.

Copyright © 2013 Pearson Canada Inc.
The right to reproduce this page is restricted to the purchasing school.

Something I know and understand before starting the Our Solar System unit.	Lesson(s) where I learned about this idea or learned more about this idea.	Important Points about Our Solar System
		Different cultures have different uses for celestial phenomena. Observations of the Moon and stars help First Nations and Métis peoples, and people from other cultures, track time and survive in a particular area.
		Both Earth and the Moon are lighted by the Sun. How much of the Moon we see lighted depends upon its position in relation to Earth and the Sun. These regular changes in lighting are called phases of the Moon.
		The Moon's surface is not smooth. It has markings, such as maria, rills, and craters on it.
		Eclipses of the Sun and Moon occur due to shadows in space. A total solar eclipse occurs when there is an exact alignment of Earth, the Moon, and the Sun, with the Moon casting its shadow on Earth. A lunar eclipse occurs when the Moon's orbit is parallel to Earth's orbit and the Moon passes through Earth's shadow.
		Each of the planets in our solar system is unique. The planets are divided into the inner planets and the outer planets. The inner planets have solid surfaces while the outer planets are "Gas Giants."
		Comets, asteroids, and meteoroids orbit the Sun. Meteoroids are space debris and when they enter Earth's atmosphere and burn up, we call them meteors. If they reach Earth, we call them meteorites.
		Stars are huge balls of hot gases. Stars form patterns in the sky that we call constellations. Astronomers have mapped about 88 constellations.

Copyright © 2013 Pearson Canada Inc.
The right to reproduce this page is restricted to the purchasing school.

Something I know and understand before starting the Our Solar System unit.	Lesson(s) where I learned about this idea or learned more about this idea.	Important Points about Our Solar System
		Canadians have contributed to space technology through tools such as the Canadarm and the James Webb Space Telescope.
		The development of technology such as the Canadarm, the Hubble Space Telescope, and space probes, has led to new discoveries and scientific knowledge about space.
		The development of materials and technology for space has proven very useful to us on Earth.

Copyright © 2013 Pearson Canada Inc.
The right to reproduce this page is restricted to the purchasing school.

Name: ____________________________

Unit 4 Key Terms

Word	I know nothing about this word.	I can spell this word correctly.	I have seen/heard it before.	I can define it as it relates to science.
altitude				
asteroid belt				
asteroids				
astronomers				
atmosphere				
axis				
Canadarm				
Canadarm2				
Cassiopeia				
Cepheus				
chromosphere				
circumpolar stars				
comets				
consensus				
constellations				
corona				
craters				
dwarf planet				
Earth				
equinoxes				
fair test				
fireballs				
Hubble Space Telescope				
James Webb Space Telescope				
Jupiter				
laser beam				
Leo				
lunar eclipse				
maria				
Mars				
Mercury				

Copyright © 2013 Pearson Canada Inc.
The right to reproduce this page is restricted to the purchasing school.

Word	I know nothing about this word.	I can spell this word correctly.	I have seen/heard it before.	I can define it as it relates to science.
meteor				
meteorites				
meteoroid				
microgravity				
Moose Mountain circle				
Neptune				
orbits				
Orion				
payloads				
penumbra				
phases				
photosphere				
planet				
radar				
Radarsat				
retrograde motion				
revolution				
revolves				
rills				
rotates				
satellite				
Saturn				
solar eclipse				
solar system				
solstices				
space probes				
sunspots				
synchronous rotation				
terrae				
umbra				
Uranus				
vapour				
variable				
Venus				

Copyright © 2013 Pearson Canada Inc.
The right to reproduce this page is restricted to the purchasing school.

Name: ________________________________

Record Keeping

Use the following tables when observing the sky.

Date:	
Weather Conditions:	
Equipment:	
Sketches:	
Notes:	

Date:	
Weather Conditions:	
Equipment:	
Sketches:	
Notes:	

Copyright © 2013 Pearson Canada Inc.
The right to reproduce this page is restricted to the purchasing school.

Name: ___________________________

Sun and Moon Finder

In this activity, you will use paper plates to create a Sun and Moon finder. It will help you observe that Earth revolves around the Sun and illustrate the rising and setting of the Moon.

Materials and Equipment

- 2 paper plates
- scissors
- pencil
- paper fastener

Procedure

1. On one plate, draw the Moon in orbit around Earth. Earth is centred in the middle of the plate, and the Sun is on the outside of the plate. Be sure to draw the positions and the appearance of the Moon (phases) correctly.

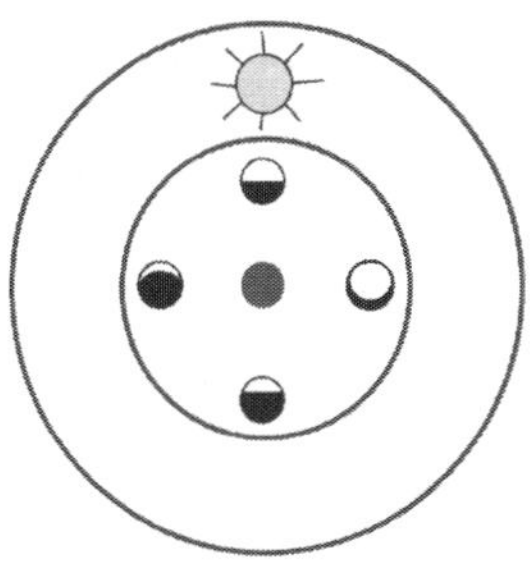

2. Make the horizon plate (or use a 3 × 5 index card). The viewpoint of the observer is looking south, so east is on the left and west is on the right. The outer edge of this plate is cut so that you can see the Sun and the Moon phases.

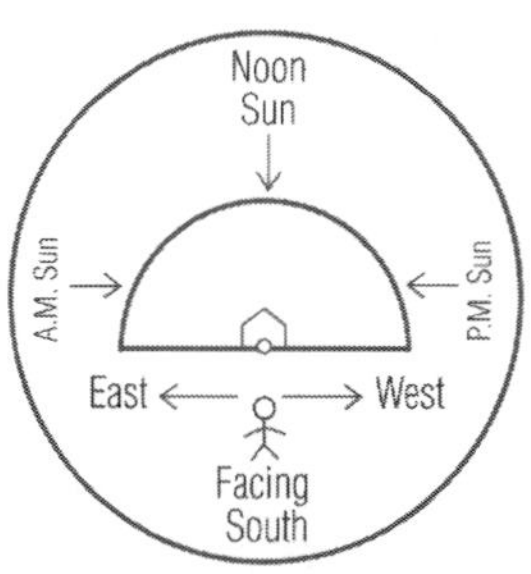

3. Place the horizon plate over the Moon plate and secure it with a paper fastener. Now it is ready to use.

Copyright © 2013 Pearson Canada Inc.
The right to reproduce this page is restricted to the purchasing school.

Using Your Sun and Moon Finder

The location of the Sun indicates the time. When the Sun is low in the east, it is morning. When the Sun is low in the west, it is evening.

If using this device as a Moon finder, focus only on one Moon phase, which depends on the location of the Sun. You can later determine when the Moon rises, transits, or sets by using the Moon finder. The full Moon always rises as the Sun sets and sets as the Sun rises. You might want to note why people are more familiar with the first quarter Moon than the last quarter Moon by considering when each of these Moons is visible.

Copyright © 2013 Pearson Canada Inc.
The right to reproduce this page is restricted to the purchasing school.

Name: ______________________________

Sun–Earth Ratio

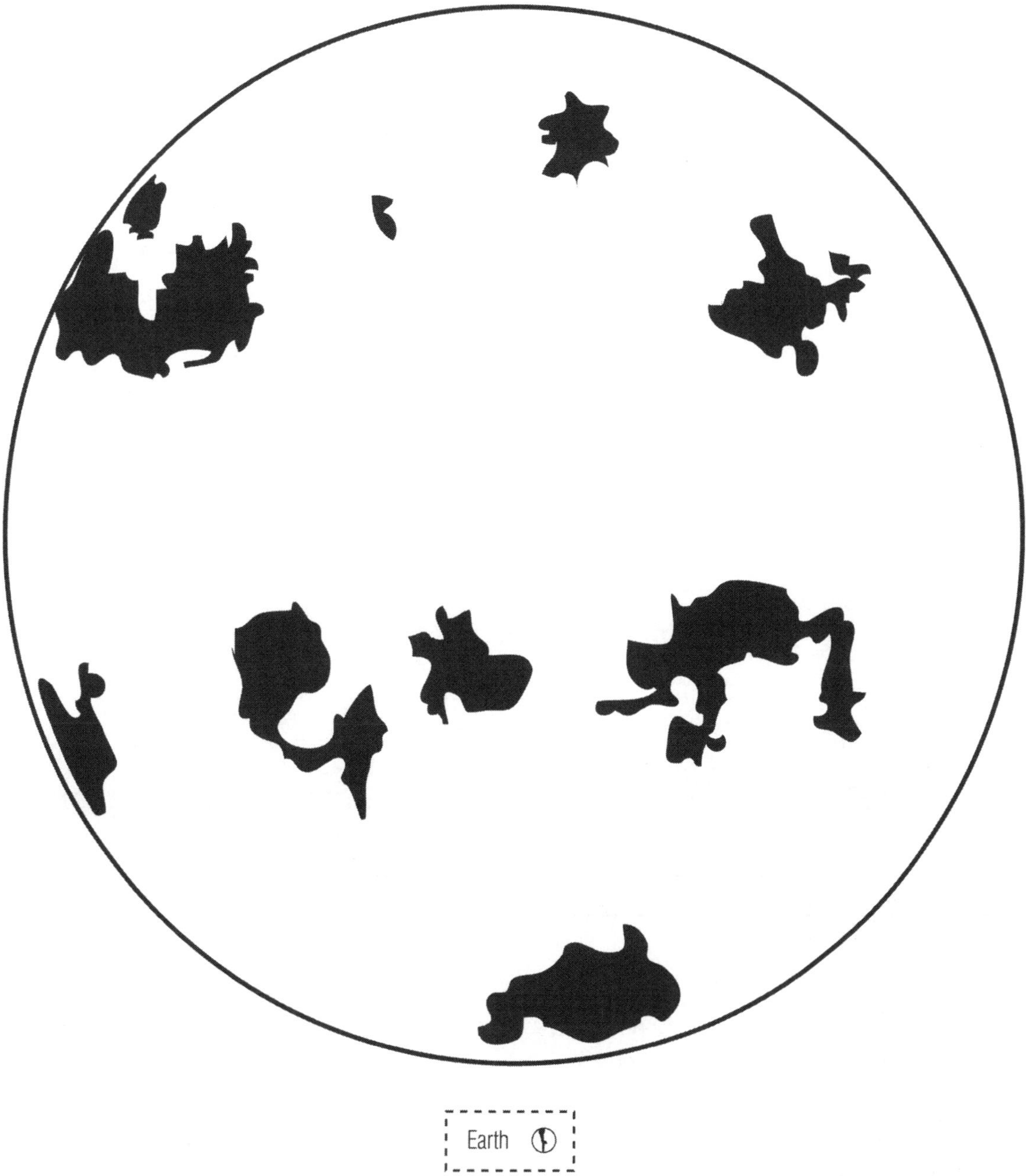

Copyright © 2013 Pearson Canada Inc.
The right to reproduce this page is restricted to the purchasing school.

Name: ______________________________

Observing the Sunset

Use the following tables when making observations of the sunset.

Time of Sunset	
Location of Sunset (description or drawing)	
Notes:	

Time of Sunset	
Location of Sunset (description or drawing)	
Notes:	

Time of Sunset	
Location of Sunset (description or drawing)	
Notes:	

Copyright © 2013 Pearson Canada Inc.
The right to reproduce this page is restricted to the purchasing school.

Name: ________________________________

The Seasons Go Round and Round

The diagram below shows Earth in orbit around the Sun. Notice that Earth is slightly tilted on its axis, at an angle of 23.5° away from the Sun.

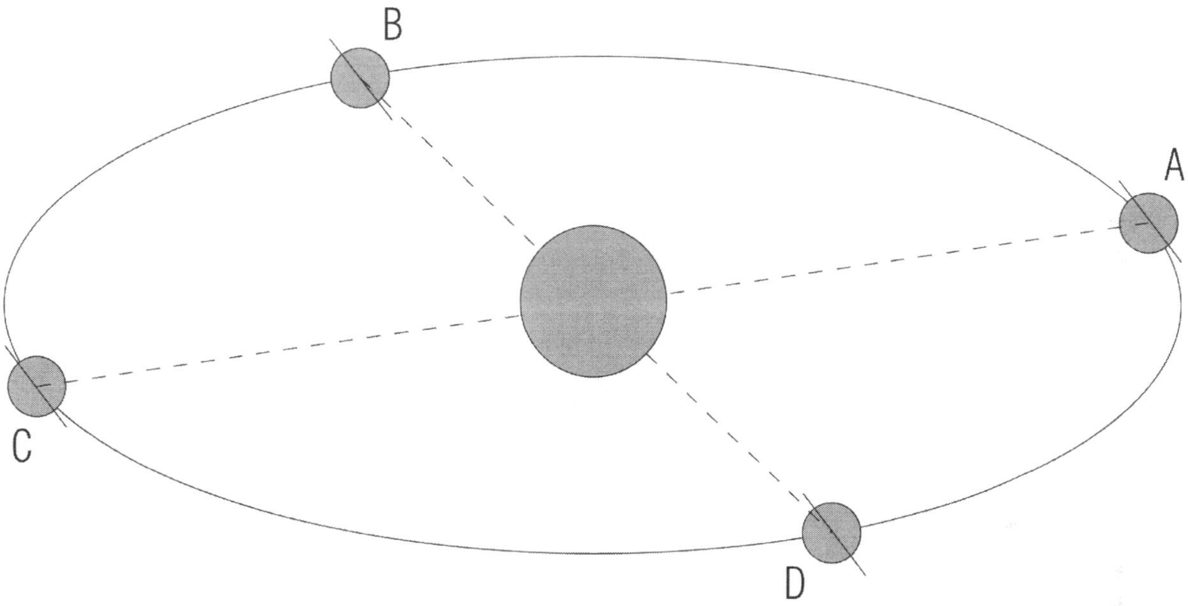

1. At point A, what would be the season in the northern hemisphere?

2. At point B, what would be the season in the northern hemisphere?

3. At point C, what would be the season in the northern hemisphere?

4. At point D, what would be the season in the northern hemisphere?

5. Are the seasons the same in the southern hemisphere? Explain your answer.

Copyright © 2013 Pearson Canada Inc.
The right to reproduce this page is restricted to the purchasing school.

Name: ___________________________

Moon Phases

In this activity, you will use paper plates to make Moon phases that you can use to follow the lunar cycle.

Materials

- 4 paper plates
- pencil
- paper fastener
- markers, crayons, or paint
- rulers
- scissors

Procedure

1. Colour one paper plate completely black. This plate represents the new Moon and will remain whole. Keep the other three plates white.
2. Cut one white plate in half. It is your quarter Moon.
3. Using a pencil and a ruler, find the centre of one of the white whole plates. Make two marks opposite to one another on either side of the plate to help make the crescent and gibbous moons.
4. Using a pencil, carefully draw an arc from one mark to another. The arc needs to be as smooth as possible. Cut along the line you drew to create your crescent and gibbous moons.
5. Place the black moon down first and then stack the "moons" as follows: crescent, quarter, gibbous, full (your remaining whole white plate). Hold all the plates together at the top and punch a hole through the centre of all the layers. You can attach them using the paper fastener.

You can use this paper plate booklet for the full 29 days of the lunar cycle by turning it upside down. The illuminated part of the Moon will now be on the opposite side.

Copyright © 2013 Pearson Canada Inc.
The right to reproduce this page is restricted to the purchasing school.

Name: ____________________________

Moon Observations

Use the following table to make your observations (your teacher may need to give you two of these pages). Draw the Moon you see each night. Note the time and sky conditions for that evening. If the Moon is not visible, predict what the Moon should look like that evening.

Month/Year:____

Moon observations				
Date/Time/Sky Conditions	**Sketch (Shape)**	**Direction**	**Altitude**	**Features**

Copyright © 2013 Pearson Canada Inc.
The right to reproduce this page is restricted to the purchasing school.

Name: ______________________________

Surface of the Moon

Use this picture to help you to create your own lunar landscape. Look at it closely to see the "seas," craters, and mountains.

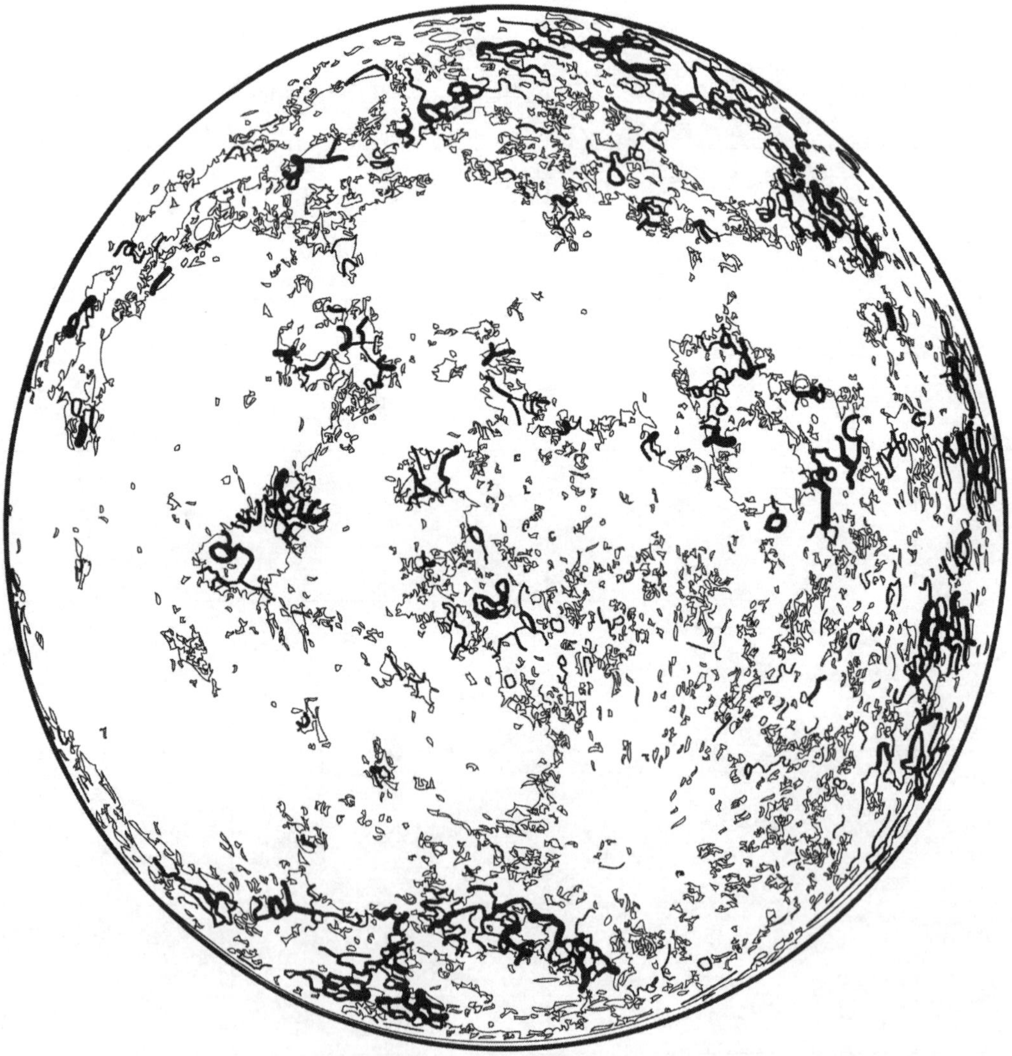

Copyright © 2013 Pearson Canada Inc.
The right to reproduce this page is restricted to the purchasing school.

Name: ______________________________

Eclipse Webquest

1. Sketch how a lunar eclipse occurs.

2. What causes the Moon to appear to be a different colour during a lunar eclipse?

3. What are the three different types of lunar eclipses?

4. Usually, how many total lunar eclipses occur every year?

5. In what phase must the Moon be in order for a lunar eclipse to occur?

Copyright © 2013 Pearson Canada Inc.
The right to reproduce this page is restricted to the purchasing school.

6. What are the names of the two parts of the Moon's shadow?

7. The shadow the Moon casts on Earth is in a "path." What is the name of this path?

8. How long does a total solar eclipse take?

9. Sketch a diagram of how a solar eclipse occurs.

10. In what phase must the Moon be in order for a solar eclipse to occur?

Copyright © 2013 Pearson Canada Inc.
The right to reproduce this page is restricted to the purchasing school.

Name: ___________________________________

Research Organizer

Answer the following questions.

1. The planet I am researching is: ____________________________________

2. Write down as many words or ideas as you can think of about your planet:

These words may help guide you in researching your topic. You can find information about your planet from the following resources:

Resource	Checked	Resource	Checked
books		CD-ROMs	
community experts		encyclopedias	
films/videos/DVDs		government agencies	
websites		journals/magazines	
newspapers		posters	

Don't forget to write down where you found your information. Information consists of the written word as well as pictures. You should record the following basic information about each of your sources:

- title or name of the source. For a website, list the http address.
- author's name (if known)
- publisher. For a website, list the person or organization that has put up the site.
- date of publication. For a website, give the date on which you visited the website.
- pages consulted

Copyright © 2013 Pearson Canada Inc.
The right to reproduce this page is restricted to the purchasing school.

Name: ______________________________

Planet Comparison Chart

1. Planet size (diameter at equator (km))

Largest							**Smallest**

2. Planet atmosphere

Inner Planets	**Outer Planets**

3. Planet rings

Planets with Rings	**Planets without Rings**

4. Period of rotation about the axis (length of the day)

Longest							**Shortest**

Additional Information

Copyright © 2013 Pearson Canada Inc.
The right to reproduce this page is restricted to the purchasing school.

Name: ________________________________

Creating Craters

Rock	Variable	Observations		
	Height	Trial 1	Trial 2	Trail 3
Rock 1				
Rock 2				
Rock 3				
Rock 4				

Sketches of the crater made by:

Rock 1	Rock 2
Rock 3	**Rock 4**

Copyright © 2013 Pearson Canada Inc.
The right to reproduce this page is restricted to the purchasing school.

Name: ______________________________

Making Your Own Constellations

Constellation and/or description:

Copyright © 2013 Pearson Canada Inc.
The right to reproduce this page is restricted to the purchasing school.

Name: ________________________________

Canadian Milestones in Space Exploration

Year	Contribution	Contributor	Reference

Copyright © 2013 Pearson Canada Inc.
The right to reproduce this page is restricted to the purchasing school.

Name: ______________________________

Living in Space Presentation Rubric

	1	2	3	4
Content	The student does not seem to understand the topic very well.	The student shows a good understanding of parts of the topic.	The student shows a good understanding of the topic.	The student shows a full understanding of the topic.
Comprehension	The student is unable to accurately answer questions posed by classmates about the topic.	The student is able to accurately answer a few questions posed by classmates about the topic.	The student is able to accurately answer most questions posed by classmates about the topic.	The student is able to accurately answer almost all questions posed by classmates about the topic.
Preparedness	The student does not seem at all prepared to present.	The student is somewhat prepared, but it is clear that rehearsal was lacking.	The student seems reasonably prepared but might have needed a couple more rehearsals.	The student is completely prepared and has obviously rehearsed.
Clarity of speech	The student often mumbles or cannot be understood.	The student speaks clearly and distinctly some (75–89 %) of the time.	The student speaks clearly and distinctly most (90–99 %) of the time.	The student speaks clearly and distinctly all (100 %) of the time.
Focus	It was difficult to tell what the topic was.	The student stays on topic some (75–89 %) of the time.	The student stays on topic most (90–99 %) of the time.	The student stays on topic all (100 %) of the time.

Copyright © 2013 Pearson Canada Inc.
The right to reproduce this page is restricted to the purchasing school.

Name: ______________________________

Design Project Planner: Space Vehicle

Group members: ____

1. Your space vehicle will be travelling on the surface of the planet ______________.

2. Important features of this planet include:

3. The challenge(s) that your vehicle will meet on this planet include(s):

4. These challenges can be met by:

Copyright © 2013 Pearson Canada Inc.
The right to reproduce this page is restricted to the purchasing school.

5. The vehicle will be investigating this part of the planet:

6. The vehicle will be able to complete its investigation because it is designed with:

7. The materials needed are:

8. Draw your design. Use the back of this page if you need more space.

Copyright © 2013 Pearson Canada Inc.
The right to reproduce this page is restricted to the purchasing school.

9. Build the model space vehicle from your design.

10. Test your design.

(a) Do you need to make any changes to your design?

(b) Draw your revised design.

11. This design is better because…

Copyright © 2013 Pearson Canada Inc.
The right to reproduce this page is restricted to the purchasing school.

Name: ______________________________

Design Project Rubric: Space Vehicle

	1	2	3	4
Modification/ Testing	Little evidence of troubleshooting, testing, or refinement	Some evidence of troubleshooting, testing, and refinements	Clear evidence of troubleshooting, testing, and refinements	Clear evidence of troubleshooting, testing, and refinements based on data or scientific principles
Knowledge	Explanations by several members of the group do not illustrate much understanding of scientific principles underlying the construction and modifications of the space vehicle.	Explanations by most group members indicate a relatively accurate understanding of scientific principles underlying the construction and modifications of the space vehicle.	Explanations by all group members indicate a relatively accurate understanding of scientific principles underlying the construction and modifications of the space vehicle.	Explanations by all group members indicate a clear and accurate understanding of scientific principles underlying the construction and modifications of the space vehicle.
Construction Materials	Inappropriate materials were selected, which contributed to a product that performed poorly.	Appropriate materials were selected.	Appropriate materials were selected and there was an attempt at creative modification to make them even better.	Appropriate materials were selected and creatively modified in ways that made them even better.
Project Log	The notebook provides very little detail about several aspects of the planning, construction, and testing process.	The notebook provides substantial detail about planning, construction, testing, modifications, and reasons for modifications.	The notebook provides a complete record of planning, construction, testing, modifications, and reasons for modifications.	The notebook provides a complete record of planning, construction, testing, modifications, reasons for modifications, and some reflection about the strategies used and the results.
Problem Solving	The student does not try to solve problems or help others solve problems. He or she lets others do the work.	The student does not suggest or refine solutions, but is willing to try out solutions suggested by others.	The student refines solutions suggested by others.	The student actively looks for and suggests solutions to problems.
Focus on Task	The student does not focus on the task.	The student focusses on the task some of the time but is easily distracted.	The student focusses on the task and what needs to be done most of the time. Other group members can count on this person.	The student consistently stays focussed on the task and on what needs to be done. Very self-directed.

Copyright © 2013 Pearson Canada Inc.
The right to reproduce this page is restricted to the purchasing school.

Name: ________________________________

Unit 4 Test

True or False

1. For the following questions, indicate whether the statement is true (T) or false (F).

a) T F The outer planets give off more energy than they receive from the Sun.
b) T F All the Gas Giants have rings.
c) T F There is at least one inner planet that has rings around it.
d) T F The Sun appears to be the same size in Neptune's sky as it does in Earth's sky.
e) T F The planet Venus has the longest day and Jupiter has the shortest day.

Multiple Choice

Circle the letter that best answers the question.

2. The Sun does a lot for Earth. One thing that it does **NOT** affect is:
a) making wind
b) making mountains
c) creating rain
d) plants making food

3. This part of the Sun's atmosphere can only be seen during a solar eclipse.
a) corona
b) chromosphere
c) core
d) photosphere

4. What event occurs around June 21 and December 21?
a) a solar eclipse
b) a lunar eclipse
c) a solstice
d) an equinox

Copyright © 2013 Pearson Canada Inc.
The right to reproduce this page is restricted to the purchasing school.

5. In the picture below, the Moon is in which of the following phases?

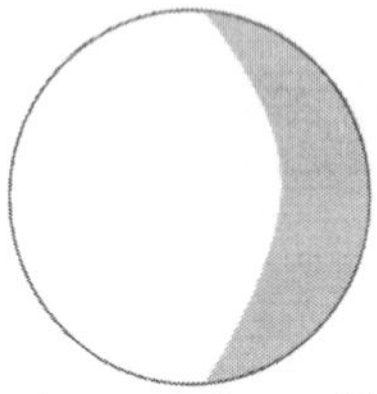

a) waxing gibbous
b) full
c) waning gibbous
d) new

6. Identify the celestial event shown in the following illustration.

a) solar eclipse
b) lunar eclipse
c) summer solstice
d) winter solstice

7. During which Moon phase will a lunar eclipse occur?
a) new
b) waxing crescent
c) full
d) waning crescent

8. Which of the following planets is NOT an inner planet?
a) Mercury
b) Mars
c) Earth
d) Jupiter

9. This planet has the greatest range of temperatures in the solar system.
a) Mercury
b) Earth
c) Jupiter
d) Neptune

Copyright © 2013 Pearson Canada Inc.
The right to reproduce this page is restricted to the purchasing school.

10. This planet has the highest mountains and deepest canyons in the solar system.
a) Mercury
b) Mars
c) Earth
d) Jupiter

11. Jupiter has bands of colour because
a) its soil has a lot of different chemicals in it
b) Jupiter reflects light differently than the other planets do
c) Jupiter is spinning so fast that its clouds, which are of different colours, spread out
d) it is surrounded by rings

12. These objects are not planets, but they orbit the Sun and are made of the same material as the inner planets.
a) comets
b) asteroids
c) meteors
d) moons

13. These objects are known as "dirty snowballs."
a) comets
b) asteroids
c) meteors
d) moons

14. This piece of space technology that NASA used on the space shuttles helped astronauts fix the Hubble Space Telescope.
a) Canadarm
b) Canadarm2
c) Radarsat
d) ISS

15. This piece of space technology helps scientists see high-quality images of Earth, no matter what the weather conditions are on Earth.
a) ISS
b) Hubble Space Telescope
c) James Webb Telescope
d) Radarsat

Copyright © 2013 Pearson Canada Inc.
The right to reproduce this page is restricted to the purchasing school.

Matching

16. Using the diagram below, match the term on the left with the letter associated with the diagram on the right.

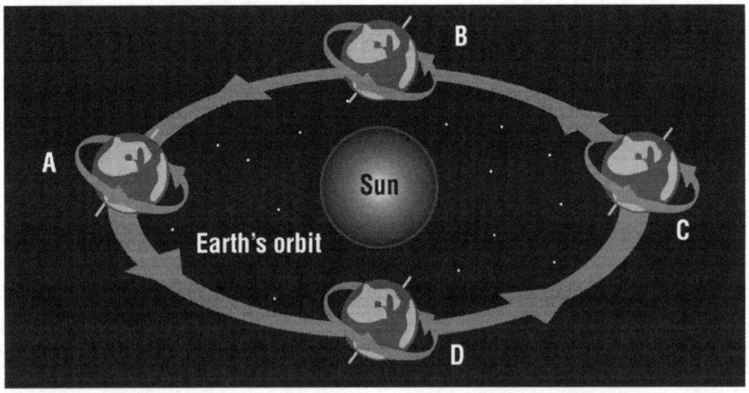

Term	**Label on diagram**
fall	A.
spring	B.
winter	C.
summer	D.

17. Match the term on the left with the correct description on the right.

maria	A. Lunar mountains, which appear as light markings on the Moon's surface
terrae	B. A bowl-shaped hole that has a rim around it
rill	C. Vast plains, which appear as dark markings on the Moon's surface
crater	D. A lunar valley, which you need binoculars or a telescope to see

Copyright © 2013 Pearson Canada Inc.
The right to reproduce this page is restricted to the purchasing school.

Fill in the Blank

18. Use the word bank to complete the following sentences.

Mars	Uranus	Mercury	Jupiter	
Earth	Neptune	Pluto	Saturn	Venus

a) Seventy percent of the surface of the planet ______________________ is covered in water.
b) The Great Red Spot of ______________________ is actually a large storm of clouds.
c) The surface of ______________________ looks a lot like the Moon because its thin atmosphere can't slow down meteors, so it has a lot of craters.
d) Scientists believe that ______________________ spins on its side because it once collided with a large object in space.
e) ______________________ was once considered a planet, but scientists now call it a dwarf planet.
f) Because of its similar size, ______________________ is called Earth's twin planet.
g) The planet ______________________ was actually discovered using mathematics.
h) The shape of ______________________ is like a squished balloon because it spins so fast and is so light.
i) The red appearance of ______________________ is caused by the iron in its soil actually rusting.

Short Answer

19. Describe the safest way to observe the Sun.

____

____

20. Why are the days longer and hotter in the summer in the northern hemisphere?

____

____

Copyright © 2013 Pearson Canada Inc.
The right to reproduce this page is restricted to the purchasing school.

21. Why is it summer in Australia when it is winter in Saskatchewan?

22. You studied different ways that other cultures recognized changes in Earth's position without the use of telescopes or satellites. These changes are most noticeable four times a year: during solstices and equinoxes. Describe one of these ancient technologies used to detect a change in Earth's position.

23. What is the difference between a new Moon and a full Moon?

24. Which type of eclipse is less noticeable and why?

25. Use a Venn diagram to show the similarities and differences between asteroids and comets.

Copyright © 2013 Pearson Canada Inc.
The right to reproduce this page is restricted to the purchasing school.

26. Explain how First Nations and Métis people have used constellations.

27. What are circumpolar stars and why is knowing what they are so important to reading a star map?

28. Discuss the pros and cons of sending equipment/technology into space to orbit Earth.

29. Describe the challenges you might face while living and working on the ISS.

Copyright © 2013 Pearson Canada Inc.
The right to reproduce this page is restricted to the purchasing school.

Answers to Unit 4 Line Masters

LM 4-7: The Seasons Go Round and Round

1. Summer
2. Fall
3. Winter
4. Spring
5. The same four seasons occur, but they are the opposite of those in the northern hemisphere. For example, when it is winter in the northern hemisphere, it is summer in the southern hemisphere.

LM 4-11: Eclipse Webquest

1. The diagram below represents a lunar eclipse.

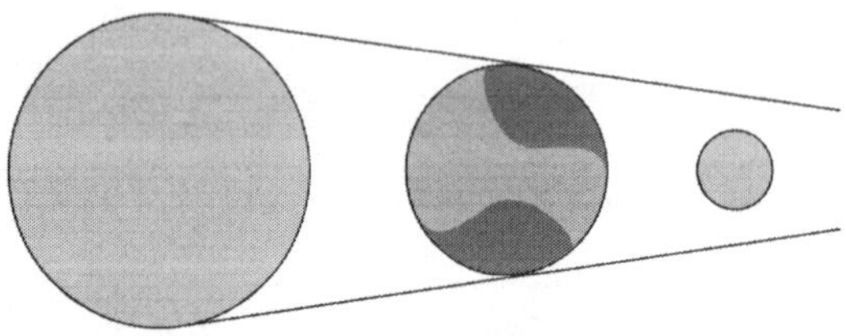

2. Sometimes the Moon will have a red colour during a lunar eclipse. The red colour is caused by dust and other pollutants that are in Earth's atmosphere. Sunlight travels through Earth's atmosphere, where the light becomes red in colour. This red light travels to the Moon, which reflects the red light. (Remember that light from the Moon is reflected light.)

3. The three different types of eclipse are:
- penumbral lunar eclipse — the Moon passes through Earth's penumbral shadow. This type of eclipse is very difficult to see.
- partial lunar eclipse — the Moon passes through part of Earth's umbral shadow. This type of eclipse is easy to see.
- total lunar eclipse — the entire Moon passes through Earth's umbral shadow. This type of eclipse is also easy to see because the Moon has a red colour.

4. There are usually between zero and three total lunar eclipses per year.

5. In order for a lunar eclipse to occur, the Moon needs to be in the full Moon phase.

6. The two different parts of the Moon's shadow are the penumbra and the umbra.

7. The shadow of the Moon on Earth's surface is known as the path of totality.

8. Most solar eclipses last about 7 min. The longest solar eclipse that has been recorded lasted 7 min 31 s.

9. Student responses should look like the following:

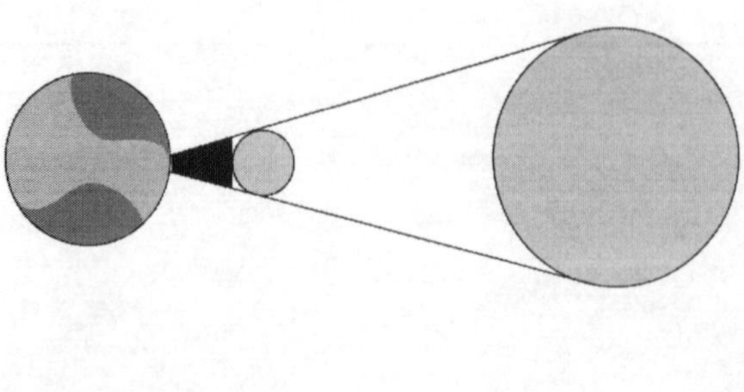

Copyright © 2013 Pearson Canada Inc.
The right to reproduce this page is restricted to the purchasing school.

10. The Moon must be in the new Moon phase.

LM 4-13: Planet Comparison Chart

1. Planet size (diameter at equator (km))

Largest							**Smallest**
Jupiter	**Saturn**	**Uranus**	**Neptune**	**Earth**	**Venus**	**Mars**	**Mercury**

2. Planet atmosphere

Inner Planets	**Outer Planets**
The inner planets have varying mixtures of gases and thicknesses of their atmospheres. Mercury: thin atmosphere of helium and sodium Venus: very thick atmosphere of carbon dioxide Earth: medium thickness atmosphere of nitrogen and oxygen Mars: atmosphere of carbon dioxide, thinner than Earth's atmosphere	The outer planets have many layers of gases in their atmospheres. All the outer planets have the gases hydrogen and helium, but Uranus and Neptune also have methane gas in their atmospheres.

3. Planet rings

Planets with Rings	**Planets without Rings**
Jupiter, Saturn, Uranus, Neptune	Mercury, Venus, Earth, Mars

4. Period of rotation about the axis (length of the day)

Longest							**Shortest**
Venus	Mercury	Mars	Earth	Uranus	Neptune	Saturn	Jupiter

LM 4-16: Canadian Milestones in Space Exploration

Student answers may include the following:

Year	**Contribution**	**Contributor**	**Reference**
1839	Determined that magnetic disturbances occur worldwide and are related to the number and strength of sunspots.	Sir Edward Sabine	All the information was found on the Canadian Space Agency's official website.
1957–1958	Churchill Research Range in northern Manitoba for launching suborbital sounding rockets is built.	Canada and the U.S.	
October 4, 1957	Canada is the first country to record *Sputnik 1*'s (the first satellite in orbit) beeps.	John Chapman and fellow scientists at Defense Research Telecommunications	
November 8, 1958	A Nike-Cajun sounding rocket is launched from the Churchill Range with the first Canadian science payload.		

Copyright © 2013 Pearson Canada Inc.
The right to reproduce this page is restricted to the purchasing school.

Year	Contribution	Contributor	Reference
June 22, 1960	The American satellite, *Transit 2A*, is launched. This is the first Canadian hardware launched into space.		
May 5, 1961	Astronaut Alan B. Shepard becomes the first American in space. The communication antenna of the spacecraft is Canadian, and is known as STEM (storable tubular extendible mechanism).	de Havilland Aircraft	
September 29, 1962	Canada becomes the third country to have a satellite in space.		
November 2, 1971	Dr. Gerhard Herzberg receives the Nobel Prize for his work in molecular spectroscopy.	Dr. Gerhard Herzberg	
August 20, 1977	*Voyager 2,* an interplanetary probe, leaves Earth. Some of the instrumentation on board is Canadian made.	NASA	
November 13, 1981	Launch of Canadarm aboard space shuttle Columbia.	NASA	
September 29, 1982	Canadian Space Astronaut program begins.	NASA	
December 5, 1983	The first Canadian astronauts are selected. They include: Roberta Bondar, Marc Garneau, Steve MacLean, Ken Money, Robert Thirsk, and Bjarni Tryggvason.	NASA	
October 5–13, 1984	Marc Garneau becomes the first Canadian in space aboard the *Challenger*.	NASA	
April 25, 1990	The Hubble Space Telescope is launched with the help of Canadarm. Black Brant 5 launches COBRA astronomy payload, which is a Canadian experiment to measure fossil radiations resulting from the original Big Bang explosion.	NASA	
October 6, 1990	High Flux Telescope (HFT), a Canadian scientific instrument, is launched to study the two poles of the Sun.	National Research Council's Herzberg Institute of Astrophysics	
Dec 14, 1990	The Canadian Space Agency is officially established.	Government of Canada	
Jan 22–30, 1990	Roberta Bondar becomes the first Canadian woman in space aboard the *Discovery*.	CSA, NASA	
Dec 2–13, 1993	Canadarm is used to repair the Hubble Space Telescope.	NASA	
July 4–6, 1997	Mars *Pathfinder* lands on Mars and two days later, the *Sojourner* Rover descends a ramp based on the first Canadian technology in space, the STEM (storable tubular extendible mechanism).	NASA	

Copyright © 2013 Pearson Canada Inc.
The right to reproduce this page is restricted to the purchasing school.

Year	Contribution	Contributor	Reference
August 26, 1998	SED Systems Inc. of Saskatoon, Saskatchewan, builds a telemetry, tracking, and command antenna system for the Rosetta mission for the European Space Agency (ESA).	ESA, SED Systems Inc.	
June 9, 1999	Canada formally agrees to be part of the International Space Station.	CSA, NASA, ESA, Government of Canada	
April 19, 2001	Chris Hadfield is the first Canadian to perform an Extra Vehicular Activity, or space walk, during his time on the space shuttle Endeavour.	CSA, NASA	
August 4, 2003	Canada's first space telescope, MOST (Microvariability and Oscillations of STars), becomes operational.	CSA	
September 9–21, 2006	Steve MacLean becomes the first Canadian to operate Canadarm2, which is instrumental in building the ISS.	CSA, NASA	
August 8–21, 2007	Dave Williams sets the record for the longest amount of time spent during a space walk (17 h and 47 min).	CSA, NASA	
May 25, 2008	Canada arrives on Mars. The Phoenix Mars Lander, which has a Canadian meteorological station aboard, lands on Mars. The station has a maple leaf on it!		

LM 4-20: Unit 4 Test

1. a) T
b) T
c) F
d) F
e) T

2. b)
3. b)
4. c)
5. c)
6. a)
7. c)
8. d)
9. a)
10. b)
11. c)
12. b)
13. a)
14. a)
15. d)

Copyright © 2013 Pearson Canada Inc.
The right to reproduce this page is restricted to the purchasing school.

16. A—summer
B—spring
C—winter
D—fall
17. A—terrae
B—crater
C—maria
D—rill
18. a) Earth
b) Jupiter
c) Mercury
d) Uranus
e) Pluto
f) Venus
g) Neptune
h) Saturn
i) Mars
19. The safest way to view the Sun is to project its image onto something.
20. The Sun's radiation on the northern hemisphere is longer during the summer months. When the Sun shines longer in an area, that area will become warmer (absorb more solar radiation). That is why the days of summer are longer and hotter.
21. Earth is at a tilt of 23.5° on its axis. Because of this tilt, one hemisphere is farther away from the Sun than its opposite hemisphere. When the southern hemisphere is tilted toward the Sun, it receives more solar radiation (heat and light). The northern hemisphere is farther from the Sun during this time, so it receives less solar radiation.
22. Answers may vary, but might include the following:
- The Ancient Chinese astronomers began tracking the solstices by measuring the shadow cast by an eight-foot (2.4-m) bamboo stalk. The day when there was no shadow was the day of the solstice.
- The Mayans built structures and monuments for observing and celebrating the changing of seasons. One of these structures was the pyramid of Kukulkan in the ancient city of Chichen Itza, Mexico. At around 4 p.m. on the spring and autumn equinoxes, the Sun cast a shadow that appeared as a slithering snake going up the pyramid. This event was important for the Mayans because it signalled that it was time to plant or harvest.
23. When the Moon is full, the surface of the Moon facing Earth is completely illuminated because the face of the Moon we see on Earth is directly opposite (at 180°) to the Sun. There is no shadow on the Moon.
When the Moon is new, the surface of the Moon facing Earth is entirely in shadow because the Moon is between Earth and the Sun (at 0°/360°). No light from the Sun illuminates the surface of the Moon that faces Earth.
24. The least noticeable eclipse is a lunar eclipse because Earth blocks the light from the Sun and casts Earth's shadow on the Moon. This shadow completely covers the Moon, making it disappear from view.
During a solar eclipse, the Moon casts the shadow. When the Moon no longer covers the Sun, the light is revealed in a bright and dramatic way.

Copyright © 2013 Pearson Canada Inc.
The right to reproduce this page is restricted to the purchasing school.

25. The diagram should look similar to the following.

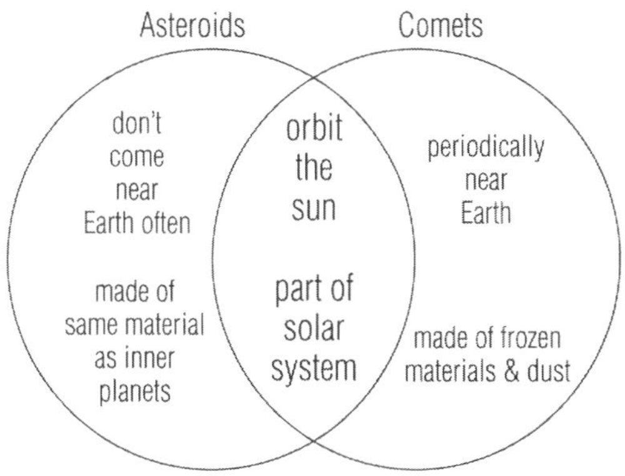

26. First Nations and Métis people used constellations
- for navigation
- for determining passage of time, for example, the race track
- for telling stories to pass on spiritual teachings and information for survival

27. Circumpolar stars are stars that are around the poles of Earth, such as the North Star, Polaris. These stars are visible during all seasons. Once they are identified in the sky, other constellations can then be easily identified using a star map.

28. Answers may vary, but may include the following:

Pros	Cons
We gain a lot of information that we can't from Earth, for example, images from the Hubble Space Telescope.	It is very expensive.
We want to look for life and explore other planets, which we can't do from Earth.	It creates a lot of space debris that can harm other equipment/technologies.
We gain a lot of information, knowledge, and technologies directly from space exploration.	Space debris could fall to Earth, causing a disaster.

29. Student answers may vary, but may include:
- Food: Taste buds change, and getting the nutrients that you need in a form that can be used in space is challenging.
- Rest: Astronauts are strapped into a bed and lack traditional night and day.
- Exercise: Microgravity affects the body, including the heart, muscles, and bone density.
- Hygiene: Self, clothing, and surroundings must be kept clean and germ free because micro-organisms multiply more quickly in space.

Copyright © 2013 Pearson Canada Inc.
The right to reproduce this page is restricted to the purchasing school.